Italian Yearbook of Human Rights 2012

P.I.E. Peter Lang

Bruxelles · Bern · Berlin · Frankfurt am Main · New York · Oxford · Wien

Editors
Interdepartmental Centre on Human Rights
and the Rights of Peoples,
University of Padua
via Martiri della Libertà, 2
35137 Padua

tel. 049.8271817; fax 049.8271816

annuario@centrodirittiumani.unipd.it
www.italianhumanrightsyearbook.eu
http://unipd-centrodirittiumani.it/en/

Italian Yearbook of Human Rights 2012

Human Rights Studies
No.3

Università degli Studi di Padova | Interdepartmental Centre on Human Rights and the Rights of Peoples

UNESCO Chair
Human Rights, Democracy and Peace

Regione del Veneto

Archivio Pace Diritti Umani
peace human rights

Cover picture: © *The ideal city (interpolation)*, 2011, Venezia, Marsilio Editori.

First Italian edition: *Annuario italiano dei diritti umani 2012*, Venezia, Marsilio Editori, 2012.

Éditions scientifiques internationales
Brussels, 2013
1 avenue Maurice, B-1050 Brussels, Belgium
info@peterlang.com; www.peterlang.com

Printed in Germany

ISSN 2294-8848
ISBN 978-2-87574-027-4
D/2013/5678/09

CIP available from the British Library, GB.

Bibliographic information published by "Die Deutsche Nationalbibliothek"
"Die Deutsche Nationalbibliothek" lists this publication in the "Deutsche Nationalbibliografie"; detailed bibliographic data is available on Internet at <http://dnb.d-nb.de>.

Table of Contents

List of Acronyms

AGCOM	The Communications Regulatory Authority (Autorità per le garanzie nelle comunicazioni)
AHD	Advance Health Care Directives (Dichiarazioni anticipate di trattamento)
ANCI	National Association of Italian Municipalities (Associazione Nazionale dei Comuni Italiani)
C.l.	Constitutional law (Legge costituzionale)
CARA	Reception Centre for Asylum Seekers (Centro di accoglienza per richiedenti asilo)
CAT	Convention against Torture and other Cruel, Inhuman or Degrading Treatment or Punishment
CDA	Reception Centre (Centro di Accoglienza)
CEDAW	Convention on the Elimination of all Forms of Discrimination against Women
CFREU	Charter of Fundamental Rights of the European Union
CFSP	Common Foreign and Security Policy of the European Union
CICLOPE	Inter-Ministerial Committee for the Coordination of the Fight against Paedophilia (Comitato interministeriale di coordinamento per la lotta alla pedofilia)
CIDU	Inter-Ministerial Committee for Human Rights (Comitato interministeriale per i diritti umani)
CIE	Identification and Expulsion Centre (Centro di identificazione ed espulsione)
CM	Committee of Ministers of the Council of Europe
CNEL	National Economy and Labour Council (Consiglio nazionale dell'economia e del lavoro)
CoE	Council of Europe
COHOM	Human Rights Working Group of the Council of the European Union
COJUR	Working Group on Public International Law of the Council of the European Union

COJUR-ICC	COJUR sub-area devoted to the International Criminal Court
CPED	International Convention for the Protection of All Persons from Enforced Disappearance
CPSA	Centre for First Aid and Reception (Centri di primo soccorso e accoglienza)
CPT	European Committee for the Prevention of Torture and Inhuman or Degrading Treatment or Punishment
CPTA	Centres for Temporary Stay and Assistance (Centri di permanenza temporanea e assistenza)
CRC	Convention on the Rights of the Child
CRPD	Convention on the Rights of Persons with Disabilities
CSDP	Common Security and Defence Policy of the European Union
D.p.c.m.	Decree of the Prime Minister (Decreto del Presidente del Consiglio dei Ministri)
D.p.r.	Decree of the President of the Republic (Decreto del Presidente della Repubblica)
ECHO	European Commission Humanitarian Aid and Civil Protection Department
ECHR	European Convention for the Protection of Human Rights and Fundamental Freedoms
ECJ	Court of Justice of the European Union
ECOSOC	United Nations Economic and Social Council
ECRI	European Commission against Racism and Intolerance
ECSR	European Committee on Social Rights
ECtHR	European Court of Human Rights
EEAS	European External Action Service
EIDHR	European Instrument for Democracy and Human Rights
EIUC	European Inter-University Centre for Human Rights and Democratisation
EP	European Parliament
ESC-R	European Social Charter (revised)
EU	European Union
EUROJUST	Judicial Cooperation Unit of the European Union
EUROPOL	European Police Office

FAO	Food and Agriculture Organisation of the United Nations
FRA	Fundamental Rights Agency of the European Union
FREMP	Working Party on Fundamental Rights, Citizens' Rights and Free Movement of Persons of the Council of the European Union
FRONTEX	European Agency for the Management of Operational Cooperation at the External Borders of the Member States of the European Union
FRP	Fundamental Rights Platform (FRA)
GA	General Assembly of the United Nations
GRECO	Group of States against Corruption
GRETA	Group of Experts on Action against Trafficking in Human Beings
HR/VP	High Representative of the Union for Foreign Affairs and Security Policy/Vice President of the European Commission
ICC	International Criminal Court
ICCPR	International Covenant on Civil and Political Rights
ICERD	International Convention on the Elimination of all Forms of Racial Discrimination
ICESCR	International Covenant on Economic, Social and Cultural Rights
ICJ	International Court of Justice
ICRMW	International Convention on the Protection of the Rights of all Migrant Workers and their Families
ILO	International Labour Organisation
INDIMI	National Institute for the Rights of Minors (Istituto nazionale per i diritti dei minori)
IOM	International Organisation for Migration
L.	Law
L.d.	Law-decree (decreto legge)
Lgs.d.	Legislative decree (decreto legislativo)
MIUR	Ministry of Education, University and Research
NATO	North Atlantic Treaty Organisation
NGO	Non-governmental Organisation
NMP	Military Protection Units (Nuclei militari di protezione)

ODIHR	Office for Democratic Institutions and Human Rights (OSCE)
OHCHR	Office of the High Commissioner of the United Nations for Human Rights
OPCAT	Optional Protocol to the Convention against Torture
OSCE	Organisation for Security and Cooperation in Europe
P.l.	Provincial law
PACE	Parliamentary Assembly of the Council of Europe
R.l.	Regional law
SIOI	Italian Society for International Organisation (Società italiana per l'organizzazione internazionale)
SPRAR	Protection System for Asylum Seekers and Refugees (Sistema di protezione per richiedenti asilo e rifugiati)
TEU	Treaty on European Union
TFEU	Treaty on the Functioning of the European Union
UN-HABITAT	United Nations Human Settlements Programme
UNACLA	United Nations Advisory Committee of Local Authorities
UNAR	Office for the Promotion of Equal Treatment and the Fight against Racial Discrimination (Ufficio per la promozione della parità di trattamento e la rimozione delle discriminazioni fondate sulla razza e sull'origine etnica)
UNDEF	United Nations Democracy Fund
UNDP	United Nations Development Programme
UNEP	United Nations Environmental Programme
UNESCO	United Nations Educational, Scientific and Cultural Organisation
UNFPA	United Nations Population Fund
UNHCR	United Nations High Commissioner for Refugees
UNICEF	United Nations Children's Fund
UNRWA	United Nations Relief and Works Agency for Palestine Refugees in the Near East
UPR	Universal Periodic Review
WHO	World Health Organisation

Italy and Human Rights in 2011

In its second edition, the *Italian Yearbook of Human Rights* aims to confirm its function as a tool which, in the mark of factual truths and with the strength of universal values, conveys a message of lawfulness, civic cohesion, solidarity and democratic inclusiveness. Politicians and civil servants at all levels can draw inspiration from the overall picture of the current human rights situation in order to fill legislative gaps and to correct shortcomings of infrastructure and policies, in the spirit of *de lege semper perficienda* – laws must perennially be perfected – and of good governance. All those who care about the increase in knowledge and culture of human rights in the world of academia, in schools and in all other walks of society can fruitfully use the Yearbook as a substantial instrument for their advocacy. This is a special reference to the "human rights defenders" as they are acknowledged by the United Nations Declaration on the Right and Responsibility of Individuals, Groups and Organs of Society to Promote and Protect Universally Recognised Human Rights and Fundamental Freedoms (9 December 1998) and who, as such, are legally entitled to take action both at the national and the international level.

The structure for the 2012 Yearbook was traced out in the 2011 edition, which was the first in the Human Rights Studies series. This has naturally simplified the preparatory work for the current edition and also allowed the research and editorial committee to enhance its practical use and sustainability.

The Yearbook has been welcome in Italy and at the international level. On 30 November 2011, the first Yearbook was presented to the President of the Republic, Giorgio Napolitano, during a private audience at the Quirinale Palace. The President, who had himself addressed the United Nations Human Rights Council on 4 March 2011, expressed his appreciation for the undertaking of the Interdepartmental Centre on Human Rights and the Rights of Peoples of the University of Padua (Human Rights Centre) and encouraged the wide circulation of the book. At the international level, thanks to the wholehearted support of Ambassador Sergio Busetto and Ambassador Laura Mirachian, the Yearbook has been presented to the Council of Europe (14 June 2012) and to the United Nations High Commissioner for Human Rights (26 June 2012). At the *Palais des Nations* Mrs Navanethem Pillay personally introduced the Yearbook in a "side event" of the UN Human Rights Council.

The *2011 Yearbook* gave a general overview of Italy's standing at that time, also using data relating to previous years.

The timespan covered by the *2012 Yearbook* is necessarily limited to one calendar year, with the consequent limits to a significant analysis of the data. However, the research and editorial committee took on the challenge of making comparisons, with the aim of highlighting any useful indication of progress in Italy's position with respect to the obligations undertaken within the worldwide human rights system and within the European regional system. The special-focus sections which follow show the results of this study, with the purpose of drawing attention to particularly important aspects for the evaluation both of progress made and of the continuing critical points and shortcomings.

One of the most significant findings to be highlighted is the increase in parliamentary activity *in re*, particularly as concerns the presentation of bills (10 in 2011 against the 6 of 2010), the number of interpellations (18 compared to 4), the questions for a written answer (234 against 81), plenary resolutions (15 as opposed to 0). A first, simple comment is that in the current difficult financial and economic situation, with its serious repercussions on the labour market and social cohesion, there is heightened sensitivity towards the vital needs of individuals and families, particularly towards the conditions of the most vulnerable groups. Naturally, the hope is that there will now be progress from the verbal attention dedicated to the issue to taking actions in terms of supportive public policies and positive measures.

Another interesting point is the legislative activity of the Regions: in 2011 48 regional laws specifically concerning human rights were passed. This is also a very significant illustration of how committed governmental bodies at sub-national level are to the joint implementation of the principle of subsidiarity and their responsibility for protecting the fundamental rights of the people closest to them. The case of Italian Regions, Provinces and Municipalities recognising the fundamental rights of the person in their statutes, simultaneously quoting the Italian Constitution and international law, is still unique worldwide, and deserves to be more widely known and developed. Its highly innovative originality lies in the fact that sub-national legal systems, in dealing with a subject which by its nature belongs to the constitutional realm, are formally and directly linked to international law, thus reinforcing the initial part of the national Constitution and confirming that "recognition of the inherent dignity and of the equal and inalienable rights of all members of the human family is the foundation of freedom, justice and peace in the world" (The Universal Declaration of Human Rights, 1948). Precisely because of their position at the forefront of the promotion and protection of human rights, local governments must be supported by States and international institutions and, as basic poles of subsidiarity, they must have at their disposal effective and visible channels of access to all levels of governance, including the world level.

There have been significant changes in university teaching and education: 118 courses specifically dedicated to human rights are run in 64 faculties of 41 different universities. Of particular note the fact that 8 of these courses are run in 7 Faculties of Economics, against 7 in 5 Faculties the previous year. As in 2010, the University of Padua leads the table, with 19 courses, followed by Turin (9), Bologna and Florence (7) and Bari (5). In all types of schools, the specific teaching of human rights is being developed in the framework of the national programme, introduced in the 2009-2010 school year, entitled *Cittadinanza e Costituzione* (Citizenship and Constitution). It should be noted that this programme is expressly mentioned as a significant good practice in the fourth European Commission against Racism and Intolerance (ECRI) report on Italy. In this context, there is growing interest in the European Charter on Education for Democratic Citizenship and Human Rights Education, adopted with recommendation of the Committee of Ministers of the Council of Europe on 11 May 2010, and in the United Nations Declaration on Human Rights Education and Training, proposed by the Human Rights Council and adopted by General Assembly resolution on 19 December 2011. These are both important strategic instruments. In particular, the United Nations Declaration, in addition to reinforcing the contents of the human right to education, as recognised by art. 26 of the Universal Declaration and corresponding art. 13 of the International Covenant on Economic, Social and Cultural Rights, raises human rights education as such to the status of a fundamental right, with the consequent duty of States to encourage the implementation of comprehensive programmes, both domestically and within a framework of international cooperation.

It should be reminded that Italy, as a Member of the Human Rights Council, was active, together with France, Morocco, Switzerland, Senegal, Slovenia and the Philippines, in a "platform" of States which supported the Council's Advisory Committee in drawing up the text of the Declaration.

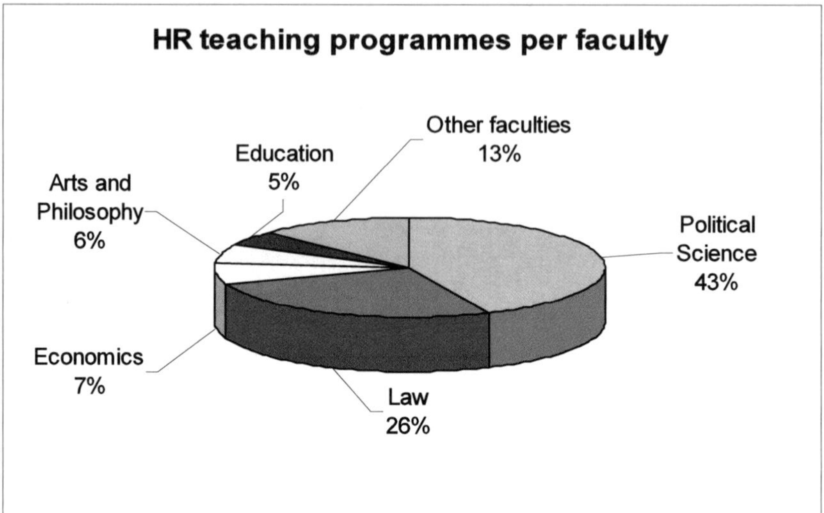

Source: based on data from the Ministry of Education, Universities and Research

Another positive note is the appointment of the Ombudsperson for Children and Adolescents, a joint decision by the Speakers of the Senate and the Chamber of Deputies.

However, 2011 is unfortunately also marred by the failure to set up the National Commission for Human Rights. The Government bill, approved in the Senate with a bipartisan vote, has been slowed down in the Chamber of Deputies by the tabling of a series of amendments, some of a substantial nature. And the institution of the National Ombudsperson is far from being established. Therefore, Italy remains devoid of the top-level structures which are indispensable to the implementation of an adequate "human rights system". This state of affairs has negative consequences both on Italy's representation at the international level and on the coordination of the numerous domestic actors, especially on the activity of the ombudspersons and children's ombudspersons operating at regional and municipal level.

There is a positive note concerning Italian case-law, which is showing ever-increasing attention to European and international norms, albeit in a context where there is no shortage of uncertainties and ambiguities for which the political *milieux* can be held responsible. This awkward situation is reflected, for example, in the field of bioethics, in the way in which Italy relates to the fundamental Oviedo Convention: it has been ratified by Italy but the instrument of ratification has not been yet deposited with the Council of Europe, with the consequence that Italy is not a Party to the Convention. The same can be said on the subject of the fight against corruption. In this case neither the Criminal Law nor the Civil Law Convention on Corruption have been ratified, despite the Italian Government having participated in their preparation; on the other hand, however, Italy is part of the Group of States against Corruption (GRECO) and is subject to the monitoring procedure performed by the latter.

A case of reluctance to adapt to international regulations, which has become chronic and is regularly flagged up by the international monitoring bodies, is that relating to the long-drawn-out issue of adding the specific crime of torture to the Italian criminal code, to which the failure to ratify the Optional Protocol to the International Convention against Torture (OPCAT) and the consequent failure to set up an appropriate mechanism for its implementation are connected.

An extremely critical situation is that concerning the behaviour of the Italian Government towards flows of migrants, particularly the refusal of entry to displaced persons from North Africa carried out in violation of specific *ius cogens* norms and principles: *non-refoulement*, prohibition of the collective expulsion of aliens, asylum rights. In this sector, too, it is urgent to move from merely reacting to waves of emergency to offering a structural response which fully respects the relevant rules of international customary and treaty law.

International monitoring has also become ever pressing as regards the way Roma and Sinti are treated and the many acts of discrimination and violence committed in Italy against people belonging to these communities.

The political debate on the requisites to qualify for Italian citizenship continued to develop during 2011. The theory which seems to be gaining strength is that the principle of equality of all members of the human family and the respect of their equal and inalienable rights, coupled with the overarching *ius humanae dignitatis*, support the *ius soli* as the ground for citizenship attribution. Further encouraged by explicit stances taken by the President of the Republic, the civil society movement in favour of immigrants' children who were born and educated in Italy automatically acquiring Italian citizenship is growing in strength.

In this same area of citizenship rights, it should be reported that the provisions contained in Chapter C of the Council of Europe Convention on the Participation of Foreigners in Public Life at Local Level, that is, the rules on the right of foreign residents to vote and to stand for election at the local level have not yet been accepted. The implementation of these norms would clearly be an effective way to counter the various forms of discrimination and xenophobia: in 2011, 799 cases of discrimination were reported, representing a 48% increase over the previous year (+ 259).

In the social rights sector and with specific reference to the provisions of the European Social Charter (revised), Italy has not yet accepted art. 25 concerning the rights of workers to the protection of their claims in the event of insolvency of their employer.

Another delay by Italy in adapting to international regulations that should be noted is the failure to ratify important treaties which contribute to shaping the central nucleus of international human rights law, in particular the Convention on the Rights of All Migrant Workers and Members of their Families and the Convention on Forced Disappearance, as well as the Protocol to the International Covenant on Economic, Cultural and Social Rights and the Third Protocol to the Convention on the Rights of the Child (signed by Italy on 28 February 2012).

A further point reported concerns the absence of Italian experts in the special procedures mechanism set up by the United Nations Human Rights Council; in the treaty bodies system set up to monitor the main Conventions on human rights, there is currently only one independent Italian expert.

The special-focus sections below contain further, more specific remarks and evaluations on thematic issues and questions that the *Yearbook* research and editorial committee considers particularly important to enhancing Italy's position in the international sphere and which combine to configure a tentative "Italian Agenda of Human Rights".

Complete and Define the Human Rights Infrastructure at the National Level

There were some noteworthy developments in setting up a national human rights infrastructure in 2011.

In Parliament, the Senate Special Commission for the Protection and Promotion of Human Rights held 32 hearings of representatives of non-governmental organisations, international institutions and individuals in the context of its survey on the current levels and mechanisms of human rights protection in Italy and in the international system. The Commission focused specifically on Italy's election to the United Nations Human Rights Council, the conditions of Roma and Sinti communities, prison conditions, and the relationship between human rights and foreign policy. The Chamber of Deputies Permanent Committee on Human Rights, on the other hand, held 13 hearings relating to two surveys, on the violation of human rights worldwide and on human rights and democracy. More specifically, they analysed issues such as the death penalty, violations of freedom of religion, violation of the rights of women and children, violation of the rights of minorities, refugees and migrants, forms of slavery and human trafficking. The Parliamentary

Commission for Children and Adolescents began a survey on the safeguarding of children's health and continued two surveys undertaken in previous years, one on child prostitution and the other on unaccompanied foreign minors. The Commission also began the study of the final report of the survey on the protection of minors in the media and adopted the final report on some aspects of the implementation of policies for children and adolescents. The Parliament-Government Observatory monitoring the Promotion and Protection of Fundamental Rights held only one meeting, dedicated to the follow-up of the Universal Periodic Review (UPR).

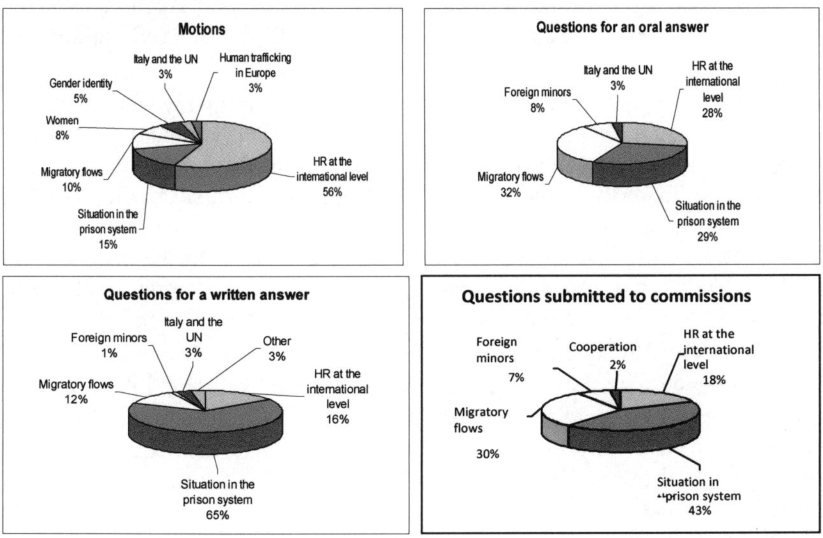

Source: openparlamento.it data

The Italian Parliament's activities concerning human rights resulted in the tabling of 10 bills regarding adaptation to international law, 39 motions (56% on the protection of human rights at the international level, 15% on the situation in prisons and 10% on migrant flows), 18 interpellations (50% on the protection of human rights at the international level and 22% on the situation in prisons), 39 questions for an oral answer (32% on migrant flows, 29% on prison conditions and 28% on the protection of human rights at the international level), 234 questions for a written answer (65% on the situation in prisons, 16% on the protection of human rights at the international level and 12% on migratory flows), 44 questions to Commissions (43% on the prison situation, 30% on migrant flows and 18% the protection of human rights at the international level), 15 parliamentary assembly resolutions (40% on the Libyan crisis, 33% on the Italian judicial and prison system and 27% on European Union policies), 8 Commission resolutions, 29 agenda proposals before the Assembly (55% on the protection of human rights at international level and 17 on the prison situation) and 2 agenda proposals before Commissions on issues concerning internationally recognised human rights.

The amount of attention dedicated by Parliament to the prison situation in Italy is justified by the data published by the Prison Administration Department (DAP). In February 2012, inmates in Italy numbered 66,832, whereas the official capacity of the 206 penal institutes was 45,742 places. The Region with the highest number of detainees is Lombardy (9,388 against an official capacity of 5,384 places in 19 institutions), followed by Campania (8,034, although the official capacity is only 5,793).

There are some particularly significant parliamentary events to report. On 19 July 2011 the Senate approved, with 230 votes in favour, 4 abstentions and none against, the bill setting up the National Commission for the Promotion and Protection of Human Rights. On October 27, the Chamber of Deputies First Commission for Constitutional Affairs began its examination of the text. It should be recorded that at the time of this *Yearbook* going to press, numerous amendments have been approved, some of which not in line with the international standards defined in the "Paris Principles".

Another new arrival is law 12 July 2011, No. 112 (Establishment of the National Ombudsperson for Children and Adolescents). This law represents a major step forward, which brings Italy, virtually at least, to the same level as many States which have already provided themselves with similar institutions some time ago. The National Ombudsperson for Children and Adolescents complements the work of the administrative and judicial bodies responsible for the wellbeing of minors.

However, Italy's adoption of this law is only a partial step forward. Apart from the criticism one could level at some specific provisions, there are two main areas in which the weakness of the new provisions and their failure to meet the parameters set up by the Paris Principles (and later interpretations) are apparent.

First of all, the overall picture of the responsibilities and duties assigned to the Ombudsperson, and the resources at his Department's disposal, lead one to express reservations as to the clarity and the actual substance of the mandate given to this institution. In effect, the responsibilities are distributed over a very wide spectrum of subjects, but they do not seem to be focused in such a way as to assure the institution itself a high profile and actual visibility. The provisions of the law include, from the substantial point of view, some positive reinforcements which can be taken as fragments of the agenda for the new institution (for example, on the issue of family law, health rights, synergy with some already-existent structures working on issues such as trafficking, paedo-pornography, emergency problems), but ignore others which deserve specific attention. For example, there is no trace of the leading role that this structure could play in relation to migrant issues, conditions of the Roma, child labour, school drop-out rates or poverty. Even the stress placed on the potential to react to emergency situations, with measures *de motu proprio* or in response to individual claims, seems functional to the figure of an Ombudsperson unlike any of the other models in Europe. It certainly does not resemble the profile of an Ombudsperson which emerges from the oldest and most consolidated experience acquired in Italy, at the regional level. The whole listening aspect – both listening to minors and to adults (parents, professionals, teachers, volunteers...) who come into contact with the Ombudsperson – appears to have been neglected in favour of the quick supplying of immediate answers. Moreover, the technical-administrative apparatus itself provided for under this law (maximum ten people), although possibly sufficient for forming a rapid-response task force for certain cases, is clearly inadequate for the task of taking on and dedicating the necessary systematic attention to the structural problems posed by a population of 10 million people under the age of 18.

And here it is the second limit of the newly-approved provisions. Although it has instituted a National Network, law 112/2011 is far from having designed an efficient overall configuration of the relationship between the central structure for the defence of children's rights and the peripheral actors working on the same front. Indeed, the law has made no noticeable effort to go into the panorama that had meanwhile been created by regional laws and the practice of the regional ombudspersons, either in terms of methodology and "style" in their actions to protect children's rights, nor in terms of a fair and realistic sharing of the "weight" of the work of monitoring and upholding the rights of children and adolescents, a weight which inevitably comes down on more heavily on the shoulders of the local (regional and sub-regional) governance system.

On November 30 2011, the Speakers of the Senate and of the Chamber of Deputies appointed Vincenzo Spadafora, previously President of the Italian Committee for UNICEF, to the position of National Ombudsperson for Children and Adolescents.

As concerns governmental actions, one of the novelties is the institution of the Ministry for International Cooperation and Integration with additional responsibility for family and youth policy, anti-drug policies, civil service, international adoptions and the fight against racial discrimination.

On this latter question, in 2011 the Office for the Promotion of Equal Treatment and the Fight against Racial Discrimination (UNAR), operating within the Department for Equal Opportunities of the Prime Minister's Office, received, as mentioned above, 799 reports on incidents of racial discrimination. Of these, 22.6% were relative to the mass media, 19.6% to employment and 16.7% to public life.

As concerns central government structures, the lack of both specialised staff and of material resources remains. In particular, it is urgent to strengthen the Human Rights Office in the Ministry of Foreign Affairs and to create an office specifically dedicated to human rights in the other Ministries, with the task, among others, of collaborating with the Inter-Ministerial Committee for Human Rights in the preparation of the periodic reports for the relevant international monitoring bodies.

A significant point which comes out at regional level is the development of legislation which, in more or less explicit terms, incorporates norms, declarations and programmes of international human rights bodies. 48 regional laws were adopted, concerning equal opportunities and gender (10), solidarity, social promotion and assistance to families (10), persons with disabilities (7), peace, human rights, development cooperation and fair trade (6), workers' rights (6), ombudspersons and children's ombudspersons (5), education to citizenship and legality (3) and migration (1).

In 2011 there were 14 Ombudspersons holding this position out of a total of 17 Regions and Autonomous Provinces which include such an institution in their respective statutes or in specific regional laws. There is a working National Coordinating Body of Ombudspersons, but the efficacy of its actions is limited by the absence of top-level offices at the national stage, specifically of the National Ombudsperson. This absence robs the Coordinating Body of the chance to be more suitably and proportionally represented at the international level, especially in the *European Ombudsman Institute* and the *International Ombudsman Institute.* In the meantime, the *Italian Ombudsman Institute*, set up in the Human Rights Centre of the University of Padua, has started operating, with the collaboration of the aforementioned National Coordinating body, supported by a specific memorandum of understanding.

In the field of university teaching, in 2011 there were 118 courses on human rights offered in 64 Faculties over 41 different Italian universities. 43% of them are run by the Faculty of Political Science (of which one third in the Faculty of Political Science of the University of Padua), 26% in the Faculty of Law, 6% in the Faculty Arts, 5% in the Faculty of Education, 7% in the Faculty of Economics and 13% in other Faculties. There are 6 university Centres for Human Rights and 5 undergraduate courses, of which one is a four-year and four are three-year courses. Of the latter, three belong to the general degree classification LM-81 Development Cooperation and one to LM-52 International Relations. There were 12 ongoing or newly-launched PhD courses in 2011 and 9 Masters.

Combat Violence Against Women and Extreme Forms of Exploitation

The question of violence against women received increasing attention in the course of 2011. This can be explained not only by the quantitative increase in the number of incidents which can be ascribed to this type of criminal behaviour, and the media coverage they get, particularly in relation to the drastic rise in murders, but also thanks to the commitments made in 2010 in the framework of the national plan against gender violence and stalking, endowed for the two-year period 2011-12 with an allocation of 20 million euros from the Department for Equal Opportunities by the 2008 budget (law 244/2007). In August 2011 a first call for proposals for an action grant was published, for projects dedicated to extending the anti-violence network nationwide. In response to the notice under which three million euros were to be assigned, 149 plans were submitted. Through a second call of proposal the Department then proceeded to create new anti-violence centres for an overall expenditure of 10 million euros shared by 116 projects. This was followed by a third call in November 2011 concerning professional training of healthcare workers.

On the trafficking front, the technical round table of the Inter-Ministerial Committee for the support of victims of trafficking, violence and serious exploitation, set up in order to adapt the *Guidelines for the development of a national and transnational system of referral* to the Italian context, continued the activities undertaken since its inception. The Inter-Ministerial Committee is coordinated by the Department for Equal Opportunities, which is the central authority responsible for coordinating the initiatives undertaken all over the Country to prevent and combat human trafficking and offer support and social reintegration to victims. On this latter issue, in July 2011 a joint call was made for applications for grants in order to run programmes for victims of trafficking and serious exploitation, based on the special programme of recovery and initial support envisaged in art. 13 of law 11 August 2003, No. 228 containing measures against human trafficking and art. 19 of the Consolidated law on immigration (lgs.d. 286/1998). The call reflects the need to structure interventions on the ground dedicated to revealing, identifying, protecting and ensuring social inclusion of the victims in one comprehensive strategy.

This call for proposals comes under the framework of concerted activities promoted by the Department for Equal Opportunities aiming at favouring initial contact with potential victims of trafficking and exploitation, and setting up a national system that will establish effective connections between the three macro-areas into which the interventions benefiting victims of trafficking can be subdivided: becoming visible, registered and being referred to the protection services; being identified, receiving protection and first-level assistance; receiving second-level support and social inclusion. In this perspective, as the call emphasises, it seemed advisable to define different specifications and operational modes for the three project areas. Interventions in favour of these beneficiaries are carried out in accordance with the definition of trafficking as a serious violation of human rights as specified in the EU directive 2011/36/EU and in the European Union plan on best practices, standards and procedures to combat and prevent human trafficking, and in conformity with the objectives of the specific Additional Protocol to the United Nations Convention against Transnational Organized Crime. Moreover, all interventions must ensure the respect of the principle of non-discrimination, be directed to the victims and potential victims discovered all over the Country, regardless of their age, nationality, gender and the type of exploitation they have suffered. As concerns the extent of the problem, it should be noted that the serious forms of exploitation of labour and, to a lesser degree, those connected to the illegal economy, are becoming progressively more central to reflections on and the organisation of action plans. There is an increase in the number of people who come into the protection system, an increase in the number of nations of origin and in the areas in which they are exploited. In the area of sexual exploitation, on the other hand, there is a tendency which is more or less in line with that recorded the previous year as to the provenance of the people involved and the ways the prostitution in the *sex business* of both young women and transsexuals is managed.

More specifically, as regards their nationality, the prostitution rings connected to situations including serious sexual exploitation and trafficking involve mainly women coming from Romania, Republic of Moldova, Bulgaria, Hungary, Nigeria, China and, referring to transsexuals, Brazil.

The main group targeted by traffickers for sexual exploitation are adults aged between 20 and 30, now also true for Nigerian prostitutes. Minors should also be considered, aged on average between 16 and 17 and a half, as shown by the data relative to the people assigned to assistance and social integration projects. Under-age girls, who seem to be particularly sought-after by clients, are usually forced to sell themselves behind closed doors so as to avoid the risk of being stopped by the police. This risk is also why prostitutes in this age-group are subject to systematic but sudden transfers from one place to another by those exploiting them, in order to drastically reduce the capacity of the police to suppress their activities.

Respect International Commitments

On 20 May 2011 the General Assembly of the United Nations elected Italy as one of the 47 Member States of the Human Rights Council for the three-year period 2011-2014. It is Italy's second mandate in this United Nations body: the first was in the three years 2007-2010. In both cases, in line with the General Assembly resolution 60/251, Italy accompanied the letter submitting its candidacy with a list of voluntary commitments it would undertake on the domestic and international fronts. A comparative analysis of the two candidacy letters, in addition to showing an increase in the number of commitments made (29 in 2011 against the 18 of 2007) allows the identification of at least two more tendencies: the prevalence of commitments to be carried out at the international level over those to be performed at the national level; the prevalence of generic statements as opposed to committing to specific actions.

In 2007, 15 of the 18 commitments were relative to the international environment, whereas three were directed to improving the human rights situation at the national level (a ratio of 5 to 1). Only two of the international commitments defined specific actions: making a donation to the new United Nations Peacebuilding Fund and signing the Convention on Enforced Disappearance (the ratification of which is still pending). In the course of its mandate, Italy achieved both these objectives. It is not possible to evaluate precisely how far Italy fulfilled its other 13 generic commitments. However, they supply useful information for identifying the strategic priorities of Italy's diplomatic activities on the human rights front. In the three-year period 2007-2010, they covered the following areas: collaboration with and strengthening the effectiveness of the work of the United Nations; promotion of the rule of law and democracy, with particular reference to Countries in post-conflict situations; protection of the rights of children, particularly those caught up in armed conflicts; increasing the support to the Human Rights Council's resolutions on combating racism and xenophobia; commitment to increasing the number of Countries party to the Convention against Torture; combating discrimination and gender-based violence; abolition of the death penalty.

All three commitments made at the national level are about specific actions, namely: complete the normative process for the implementation of the Statute of the International Criminal Court; ratify and implement the Optional Protocol to the Convention against Torture and other Cruel,

Inhuman or Degrading Treatment or Punishment; institute the independent National Commission for the Promotion and Protection of Human Rights and Fundamental Freedoms. It must be recorded that to date none of these commitments has been fully satisfied.

The commitments undertaken in 2011 show slightly more attention to the Italian context but, at the same time, a significant increase in the generic nature of the objectives set. It is true that the disproportion between international and national commitments has decreased slightly, going from a ratio of 5 to 1 to approximately 3 to 1, with 20 commitments to achieve internationally, 6 domestically and 3 to be carried out both nationally and internationally. On the other hand, whereas in 2007 about a quarter of the commitments made described specific actions, in 2011 this was the case only for 2 objectives out of 29 (approximately 7%). In detail, none of the international commitments refers to specific actions, so it will not be simple to monitor Italy's performance at the end of its mandate in the Human Rights Council in 2014. However, a comparison with the strategic priorities of 2007 allows the identification of a strong element of continuity in Italian diplomatic action in relation to the promotion of human rights. Indeed, all the priorities identified in 2007 were repeated, apart from the fight against torture; further objectives were added, relating to the following areas: supporting initiatives to fight discrimination based on religion or creed; promotion of the rights of persons with disabilities; protection of human rights in counter-terrorism activities; fighting human trafficking.

The two specific commitments undertaken at the domestic level concern the updating of the National action plan against racism, adopted in 2006, and the full implementation of all the recommendations accepted by Italy in the context of the Human Rights Council's Universal Periodic Review. None of the commitments undertaken in 2007 (and not fulfilled) was reiterated, apart from the creation of national institutions for human rights, which was moreover included, in a much more generic form than previously, in the recommendations accepted by Italy in the UPR.

Italy's voluntary pledges and commitments on human rights

	2007		2011	
	Generic	Specific	Generic	Specific
International level	**13** – close cooperation with the United Nations (6) – rule of law and democracy (2) – children rights (1) – fight against racism and xenophobia (1) – fight against torture (1) – fight against gender discrimination and violence (1) – abolition of death penalty (1)	**2** – contributing to the United Nations Peacebuilding Fund – signing of the Convention on Enforced Disappearance	**20** – close cooperation with the United Nations (7) – rule of law and democracy (2) – children rights (2) – fight against racism and xenophobia (1) – fight against torture (1) – fight against gender discrimination and violence (1) – abolition of death penalty (1) – fight against discrimination on the basis of religion or belief (3) – rights of persons with disabilities (1) – respect for human rights in the struggle against terrorism (1) – fight against human trafficking (1)	-
National level	–	**3** – implementation of the Statute of the International Criminal Court – ratification of the Optional Protocol to the Convention against Torture – Establishment of the National Independent Commission on Human Rights	**4** – implementation of specific legislation to counter expressions of racism and xenophobia – implementation of legislation to counter gender violence – implementation of the Convention on the Rights of Persons with Disability – strengthening civil society	**2** – updating the National action plan against racism – implementation of UPR recommendations
Both international and national	–	–	**3** – promoting educational measures to help eradicate all forms of discrimination – fight against child pornography – protection of victims of human trafficking	–
Total (partial)	*13*	*5*	*27*	*2*
Total (generic + specific)	**18**		**29**	

The implementation of the recommendations made to Italy during the UPR presents a particularly complex objective for Italy, as it requires the following elements to come together simultaneously: sufficient political will, the design of a clear and definite road map, the allocation of sufficient resources, as well as the collaboration, in a coordinated manner, of the different bodies and organisations responsible for the whole cycle of public policies at the various levels of governance.

Italy was reviewed in 2010 (7th session) and will be reviewed again in 2014, during the 20th session of the UPR Working Group. In the course of the first review, 92 recommendations were made to Italy, of which it fully accepted 78, partially accepted 2 and rejected 12. Some of the main themes on which recommendations were made were: the rights of migrants (20% of the recommendations); the rights of minorities (18%); racial discrimination (14%); becoming party to additional international instruments (14%); creating a National Institution for Human Rights (10%); children's rights (10%).

It is now a question of following up on these recommendations by introducing suitable regulatory bills and policies. The implementation of recommendations is the most critical part of the whole UPR process: indeed it will be the outcome of this stage that determines the effectiveness and the credibility of the whole review mechanism, as well as testing the real commitment of States to the strengthening of human rights. Hence the importance of closely monitoring the recommendation implementation stage.

To encourage this process in Italy, it could be useful to look to some examples of good practice by other States. Some of them, reviewed in 2008-2009 for example, have produced mid-term monitoring reports which supply updates on the status of implementation of the recommendations at two years from their respective UPRs. Among others, Argentina, Azerbaijan, Benin, Bolivia, Chile, Colombia, Ecuador, Finland, France, Japan, Netherlands, Poland, Portugal, Romania, Spain, Switzerland, Ukraine and the United Kingdom. These reports list both their legislative actions and the national action plans adopted as a consequence of the recommendations received and accepted. At the institutional level, the examples of France and the United Kingdom should be noted, where their respective independent national institutions for human rights have been directly involved in the monitoring and steering activities; and that of Poland, which has instituted an inter-ministerial human rights committee, charged with coordinating the Government's activities in this area. Again, in Switzerland, civil society has been fully involved in the implementation stage of the recommendations, through regular meetings and consultations with government representatives.

Finally, in many Countries, civil society itself has set up common networks and platforms which are very active in lobbying and as observatories of their Government's performance in implementing the UPR recommendations (for example, in Bangladesh, Cambodia, India and Kenya); some NGOs have also developed their own "conformity indices", which measure the degree of implementation of the recommendations by the States (this is the case of UPR Info, an NGO based in Geneva).

Italy continues to pay the price of its structural shortcomings, due in particular to the lack of an independent human rights institution which, as is the case in other Countries, could act as the coordinating point for monitoring activities relative to the implementation of the UPR recommendations.

And once again, it is civil society that takes the initiative. Particularly important is the role of the *Comitato per la promozione e protezione dei diritti umani* (Committee for the promotion and protection of human rights), a network of over 80 NGOs which published a report in 2011 entitled *L'Italia ad un anno dalle raccomandazioni del Consiglio delle Nazioni Unite per i diritti umani* (Italy one year after the United Nations Human Rights Council recommendations). The report gives an update on the degree of implementation by Italy of the 92 recommendations received during the Universal Periodic Review, with a special focus on the following aspects: civil and political rights and international instruments; national legislation; National Institution for Human Rights; human rights education; the rights of migrants, refugees and asylum-seekers; racism and xenophobia; women's rights; discrimination based on sexual orientation; the rights of minors; overcrowding of prisons; torture; human trafficking; independence of the media; status of public development aid.

Through this report, the Committee intended to ask the Government to follow the example of other European Union Countries and prepare a mid-term follow-up review, to make it public by sending it to the Office of the United Nations High Commissioner for Human Rights and to support the diffusion of the contents of the recommendations and of the Universal Periodic Review mechanism throughout Italy.

Eliminate Discrimination against Roma and Sinti

One of the most problematic issues which have been repeatedly brought up by the international institutions is that regarding the status and treatment of people belonging to the Roma, Sinti and Travellers communities in Italy. Roma and Sinti are often the victims of multiple discrimination inasmuch as they belong to communities which are discriminated against and at the same time, they fall into other particularly vulnerable social groups.

Despite the lack of official statistics and the evident practical difficulties which make it impossible to gather reliable data (see, for example, the *Rapporto Conclusivo dell'indagine sulla condizione di rom, sinti e camminanti in Italia* [Final report from the survey on the conditions of Roma, Sinti and Travellers in Italy], published in 2011 by the Italian Senate's Special Commission for the Protection and Promotion of Human Rights, pp. 17-20), numerous organisations, national and international, from civil society and from international and European institutions, have at various times supplied estimates, rarely matching one another, of the numbers of Roma present in Italy. According to the Council of Europe "Roma and Travellers" Division, based on data updated to 14 September 2010, the total number of people belonging to these minorities in Italy oscillate between 110,000 and 170,000, with the average reckoned to be of around 140,000 people: about 0.23% of the total population of Italy (the European average is about 1.36%). This data puts Italy in the 14th place for the number of members of these groups in "great geographical Europe", represented by the Council of Europe, where Turkey, Romania and the Russian Federation occupy the top three positions.

It is worth remarking that this complex problem is common to the vast majority of European Countries, as is implicitly proven by the adoption of two important regional-level policy documents in 2011: within the European Union framework, the communication from the Commission to the European Parliament, the Council and the European Economic and Social Committees, to define an *EU framework for National Roma Integration Strategies up to 2020* (COM(2011)173 final), within the Council of Europe, the *European Commission against Racism and Intolerance (ECRI) General Policy recommendation No. 13* (CRI(2011)37).

In Italy, it should be reported that a series of "security pacts" between the Government and regional authorities were adopted, in accordance with art. 1(439) of law 296/2006 (2007 Budget Act) which, in allowing "the enactment of extraordinary programmes to increase police services, urgent technical assistance and the security of citizens", set the regulatory basis – subsequently strengthened by later security measures, such as the decree on the so-called "nomad emergency" (d.p.c.m. 21 May 2008 and subsequent decrees extending it) and the 2008 "security package" (law 125/2008) – which in practice legalised discriminatory treatment (census of Roma camps, the practice of "forced evictions") of Roma and Sinti as well as other social groups such as migrants, asylum-seekers and other minorities. These measures were also the cause of greater problems for many members of these communities trying to obtain the identity documents they needed to acquire the status of regular residents.

Among the numerous recommendations from international organisations, two *decisions* by the European Committee of Social Rights (adopted in 2006 and 2010 respectively) should be noted, concerning two collective complaints presented by international NGOs dedicated to the protection of the rights of members of the Roma and Sinti communities (*European Roma Rights Centre v. Italy*, complaint 27/2004 and *Centre on Housing Rights and Evictions v. Italy*, complaint 58/2008). Both these *decisions* recognised that the Italian authorities had violated the rights mentioned in the respective complaints, which were, *inter alia*, the right to suitable housing, the right to protection from poverty and social exclusion and the principle of non-discrimination. In the light of these *decisions*, the Italian authorities are bound to implement measures which will allow the situation of the Roma and Sinti communities to be brought in line with the provisions of the European Social Charter (revised) which Italy accepted back in 1999.

In relation to the United Nations system, it is worth pointing out that, out of the 92 recommendations made to Italy in the recent Universal Periodic Review (v. *supra*), 10 of them explicitly address the conditions of Roma, Sinti and Travellers. Of these, 8 have been accepted by Italy (with reference to issues such as combating racism and discrimination and the need to integrate these communities through positive actions in the fields of education, work, housing and social services); 2 were rejected, those relating to the request to recognise Roma and Sinti as a national minority, hence subject to the protection provisions included in domestic law and international regulations on this issue. Over the course of 2011 some minor progress can be seen, but amidst a long list of critical and worrying situations, that must be resolved urgently.

Among the *positive developments* it is possible to mention the initiatives of NGOs and local authorities which have started up good practices with particular reference to inclusiveness and the active participation of Roma children in the school system, also thanks to actions designed to overcome physical barriers (such as the distance from the Roma camps to schools) which prevent Roma minors from accessing schools and being regularly present throughout the education system. In 2010 the Observatory for security against discriminatory acts (OSCAD) was set up in the State Police Department, followed by the signature of a memorandum of understanding between the Observatory and the UNAR, aiming to optimise their cooperation for the protection of minorities from all forms of discrimination, and also to collect data and information in these areas (the lack of which is frequently highlighted at the international level). In June 2010, Italy joined the Council of Europe's *DOSTA!* Campaign against racial prejudice towards the Roma under UNAR coordination. Significant also the aforementioned final report from the survey on the conditions of the Roma and Sinti carried out by the Special Commission of the Senate – the first official document from the Italian Parliament on these issues – as well as the organisation of a series of institutional activities to raise awareness of these issues among the general public.

As concerns the contested security measures adopted as of 2006, a significant ruling was the No. 6050, dated 16 November 2011, pronounced by the Council of State (see Part IV, Human Rights in Italian Case-law, V, B), which partially repealed the decrees on the "nomad emergency", confirming the illegitimacy of the measures implemented by the Italian authorities, on the basis of the non-existence of the requisites for declaring a state of emergency in order to manage the Roma and Sinti situation in Italy. However, in April 2012 the Government presented an appeal to the Court of Cassation (the Italian Supreme Court), requesting the reversal of the Council of State ruling.

Alongside a limited number of positive aspects, there are many *critical issues.*

One of the most urgent issues highlighted by the main international monitoring bodies is that of the right to adequate housing. First of all, the widespread practice of forced dismantling of informal settlements is censured, and particularly the discriminatory ways in which this is carried out, in clear violation of international human rights law and of the European standards accepted by Italy (violation of the human dignity of the people "evicted", failure to supply housing or compensation in lieu, destruction of personal belongings of the people living in the settlements, substantial impunity of those responsible for the violence used during such operations). Attention is also focused on the poor conditions of the housing in the settlements, even in the so-called "equipped" camps, as well as on the essential need that the housing solutions offered by the authorities must not lead to further segregation and marginalisation, but should favour Roma and Sinti integration into Italian society.

Another issue which causes increasing concern on the part of international institutions is the increase in the number of *violent hate crimes* against Roma committed both by private citizens and by members of the police forces, without these incidents being property investigated and punished by the appropriate authorities. The recent conclusions presented by various European organisations deploring the use of expressions of hatred and racism by Italian politicians at all levels towards Roma, Sinti, immigrants and other social, cultural and religious groups have become particularly significant. In this context, the remarks made public by Thomas Hammarberg, Council of Europe Commissioner for Human Rights, following his visit to Italy in May 2011 attracted particular attention from the media. He said he was deeply shocked by the use of election posters which used anti-Roma rhetoric for political ends in the campaign for municipal elections in Milan. According to the Commissioner, behaviour of this kind has the effect of lending legitimacy to prejudice and discrimination against these groups of people, undermining the hard work of Italian civil society to foster their inclusion and reduce the causes at the root of the negative stereotypes of them. On the basis of his experience in Milan, Hammarberg also published a *human rights comment* which showed how the Italian case is a typical example of behaviour common to many European Countries and he stressed, on one hand, the need to put an immediate end to shows of this kind and, on the other, the special responsibility that political and institutional representatives have to lead the fight against discrimination and favour the inclusion of all sectors of society. Discriminatory events of this nature, it is well to repeat, do not only harm those who belong to the Roma and Sinti communities, but also other social groups such as migrants and asylum-seekers who, as the ECRI stresses in its fourth report on Italy, are systematically associated with a threat to security and consequently subjected to a hostile attitude towards them. Alongside their concerns for the hatred shown towards Roma, Sinti and migrants in Italian political discourse, the international institutions made critical comments on the partisan bias and sensationalism of some Italian mass media, and their use of aggressive and stereotyped language which contributes to the forming of public opinion which accepts the above-mentioned discriminatory measures and accustoms them to the violence used against certain vulnerable communities.

Another critical issue is that of the legal status of many Roma and Sinti communities living in Italy. Many descendants of Roma families originating from former Yugoslavia are not only devoid of citizenship, but also without any recognition of their statelessness. Very few of them, after the break-up of former Yugoslavia, returned to their lands of origin to request recognition of their statelessness and their children, although born in Italy, cannot be recognised as stateless because, under Italian law, that would require proof of the statelessness of their parents. And neither can the Italian law on citizenship, which attributes Italian nationality to people born in Italy to a stateless couple, be applied. This condition of de-facto statelessness now affects over 15,000 Roma born in Italy, according to the Council of Europe report. The legal status of these people, together with the implementation of the disputed security measures described above, constitute the basis of many "irregular" situations which are subject to criminal proceedings and expulsion orders.

To enhance the protection of the rights of Roma and Sinti, it is first of all indispensable to implement a radical change of approach to this issue, replacing a management of the situation centred entirely on emergencies and the question of public order with actions to favour their inclusion and combating discrimination, as well as improving their standard of living, especially as regards their housing, access to health and social care, to schooling and to the labour market. As reiterated by several international organisations and in line with the Council of Europe and European Commission's suggestions, the definition of a specific and comprehensive framework of regulations for the social inclusion and protection of the members of these communities can no longer be delayed. This should be achieved through consultations with the community members themselves, also dedicating further human and economic resources and a more decisive role to the UNAR, the recent development of which has been welcomed by international organisations. More specifically, as was moreover requested in one of the two recommendations addressed to Italy but rejected during the UPR, the Roma and Sinti present in Italy should be officially recognised as a minority, thus guaranteeing them the same protection as is provided for those belonging to recognised linguistic minorities. Action along this line would require an amendment of law 482/1999 (Provisions for the protection of the historic linguistic minorities), which only recognises and protects the linguistic minorities which have historically settled in a certain limited territorial area and therefore excludes the Roma and Sinti communities, scattered all over Italy.

In conclusion, Italy is urgently requested to multiply its efforts to pursue the adoption of uniform regulations and set up structured consultation mechanisms, at both the local and national level, with the Roma and Sinti communities present in the area and with the relevant civil society organisations.

Guarantee the Respect of Human Rights in the Handling of "Mixed" Migrant Flows from North Africa

One of the particularly sensitive issues for Italy which emerged in 2011, and on which many international human rights organisations have expressed their concern and reported numerous critical areas, is that of the handling of the massive flow of irregular migrants, asylum-seekers and refugees caused by the uprisings in North African Countries and by the conflict in Libya.

According to UNHCR data, almost 60,000 immigrants reached Italian shores in the course of 2011. Of these, about 26,000 were Tunisian citizens and had come to Italy mainly for economic reasons; the others, who had departed from Libya, were mostly non-Libyan citizens fleeing from the ongoing conflict. According to data supplied by the Italian Civil Protection, in October 2011, the people housed in the various structures made available by the regional administrations (excluding Abruzzo) numbered just over 21,000.

In this context, despite acknowledging the exceptional dimensions of the migratory pressure to which Italy was subjected, and appreciating the State's efforts to supply aid and humanitarian assistance, many international bodies, including UNHCR, IOM and the Council of Europe (Parliamentary Assembly and Committee of Ministers) pointed out some problematic issues relative, on one hand, to the reception and access conditions to international protection for potential beneficiaries, and on the other, to the interception on the high seas and aid at sea in connection with the principle of *non-refoulement.*

Specifically, the criticisms most often made were of the inadequacy of the infrastructures made available for the reception of migrants, the prolonged holding there and the insufficient speed in transferring them (particularly the most vulnerable categories such as unaccompanied minors and asylum-seekers) from Lampedusa towards other centres charged with assisting them, factors which contributed to the creation of a real humanitarian emergency on the island, with consequent tension between migrants and the local population. As concerns access to forms of international protection, some shortcomings were reported in the speed of processing and the type of reception and support provided for those waiting to have their claim examined or, in the case of their claim being rejected, who have presented an appeal.

It is felt appropriate to remark here that although, on the one hand, the tardiness of the asylum procedure could be blamed on the exponential increase in the number of requests presented in 2011 (34,100 according to the UNHCR), the Italian Government's decision (d.p.c.m. 5 April 2011) to grant a six-month residence permit for humanitarian reasons (extended for a further six months by d.p.c.m. 6 October 2011), exclusively to citizens arriving from North Africa and who entered Italy between 1 January and 5 April 2011 had some negative consequences. As a matter of fact for all those who arrived after the date specified, the only chance of having any form of protection recognised them was to present a claim for international protection, even if there were none of the pre-requisites for so doing. The response to these claims for asylum, mostly presented by foreign workers with stable residence in Libya prior to the conflict, and thus not in need, *strictu sensu*, of international protection (as they are not Libyan citizens), but on the other hand cannot or do not always want to be repatriated to their own Countries of origin nor to Libya until the situation has not entirely stabilised, has in most cases been one of rejection. Numerous Italian organisations working on the promotion and protection of human rights have recently advised the Italian authorities to adopt a "political" stance towards this group of people, thus avoiding an avalanche of appeals and the inevitable subsequent clogging up of the Italian asylum system.

On the question of the operations to intercept and aid migrants at sea, the UNHCR and the Council of Europe have addressed clear recommendations to Italy and other coastal Countries, in particular as regards their obligation to render aid and the need to systematically respect the human rights of all people intercepted, avoiding all type of practice which could be assimilated to *refoulement*. Such close attention to the issue of rendering aid on the high seas is explained by the shocking number of human lives lost in the attempt to reach Italian or Maltese shores (UNHCR estimates 1,500 deaths in 2011), tragedies on which international bodies (the Parliamentary Assembly and the European Parliament) are starting to produce reports and fact-finding investigations in order to apportion responsibilities, and in some cases also concerning events which could be blamed on omissions by the Italian authorities.

Among the positive notes to be made in the area of Italy's general efforts to receive migrants coming from North Africa, the actions and mobilisation of a certain number of civil society organisations, but also of regional and municipal administrations should be recorded, as well as the mobilisation of human and financial resources by the central government. The launch of a reception plan (12 July 2011), in agreement with regional and municipal authorities, constituted the basis for a generalised effort to achieve a fair distribution of the migrants over the whole of Italy, also envisaging the involvement, albeit marginal, of the Protection System for Asylum-seekers and Refugees (SPRAR) network.

Another critical area concerning the minimum reception conditions, the inadequacy of the structures and the very limited resources dedicated to integration programmes for asylum-seekers, shows that there is a certain inconsistency in the policy for handling the flows, and the relative measures. State policies have in practice created a situation of unequal treatment between those who came to Italy prior to 5 April 2011 (the latest date the Government allowed residence permits for humanitarian purposes to be granted, per art. 20 of the lgs.d. 286/1998) and those arriving afterwards, despite their being in virtually identical situations (the events from which these people were fleeing, considered as the legal basis for affording temporary protection, were in many cases the same). Moreover, taking a broader perspective, it can be seen that State actions on immigration have for many years been delegated to regulating emergency situations. Indeed, since 2002 states of emergency have been declared, extended and repeated as a means of dealing with the exceptional influx of non-EU citizens to Italy, whereas the influx of migrants and refugees appears to have become a structural issue, up to a point foreseeable and circumstantial, the handling of which should be assigned to normal instruments.

Finally, one of the most urgent issues the Italian Government must face in the near future is the handling of those whose residence permits for humanitarian reasons reach their expiry date as well as those coming from Libya, Libyan citizens and non-Libyans, whose asylum claims are rejected. Plans will have to be made for their integration, voluntary repatriation or expulsion by deportation.

Foster the Implementation of International Principles and Norms on Bioethics and Bio-law

The situation of Italy in relation to international instruments dedicated to bio-law issues has for some years stood out for the singularity of its position towards the 1997 Oviedo Convention on Human Rights and Biomedicine. Despite having ratified both the Convention and the 1998 Optional Protocol on the Prohibition of Cloning of Human Beings in law 28 March 2001, No. 145, Italy does not figure as Party to the Convention because it has not proceeded to depositing the relative instrument of ratification. In the context of the ratification law, the Parliament has delegated to the Government to adopt the decrees implementing the provisions necessary to adapt Italian law to the principles and provisions of the Convention and the Protocol. However, the time limit set for the Government in order to adopt such decrees, although extended several times, has always been left to expire.

Despite the absence of implementing legislation, many of the provisions of the Convention, which cover fundamental issues such as consent, private life and right to information, the human genome, scientific research, the harvesting of organs and tissues from living donors for transplant purposes, have in any case been applied in Italy in a certain measure. An example to consider is the updated edition of the medical code of conduct which came into effect in 2006, the content of which is almost totally based on the articles of the Convention, as well as on widespread practice in case-law. And indeed it has been case-law, both ordinary and constitutional, which over recent years has intervened on the issue of "end-of-life" which for Italy is probably the main obstacle to the completion of the Oviedo Convention ratification process: the so-called "living will" or advance health care directive (AHD). The right of individuals to give instructions as to the type of medical treatment they are to receive at a time at which they are unable to express their wishes has several times been brought before the Italian courts and has been at the centre of Italian political debate following some particularly painful and controversial cases. The legal cases have centred particularly on the possibility of an individual appointing a third party (an *amministratore di sostegno*, or judicially-appointed guardian) as caretaker with a durable proxy for health care decisions regarding him/her when he/she is no longer able to do so (as per art. 404 and subsequent articles of the Italian civil code). Italian case-law, referring to articles 2, 3, 13 and 32 of the Italian Constitution and articles 1-3 of the Charter of Fundamental Rights of the European Union (CFREU), and having recognised free and informed consent as a "full-scale right of the person", both as concerns the right to self-determination and as concerns the right to healthcare (judgement 438/2008 of the Constitutional Court), Italian case-law did not exclude, in the cases in point, the compatibility of advance health care directives with the Italian legislation.

In the absence of a comprehensive set of regulations covering the issue of "living wills" which gives the individual, their family and their doctors certainties as to their rights and duties in this sensitive issue, some indications of the Italian legislator's orientation in this area can be found in the bill "Provisions on therapeutic alliances, informed consent and advance health care directives", approved by the Chamber of Deputies on 12 July 2011 and referred to the 12th Standing Commission (Health and Hygiene) in the Senate. Skimming through the text of the bill, one can more or less see the ways future AHDs would be applied and their limitations, as they will not be considered binding for the doctor (art. 7) and they can become applicable only after the absence of cerebral activity has been ascertained (art. 3). Moreover, art. 3 also states that such advance directives may not cover the supply of nutrition and hydration.

The point of potential non-conformity with the Oviedo Convention seems to be that relative to the binding nature of AHDs from a legal standpoint, which is excluded in the Italian bill, whereas art. 9 of the Convention reads "The previously expressed wishes relating to a medical intervention by a patient who is not, at the time of the intervention, in a state to express his or her wishes shall be taken into account". However, a contrast thus described, if there is one, would not prevent Italy from completing the ratification process of the Convention, considering art. 36 of the same, which includes the possibility for a State to express reservations on the treaty if a law currently applicable in that state (this is not yet the case in Italy) is out of line with such provisions. Appeals for the ratification process to be completed were made by the National Committee for Bioethics (a motion was approved in plenary session on 24 February 2012) and by the Council of Europe Parliamentary Assembly (resolution No. 1859 of 25 January 2012 concerning informed consent).

As a concluding remark, it is interesting to note that, in the absence of a law regulating the issue of living wills, many Italian Municipalities have set up registers of advance healthcare directives. Such directives, which can neither exclude nor replace action by the legislator, are considered useful instruments which, should they be needed, will avoid the burden of having to reconstruct that person's wishes *a posteriori*.

Implement the Rome Statute Establishing the International Criminal Court

Despite the strong commitment of Italy during the process instituting the International Criminal Court (ICC) and the prompt ratification, already back in 1999, of the relative instrument (the Rome Statute), today there has still been no implementing legislation. In the course of 2011, the parliamentary process regarding "regulations for the adaptation to the provisions of the Rome Statute" (C.1439-A) had a significant burst of speed, although it had been reduced to the mere procedural aspects concerning legal cooperation with the Court. However, Italy has still not managed to definitively approve a legislative instrument which is absolutely necessary to making the principle of complementarity governing and regulating the jurisdiction of the International Criminal Court come into effect. The absence of an implementing legislation, which at this stage implies the impossibility for Italy to satisfy even the simplest requests for collaboration under Chapter IX of the Rome Statute, such as, for example, the handing over to the Court of a person on Italian soil for whom an international arrest warrant has been issued, stands out in an ever more alarming way, also in the light of the growing interest shown by the European Union, and especially by the EU Council, in the promotion of an efficient and effective functioning of the ICC.

Develop a Dialogue between Italian Courts and International Courts for Greater Guarantees of the Respect of Human Rights

Again, over the course of 2011 the process of actually integrating the Italian legal system into the context of that of the European Union and of the international community in general, with particular reference to the recognition and protection of human rights was further developed. On this matter, domestic norms are ever more clearly perceived by legal practitioners as being closely interconnected with the norms contained in European Union sources and international law, while there are continually increasing opportunities for positive osmosis, that is, chances to strengthen the guarantee of the human person.

The case-law of the Italian courts illustrates the growing awareness on the part of the judiciary of the structuring force of pronouncements oriented by human rights, indeed there are several examples of Italian courts which have elaborated new ideas and innovative interpretations on the question of fundamental rights, which could also have repercussions beyond the national boundaries – even if they are not always confirmed by the case-law of national courts in other Countries or in international courts. Among others, one such is the *Ferrini* case, which affirmed the primacy of the right of redress of the victims of international crimes against *jus cogens* norms over the principle of sovereign immunity of States. The International Court of Justice, with a ruling in February 2012 – hence outside the scope of this Yearbook – rejected this interpretation, ruling in favour of the State which appealed it, Germany v. Italy in 2008. There is no doubt, however, that the reading of international law given by the Italian Supreme Court in the *Ferrini* case and in other similar rulings, although considered unfounded under current international law, shows the potential for expansion of legal principles considering the primacy of fundamental rights in the framework of international public law.

Another example of how the Italian courts have given weight to an approach orientated towards the highest consideration of human rights is the Turin court's judgement in the *Thyssen Krupp* case. The ruling – which, it is worth recalling, is only relative to the Court of First Instance – found the top managers of the steel-working multinational guilty of murder because they ignored workplace health and safety measures for purely economic reasons. The guilty sentence recognises the intent (using the formula *dolus eventualis*), not mere negligence. In this way it established a principle which, if confirmed in the higher courts, will contribute to strengthening the defence of the right to health and personal safety in the workplace, with major implications for the whole range of economic and social rights. Other cases which are in some way comparable – but have not been concluded during the year under consideration – can be interpreted in the same way: for example, the case accusing the top management of Eternit of having kept the asbestos-processing plants in action despite being aware of the cancerous effects that contact with asbestos had on the workers. These and other proceedings are good illustrations of the transformational reach that a perspective directed towards the protection of human rights – including economic and social rights: the right to health, to work, to the environment, etc. – can have on the evolution of the juridical conscience and on the administration of justice.

In the course of 2011, the judiciary made several important pronouncements which reaffirmed the primacy of the fundamental rights of the person in situations where political reasoning connected with "security" or "emergencies" had claimed absolute primacy. And so the review of recent legislation on immigration proceeded, and saw substantially convergent work by ordinary justice and administrative justice, trial judges and the Court of Cassation, the Italian Constitutional Court and Court of Justice of the European Union. In particular, the Constitutional Court repealed certain provisions which were ruled a disproportionate interference with the exercise of the right to marry of illegal immigrants in Italy. The ruling by the European Court of Justice (*El Dridi* case) which pointed out the immediate applicability of the EU returns directive, despite Italy's failure to transpose it, and ordered that certain domestic norms which limit the personal freedom of irregular immigrants should not be applied, was promptly reflected in the actions of the Italian judiciary. Similar observations can be made as concerns bringing the recent provisions on the "nomad emergency" and asylum-seekers back within a framework placing the respect of individual rights at the centre. In some cases, the reiterated rulings have produced encouraging recognition on the legislative front, too (an example is the substantial turnaround enacted by law 129/2011 on the question of unaccompanied minors).

Despite these important signs of maturity on the part of the Italian judiciary, certain points of friction still remain, and in some ways are getting worse, between how law is actually applied in Italy and international human rights standards as they are understood and applied in the case-law of the international courts – particularly by the European Court of Human Rights. Moreover, the confirmation of a distinctive national profile of the way of understanding and applying human rights need not necessarily be judged negatively. The existence of points of friction is indeed symptomatic of the consolidation, within the Country, of a more mature and aware position as regards the practical terms in which human rights issues come into play within the national community. In the well-known "Crucifix case", for example, the tenacity with which the Italian Government defended its position before the European Court of Human Rights contributed to the recognition of the legitimacy of a particular way of using the "national margin of appreciation" which, however debatable and controversial, nonetheless contributes to rendering the mechanism protecting freedom of education and the freedom of religion itself provided by the European Court of Human Rights more complex, more pluralist and more sophisticated. Other fronts of open or latent contrast between the orientation expressed by Italian case-law and the consolidated positions of the Strasbourg Court have emerged concerning the power of the Government and the legislator to introduce provisions which put an end to a large number of disputes by issuing partially retroactive "authoritative interpretations" of the norms being challenged. Such interventions, although justified by the Italian Constitutional Court, do not appear to fully respect the independence of the judiciary, especially when the consequence is the cutting short of proceedings in which the public administration might incur financial loss or when they concern judicial issues considered politically sensitive (as in the changes to the terms of the statute of limitations in criminal law). Some disparities between the approach favoured by the international courts and the established practice of the Italian courts (or the legal provisions that national judges have to apply) are still found over the issue of just satisfaction for the excessive length of trials and payment of indemnities for expropriation in cases of so-called indirect expropriation. On the other hand, there has been progress on the possibility of reopening criminal cases on which a final ruling has been made, in cases where the Court of Strasbourg has recognised that the way the trial was conducted did not meet European standards of what constitutes a fair trial. The Constitutional Court has issued a remedial interpretation which extends the norms on judicial review to the cases in point.

There are still worrying differences in approach found between the practice of the European Court of Human Rights and Italian case-law on several issues. One of these concerns the effectiveness of investigations into cases where suspect perpetrators of crime have been killed by police officers (the ruling of the Grand Chamber of their non-violation in the *Giuliani* case was followed by that on the *Alikaj* case, which the Government did not appeal, and which on the contrary established that article 2 of the European Convention on Human Rights had been violated). A second aspect relates to the respect of the right not to suffer torture or inhuman treatment or punishment in connection with the expulsion or return of foreign citizens to non-European Countries in which such practices are known to be used. The scarce protection offered by the Italian legal system as a whole in this kind of situation is aggravated by the unacceptable decision, censured by the Court of Strasbourg, to ignore, in some cases, requests for the suspension of the expulsion procedure made by the Court itself. Although the *Hirsi* case – relative to the deplorable practice of pushing back refugees from North Africa, among whom potential asylum-seekers, on the high seas – is not one on which judgement was reached in 2011, the issue of the failure to respect the right not to suffer inhuman treatment following the issue of expulsion orders, with insufficient investigation into the consequences, was once again a dramatic problem in 2011. Moreover, there is still a gap between the standards of case-law in Strasbourg and that in Italy as concerns parliamentary privilege: the current legislation in Italy, which offers members of Parliament immunity in the exercise of their political functions even to the detriment of the right of the non-parliamentary citizen to take legal action against abusive and defamatory speech by the politician, is disproportionately weighted in favour of politicians. A final point to remember is that, according to the Court of Justice of European Union, current legislation on compensation for judicial errors does not offer sufficient protection to citizens who are the victims of such forms of miscarriage of justice. The ongoing stalemate as regards bills to reform this area and the misleading tracks that political debate on the matter sometimes follows, constitute further grounds for concern.

Structure of the Yearbook 2012

The *Italian Yearbook of Human Rights 2012* is divided into four main Parts, sub-divided into chapters, dedicated to the implementation of human rights law in Italy, to the national human rights infrastructure, to Italy's dialogue with the international human rights institutions, to human rights in Italian case-law and the international case-law concerning Italy. Their consecutive reading should yield a comprehensive picture of the human rights situation in the Country, both in a normative, "infrastructural" light and as regards the real enactment of policies and initiatives fostering human rights promotion and protection. The degree of detail and in-depth discussion pursued in each Part of the *Yearbook* may hopefully allow to make transversal, targeted readings, which can be developed by consulting the index and the table of cases.

The information provided in the first three Parts are taken from documents of public knowledge, mostly traceable to the official websites of the various organisations considered. A specific database on the Italian version of the Archive "Peace Human Rights" website (www.annuarioitalianodirittiumani.it) provides access to all the documents cited in this and in the previous edition of the Yearbook.

Part I of the *Yearbook* illustrates the degree to which international and European norms have been included in the internal law system. The review progresses systematically, starting from the universal level (United Nations, UNESCO, ILO, international humanitarian law instruments) and finally reaching the regional level, constituted by the Council of Europe and the European Union. The same progressive criterion is used in presenting the internal legislation which acknowledges principles and obligations contained in the international legal instruments at the national, regional and local levels.

Part II is dedicated to Italy's human rights infrastructure, and is divided into three chapters. The first presents the structure, functions and activities of parliamentary, governmental and judiciary bodies, independent authorities, civil society organisations and academic institutions. The second chapter refers to the sub-national level, and presents the variegated local and regional human rights infrastructure, and the related national coordinating structures. The third chapter concentrates on the activities of the Region of Veneto in the fields of human rights, peace and international solidarity. The particular emphasis on this exemplary sub-national reality is inspired by the pioneering commitment of the Region of Veneto, started with regional law No. 18 of 1988, in promoting a culture of human rights and peace.

Part III focuses on Italy's position in relation to the international and European monitoring machinery: Committees, Commissions, Special Rapporteurs and Representatives, etc. Ample space is given to the assessments and recommendations addressed to the Italian Government by those bodies, as the result of specific missions and activities of periodic reporting. Further focus is on Italy's role within those organisations, and on contribution given by its representatives in promoting human rights both at regional and global level. This Part is divided into five chapters. The first focuses on the United Nations system and, specifically, on the activities of the General Assembly, the Human Rights Council, the treaty bodies, specialised Agencies, Programmes and Funds (UNESCO, OIL, FAO, UNDP, etc.) as well as of international organisations with a consultative status with the General Assembly (IOM). The second chapter is devoted to the Council of Europe and offers a comprehensive overview of activities and initiatives that have involved the main bodies for the promotion and protection of human rights established by the pan-European Organisation: particular attention is set on the action of the Parliamentary Assembly, the European Committee on Social Rights, the Commissioner for Human Rights, the European Commission against Racism and Intolerance (ECRI) and the Advisory Committee on the Framework Convention for the Protection of National Minorities. The third chapter, specifically dedicated to the European Union, presents the most significant activities realised by European institutions and bodies in human rights matters, both within the EU and in the relationship with third Countries. This chapter complements the data presented in Part I (as regards norms) and in Part IV (as regards case-law) with reference to the European Union action in 2011. The fourth chapter refers to the Organisation for Security and Cooperation in Europe (OSCE), and its bodies committed to promoting the human dimension of security, in particular the Representative on Freedom of the Media. The fifth and final chapter of Part III examines international humanitarian and criminal law, highlighting the degree of Italy's adaptation to it, and listing international peace missions that took place in 2011 involving participation by Italian security forces.

Finally, Part IV provides a selection from national and international case-law regarding Italy during 2011. In its three chapters, cases are subdivided according to the topics addressed by the various judgements.

The chapters deal respectively with internal case-law of the Constitutional Court, the Court of Cassation, national courts and administrative justice, the case-law of the European Court of Human Rights and the case-law of the Court of Justice of the European Union as regards claims brought against Italy. A targeted reading of the case-law can also be made by looking up single cases appearing in the table of cases at the end of this volume.

Toward an Italian Agenda of Human Rights

The recommendations Italy has received internationally, some of which either shared by several monitoring bodies or reiterated in the course of time, taken together with the analysis of the more critical aspects identified in this Yearbook, allow formulating a possible, tentatively organic "Agenda of human rights". The wish is that the Agenda, which is presented below, could provide policy-makers with a useful orientation tool with regards to the main initiatives that are to be realised in Italy at the normative, infrastructural and policy levels.

Italian Agenda of Human Rights

Normative Level

1. Ratify the following legal instruments (United Nations and Council of Europe):

- International Convention on the Protection of the Rights of All Migrant Workers and Members of Their Families.
- International Convention for the Protection of All Persons from Enforced Disappearance.
- Optional Protocol to the International Covenant on Economic, Social and Cultural Rights.
- Optional Protocol to the Convention against Torture and Other Cruel, Inhuman or Degrading Treatment or Punishment.
- Optional Protocol to the Convention on the Rights of the Child on a Communications Procedure.
- Protocol No. 12 to the Convention for the Protection of Human Rights and Fundamental Freedoms.
- Council of Europe Convention on Preventing and Combating Violence against Women and Domestic Violence.
- Civil Law Convention on Corruption.
- Criminal Law Convention on Corruption and Additional Protocol.
- European Convention on Nationality.

2. Accept art. 25 of the European Social Charter (revised), which recognises the right of workers to the protection of their claims in the event of the insolvency of their employer.

3. Withdraw the declaration which excludes the application, for Italy, of Chapter C of the European Convention on the Participation of Foreigners in Public Life at Local Level and, accordingly, to provide for the introduction of active and passive voting rights in local elections for foreigners residing in the Country for a certain number of years.

4. Incorporate the aggravating circumstances for hate motivation in art. 61 of the criminal code.

5. Incorporate the crime of torture into domestic legislation.

Infrastructural Level

6. Plug the structural macro-gap regarding the lack of independent national human rights institutions, consistent with the Paris Principles adopted by the United Nations.

7. Establish a national, independent and adequately funded preventive mechanism against torture.

8. Clarify the division of labour among the Inter-Ministerial Committee for Human Rights, the National Ombudsperson for Children and Adolescents and the (future) National Commission for the Promotion and Protection of Human Rights.

9. Give top expression to the Network of Regional Ombudsperson by establishing the National Ombudsperson.

10. Foster coordination among the Independent Authorities dealing with fundamental rights issues within the national human rights system.

11. Provide all Ministries with an *ad hoc* human rights office.

12. Increase the number of staff with specific skills in human rights within the Ministry of Foreign Affairs and update diplomats' training on the European Union guidelines on human rights.

Implementation of International Obligations and Commitments

13. Comply with specific voluntary pledges and commitments, at the national level, undertaken by Italy upon the presentation of the two candidatures at the United Nations Human Rights Council, and in particular:

- complete the normative process for the implementation of the Statute of the International Criminal Court,
- update the National action plan against racism,
- implement, in a timely manner, all accepted recommendations in connection with the Universal Periodic Review.

14. Start up a monitoring process concerning the stage of implementation of the Universal Periodic Review recommendations with the aim of realising a mid-term report, to be drafted with the full participation of civil society organisations.

15. Submit overdue reports to United Nations treaty bodies, in particular:

- V report to the Committee on economic, social and cultural rights (overdue since June 2009).
- VI report to the Committee on civil and political rights (overdue since October 2009).
- VI report to the Committee against torture (overdue since July 2011).
- I report to the Committee on the rights of persons with disabilities (overdue since June 2011).

16. Fully comply with interim measures issued by the European Court of Human Rights and improve the capacity to adapt the domestic system to human rights standards defined by the Court, in areas such as:

- use of lethal force by law enforcement officials and effectiveness of related investigations,
- prohibition of torture and other cruel or inhuman treatments in connection to expulsions or push back of aliens toward States where such practices exist,
- parliamentary immunity,
- protection of the rights of detainees,
- recourse to retroactive laws which impinge over the legitimate expectations concerning an existing legal dispute,
- scrupulous compliance with the principle of the best interest of the child in proceedings concerning minors and, in particular, in cases of international child abduction.

17. Find a definitive solution to the excessive length of judicial proceedings, including those set up to remedy to excessively long ones.

18. Implement, with no delay, European Union directives on human rights-related issues and comply with European Court of Justice rulings.

Adoption of Policies

19. Hold an annual parliamentary debate on human rights.

20. Adopt the following national plans of actions, providing them with adequate monitoring and assessing tools:

- National plan of action against trafficking in human beings.
- National plan of action to combat violence against women.

- National plan of action to improve the human rights conditions of persons deprived of their liberty.
- National Roma integration strategy (under the Communication from the European Commission 173/2011).
- National plan of action for the human rights promotion of persons with disabilities.
- National programme on education for democratic citizenship and on human rights education and training.

21. Ensure that due attention is paid to the human rights dimension in the framework of economic, fiscal and budgetary policies, as well as in labour and job-related policies.

Initiatives in Specific Fields

Rights of Women

22. Strengthen women's representation in the highest decision-making positions of institutional bodies, including the Parliament and Regional Councils, public administration, including the diplomatic service, and the private sector.

23. Adopt coordinated policies to promote the effective equality between men and women in relation to job conditions.

Rights of Children

24. Introduce a comprehensive legal provision establishing the right of the child to be heard that would be applicable to all courts, administrative bodies, institutions, schools, childcare institutions and families in matters affecting children, and provide adequate safeguards and mechanisms for ensuring that such participation can be carried out effectively.

25. Effectively implement the National plan of action and intervention for the protection of rights and development of subjects in developmental age (2010-2011) through the allocation of adequate funds and the setting-up of a specific monitoring and evaluation system.

26. Amend the criminal code to expressly prohibit and criminalise the recruitment and use in hostilities of persons under the age of 18 by the armed forces and armed groups.

27. Prohibit and criminalise in domestic legislation the sale of small arms and light weapons to Countries where children are involved in armed conflict.

28. Review domestic law and ensure that it prohibits the expulsion of persons under the age of 18, even for reasons of public order and State security, where

there are substantial grounds for believing that there is a real risk of irreparable harm to the child.

Rights of Migrants, Refugees and Asylum Seekers

29. Fully respect the *jus cogens* principle of *non-refoulement*.

30. Respect the right of asylum seekers to an individual examination of their asylum claim, as well as to immediate access to asylum procedures and other national and international forms of protection.

31. Deal with migrations as a structural phenomenon through ordinary tools, discontinuing the emergency and securitarian approach.

32. Adopt broad policies aiming at integrating the resident foreign population and provide for the widening of political participation, also in order to reconsider the citizenship law under the principle of *ius humanae dignitatis*.

33. Resolve the *de facto* statelessness of more than 15,000 Roma who were born in Italy from parents coming from former Yugoslavia territories.

Part I

Implementation of International Human Rights Law in Italy

International Human Rights Law

The first Part of the Yearbook is divided into two chapters. The first is devoted to the review of the major international human rights instruments that Italy has ratified as well as to the identification of both those international instruments signed but not ratified by the Country and those that have not been subjected to any initiative of acceptance yet. The framework of Italy's international obligations takes into consideration the universal conventions adopted within the system of the United Nations, the conventions of the Council of Europe as well as the European Union treaties and secondary law. Accordingly, the information provided are preliminary to the presentation of the national normative apparatus – Constitution, national and regional laws – which is the subject of the following chapter.

There are 132 international legal instruments in force dedicated to protecting and promoting human rights, according to the listing annually edited by UNESCO (*Major Human Rights Instruments*). Among them, 60 are universal in scope and 72 are regional, whereof 39 have been adopted by the Council of Europe (CoE), 11 by the African Union (AU) and 22 by the Organisation of American States (OAS). This legal framework is enriched by several other instruments of soft law, which help orienting States' policies, often with a high degree of effectiveness.

In addition to the conventions indicated by UNESCO, the Yearbook lists other legal instruments that have particular relevance for the topics dealt with in this 2012 edition. In particular, this chapter considers 61 conventions of the United Nations, to which are added 15 conventions on disarmament and non-proliferation, and 50 conventions of the Council of Europe.

In the charts below, the international instruments which establish obligations for Italy are grouped according to the international organisation adopting those instruments, and to thematic area. For each treaty, the official title, the date of adoption and the date of its coming into force are detailed as well as the date of Italy's signature and deposit of the ratification instrument, if applicable. It is to be noted that the date of deposit does not coincide with the normally preceding one in which the Italian Parliament has adopted the law that authorises the ratification of the treaty and issues the order of execution.

I. Legal Instruments of the United Nations

The following charts indicate the main instruments touching on human rights (variously designated as conventions, protocols, covenants or treaties) adopted by the United Nations and its specialised Agencies, in particular the United Nations Educational, Scientific and Cultural Organisation (UNESCO) and the International Labour Organisation (ILO).

These conventions are divided into three main categories: general instruments, instruments concerning particular subjects (prohibition and prevention of discrimination, genocide, war crimes, crimes against humanity, terrorism, torture, slavery, human trafficking, forced labour, freedom of expression, education), and instruments concerning the protection of social groups (foreigners, refugees, displaced or stateless persons, workers, women, children, persons with disabilities, victims of armed conflict). A further category is that constituted by the legal instruments on disarmament and non-proliferation that are presented in the following section.

A. Conventions Ratified by Italy

Treaty Title	**Adoption**	**Entry into force (as of 31/12/2011**	**Signature**	**Deposit of instrument of ratification**
a) General Instruments				
International Covenant on Economic, Social and Cultural Rights	16/12/1966	03/01/1976	18/01/1966	15/09/1978
International Covenant on Civil and Political Rights	16/12/1966	23/01/1976	18/01/1966	15/09/1978
Optional Protocol to the International Covenant on Civil and Political Rights	16/12/1966	23/03/1976	30/04/1976	15/09/1978
Second Optional Protocol to the International Covenant on Civil and Political Rights, aiming at the abolition of the death penalty	15/12/1989	11/01/1991	13/02/1990	14/02/1995
b) Instruments concerning particular subjects				
Prevention of discrimination				
International Convention on the Elimination of All	07/03/1966	04/01/1969	13/03/1968	05/01/1976

Forms of Racial Discrimination				
ILO Convention (No. 100) concerning Equal Remuneration for Men and Women Workers for Work of Equal Value	29/06/1951	23/05/1953		08/06/1956
ILO Convention (No. 111) concerning Discrimination in Respect of Employment and Occupation	25/06/1958	15/06/1960		12/08/1963
Genocide, war crimes, crimes against humanity				
Convention on the Prevention and Punishment of the Crime of Genocide	09/12/1948	12/01/1951		04/06/1952
Rome Statute of the International Criminal Court	17/07/1998	01/07/2002	18/07/1998	26/07/1999
Terrorism				
Convention for the Suppression of Terrorist Bombings	15/12/1997	23/05/2001	04/03/1998	16/04/2003
Convention for the Suppression of the Financing of Terrorism	09/12/1999	10/04/2002	13/12/2000	27/03/2003
Torture and other cruel, inhuman or degrading treatment or punishment				
Convention against Torture and Other Cruel, Inhuman or Degrading Treatment or Punishment	10/12/1984	26/06/1987	04/02/1985	12/01/1989
Slavery, traffic in persons, forced labour				
Protocol amending the Slavery Convention signed at Geneva on 25 September 1926	07/12/1953	07/12/1953		04/02/1954
Supplementary Convention on the Abolition of Slavery, the Slave Trade, and Institutions and Practices Similar to Slavery	07/09/1956	30/04/1957	07/09/1956	12/02/1958

Convention for the Suppression of the Traffic in Persons and of the Exploitation of the Prostitution of Others	21/03/1950	25/07/1951		18/01/1980
ILO Convention (No. 29) concerning Forced or Compulsory Labour	21/06/1930	01/05/1932		18/06/1934
ILO Convention (No. 105) concerning the Abolition of Forced Labour	25/06/1957	17/01/1959		15/03/1968
Freedom of information and expression				
UNESCO Convention on the Protection and Promotion of the Diversity of Cultural Expressions	20/10/2005	18/03/2007		19/02/2007
Education				
UNESCO Convention against Discrimination in Education	14/12/1960	22/05/1962		06/10/1966
UNESCO Protocol Instituting a Conciliation and Good Offices Commission to be Responsible for Seeking the Settlement of any Disputes which may Arise between States Parties to the Convention against Discrimination in Education	10/12/1962	24/10/1968		06/10/1966
c) Instruments concerning the protection of social groups				
Foreigners, refugees, stateless				
Convention relating to the Status of Refugees	28/07/1951	22/04/1954	23/07/1952	15/11/1954
Protocol relating to the Status of Refugees	31/01/1967	04/10/1967		26/01/1972
Convention relating to the Status of Stateless Persons	28/09/1954	06/06/1960	20/10/1954	03/12/1962
Workers				
ILO Convention (No. 11) concerning the Rights of	12/11/1921	11/05/1923		08/09/1924

Association and Combination of Agricultural Workers				
ILO Convention (No. 87) concerning Freedom of Association and Protection of the Right to Organise	09/07/1948	04/07/1950		13/05/1958
ILO Convention (No. 98) concerning the Application of the Principles of the Right to Organise and to Bargain Collectively	01/07/1949	18/07/1951		13/05/1958
ILO Convention (No. 122) concerning Employment Policy	09/07/1964	15/07/1966		05/05/1971
ILO Convention (No. 135) concerning Protection and Facilities to be Afforded to Workers' Representatives in the Undertaking	23/06/1971	30/06/1973		23/06/1981
ILO Convention (No. 141) concerning Organisations of Rural Workers and Their Role in Economic and Social Development	23/06/1975	24/11/1977		23/06/1981
ILO Convention (No. 151) concerning Protection of the Right to Organise and Procedures for Determining Conditions of Employment in the Public Service	27/06/1978	25/02/1981		28/02/1985
Women				
Convention on the Political Rights of Women	31/03/1953	07/07/1954		06/03/1968
Convention on the Elimination of All Forms of Discrimination against Women	18/12/1979	03/09/1981	17/07/1980	10/06/1985
Optional Protocol to the Convention on the Elimination of Discrimination against Women	06/10/1999	22/12/2000	10/12/1999	22/09/2000

Children				
Convention on the Rights of the Child	20/11/1989	02/09/1990	26/01/1990	05/09/1991
Optional Protocol to the Convention on the Rights of the Child on the Involvement of Children in Armed Conflict	25/05/2000	12/02/2002	06/09/2000	09/05/2002
Optional Protocol to the Convention on the Rights of the Child on the Sale of Children, Child Prostitution and Child Pornography	25/05/2000	18/01/2002	06/09/2000	09/05/2002
ILO Convention (No. 138) concerning Minimum Age for Admission to Employment	26/06/1973	19/06/1976		28/07/1981
ILO Convention (No. 182) concerning the Prohibition and Immediate Action for the Elimination of the Worst Forms of Child Labour	17/06/1999	19/11/2000		07/06/2000
Persons with disabilities				
Convention on the Rights of Persons with Disabilities	13/12/2006	03/05/2008	30/03/2007	15/05/2009
Optional Protocol to the Convention on the Rights of Persons with Disabilities	13/12/2006	03/05/2008	30/03/2007	15/05/2009
Fighters, prisoners and civilians				
Geneva Convention (I) for the Amelioration of the Condition of the Wounded and Sick in Armed Forces in the Field	12/08/1949	21/10/1950	08/12/1949	17/12/1951
Geneva Convention (II) for the Amelioration of the Condition of Wounded, Sick and Shipwrecked Members of Armed Forces at Sea	12/08/1949	21/10/1950	08/12/1949	17/12/1951

Geneva Convention (III) relative to the Treatment of Prisoners of War	12/08/1949	21/10/1950	08/12/1949	17/12/1951
Geneva Convention (IV) relative to the Protection of Civilian Persons in Time of War	1208/1949	21/10/1950	08/12/1949	17/12/1951
Protocol Additional to the Geneva Conventions of 12 August 1949, and relating to the Protection of Victims of International Armed Conflicts (Protocol I)	08/06/1977	07/12/1978	12/12/1977	27/02/1986
Protocol Additional to the Geneva Conventions of 12 August 1949, and relating to the Protection of Victims of Non-International Armed Conflicts (Protocol II)	08/06/1977	07/12/1978	12/12/1977	2702/1986
Protocol additional to the Geneva Conventions of 12 August 1949, and relating to the Adoption of an Additional Distinctive Emblem (Protocol III)	08/12/2005	14/01/2007	08/12/2005	29/01/2009

B. Conventions Signed by Italy but Not (yet) Ratified

Treaty Title	**Adoption**	**Entry into force (as of 31/12/2011)**	**Signature**	**Deposit of instrument of ratification**
a) General Instruments				
Optional Protocol to the International Covenant on Economic, Social and Cultural Rights	10/12/2008	Not yet in force	28/09/2009	
b) Instruments concerning particular subjects				
Terrorism				
International Convention for the Suppression of Acts of Nuclear Terrorism	13/04/2005	07/07/2007	14/09/2005	

Torture and other cruel, inhuman or degrading treatment or punishment				
Optional Protocol to the Convention against Torture and Other Cruel, Inhuman or Degrading Treatment or Punishment	18/12/2002	22/06/2006	20/08/2003	
International Convention for the Protection of All Persons from Enforced Disappearance	20/12/2006	23/12/2010	03/07/2007	
c) Instruments concerning the protection of social groups				
Women				
Convention on Consent to Marriage, Minimum Age for Marriage and Registration of Marriages	10/12/1962	09/121964	20/12/1963	

C. Conventions Not Signed by Italy

Treaty Title	**Adoption**	**Entry into force (as of 31/12/2011)**	**Signature**	**Deposit of instrument of ratification**
b) Instruments concerning particular subjects				
Prevention of discrimination				
International Convention on the Suppression and Punishment of the Crime of Apartheid	30/11/1973	18/07/1976		
ILO Convention (No. 156) concerning Equal Opportunities and Equal Treatment for Men and Women Workers: Workers with Family Responsibilities	23/06/1981	11/08/1983		
International Convention against Apartheid in Sports	10/12/1985	03/04/1988		
OIL Convention (No. 169) concerning Indigenous and Tribal Peoples in Independent Countries	27/06/1989	05/09/1991		
Genocide, war crimes, crimes against humanity				
Convention on the Non-applicability of Statutory Limitations to War Crimes and Crimes against Humanity	26/11/1968	11/11/1970		

Education				
UNESCO Convention on Technical and Vocational Education	10/11/1989	29/08/1991		
c) Instruments concerning the protection of social groups				
Foreigners, refugees, stateless				
Convention on the Reduction of Statelessness	30/08/1961	13/12/1975		
Workers				
International Convention on the Protection of the Rights of All Migrant Workers and Members of Their Families	18/12/1990	01/07/2003		
Women				
Convention on the Nationality of Married Women	20/02/1957	11/08/1958		

II. Legal Instruments on Disarmament and Non-proliferation

A. Conventions Ratified by Italy

Treaty Title	**Adoption**	**Entry into force (as of 31/12/2011)**	**Signature**	**Deposit of instrument of ratification**
Protocol for the Prohibition of the Use of Asphyxiating, Poisonous or Other Gases, and of Bacteriological Methods of Warfare	17/06/1925	08/02/1928	17/06/1925	03/04/1928
Treaty Banning Nuclear Weapon Tests in the Atmosphere, in Outer Space and Under Water	05/08/1963	10/10/1963	08/08/1963	10/12/1964
Nuclear Non-proliferation Treaty	01/07/1968	05/03/1970	28/01/1969	02/05/1975
Convention on the Prohibition of the Development, Production and Stockpiling of Bacteriological (Biological) and Toxin Weapons and on their Destruction	10/04/1972	26/03/1975	10/04/1972	30/05/1975

Convention on Prohibitions or Restrictions on the Use of Certain Conventional Weapons Which May be Deemed to be Excessively Injurious or to Have Indiscriminate Effects	10/10/1980	02/12/1983	10/04/1981	20/01/1995
Protocol on Non-Detectable Fragments (Protocol I)	10/10/1980	2/12/1983	10/04/1981	20/01/1995
Protocol on Prohibitions or Restrictions on the Use of Mines, Booby-Traps and Other Devices (Protocol II), as amended by the Review Conference	10/10/1980	02/12/1983	10/04/1981	20/01/1995
Protocol on Prohibitions or Restrictions on the Use of Incendiary Weapons (Protocol III)	10/10/1980	02/12/1983	10/04/1981	20/01/1995
Protocol on Blinding Laser Weapons (Protocol IV)	13/10/1995	30/07/1998		13/01/1999
Protocol on Explosive Remnants of War (Protocol V)	28/11/2003	12/11/2006		11/02/2010
Amendment article 1 of the Convention on Prohibitions or Restrictions on the Use of Certain Conventional Weapons Which May be Deemed to be Excessively Injurious or to Have Indiscriminate Effects	21/12/2001	18/05/2004		01/09/2004
Convention on the Prohibition of the Development, Production, Stockpiling and Use of Chemical Weapons and on Their Destruction	13/01/1993	29/04/1997	13/01/1993	08/12/1995
Comprehensive Nuclear Test-Ban Treaty	10/09/1996	not yet in force	24/09/1996	01/02/1999
Convention on the Prohibition of the Use, Stockpiling, Production and Transfer of Anti-personnel Mines and on their Destruction	18/09/1997	01/03/1999	03/12/1997	23/04/1999
Convention on Cluster Munitions	30/08/2008	01/08/2010	03/12/2008	21/09/2011

III. Legal Instruments of the Council of Europe

The following charts indicate the major legal instruments adopted by the Council of Europe: general instruments, instruments concerning particular subjects (bioethics, corruption, culture, terrorism, torture, etc.)

and instruments concerning the protection of social groups (foreigners, refugees, displaced or stateless persons, migrant workers, women, children, persons belonging to minorities).

The Italian Parliament, with l. 28 March 2001, No. 145 (Official Gazzette 24 April 2001, No. 95), has authorised the ratification and execution of the Oviedo Convention and of the 1998 Protocol on the Prohibition of Cloning Human Beings, delegating the Government to adopt measures to adapt the Italian legal system to the principles and provisions of both the Convention and the Protocol. However, to this day, the related instrument of ratification has not been yet deposited with the Secretariat General of the Council of Europe and, accordingly, consistent with art. 33(4) of the Oviedo Convention, Italy is not contracting party to the treaty.

A. Conventions Ratified by Italy

Treaty Title	**Adoption**	**Entry into force (as of 31/12/2011)**	**Signature**	**Deposit of instrument of ratification**
a) General instruments				
Convention for the Protection of Human Rights and Fundamental Freedoms	04/11/1950	03/09/1953	04/11/1950	26/10/1955
Protocol to the Convention for the Protection of Human Rights and Fundamental Freedoms	20/03/1952	18/05/1954	20/03/1952	26/10/1955
Protocol No. 4 to the Convention for the Protection of Human Rights and Fundamental Freedoms, securing Certain Rights and Freedoms other than those already included in the Convention and in the first Protocol thereto	16/09/1963	02/05/1968	16/09/1963	27/05/1982
Protocol No. 6 to the Convention for the Protection of Human Rights and Fundamental Freedoms concerning the Abolition of the Death Penalty	28/04/1983	01/03/1958	21/10/1983	29/12/1988
Protocol No. 7 to the Convention for the Protection of Human Rights and Fundamental Freedoms	22/11/1984	01/11/1988	22/11/1984	07/11/1991

Protocol No. 13 to the Convention for the Protection of Human Rights and Fundamental Freedoms, concerning the Abolition of the Death Penalty in all Circumstances	03/05/2002	01/07/2003	03/05/2002	03/03/2009
Protocol No. 14 to the Convention for the Protection of Human Rights and Fundamental Freedoms, amending the Control System of the Convention	13/05/2004	01/06/2010	13/05/2004	07/03/2006
European Agreement relating to Persons participating in Proceedings of the European Commission and Court of Human Rights	06/05/1969	17/04/1971	08/01/1974	06/01/1981
European Agreement relating to Persons Participating in Proceedings of the European Court of Human Rights	05/03/1996	01/01/1999	05/03/1996	06/03/1998
European Social Charter	18/10/1961	26/02/1965	18/10/1961	22/10/1965
Additional Protocol to the European Social Charter	05/05/1988	04/09/1992	05/05/1988	26/05/1994
Protocol amending the European Social Charter	21/10/1991	not yet in force	21/10/1991	27/01/1995
Additional Protocol to the European Social Charter Providing for a System of Collective Complaints	09/11/1995	01/07/1998	09/11/1995	03/11/1997
European Social Charter (revised)	03/05/1996	01/07/1999	03/05/1996	05/07/1999
Convention for the Protection of Individuals with regard to Automatic Processing of Personal Data	28/01/1981	01/10/1985	02/02/1983	29/03/1997
Convention on Cybercrime	23/11/2001	01/07/2004	23/11/2001	05/06/2008
Council of Europe Convention on Action against Trafficking in Human Beings	16/05/2005	01/02/2008	08/06/2005	29/11/2010

b) Instruments concerning particular subjects				
Terrorism				
European Convention on the Suppression of Terrorism	27/01/1977	04/08/1978	27/01/77	28/02/86
Torture				
European Convention for the Prevention of Torture and Inhuman or Degrading Treatment or Punishment	26/11/1987	01/02/1989	26/11/1987	29/12/1988
Protocol No. 1 to the European Convention for the Prevention of Torture and Inhuman or Degrading Treatment or Punishment	04/11/1993	01/03/2002	30/10/1996	08/03/1999
Protocol No. 2 to the European Convention for the Prevention of Torture and Inhuman or Degrading Treatment or Punishment	04/11/1993	01/03/2002	30/10/1996	08/03/1999
c) Instruments concerning the protection of social groups				
Foreigners, refugees, stateless				
European Agreement on Transfer of Responsibility for Refugees	16/10/1980	01/12/1980	07/07/1981	08/11/1985
Convention on the Participation of Foreigners in Public Life at Local Level	05/02/1992	01/05/1997	05/02/1992	26/05/1994
Migrant workers				
European Convention on the Legal Status of Migrant Workers	24/11/1977	01/05/1983	11/01/1983	27/02/1995
Minorities				
Framework Convention for the Protection of National Minorities	01/02/1995	01/02/1998	01/02/1995	03/11/1997
Children				
European Convention on the Exercise of Children's Rights	25/01/1996	01/07/2000	25/01/1996	04/07/2003

B. Conventions Signed by Italy

Treaty Title	**Adoption**	**Entry into force (as of 31/12/2011)**	**Signature**	
a) General Instruments				
Protocol No. 12 to the Convention for the Protection of Human Rights and Fundamental Freedoms	04/11/2000	01/04/2005	04/11/2000	
b) Instruments concerning particular subjects				
Bioethics				
Convention for the Protection of Human Rights and Dignity of the Human Being with regard to the Application of Biology and Medicine: Convention on Human Rights and Biomedicine	04/04/1997	01/12/1999	04/04/1997	
Additional Protocol to the Convention for the Protection of Human Rights and Dignity of the Human Being with regard to the Application of Biology and Medicine, on the Prohibition of Cloning Human Beings	12/01/1998	01/03/2001	12/01/1998	
Additional Protocol to the Convention on Human Rights and Biomedicine, concerning Transplantation of Organs and Tissues of Human Origin	24/01/2002	01/05/2006	28/02/2002	
Additional Protocol to the Convention on Human Rights and Biomedicine, concerning Biomedical Research	25/01/2005	01/09/2007	25/01/2005	
Council of Europe Convention on the Counterfeiting of Medical Products and Similar Crimes involving Threats to Public Health	28/10/2011	not yet in force	28/10/2011	
Corruption				
Criminal Law Convention on Corruption	04/11/1999	01/11/2003	04/11/1999	

Civil Law Convention on Corruption	27/01/1999	01/07/2002	27/01/1999	
Additional Protocol to the Criminal Law Convention on Corruption	15/05/2003	01/02/2005	15/05/2003	
Terrorism				
Protocol amending the European Convention on the Suppression of Terrorism	15/05/2003	not yet in force	15/05/2003	
Council of Europe Convention on the Prevention of Terrorism	16/05/2005	01/06/2007	08/06/2005	
Council of Europe Convention on Laundering, Search, Seizure and Confiscation of the Proceeds from Crime and on the Financing of Terrorism	16/05/2005	01/05/2008	08/06/2005	
c) Instruments concerning the protection of social groups				
Minorities				
European Charter for Regional or Minority Languages	05/11/1992	01/03/1998	27/06/2000	
European Convention on Nationality	06/11/1997	01/03/2000	06/11/1997	
Children				
Convention on Contact concerning Children	15/05/2003	01/09/2005	15/05/2003	
Council of Europe Convention on the Protection of Children against Sexual Exploitation and Sexual Abuse	25/10/2007	01/07/2000	07/11/2007	

C. Conventions Not Signed by Italy

Treaty Title	**Adoption**	**Entry into force (as of 31/12/2011)**		
b) Instruments concerning particular subjects				
Prevention of discrimination				
Additional Protocol to the Convention on Cybercrime, concerning the Criminalisation	28/01/2003	01/03/2006		

of Acts of a Racist and Xenophobic Nature committed through Computer Systems				
Genocide, war crimes, crimes against humanity				
European Convention on the Non-Applicability of Statutory Limitation to Crimes against Humanity and War Crimes	25/01/1974	27/06/2003		
Bioethics				
Additional Protocol to the Convention on Human Rights and Biomedicine, concerning Genetic Testing for Health Purposes	27/11/2008	not yet in force		
Culture				
Council of Europe Framework Convention on the Value of Cultural Heritage for Society	27/10/2005	01/06/2011		
b) Instruments concerning the protection of particular groups				
Victims of crime				
European Convention on the Compensation of Victims of Violent Crimes	24/11/1983	01/02/1988		
Foreigners, refugees, stateless				
Council of Europe Convention on the Avoidance of Statelessness in relation to State Succession	19/05/2006	01/05/2009		
Women				
Council of Europe Convention on Preventing and Combating Violence against Women and Domestic Violence	11/05/2011	not yet in force		
Children				
European Convention on the Adoption of Children (revised)	27/11/2008	01/09/2011		

IV. European Union Law

A. Treaties

In the new EU legal framework characterised by the entry into force on 1 December 2009 of the Treaty on the European Union (TEU) and the Treaty on the Functioning of the European Union (TFEU) (the so called Lisbon Treaty), the Charter of Fundamental Rights of the European Union (CFREU) has become legally binding. The Preamble of the TEU mentions the 1961 European Social Charter of the Council of Europe (revised in 1999) and the 1989 Community Charter of Fundamental Social Rights of Workers. Both instruments are also recalled by the TFEU in the context of Title X on the Social Policy (art. 151).

Negotiations between the European Union and the Council of Europe on the EU accession to the European Convention on Human Rights (ECHR) have been under way throughout 2011. Thanks to the EU accession to the ECHR, legally imposed by article 6 TEU and now technically possible after the entry into force of Protocol 14 amending article 59 ECHR, individuals who deem their rights have been violated by the European institutions will have the possibility, after exhaustion of domestic remedies, to file complaint against the EU before the European Court of Human rights (ECtHR).

In order to prepare the necessary legal instrument for the EU accession to the ECHR, in 2010 the Committee of Ministers of the Council of Europe gave an ad-hoc mandate to its Steering Committee for Human Rights. The Steering Committee then entrusted an informal working group composed of 14 Independent Experts with the task of drafting such legal instrument(s). The informal working group, together with the European Commission, elaborated a draft agreement on the accession of the EU to the ECHR, a draft rule and a draft explanatory report of the agreement.

The draft agreement on accession (CDDH-UE(2011)16 final), consisting of 12 articles, tackles both substantial and procedural issues related to the EU accession to the ECHR such as the participation of the EU in the expenditure related to the Convention or the participation of the EU in the bodies of the Council of Europe. According to article 1 of the draft agreement, the EU will not only accede to the ECHR but also to Protocol No. 1 and 6 to the Convention. Paragraph 2 of article 59 ECHR shall be then amended in order to allow the EU to accede to the other Protocols. As for the relationship between the jurisdictions of the two European Courts (ECtHR and Court of Justice of the European Union), the draft agreement stipulates that, if the Court of Justice (ECJ) has not previously assessed the compatibility of a EU law provision with a Convention right, sufficient time shall be afforded to the ECJ to make such an assessment before the pronouncement of the Strasbourg Court. In this connection though, the draft agreement leaves open the issue related to the compatibility of inter-party cases (art. 33 ECHR) with article 344 TFEU concerning the exclusive competence of the ECJ to interpret EU law. Moreover, as to avoid the risk of the ECHR dealing with issues concerning the division of competences between the Union and the Member States, the draft agreement established the so-called co-respondent mechanism. As for the election of judges, a delegation of the European Parliament composed of 18 members will be entitled to participate, with the right to vote, in the sittings of the Parliamentary Assembly of the Council of Europe on an equal footing with the other Contracting parties. The participation of the European Union in the Committee of Ministers of the CoE is then governed by article 7 of the draft agreement.

On 14 October 2011, considering the persistent disagreement on some outstanding issues and in the absence of a common position among the EU Member States, the Steering Committee for Human Rights of the CoE agreed to transmit its final report (CDDH(2011)009) to the Committee of Ministers for consideration and further guidance.

B. EU Law in 2011

During the year 2011, the European Parliament and the Council of the EU adopted a number of regulations, directives and decisions particularly relevant to human rights issues regarding both the external and the internal dimension. For its part, the European Commission presented communications and legislative proposals.

In 2011 several directives on issues such as immigration, asylum and international protection have been adopted. Particularly relevant in this regards are: directive 2011/51/EU of the European Parliament and of the Council, 11 May 2011, amending and extending the scope of Council directive 2003/109/EC to beneficiaries of international protection; directive 2011/98/EU of the European Parliament and of the Council, 13 December 2011, on a single application procedure for a single permit for third-Country nationals to reside and work in the territory of a Member State and on a common set of rights for third-Country workers legally residing in a Member State; directive 2011/95/EU of the European Parliament and of the Council, 13 December 2011, on standards for the qualification of third-Country nationals or stateless persons as beneficiaries of international protection, for a uniform status for refugees or for persons eligible for subsidiary protection, and for the content of the protection granted.

Critical measures in the field of human trafficking and smuggling include: directive 2011/36/EU of the European Parliament and of the Council, 5 April 2011, on preventing and combating trafficking in human beings and protecting its victims and the Commission decision 2011/502/EU, 10 August 2011, on setting up the Group of Experts on Trafficking in Human Beings. Worth to note in connection with these issues are directive 2011/92/EU of the European Parliament and of the Council, 13 December 2011, on combating the sexual abuse and sexual exploitation of children and child pornography and directive 2011/99/EU of the European Parliament and of the Council, 13 December 2011, on the European protection order. The European Commission also addressed the issue of Roma with a Communication on the EU Framework for National Roma Integration Strategies up to 2020 (COM(2011)173 final).

In 2011 regulations have been adopted in order to impose special conditions governing the import of feed and food originating in or consigned from Japan following the accident at the Fukushima nuclear power station. In addition, EU regulations have been adopted in order to update the list of individuals and organisations subject to sanctions in execution of United Nations Security Council resolutions against the terrorist network of Al-Qaeda and the Taleban, and to update the punitive measures against other terrorist organisations. In 2011 regulations have been adopted in order to renew measures against persons wanted by the International Tribunal for the Former Yugoslavia as well as to implement restrictive measures established by the United Nations against Countries such as Belarus, Libya, North Korea, Myanmar, Guinea, Iran, Syria, Sudan, the Democratic Republic of the Congo, Somalia, Ivory Cost and Zimbabwe. With some decisions adopted in the context of the Common Foreign and Security Policy, the Council has also established restrictive measures directed against certain persons and entities in view of the situation in Tunisia (2011/72/CFSP of 31 January 2011); set up the European Union military operation in support of humanitarian assistance operations in response to the crisis situation in Libya (EUFOR Libya) (2011/210/CFSP, 1 April 2011); adopted the new EU Common Position on the International Criminal Court (2011/168/CFSP, 21 March 2011).

Other regulations adopted included: regulation (EU) No. 1168/2011 of the European Parliament and of the Council, 25 October 2011, concerning the reform of the European Agency for the Management of Operational Cooperation at the External Borders of the Member States of the European Union (FRONTEX); Commission implementing regulation 1352/2011, 20 December 2011, concerning trade in certain goods which could be used for capital punishment, torture or other cruel, inhuman or degrading treatment or punishment; regulation 211/2011 of the European Parliament and of the Council, 16 February 2011, on the citizens' initiative.

On March 2011 the EU acceded to the 2007 Hague Convention on the International Recovery of Child Support and other Forms of Family Maintenance. With Council decision 2011/640/CFSP of 12 July 2011 the Council signed an agreement with the Republic of Mauritius on the conditions of transfer of suspected pirates and associated seized property from the European Union-led naval force to the Republic of Mauritius and on the conditions of suspected pirates after transfer.

In Italy, the implementation of European law is ensured by a bill (the so-called "Community law") to be introduced by 31 December each year by the Minister of European Affairs. In 2011, 12 directives have been implemented by legislative decree while 46 have been implemented by administrative regulations. None of them is particularly relevant to human rights. On December 2011 the Italian Parliament passed the "Community law 2010" (l. 15 December 2011, No. 217) while the bill on the "Community law 2011" (A.C. 4623), presented before the Chamber of Deputies on 19 September 2011 is still under review. The latter provides a list of directives to be implemented by the Government among which there are: Council directive 2010/18/EU, 8 March 2010, implementing the revised Framework Agreement on parental leave; directive 2010/41/EU of the European Parliament and of the Council, 7 July 2010, on the application of the principle of equal treatment between men and women engaged in an activity in a self-employed capacity; directive 2010/64/EU of the European Parliament and of the Council, 20 October 2010, on the right to interpretation and translation in criminal proceedings and directive 2011/36/EU of the European Parliament and of the Council, 5 April 2011, on preventing and combating trafficking in human beings and protecting its victims.

On 23 December 2011, the "Community law 2012" has been approved by the Council of Ministers and then introduced before the Parliament. It provides, among other things, a list of directives to be implemented by the Government including directive 2011/24/EU on the application of patients' rights in cross-border healthcare; directive 2011/51/EU on international protection; directive 2011/77/EU on the protection of copyright and directive 2011/83/EU on consumer rights.

In 2011 Italy has received 72 letter of formal notice by the European Commission for its failure to comply with EU law. As 31 December 2011, data provided by the Department of Political Affairs of the Presidency of the Council of Ministers showed that 136 infringement procedures were pending against Italy (among which 54 opened in 2011).

As for the development of some infringement procedures particularly relevant for human rights, on 16 December 2011 the European Commission decided to address to Italy two "reasoned opinions" (ex art. 258 TFEU) requesting it to end discrimination against workers with professional experience (No. 2009/4646) and qualifications (No. 2010/4038) from another Member State. Always in regards of equal treatment in employment and occupation, on 4 April 2011 the European Commission referred Italy to the Court of Justice of the European Union because of its failure to correctly implement Council directive 2000/78/EC and in particular article 5 which establishes that employers shall take appropriate measures in order to provide reasonable accommodation for disabled persons (No. 2006/2441). On 24 November 2011, the European Commission opened another infringement procedures against Italy because it failed to correctly implement Council directive 2004/80/EC on compensation to crime victims which requires Member States to establish a scheme on compensation to victims of violent international crimes.

Italian Law

I. The Constitution of the Italian Republic

> "The Republic recognises and guarantees the inviolable rights of the persons, both as an individual and in the social group where the human personality is expressed. The Republic expects that the fundamental duties of political, economic and social solidarity be fulfilled" (art. 2).
>
> "All citizens have equal social dignity and are equal before the law, without distinction of sex, race, language, religion, political opinion, personal and social conditions.
>
> It is the duty of the Republic to remove those obstacles of an economic or social nature which constrain the freedom and equality of citizens, thereby impeding the full development of the human person and the effective participation of all workers in the political, economic and social organisation of the Country" (art. 3).
>
> "The Italian legal system conforms to the generally recognised principles of international law. The legal status of foreigners is regulated by law in conformity with international provisions and treaties. A foreigner who, in his home Country, is denied the actual exercise of the democratic freedoms guaranteed by the Italian constitution shall be entitled to the right of asylum under the conditions established by law. A foreigner may not be extradited for a political offence" (art. 10).
>
> "Italy rejects war as an instrument of aggression against the freedom of other peoples and as a means for the settlement of international disputes. Italy agrees, on conditions of equality with other States, to the limitations of sovereignty that may be necessary to a world order ensuring peace and justice among the Nations. Italy promotes and encourages international organisations furthering such ends" (art. 11).

The entire First Part of the Constitution (art. 13-54) is dedicated to the fundamental rights and duties of the persons. The inviolable rights recognised therein are classified according to four areas: civil relations (art. 13-28), ethical and social relations (art. 29-34), economic relations (art. 35-47) and political relations (art. 48-54). On 7 March 2011, the Italian Government has presented before the Parliament a constitutional law bill (A.C. 4144) concerning amendments of art. 41 (economic initiative), 97 (public administration) and 118 (administrative function). The bill is currently under the review of the Constitutional Affairs Commission of the Chamber of Deputies.

On 7 April 2011 the Italian Government has presented to the Parliament another constitutional law bill (A.C. 4275) aiming at reforming Title IV of Part Two of the Constitution (art. 101-113). The most significant proposals contained in the bill, whose goal is to reform the Italian justice system, are: the separation of career path for judges and prosecutors; the splitting of the High Council of the Judiciary into two bodies (one for judges and one for prosecutors); the setting up of a High Disciplinary Court responsible for disciplinary measures, with separate sections for judges and prosecutors; the introduction of the personal liability of magistrates for cases of miscarriage of justice; new criteria to be established by law governing the obligation to institute criminal proceedings. Currently, the bill is under joint review of the Constitutional Affairs and Justice Commissions of both Chambers of the Italian Parliament.

II. National Legislation

During the year 2011, the Parliament and the Government passed a number of legislative acts (laws, law-decrees, legislative decrees) regarding issues addressing, directly or indirectly, internationally recognised human rights. The list of legislative acts which follows is structured according to the international instruments classification:

a) general legislative acts (State and sub-State institutions; judiciary in general);

b) legislative acts dealing with specific issues (public order and security; peace keeping missions and international cooperation; crimes, criminal jurisdiction and detention; education, culture and mass media; environment protection, health; property right, freedom of enterprise);

c) legislative acts devoted to the protection of social groups (minorities; children and adolescents; victims of disasters; migrants, refugees and asylum seekers; equal opportunities, gender; persons with disabilities; workers).

a) General legislative acts

State and sub-State institutions

Lgs.d. 6 September 2011, No. 149 (Sanctionatory and rewarding mechanisms for Municipalities, Provinces and Regions according to articles 2, 17 and 26 of l. 5 May 2009, No. 42).

The judiciary in general

L. 14 September 2011, No. 148 (Conversion into law, with amendments, of law-decree 13 August 2011, No. 138, on urgent measures for the financial stability and development. Parliamentary delegation to the

Government for the re-organisation of the territorial distribution of judicial offices).

L. 29 December 2011, No. 218 (Amendments to article 645 and interpretation of article 165 of the code of civil procedure regarding challenges to injunctive decrees).

b) Legislative acts dealing with specific issues

Public order and security

Lgs.d. 6 September 2011, No. 159 (Code of anti-mafia laws and prevention measures, as well as new provisions on anti-mafia documentation, according to articles 1 and 2 of l. 13 August 2010, No. 136).

Peace keeping missions and international cooperation

L. 22 February 2011, No. 9 (Conversion into law, with amendments, of law-decree 29 December 2010, No. 228, on measures to extend development cooperation activities and interventions in support of peace and stabilisation processes, as well as international operations of Italian armed forces and the police).

L. 2 August 2011, No. 130 (Conversion into law, with amendments, of law-decree 12 July 2011, No. 107, on measures to extend development cooperation activities and interventions in support of peace and stabilisation processes, as well as international operations of Italian armed forces and the police and measures to implement United Nations Security Council resolutions 1970 (2011) and 1973 (2011). Urgent measures to fight piracy.)

Lgs.d. 29 December 2011, No. 215 (Measures to extend international operations of Italian armed forces and the police, development cooperation activities and participation to initiatives of international organisations in support of peace and stabilisation processes, as well as urgent measures for the administration of defence).

Crimes, criminal jurisdiction and detention

L. 21 April 2011, No. 62 (Amendments to the code of criminal procedure and to l. 26 July 1975, No. 354, as well as other provisions for the protection of the relationship between incarcerated mothers and their under age children).

L. 14 June 2011, No. 97 (Ratification and order of execution of the Agreement between the Italian Republic and the Republic of Albania, supplementing and facilitating the application of the provisions contained in the European Convention of Extradition of 13 December 1957 and the European Convention on Mutual Assistance in Criminal Matters of 20 April 1959, made in Tirana on 2 December 2007 through an exchange of note carried out in Tirana on 18-19 September 2008).

Lgs.d. 18 July 2011, No. 140 (Provisions implementing the special statute of the Autonomous Region of Sardinia on the correctional health care system).

Lgs.d. 22 December 2011, No. 211 (Urgent measures to counter the overcrowding of detention facilities).

Culture and mass media

L. 26 May 2011, No. 75 (Conversion into law, with amendments, of law-decree 31 March 2011, No. 34, on urgent provisions to support cultural activities; intersections of the press and media sectors; rationalisation of the radio electric spectrum; moratorium on nuclear energy; shareholding to the "Cassa depositi e prestiti"; bodies of the national health system located in the Region Abruzzo).

Environment protection, health

Lgs.d. 11 February 2011, No. 21 (Modifications of lgs.d. 20 November 2008, No. 188, implementing directive 2006/66/CE on batteries and accumulators that repeals directives 91/157/EEC and implementing directive 2008/103/CE).

Property right, freedom of enterprise

L. 11 November 2011, No. 180 (Statute of corporation. Provisions for the protection of the freedom of enterprise).

c) Legislative acts devoted to the protection of social groups

Minorities

Lgs.d. 14 September 2011, No. 172 (Provisions implementing the special statute of the Autonomous Region Trentino-Alto Adige which amend art. 32, paragraph 3, d.p.r. 15 July 1988, No. 574, on the protection of the Ladina community in the Autonomous Province of Trent).

Children and adolescents

L. 12 July 2011, No. 112 (Establishment of the National Ombudsperson for Children and Adolescents).

L. 21 April 2011, No. 62 – see above, Crimes, criminal jurisdiction and detention.

Victims of disasters

L. 14 June 2011, No. 101 (Designation of the National day of remembrance of the victim of natural and industrial disasters caused by man negligence).

Migrants, refugees and asylum seekers

L. 2 August 2011, No. 129 (Conversion into law, with amendments, of law-decree 23 June 2011, No. 89, on urgent measures to finalise the implementation of directive 2004/38/CE on the right of citizens of the Union to move and reside freely within the territory of the Member States and to implement directive 2008/115/CE on the returning of illegally staying third-Country nationals).

Equal opportunities, gender[*]

Lgs.d. 26 March 2001, No. 151 (Consolidated act on the protection and support for motherhood and fatherhood, as provided for in art. 15, l. 8 March 2000, No. 53).

L. 4 April 2001, No. 154 (Measures against violence in family relations).

Lgs.d. 9 July 2003, No. 216 (Implementation of directive 2000/78/CE for equal treatment in employment and occupation).

L. 11 August 2003, No. 228 (Measures against trafficking in human beings).

L. 9 January 2006, No. 7 (Provisions for the prevention and prohibition of any female genital mutilation practice).

Lgs.d. 11 April 2006, No. 198 (Code for equal opportunities between men and women).

Lgs.d. 29 February 2009, No. 11 (Urgent measures on public security and to counter sexual violence as well as persecutory acts. Converted with l. 23 April 2009, No. 38).

III. Municipal, Provincial and Regional Statutes

Since 1991, after the adoption of law 8 June 1990, No. 142 (Local authorities system), the so called "peace human rights norm", originally contained in art. 1 of Veneto regional law 30 March 1988, No. 18 (updated today by regional law 55/1999) on "Regional measures for the promotion of a culture of peace", has been included in the statutes of several Italian Municipalities, Provinces and Regions (see *2011 Yearbook* for statistics, pp. 65-69). The original wording of this norm reads:

> The Municipality [...] [the Province...], consistent with the Constitutional principles sanctioning the repudiation of war as a means of resolving international controversies, and the promotion of human rights, the democratic freedoms and international cooperation, recognises peace as a fundamental human and peoples' right. To this end it promotes the culture of peace through cultural, research, education, cooperation and information initiatives aimed at making the Municipality a land of peace.
>
> In order to achieve these goals, the Municipality will take direct initiatives and foster the initiatives by local authorities, associations, cultural institutions, volunteers and international cooperation groups.

Moreover, there are also many statutes, at the municipal, provincial and regional levels, that make explicit references to international provisions and principles on human rights and territorial self-government, in particular the Charter of the United Nations, the Universal Declaration of Human Rights, the International Covenant on Civil and Political

[*] For this specific domain, legislative acts adopted before 2011 are also recalled.

Rights, the International Covenant on Economic, Social and Cultural Rights, the International Convention on the Rights of the Child, the EU Charter of Fundamental Rights and the European Charter on Local Self-Government.

IV. Regional Laws

This section lists the laws on human rights, equal opportunities, development cooperation, fair trade, migrations, ombudspersons, rights of children, rights of workers and rights of persons with disabilities, adopted by the Councils of Italian Regions and Autonomous Provinces in 2011. The laws are divided according to topics and listed, within each authority, in chronological order. A comprehensive list of the main regional laws adopted on these subjects until 2010 is provided in the *2011 Yearbook* (pp. 69-77).

Peace, human rights, development cooperation, fair trade

R.l. Calabria 18 July 2011, No. 21 (Modifications and integrations to the r.l. 4/2007 (Cooperation and international relations of Calabria)).

R.l. Calabria 18 July 2011, No. 23 (Provisions for the support of local exchange communities and for the promotion of quality food products from short distribution chain).

R.l. Emilia-Romagna 13 November 2011, No. 35 (Participation of the Region Emilia-Romagna to the establishment of the Fondazione Scuola di Pace of Monte Sole).

R.l. Liguria 27 December 2011, No. 36 (Further provisions for the rationalisation of the Regional health service and of social services and international cooperation).

R.l. Tuscany 2 May 2011, No. 14 (Modifications to r.l. 14 October 2002, No. 38 (Provisions for the protection and valorisation of political, cultural and historical heritage of Antifascism and of the Resistance and for the promotion of a culture of liberty, democracy, peace and cooperation among peoples)).

R.l. Umbria 10 February 2011, No. 1 (Provisions for the support of local exchange communities and for the promotion of quality agricultural and food products from short distribution chain).

Equal opportunities, gender

R.l. Basilicata 7 June 2011, No. 11 (Women's spaces of dialogue for the modification and integration of r.l. 26 November 1991, No. 27).

P.l. Bolzano 19 July 2011, No. 7 (Modification of p.l. 8 March 2010 No. 5 (Law of the Autonomous Province of Bolzano on the equalisation and promotion of women and modifications of the provisions in force).

R.l. Calabria 27 April 2011, No. 15 (Modification of r.l. 19 April 1995, No. 22 (Establishment of Project Woman) and successive modifications and integrations).

R.l. Campania 11 February 2011, No. 2 (Measures for the preventing and combating gender-based violence).

R.l. Campania 10 November 2011, No. 17 (Provisions to guarantee effectiveness, saving and equal opportunities).

R.l. Emilia-Romagna 15 July 2011, No. 8 (Establishment of the Regional Commission for the promotion of full equal opportunity conditions between women and men).

R.l. Lombardy 29 April 2011, No. 8 (Establishment of the Council for equal opportunities).

P.l. Trent 1 August 2011, No. 11 (Measures to foster the employment of women).

R.l. Tuscany 10 February 2011, No. 4 (Modifications to r.l. 2 April 2009, No. 16 (Gender Citizenship)).

R.l. Tuscany 19 September 2011, No. 43 (Modifications to art. 10 of r.l. 15 December 2009, No. 76 (Regional Commission for equal opportunities)).

Migrations

P.l. Bolzano 28 October 2011, No. 121 (Integration of foreign women and men nationals).

Ombudspersons and children's ombudspersons

P.l. Bolzano 19 September 2011, No. 101 (Modification of p.l. 4 February 2010, No. 3 (The Ombudsperson in the Autonomous Province of Bolzano)).

R.l. Calabria 6 April 2011, No. 13 (Modifications and integrations to r.l. 16 January 1985, No. 4 (Establishment of the Regional Ombudsperson of the Region of Calabria)).

R.l. Emilia-Romagna 27 September 2011, No. 13 (New provisions on public authorities. Modification of r.l. 16 December 2003, No. 25 (Provisions concerning the Regional Ombudsperson). Abrogation of r.l. 21 March 1995, No. 15 (New regulation concerning the Ombudsperson), of r.l. 17 February 2005, No. 9 (Establishment of the Ombudsperson for children and adolescents) and of r.l. 19 February 2008, No. 3 (Provisions for the protection of the persons convicted in the prisons of the Region Emilia-Romagna)).

R.l. Sardinia 7 February 2011, No. 8 (Establishment of the Regional Ombudsperson for children and adolescents).

R.l. Valle d'Aosta 1 August 2011, No. 19 (Modifications to r.l. 28 August 2001, No. 17 (regulation on functioning of the Ombudsperson's office). Abrogation of r.l. 2 March 1992, No. 5 (Establishment of the Ombudsperson)), and of r.l. 23 July 2010, No. 22 (New regulation concerning the organisation of the regional administration and of the bodies of Valle d'Aosta. Abrogation of r.l. 23 October 1995, No. 45) and of other laws concerning personnel).

Persons with disabilities

R.l. Abruzzo 3 August 2011, No. 26 (Modifications to r.l. 13 April 1995, No. 49 (Contribution to the Council of the Italian Union of the Blind to purchase tiflotecnic electronic devices in favour of the blind).

P.l. Bolzano 13 May 2011, No. 3 (Provisions concerning assistance, charity, administrative procedure, overcoming and removal of architectural barriers, hygiene, health and subsidised housing).

R.l. Calabria 20 December 2011, No. 44 (Provisions in support of not self-sufficient persons – Fund for not self-sufficiency).

R.l. Sicily 4 November 2011, No. 23 (Promotion of Italian Sign Language (LIS). Measures to cope with the situation of emergency in the islands of Lampedusa and Linosa).

P.l. Trent 16 March 2011, No. 4 (Provisions for the promotion and the circulation of support administration for the protection of fragile persons).

P.l. Trent 16 March 2011, No. 5 (Modifications of the p.l. on transportations: measures in favour of disabled persons).

P.l. Trent 26 October 2011, No. 14 (Measures in favour of individuals with specific learning disorders).

Workers' rights

R.l. Apulia 29 September 2011, No. 25 (Provisions concerning authorisation and accreditation for employment services).

R.l. Calabria 20 December 2011, No. 45 (Modification of r.l. 26 February 2010, No. 11 (Regional measures in favour of the relatives of workers who died or who have become severely disabled as a consequence of incidents at the workplace).

R.l. Liguria 11 March 2011, No. 5 (Further modifications to r.l. 1 August 2008, No. 30 (Regional provisions for the promotion of labour) and successive modifications and integrations).

R.l. Piedmont 11 October 2011, No. 20 (Modifications to r.l. 22 December 2008, No. 34 (Provisions for the promotion of employment and of the quality, safety and regularity of labour)).

R.l. Sicily 20 July 2011, No. 15 (Provisions concerning support to companies and to the inclusion of underprivileged individuals. Provisions concerning surveillance of cooperative bodies and the personnel of the Sicilian aqueduct authority).

P.l. Trent 6 October 2011, No. 13 (Solidarity fund for the relatives of the victims of fatal accidents while working or volunteering).

Solidarity, social promotion and assistance to families

R.l. Abruzzo 24 June 2011, No. 17 (Reorganisation of the Public institutions of assistance and charity and regulation of the Public companies of social services).

R.l. Lombardy, 13 December 2011, No. 20 (Relief and security humanitarian initiatives of the Regional Council in favour of populations affected by calamities and catastrophes).

R.l. Marche 1 August 2011, No. 16 (Modification to r.l. 13 October 2008, No. 28 (Integrated regional system of the measures in favour of adults and children subjected to provisions of the Judicial and in favour of former detainees)).

R.l. Molise 9 September 2011, No. 24 (Modification to r.l. 3 December 2004, No. 31 (Provisions concerning the promotion, recognition and development of associations of social promotion)).

P.l. Trent 2 March 2011, No. 1 (Integrated system of structural policies for the promotion of family wellbeing and birth).

R.l. Trentino-Alto Adige 14 July 2011, No. 5 (Support during the *iter* towards pensions in favour of those who benefit of mobility and extension of anti-crisis measures).

R.l. Trentino-Alto Adige 26 September 2011, No. 7 (Modifications to r.l. 21 September 2005, No. 7 and successive modifications concerning "New system of public institutions of assistance and charity – Public companies of social services").

R.l. Tuscany 14 June 2011, No. 23 (Modifications to r.l. 24 February 2005, No. 41 (Integrated system of measures and services for the protection of social citizenship rights)).

R.l. Umbria 4 November 2011, No. 13 (Integration of r.l. 16 February 2010, No. 13 (regulation of services and measure in favour of the family)).

R.l. Veneto 26 May 2011, No. 11 (Measure to fight poverty and social problems through the redistribution of food surplus).

Education to citizenship and legality

R.l. Emilia-Romagna 9 May 2011, No. 3 (Measures for the coordinated implementation of the regional policies in favour of the prevention of organised crime and mafia, as well as for the promotion of the culture of legality and of responsible citizenship).

R.l. Lombardy 14 February 2011, No. 2 (Actions oriented towards the education to legality).

P.l. Trent 21 December 2011, No. 15 (Promotion of the culture of legality and of responsible citizenship for the prevention of organised crime).

Part II

The Human Rights Infrastructure in Italy

National Bodies with Jurisdiction over Human Rights

International human rights law requires States to set up structures adequately specialised in promoting and protecting fundamental rights. In this regard, a distinction shall be made between, on one hand, strictly governmental bodies and, on the other, independent structures directly emanating from civil society. The latter in particular, through channels different from those classically used by governmental powers, aim at participating in policy-making, promoting and developing a human rights culture as well as preventing violations.

In this Part the composition, mandate and activities of the following institutions will be illustrated:

– *Parliamentary bodies*: the Special Commission for the Promotion and Protection of Human Rights of the Italian Senate; the Permanent Committee on Human Rights instituted within the Foreign Affairs Commission (III) of the Italian Chamber of Deputies; the Parliamentary Commission for Children and Adolescents; the Parliament-Government Observatory Monitoring the Promotion and Protection of Fundamental Rights.

– *Governmental bodies* established within: the Prime Minister's Office (Committee of Ministers for Orientation and Strategic Guidance for the Protection of Human Rights; Department for Equal Opportunities; Commission for International Adoptions; National Committee on Bioethics; Inter-Ministerial Committee for Human Rights; National Commission for UNESCO); the Ministry of Labour and Social Policies (National Observatory for Children and Adolescents; National Observatory Monitoring the Condition of Persons with Disabilities; Committee on Foreign Minors); as well as the departments and bureaus of the Ministry of Justice specifically involved in human rights matters.

– *Judicial authorities*: the Constitutional Court and the Court of Cassation, acting as the supreme judge of legitimacy;

– the *National Economy and Labour Council (CNEL)* as a constitutional body;

– *Independent authorities*: the Communications Regulatory Authority; the Data Protection Authority; the Committee Guaranteeing the Implementation of the Law on Strikes Affecting Essential Public Services; the National Ombudsperson for Children and Adolescents.

Finally, Italy's national human rights infrastructure is completed by academic institutions promoting not only research, but also education and training in human rights issues, and by several non-governmental organisations, some of which function through networking.

I. Parliamentary Bodies

A. Senate of the Republic: Special Commission for the Protection and Promotion of Human Rights

The Senate's Special Commission for the Protection and Promotion of Human Rights was set up during the 14th legislature (motion 20, 1 August 2001) and is the fruit of long experience by the Committee against Capital Punishment (1996-2001). Since the Commission is not of a permanent nature, it must be instituted formally at the beginning of each legislature and the Senate did so both during the 15th legislature (motion 20, 12 July 2006) and the 16th legislature (motion 13, 26 June 2008). In the latter motion, the Senate decided to proceed with the establishment of a permanent human rights commission.

The Commission has the task of studying, observing and taking initiatives on issues concerning the protection and promotion of internationally recognised human rights. To this end, it can establish relations with institutions of other Countries and with international bodies; carry out missions in or outside Italy, in particular with foreign Parliaments, even – if necessary – in order to establish agreements fostering human rights or to facilitate other forms of collaboration; it can carry out informational procedures and formulate proposals and Assembly reports; and provide its advisory opinions on proposed legislation as well as on matters deferred to other commissions.

The incumbent Commission is made up of 25 members, present in proportion to the numerical presence of the various parliamentary groups to which they belong. Among these members, the Commission elects the bureau, made up of the Chair, two Vice Chairs and two Secretaries. In 2011 the Commission was composed as follows: *Chair*: Pietro Marcenaro; *Vice Chairs*: Lorenzo Bodega, Ulisse Di Giacomo; *Secretaries*: Franco Mugnai, Marco Perduca; *Members*: Silvana Amati, Emanuela Baio, Franco Cardiello, Emilio Colombo, Barbara Contini, Roberto Della Seta, Egidio Digilio, Roberto Di Giovan Paolo, Salvo Fleres, Andrea Fluttero, Cosimo Gallo, Mariapia Garavaglia, Cosimo Latronico, Rita Levi-Montalcini, Massimo Livi Bacci, Rosa Angela Mauro, Colomba Mongiello, Francesco Pardi, Fedele Sanciu, Giancarlo Serafini.

In 2011, in the ambit of the inquiry into the various levels and systems of human rights protection currently in place in Italy and abroad (launched on 13 January 2009), the Commission held 32 hearings (there were 35 in 2010) of representatives from associations, organisations and institutional bodies, and of individual experts. More specifically, the Commission focused on four lines of inquiry.

– *Italy's election to the United Nations Human Rights Council.* Two sessions were devoted to this topic. On 15 June 2011, the Commission heard Professor Antonio Papisca, professor of International Organisation of Human Rights and Peace at the Faculty of Political Sciences, University of Padua, together with Carola Carazzone, spokesperson of the Commission for the Promotion and Protection of Human Rights, and Riccardo Noury, spokesperson of the Italian section of Amnesty International. On 16 June the Commission heard Vincenzo Scotti, Under Secretary of State for foreign affairs.

– *Condition of the Roma and Sinti in Italy.* On 9 February, the Commission unanimously approved the *Rapporto sulla condizione di rom e sinti in Italia* ("Report on the Condition of the Roma and Sinti in Italy"), the result of an inquiry begun the previous year. The first official document produced by the Italian Parliament on this theme, it contains an analytic description of the situation of the Roma and Sinti in Italy, their numbers and demographic structure, and their living, work and health conditions. The report was then presented in Naples, in the presence of Mayor Rosa Russo Jervolino (1 April 2011); in Turin, in the presence of Mayor Sergio Chiamparino (4 April 2011), and again in Turin (13 May 2011) at the Book Fair; in Milan, at Don Colmegna's Casa della Carità, at an event moderated by the journalist Gad Lerner (15 April 2011); in Florence, in the Aula Magna of the social sciences complex, with contributions, amongst others, from Senator Massimo Livi Bacci and from Franca Alacevich, Dean of the Faculty of Political Sciences at the University of Florence (19 May 2011); in Rome, on 14 June, at the Community of Sant'Egidio, in the presence of Andrea Riccardi, the current Minister for International Cooperation. Finally, a workshop on the Roma and Sinti issue was held at the Senate on 6 December, attended by representatives from various institutional bodies and many members of the communities concerned. The event provided an occasion for preliminary reflections leaning towards the development of a national strategy.

– *Prison conditions.* In the course of 2011, the Commission began to conduct an inquiry into human rights in the prison system, by holding hearings with non-governmental bodies, prison officers' unions, representatives from the Department of Prison Administration, and by making visits to a number of Italian prisons (Ucciardone, Palermo; Favignana; Lanza, Catania; Dozza, Bologna; Poggioreale, Naples; Nisida; Regina Coeli, Rome), and reception centres (the Lampedusa reception centre, the Villaggio della Solidarietà in Mineo, the Identification and Expulsion Centres of Santa Maria Capua Vetere and Ponte Galeria, Rome).

– *Human rights and foreign policy.* The final strand of inquiry undertaken by the Commission in 2011 set out to investigate the relationship between human rights and foreign policy. To analyse this question, the Commission heard representatives from institutional bodies (the former Ministers of Foreign Affairs Lamberto Dini and Massimo D'Alema; Bernard Kouchner, the former French Foreign Minister; Kamel Jendoubi, President of the Independent Electoral Commission, Tunisia, and a member of the Euro-Mediterranean Network for the Defence of Human Rights), diplomats (Laura Mirachian, Italy's permanent representative at international organisations in Geneva; David H. Thorne, US Ambassador to Italy), and prominent members of international civil society, such as the Iranian lawyer and Nobel Peace Prize winner, Shirin Ebadi.

Other issues dealt with in the course of the year were: the situation of migrants and asylum-seekers in Italy, coming from Tunisia and then from Libya, with particular attention towards the condition of minors; the situation of Countries like Iran, Tunisia and Libya, with particular attention towards the unrest and outcomes of the Arab Spring; the condition of Palestinian refugees (through the hearing of Filippo Grandi, Commissioner-General of UNRWA, the United Nations Relief and Works Agency for Palestine Refugees in the Near East); the rights of homosexuals, that is to say, the fight against discrimination and intolerance; and the kidnapping of Francesco Azzarà, the logistician of the NGO Emergency abducted in Nyala, Darfur, in August 2011.

On 25 January, the Commission also organised, together with the US Embassy in Italy and Cittadinanza Attiva, a conference entitled *I nuovi cittadini. Dai luoghi comuni ai beni comuni: l'immigrazione tra diritti, responsabilità, cittadinanza e partecipazione* ("New Citizens. From Commonplaces to Common Assets: Rights, Responsibilities, Citizenship and Participation in the Field of Immigration").

On 3 and 4 April 2011, the Commission, together with the Italian Centre for Peace in the Middle East, organised an international meeting on *Minoranze etniche e religiose nell'area statuale mediterranea* ("Ethnic and Religious Minorities in the Mediterranean States"), devoted to the theme of religious freedom. Finally, on 2 November 2011, in the Sala Nassiriya of Palazzo Madama, the Commission organised a meeting to pay tribute to the memory of the Italian jurist Antonio Cassese, who died on 22 October.

B. Chamber of Deputies: Permanent Committee on Human Rights

The international protection of human rights is one of the focal point of the activities carried out by the Commission for Foreign and European Union Affairs (3rd Commission) of the Chamber of Deputies. Using hearings as its main instrument, the Commission ensures continual updating for Parliament on the status of human rights in various parts of the world and, with this goal in mind, in July 2008 it created the Permanent Committee on Human Rights, chaired by Furio Colombo.

During 2011, besides continuing the inquiry begun on 1 October 2008 into human rights violations around the world, with particular reference to safeguarding minorities, the Foreign Affairs Commission charged the Permanent Committee on Human Rights with the task of conducting an inquiry into human rights and democracy. One of the aims was to evaluate the adequacy of Italian foreign policy regarding the goals of peace and stability (resolution of 2 March 2011), with reference to areas of recent or fragile democratisation. The aim of the preliminary work was to highlight areas of particular difficulty and of progress, and to shed light on the role played by cultural and religious factors in the field of human rights. More specifically, the following issues were investigated: death penalty; violations of religious freedom; violations of the rights of women and minors; violations of the rights of minorities, refugees and migrants; forms of slavery and human trafficking.

Two hearings were held in 2011 in the ambit of the inquiry into human rights violations around the world: of Monsignor Shlemon Warduni, the Chaldean Patriarchal Vicar of Baghdad, with regard to the safeguarding of religious freedom, and with particular reference to Christians and persecuted minorities (19 January); and of representatives from the NGO Associazione Migrare – Osservatorio sul Fenomeno dell'Immigrazione, on the situation in Somalia (25 January).

In 2011, the following 11 hearings were held in relation to the inquiry into human rights and democracy:

– 15 March (a.m.): Vermondo Brugnatelli, President of the Associazione Culturale Berbera, on the situation in Libya and North Africa;

– 15 March (p.m.): Tareq Heggy, democracy activist in Egypt and the Arab nations;

– 29 March: Maria Grazia Giammarinaro, the OSCE's Special Representative and Coordinator for Combating Trafficking in Human Beings;

– 5 April: Laura Boldrini, spokesperson for UNHCR, the UN Refugee Agency, on the humanitarian situation in Libya;

– 18 May: Judith Sunderland, representative of Human Rights Watch, on racist and xenophobic violence in Italy;

– 9 June: Enzo Cucco, coordinator of the organising committee of the 15th Annual Conference of the European section of the International Lesbian, Gay, Bisexual, Trans and Intersex Association – ILGA-Europe (Turin, 27-30 October 2011); Giuseppina La Delfa, National President of Famiglie Arcobaleno; Andrea Maccarone, representative in Italy of the European Pride Organisers' Association; Porpora Marcasciano, National President of the Movimento Identità Transessuale; Paolo Patanè, National

President of Arcigay; Antonella Porfido, representative of Arcilesbica; Sergio Rovasio, National Secretary of the Associazione Radicale Certi Diritti, on the rights of gay, lesbian and transsexual people;

– 28 June: Shukri Said, human rights activist in Somalia;

– 12 July: Father Moissié Zerai, President of the Habeshia Agency, on the situation of asylum-seekers and refugees from Eritrea;

– 29 September: Djimi El Ghalia and Francesca Doria, human rights defenders working in the Western Sahara, and Luciano Ardesi, President of the National Association of Solidarity with the Sahrawi People;

– 9 November: Sebastiano Maffettone, Director of the Department of Political Science at the Libera Università Internazionale degli Studi Sociali (LUISS), on definitions and theories in the field of democracy and human rights;

– 21 December: Shady Hamadi, human rights activist in Syria.

C. Bicameral Bodies: Parliamentary Commission for Children and Adolescents

The Parliamentary Commission for Children and Adolescents was set up by law 23 December 1997, No. 451, although its denomination and competencies were modified by law of 3 August 2009, No. 112.

Essentially, the Commission is entrusted with a supervisory and policy-making role related to the enforcement of international obligations and domestic law on children's rights. In particular, in exercising its consultative powers, the Commission gathers data, fosters the exchange of information and promotes effective synergies with bodies and institutions both in and outside Italy involved in protecting children and adolescents; with associations, non-governmental organisations and all other subjects operating in the field; and with groups dealing with adoptions and foster care. It may also present to the two Houses of Parliament observations and proposals concerning the effects of current legislation, its gaps, and anything needed in order to ensure compliance with European Union law and with the rights enshrined in the United Nations Convention on the Rights of the Child.

The Commission is composed of 20 Senators and 20 Representatives appointed, respectively, by the Chair of the Italian Senate and the Chair of the Italian Chamber of Deputies, proportionately to the total number of members in the various parliamentary groups. The Commission then elects its Chair, two Vice Chairs and two Secretaries. In 2011 the Commission was composed as follows: *Chair*: Alessandra Mussolini; *Vice Chairs*: Annamaria Serafini, Gabriella Carlucci; *Secretaries*: Laura Allegrini, Marco Calgaro; *members from the Chamber of Deputies*: Mariella Bocciardo, Sandro Brandolini, Luisa Capitanio Santolini, Daniela Cardinale (replaced by Maria Letizia De Torre after 10 October 2011), Giulia Cosenza, Anita Di Giuseppe, Arturo Iannaccone, Beatrice Lorenzin, Barbara Mannucci, Donella Mattesini, Gabriella Mondello, Alessandro Pagano, Massimo Polledri,

Mariarosaria Rossi, Daniela Sbrollini, Amalia Schirru, Sandra Zampa; *Members from the Senate*: Irene Aderenti, Emanuela Baio Dossi, Alberto Balboni, Giorgio Bornacin, Giuliana Carlino, Mauro Ceruti, Stefano De Lillo, Giuseppe Esposito, Alessandra Gallone, Antonio Gentile, Rita Ghedini, Mirella Giai, Claudio Gustavino, Piergiorgio Massidda (until 21 December 2011), Donatella Poretti, Fabio Rizzi, Maria Rizzotti, Luciana Sbarbati.

During 2011, the Commission began an *Inquiry into the Protection of the Health of Minors, with Particular Reference to the Harmful Effects of Benzopyrene-related Atmospheric Pollution*. Hearings were held for Angelo Cecinato, a manager from the Environmental Pollution Institute of the National Research Council (CNR), and Loredana Musmeci, Director of the Environment and Primary Prevention Department of the Istituto Superiore di Sanità (4 October); and of Gianluigi De Gennaro, Professor of Environmental Chemistry at the Department of Chemistry, University of Bari (18 October).

The Commission also continued two inquiries begun in previous years, holding the following hearings:

– *Inquiry into Child Prostitution* (begun in 2008). Hearings of Paolo Ramonda, President of the Associazione Papa Giovanni XXIII (22 February); Chiara Finocchietti, Vice President of Azione Cattolica (15 March); Giancarlo Perego, Director General of the Fondazione Migrantes, and José Oropeza, Head of Mission of the International Organisation for Migration in Italy (5 April).

– *Inquiry into Unaccompanied Foreign Minors* (begun in 2008). Hearings of: representatives from the Comunità Papa Giovanni XXIII (19 July); Roberto Maroni, Minister of the Interior (27 September); Natale Forlani, Director General for Immigration and Integration Policies at the Ministry of Labour and Social Policies, and Ernesto Tomei, Professor of Radiology at the University of Rome La Sapienza (25 October).

In September the Commission began to examine the final report of the *Inquiry into the Protection of Minors in Means of Communication* (begun in 2008).

On 8 February 2011, the final report of the *Inquiry into Some Aspects of the Implementation of Policies in Favour of Children and Adolescents* (begun in 2010) was adopted with a majority vote. The report focused on the following aspects in particular: the cultural framework for childhood policies; coordination of policies at a central, regional and integrated level; reinforcement of human rights protection; resources for policies in favour of minors; federalism and respect for the principle of non-discrimination; reform of child and family law; prevention of abuse and mistreatment.

D. Parliament-Government Observatory Monitoring the Promotion and Protection of Fundamental Rights

The Observatory is a consultative body created on 7 July 2009. It meets when necessary in order to report on Italy's international activity in the field of human rights. Members of the Observatory include representatives from the Senate's Special Commission for the Protection and Promotion of Human Rights, from the Chamber of Deputies Permanent Committee on Human Rights, from the Ministry of Foreign Affairs and from the Inter-Ministerial Committee for Human Rights.

The fifth meeting of the Observatory was held on 24 February 2011. It dealt with issues arising from the Universal Periodic Review, with particular attention to the establishment, in Italy, of an independent national institution for human rights; the questions discussed at the UN General Assembly, such as the abolition of the death penalty, female genital mutilation and the protection of religious freedom; the emergency in Libya, also in the light of problems connected with the terms of the "friendship treaty" between Italy and Libya.

E. Parliamentary Initiatives concerning Human Rights

Presented below is a synthetic outlook of the main human rights initiatives taken by the Italian Parliament in 2011, subdivided into bills, motions, interpellations, questions for an oral answer, questions for a written answer, questions submitted to Commissions, resolutions made by Commissions and agenda proposals submitted to the Assembly. The reference source is the *openparlamento* website (http://parlamento.openpolis.it). As far as bills are concerned, the proposer or first signer, the code (the letter 'C' indicates that the initiative was presented in the Chamber of Deputies, the letter 'S' that it was presented in the Senate), the title, the date of presentation and the most recent update are listed for each initiative.

The Italian Parliament was more active on human rights issues in 2011 than in the previous year. A total of 9 bills were presented to bring Italian human rights legislation into line with international norms (compared to 6 in 2010). There were also 39 motions (compared to 32 in 2010), 18 interpellations (compared to 4 in 2010), 39 questions for an oral answer (compared to 6 in 2010), 234 questions for a written answer (compared to 81 in 2010), 44 questions submitted to Commissions (compared to 18 in 2010), 15 parliamentary resolutions (there were none in 2010), 8 Commission resolutions (compared to 6 in 2010), 29 agenda proposals submitted to Parliament (compared to 6 in 2010) and 2 agenda proposals submitted to Commissions (compared to 3 in 2010) on themes concerning internationally recognised human rights.

Bills

Date	Initiative	Latest update
18/02/2011	Gabriella Carlucci (UDC) and others – C.4099 Amendment to article 1 of the civil code concerning the recognition of the legal personality to every human being	15/03/2011 Assigned (review not yet begun)
05/05/2011	Franco Frattini – S.2720 Establishment of the National Commission for the promotion and protection of human rights	20/07/2011 Approved as a unified text
25/05/2011	Salvatore Fleres (CN) and others – S.2744 Provisions for the relations between detainees and the authorities on the rights of detainees in the interests of justice	15/06/2011 Assigned (review not yet begun)
20/07/2011	Barbara Contini (ApI-FLI) and others – C.4534 Establishment of the National Commission for the promotion and protection of human rights	28/03/2012 Under review in Commission
21/09/2011	Pietro Marcenaro (PD) – S.2915 Law to reduce prison overcrowding	06/03/2012 Assigned (review not yet begun)
03/11/2011	Nunzio Francesco Testa (UDC) – C.4753 Provisions for the recognition of the rights of persons with epilepsy	03/11/2011 Still to be assigned
09/11/2011	Matteo Mecacci (PD) – C.4765 Ratification and execution of the Optional Protocol to the United Nations Convention against Torture and other Cruel, Inhuman or Degrading Treatment or Punishment	11/01/2012 Assigned (review not yet begun)
24/11/2011	Rita Bernardini (PD) – C.4798 Amendments to the criminal code and the code of criminal procedure and other provisions, as well as delegation to the Government, to reduce prison overcrowding	14/12/2011 Assigned (review not yet begun)

Particularly worthy of mention is that, on 19 July, the Senate approved, with 230 votes in favour, 4 abstentions and no votes against, bill No. 2720, establishing the National Commission for the Promotion and Protection of Human Rights (Proposers: Carlo Vizzini, PdL, and Maria Fortuna Incostante, PD). On 27 October, the Chamber of Deputies' Commission for Institutional Affairs began to examine the text of the bill.

Motions

Of the 39 motions presented in the course of the year, 22 concerned the protection of human rights at an international level (with particular reference to Belarus, the Countries of the Mediterranean Basin and the Middle East, China, Countries of the Horn of Africa); 6 related to the situation in the prison system; 4 regarded the respect of human rights in the management of migratory flows; 3 concerned women's rights; 2 related to the respect of human rights regarding sexual orientation and gender identity; 1 concerned Italy and the United Nations; and 1 human trafficking in Europe.

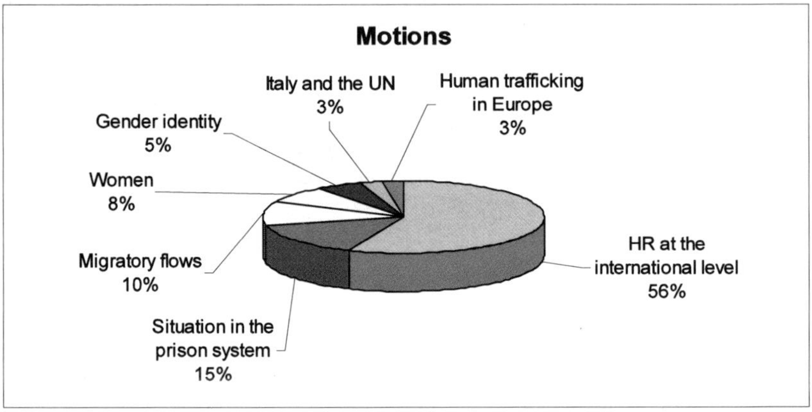

Interpellations

Of the 18 interpellations presented, 9 (50%) concerned the protection of human rights at an international level (with particular reference to Cuba, Pakistan, the Mediterranean Countries, China and the Countries of the Horn of Africa); 4 concerned the situation in the prison system; 4 related to the respect of human rights in the management of migratory flows; and 1 concerned the rights of persons with disabilities.

Questions for an Oral Answer

Of the 39 questions presented for an oral answer, 13 concerned the respect of human rights in the management of migratory flows; 12 were about the situation in the prison system; 11 regarded the protection of human rights at an international level (with particular reference to Belarus, Iran, Afghanistan, the Mediterranean Basin Countries, Nigeria and Sudan); 3 related to the rights of unaccompanied foreign minors; 1 was about Italy and the United Nations.

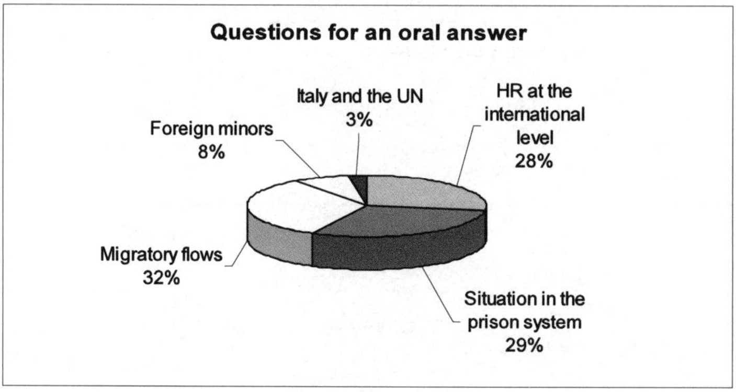

Questions for a Written Answer

Of the 234 questions presented for a written answer, 152 concerned the situation in the prison system; 37 related to the protection of human rights at an international level (with particular reference to Belarus, the Countries of the Mediterranean Basin and the Middle East, China, Afghanistan, Pakistan, Cuba, Iran, Hungary, North Korea, Sudan, Nigeria, Burma); 28 were about the respect of human rights in the management of migratory flows; 7 concerned Italy and the United Nations; 3 regarded the rights of unaccompanied foreign minors; 2 were about labour exploitation; 2 about health rights; 1 about human rights and the armed forces; 1 about the situation in Italy regarding discrimination and racism; and 1 concerned the National Institution for the Promotion and Protection of Human Rights.

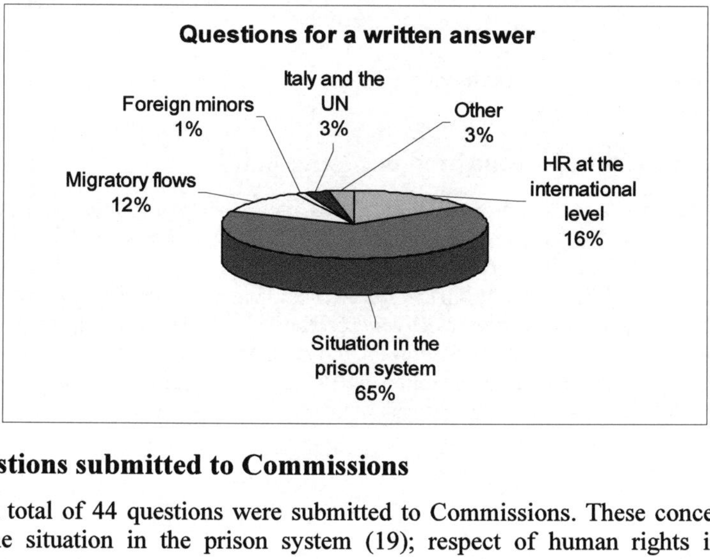

Questions submitted to Commissions

A total of 44 questions were submitted to Commissions. These concerned: the situation in the prison system (19); respect of human rights in the management of migratory flows (13); the protection of human rights at an international level, with particular reference to Cuba, Uganda, the Countries of the Mediterranean basin and the Middle East, Sudan and Eritrea (8); the rights of unaccompanied foreign minors (3); Italian development cooperation (1).

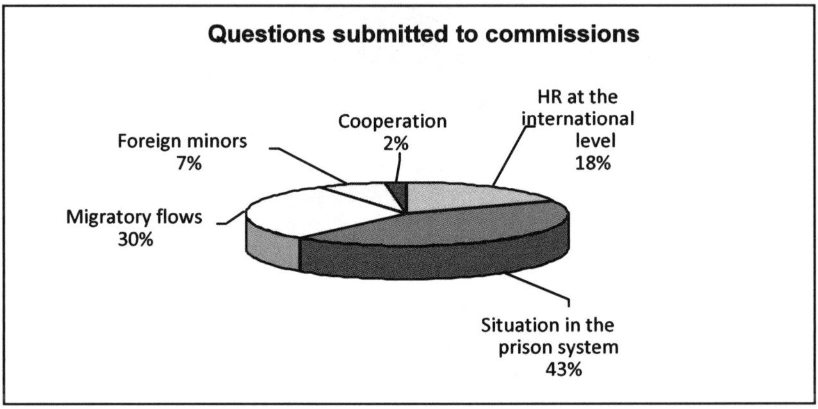

Assembly Resolutions

Of the 15 resolutions presented in the Assembly, 6 concerned the crisis in Libya (40%), 5 were about the judicial and prison system in Italy (33%), and 4 regarded the policies of the European Union (27%).

Commission Resolutions

The 8 Commission resolutions related to the protection of human rights at an international level.

Agenda Proposals submitted to the Assembly

A total of 29 agenda proposals were presented in the Assembly. Of these, 16 concerned the protection of human rights at an international level, with particular reference to Sudan, Syria, the Western Sahara, Libya, the Countries of the Horn of Africa, the African, Caribbean and Pacific group of Countries, Indonesia, Qatar, Kuwait; 5 related to the situation in the prisons; 4 were about the respect of human rights in the management of migratory flows; 2 regarded national human rights infrastructure; and 2 concerned the way to adapt to international instruments.

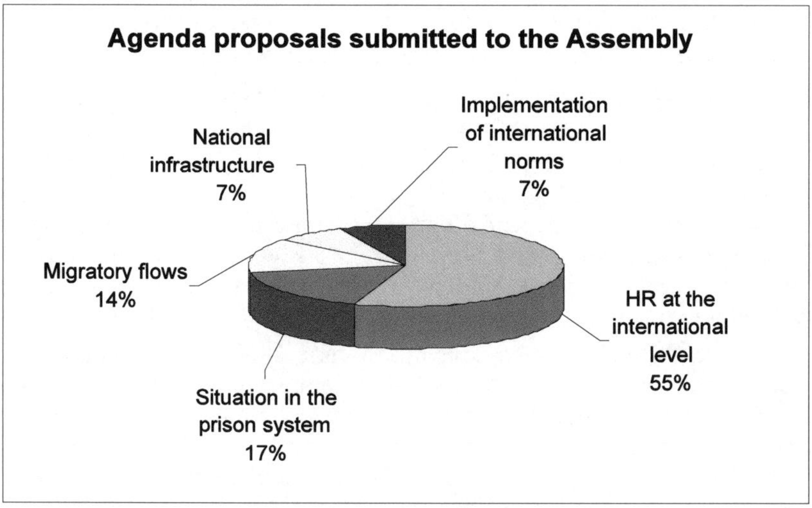

II. Prime Minister's Office (Presidency)

The organisation of the Prime Minister's Office is regulated by the prime ministerial decree (d.p.c.m.) of 1 March 2011. A number of departments and offices form part of the Prime Minister's Office (the so-called "general structures"), and the Prime Minister draws on them for guideline and coordination functions regarding specific political and institutional fields. Of particular importance for human rights is the Department for Equal Opportunities.

A number of committees and commissions with specific tasks of economic and social relevance operate within the ambit of the Prime Minister's Office. These include the Commission for International Adoptions and the National Committee on Bioethics.

In addition, in 2007 the Committee of Ministers for Orientation and Strategic Guidance for the Protection of Human Rights was established, in order to ensure effective policy and coordination between ministries in relation to the protection of human rights.

Finally, in November 2011, the Government led by Mario Monti established, as part of the Prime Minister's Office, the Ministry for International Cooperation and Integration, with the following delegated responsibilities: international cooperation, integration, family, youth and anti-drug policies, civil service, international adoptions, and measures to combat racial discrimination. The Ministry is headed by Andrea Riccardi.

A. Committee of Ministers for Orientation and Strategic Guidance for the Protection of Human Rights

The Committee was established on 13 April 2007 by a decree of the Prime Minister (d.p.c.m.) and is composed as follows: Prime Minister, Minister of Rights and Equal Opportunities, Minister of Foreign Affairs, Minister of Defence, Minister of Justice, Minister of Interior, Minister of Education, University and Research, Minister of Labour and Social Policies, Minister of Social Solidarity, Minister of European Policies, Minister of Family Policy, Undersecretary of State to the Presidency of the Council of Ministers – Secretary to the Council of Ministers.

Since 2008, in virtue of d.p.c.m. 13 June 2008, the Committee has been chaired by the Minister for Equal Opportunities. The Committee adopts guidelines and orientation relating to human rights issues, and serves as steering and coordinating body of the Inter-Ministerial Committee for Human Rights (CIDU) and other bodies carrying out institutional activities in the field of human rights.

Data are lacking on the actual functioning of this Committee.

B. Department for Equal Opportunities: UNAR and Observatory for the Fight against Paedophilia and Child Pornography

The Department for Equal Opportunities, instituted under the auspices of the Presidency of the Council of Ministers, is dedicated to planning and coordinating legal, administrative and research initiatives in all areas pertaining to equal opportunities policies. It was directed by the Minister-without-portfolio for Equal Opportunities Maria Rosaria Carfagna until October 2011. Since November 2011, with the new Government led by Mario Monti, the Minister of Labour and Social Policies Elsa Fornero is entrusted with the direction of the Department.

The Department was instituted by d.p.c.m. No. 405 of 28 October 1997, later amended by d.p.c.m. of 30 September 2004. It is composed of four offices: Office of International Affairs and Social Measures; Office of General Affairs and Protection Measures; Office for Equality and Equal Opportunities, Strategic Intervention and Communications; Office for the Promotion of Equal Treatment and the Fight against Racial Discrimination (UNAR).

UNAR was established by legislative decree No. 215 of 9 July 2003, in compliance with the European Community directive 2000/43/CE. Its mission is to guarantee observance of the principle of equal treatment of individuals, to monitor the efficacy of current instruments against discrimination, and to help abolish forms of discrimination based on race or ethnic origin, while analysing their diversified impact on gender, and their connection with racism.

During 2011, according to data provided by the UNAR in its *Report to the Prime Minister on Activities in 2011*, the office received 799 well-founded reports, that is to say, preliminary investigations which, following more in-depth examination, revealed clear-cut cases of racial discrimination (259 more than in 2010, an increase of 48%). The geographical distribution of these reports, and a comparison with the 2010 data, is shown in the following chart.

Pertinent complaints according to Region and geographical area: 2010-2011 (%)

		2010	2011	Diff. 2011-2010
Region	Piedmont	4.4	4.1	-0.3
	Valle d'Aosta	-	-	-
	Lombardy	18.8	21.0	2.2
	Liguria	3.5	2.4	-1.1
	Trentino-Alto Adige	1.5	0.6	-0.9
	Veneto	11.6	12.2	0.6
	Friuli Venezia Giulia	2.2	2.4	0.2
	Emilia Romagna	9.6	10.8	1.2
	Tuscany	10.6	10.4	-0.2
	Umbria	1.5	1.4	-0.1
	Marche	2.2	1.5	-0.7
	Lazio	19.8	19.0	-0.8
	Abruzzo	1.7	1.1	-0.6
	Molise	3.5	0.1	-3.4
	Campania	2.7	3.4	0.7
	Apulia	0.2	4.3	4.1
	Basilicata	-	0.3	0.3
	Calabria	2.2	1.0	-1.2
	Sicily	3.0	2.2	-0.8
	Sardinia	1.0	1.8	0.8
	Tot.	100	100	-
Geographical area	North-West	26.7	27.5	0.8
	North-East	24.9	25.9	1.0
	Centre	34.1	32.3	-1.8
	South and Islands	14.3	14.3	0.0
	Tot.	100	100	-

Source: UNAR, Report to the Prime Minister on Activities in 2011

Of the well-founded reports that were received, 369 (46.2%) were resolved through a conciliation procedure (in 2010 the percentage was 75%); in 31.4% of cases, a preliminary inquiry is still under way (in 2010 the percentage was 13%), while in 9% of cases (compared to 7.4%

in 2010), legal proceedings monitored by the office are in course. The complexity of preliminary inquiries in 2011 seems to be greater than in the previous year. Some cases have been referred to the Observatory for Security against Discriminatory Acts and to the Postal Police (both under the aegis of the Ministry of the Interior), or to the National Equality Advisor.

The break-down of reported cases is as follows: 22.6% concern the mass media (up 2.6% on 2010), while other areas regard work (19.6%, +8.3%), public life (16.7%, -1.1%), the provision of services by public authorities (10.9%, -5.1%), leisure (9.8%, +1.8%), housing (6.3%, -2.6%), the provision of services by commercial enterprises (4.3%, -1.1%), the school system and education (2.8%, -0.5%), public transport (2.5%, +0.1%), police forces (1.8%, -0.6%), health services (1.8%, +0.7%) and the provision of financial services (1%, -2.3%).

However, despite the increase in preliminary inquiries, the UNAR has not received additional human resources with respect to the staffing levels envisaged by the prime ministerial decree of 11 December 2003. Those levels actually diminished in 2010 and 2011, and, as of 31 December 2011, are approximately 50% of the staffing levels established by the law.

During 2011, the UNAR continued its work to build up an extended network of *territorial centres* to combat racism. Begun in 2009, and operating in synergy with local, regional and civic bodies, the aim is to develop the centres and observatories envisaged by art. 44 of lgs.d. No. 286 of 25 July 1998 (Consolidated immigration act). In particular, with the decree approved on 24 October 2011, the UNAR arrived at the definition of a shared model for inter-institutional cooperation between Regions, Provinces and Municipalities capable of responding to the normative projections of the Consolidated law on immigration.

In July 2011, the UNAR issued notice regarding the setting up of a project to establish a research centre to monitor cases of xenophobia and racial discrimination (CERIDER), which, it is planned, will become operational as from the second quarter of 2012.

The following awareness-raising, advocacy and information activities were carried out in 2011: *7th Week of Action Against Racism* (14-21 March 2011), which involved over 100 initiatives across the Country, undertaken together with local bodies and NGOs; the Council of Europe's *DOSTA* campaign to combat harmful prejudices regarding the Roma and Sinti communities; *Foreign Women Against All Forms of Discrimination*, a campaign to fight complex forms of discrimination; the *3rd National Anti-violence Week*, promoted in all Italian schools in the month of October; the *1st Week of Action Against Racism in the Workplace* (14-21 March 2011); promotion of the *Equal Opportunities*

Charter, a declaration of intent that companies sign voluntarily in order to contribute to the struggle against all forms of discrimination in the workplace (gender, disability, ethnic origin, religious faith, sexual orientation), through the organisation of a network of regional roundtables for the implementation of the Charter, and of four events respectively in Modena, Bologna, Palermo and Messina. The Charter was adopted in 2009 by the promoting committee, which includes the Sodalitas Foundation, the Italian Association of Family-run Businesses (AIDAF), the Association of Female Businesspeople and Company Managers (AIDDA), Impronta Etica, the Christian Union of Business Managers (UCID), the Office of the National Equality Advisor, with the support of the Ministry of Labour, Health and Social Policies, and of the Ministry for Equal Opportunities (www.cartapariopportunita.it).

In November 2011 the UNAR was formally appointed by the Government to act as *national focal point* in the development and coordination of the National Strategy for the Inclusion of Roma, Sinti and Traveller Communities through to 2020, pursuant to European Commission communication No. 173/2011. The general goal of the strategy is to promote parity of treatment and the economic and social inclusion of the Roma, Sinti and Traveller communities in society; to bring about a lasting and sustainable improvement in their living conditions; and to encourage effective and permanent responsibilisation, participation in their social development and the full exercising of citizenship rights guaranteed by the Italian Constitution and the international agreements. To this end, the UNAR began to seek the active involvement of the most significant institutional and associative players, and to coordinate steps to promote socio-economic inclusion policies and services for the benefit of Roma, Sinti and Traveller communities.

The following bodies also form part of the Department for Equal Opportunities: the Committee for the Prevention of Female Genital Mutilation; the Inter-Ministerial Committee to Support Victims of Human Trafficking, Violence and Severe Exploitation; the Observatory on Human Trafficking; the Committee to Evaluate the Legitimacy to Act on Behalf of People with Disabilities; the Committee for Equal Opportunities between Men and Women; the Public Investments Evaluation and Verification Group; the Health Study Committee; the Committee for Female Entrepreneurship; the Inter-Ministerial Committee for the Coordination of the Fight against Paedophilia (CICLOPE); the Observatory for the Fight against Paedophilia and Child Pornography.

The Observatory for the Fight against Paedophilia and Child Pornography was set up in line with law No. 269 of 3 August 1998, as modified by law No. 38 of 6 February 2006. Its task is to gather and monitor data and information regarding activities conducted by governmental bodies to prevent and stamp out child abuse and sexual exploitation. One of the Observatory's other major responsibilities is to draw up a *National Plan to Prevent and Fight Child Abuse and Sexual Exploitation*, to be submitted to the CICLOPE for approval.

In the course of 2011, the Observatory pursued its commitment to set up a database to monitor child abuse and sexual exploitation, child pornography, and related activities to prevent and fight the phenomena, gathering together information supplied by the relevant governmental bodies. The Observatory also took part in a wide range of initiatives, including:

– the European programme *Safer Internet 2009-2013*, an intervention plan regarding new media and child protection;

– the European Commission programme *Prevention and Fight Against Crime 2007-2013*, with a project entitled *Development of a Methodology to Identify and Support Children Who Have Been Sexually Exploited for the Production of Pornographic Images.* The project was run in conjunction with Save the Children, the Italian Association of Services to Combat the Mistreatment and Abuse of Children (CISMAI), and the Postal and Communications Police;

– the European Commission's *Daphne III* programme, running from 2007 to 2013, the aim of which is to fund projects submitted by institutional and other subjects and designed to help protect children, young people and women against any form of violence.

C. Commission for International Adoptions

Art. 6 of the Hague Convention on the Protection of Minors and Cooperation in Respect of Intercountry Adoption, adopted on 29 May 1993 and entered into force on 1 May 1995, requires State parties to establish a central authority guaranteeing that adoptions of foreign children occur in respect of the principles established by the Convention itself. In order to comply with this requirement, Italy, via ratifying law 31 December 1998, No. 476, instituted the Commission for International Adoptions, operative through the Presidency of the Council of Ministers. The Commission is Italy's central authority implementing the Hague Convention.

The Commission is composed of a Chair, appointed by the President of the Council of Ministers (in 2011 Minister in charge of international adoptions Andrea Riccardi succeeded Minister Carlo Giovanardi), and by the following members: three representatives of the Presidency of the Council of Ministers; a representative of the Ministry of Foreign Affairs; a representative from the Ministry of Education; a representative from the Ministry of Labour and Social Policies; a representative from the Ministry of Interior; two representatives from the Ministry of Justice; a representative from the Ministry of Health; a representative from the Ministry of Economy; four representatives from the Conference between State and Regions (*Conferenza Stato-Regioni*); three representatives from family associations; experts in the field.

During 2011, the Commission authorised the entry of 4,022 children (just 2.6% lower than the previous year's figure of 4,130) into Italy, from 57 Countries. A total of 3,154 couples successfully completed the adoption procedure, compared to 3,241 in 2010. The average wait for an international adoption (calculated from the date on which the authorised body is charged with the task until the authorisation to enter, which is the responsibility of the Commission, is issued) was 25 months, one month less than 2010.

In 2011, 57.5% of the adopted children were male and 42.5% female. The average age was 6.1 years, slightly up on the figure for 2010 (6 years). More specifically, over a third of the children adopted in 2011 (36.1%) were aged between 1 and 4, 45.2% were between 5 and 9, 13.3% were 10 years old or above, while just 5.4% were below one year of age.

As regards the origin of the foreign minors who entered Italy in 2011 for adoption, the greatest number of minors came, as in 2010, from the Russian Federation – 781 minors, amounting to 19.42% of the total. Then came Colombia, with 554 minors (13.77%), Brazil with 304 (7.56%), Ukraine with 297 (7.38%), Ethiopia with 296 (7.36%), Poland with 181 (4.50%) and India with 148 (3.68%).

Of the total number of children adopted, 13.4% have special needs (children with severe and often incurable pathologies, for instance neurological and mental difficulties), or particular needs (where recovery over time is predicted), a slight drop with respect to the figure for 2010 (15.5%).

In 2011 the Commission published a study entitled *L'Italia e il Brasile per il benessere dell'infanzia nelle adozioni internazionali* ("Italy and Brazil for the best interests of the child in international adoptions").

D. National Committee on Bioethics

The National Committee on Bioethics carries out roles of consultancy *vis-à-vis* the Government, Parliament and other institutions, formulating opinions and motions on legislative and administrative instruments dealing with bioethical issues. It also has the role of information and awareness-raising in relation to ethical and legal problems that may arise in connection with progress in scientific research and technological applications on life.

The Committee was established by the d.p.c.m. of 28 March 1990. It is composed of the following bodies: President (Francesco Paolo Casavola,

President Emeritus of the Constitutional Court); Vice Presidents (Riccardo Di Segni, Chief Rabbi of Rome; Lorenzo d'Avack, Professor of Philosophy of Law; Luca Marini, Professor of International Law; Laura Palazzoni, Professor of Philosophy of Law); Office of the President (made up of the President and the Vice Presidents); Assembly.

One of the tasks of the Committee is to produce studies and make recommendations that can also be used for legislative purposes. The Committee's documents offer in-depth focus and reflection on ethical and legal issues that arise as knowledge in the field of the life sciences advances. According to their nature and purpose, the documents are classified as: *opinions* (approved in the Committee's assembly on the basis of inquiries conducted by working groups); *motions* (urgent documents approved with a two-thirds majority of those present in the assembly); *responses* (documents in which the Committee makes recommendations on issues about which its opinion has been sought by other bodies or physical persons).

No motions or responses were approved in 2011. The following opinions were approved: Note on the Pharmacist's Conscientious Objection to the Sale of Emergency Contraceptive Products (25 February); Pharmacological Trials in Developing Countries (27 May); Knowing One's Biological Origins in Heterologous Medically Assisted Procreation (25 November); Orphan Drugs for Persons Affected by Rare Illnesses (25 November).

III. Ministry of Foreign Affairs

The Ministry of Foreign Affairs has a number of directorate-generals (DGs) and offices that deal specifically with human rights, disarmament and cooperation. Until October 2011, the delegated responsibility for issues arising in the United Nations and for questions regarding human rights and fundamental freedoms was held by the Under Secretary Enzo Scotti. In November 2011, with the formation of the Government led by Mario Monti, this role was assumed by Under Secretary Staffan de Mistura.

Particularly worthy of note is Office II – Human rights advocacy and international humanitarian law, Council of Europe, which falls within the DG for Political Affairs and Security. Other offices in the same DG are: Office I – The United Nations system and the institutional reform process, peacekeeping operations and preventive diplomacy; Office V – Disarmament, arms control and nuclear, biological and chemical non-proliferation, Office of the National authority for the banning of chemical weapons; Office VI – Organisation for Security and Cooperation in Europe. The theme of human rights also relates across the board to the DG for Global Affairs (Office IV – Energy, environmental protection and sustainable global development policies), the DG for the European Union (Office III – European space of freedom, security and justice, the free movement of people and migratory flows towards the European Union) and the DG for Development Cooperation (Office I – Development of cooperation policies within the European Union; Office II – Multilateral development cooperation; Office VI – Emergency and humanitarian aid; Office VIII – Planning and monitoring of the cooperation budget; gender issues, the rights of children and people with disabilities).

A. Inter-Ministerial Committee for Human Rights (CIDU)

The Inter-Ministerial Committee for Human Rights (CIDU), established by decree of the Minister of Foreign Affairs on 15 February 1978, No. 519, is particularly important; its composition was updated by d.c.p.m. on 11 May 2007. It is chaired by an agent of the diplomatic service appointed by the Minister of Foreign Affairs: in 2011, Diego Brasioli.

The CIDU's members include representatives of the Presidency of the Council of Ministers, of various Ministries and of several institutions (such as the National Council on Economy and Labour (CNEL); the Association of Italian Municipalities (ANCI); the Conference of Presidents of the Regions and Autonomous Provinces; the Union of Italian Provinces (UPI); the National Commission for UNESCO; the Italian Committee for UNICEF; the Italian Society for International Organisation (SIOI); as well as three eminent personalities in the field of human rights.

The CIDU has the following tasks: to promote measures necessary for ensuring full compliance with international obligations already assumed, or that must be assumed by Italy upon ratification of the conventions it has signed; to monitor nation-wide compliance with international agreements; to draft all reports Italy is requested to submit to the United Nations and other multilateral bodies; to prepare the yearly report on the status of human rights promotion and protection in Italy the Ministry of Foreign Affairs must present to the Parliament in accordance to art. 1, law 19 March 1999, No. 80; to maintain and develop pertinent relations with organisations of civil society which are actively involved in promoting and protecting human rights.

On 11 November 2011 the Ministry of Foreign Affairs delivered to the Office of the President of the Chamber of Deputies a report on the Committee's activities in relation to the protection and respect of human rights in Italy in the course of 2010 (doc. CXXI, No. 4). The report details the results of the collaborative activities conducted with UN, Council of Europe and European Union bodies with regard to the presentation of the periodic reports envisaged by the international human rights instruments to which Italy is a party, and the visits arranged by these organisations in order to obtain specific information or to directly appraise the situation in areas considered to be particularly sensitive for human rights.

The activities carried out by CIDU in 2010 are as follows:

United Nations

– drafting of the 6th report on the implementation of the International Covenant on Civil and Political Rights;

– drafting of the 5th report on the implementation of the International Covenant on Economic, Social and Cultural Rights;

– preparation of the discussion of the 6th periodic report regarding the Convention on the Elimination of All Forms of Discrimination against Women;

– organisation of Italy's participation in the Universal Periodic Review;

– drafting of the National action plan on women, peace and security.

Council of Europe

– drafting of the response to the 2009 report of the European Committee for the Prevention of Torture;

– *ad hoc* visit to Italy of the European Committee for the Prevention of Torture (14-18 June 2010);

– periodic visit of the European Commission against Racism and Intolerance (22-26 November 2010).

Organisation for Security and Cooperation in Europe

– visit of the High Commissioner on National Minorities, Knut Vollebaek (November 2010).

European Union

– drafting of the response to the report of the EU Fundamental Rights Agency (FRA).

The annual report also sums up Italy's responses, via CIDU, to the requests for information and the questionnaires sent by various bodies of the United Nations, the Council of Europe and the Organisation for Security and Cooperation in Europe (OSCE). In connection to this, replies were given to the following requests and questionnaires:

– letter from the President of the European Committee for the Prevention of Torture, regarding the situation on Lampedusa (February 2010);

– joint questionnaire from UN Special Rapporteurs on the rights of migrants and the right to education (March 2010);

– request for information from the UN Special Rapporteurs on the right to adequate housing and on contemporary forms of racism, and the independent expert on minority issues, in relation to Rome City Council's "Roma plan" (June 2010);

– request for information from the United Nations Office of the High Commissioner for Human Rights in relation to the national framework for the implementation of the Convention on the Rights of Persons with Disabilities (October 2010).

The report also contains information about CIDU's study and research activities, and its relations with the academic world and with civil society organisations:

– hearing of CIDU before the Chamber of Deputies' Permanent Observatory on Xenophobia and Racism (16 September 2010);

– drafting of a bill for the establishment of a National Commission for the Promotion and Protection of Human Rights;

– relations with the academic world: meeting with the Under Secretary for Foreign Affairs, Scotti, and the Conference of the Deans of Political Science faculties, to evaluate possible forms of cooperation (July 2010);

– relations with civil society: involvement of non-governmental organisations in the monitoring group of the United Nations Convention on the Rights of the Child, in the drawing up of the National action plan on women, peace and security, and in the Universal Periodic Review process; attendance of the president of CIDU at the conference promoted by the Italian Institute for Asia and the Mediterranean, in conjunction with the New Friendship and Cooperation Association Italy-Morocco, on the theme: *The Arab World Engages with Reform. Morocco: A Model?*

B. Italian National Commission for UNESCO

The Commission was established by inter-ministerial decree on 11 February 1959, at the Ministry of Foreign Affairs, two years after Italy entered the Organisation, and pursuant to art. 7 of the UNESCO Charter.

Its composition has been regulated and updated by a series of successive decrees, the most recent one dating back to 24 May 2007. Members of the Commission include representatives from Parliament, the Presidency of the Council of Ministers, various Ministries, public and private agencies, local authorities and civil society.

The Commission's mission is to promote the implementation of UNESCO programmes in Italy; to spread the ideals of the Organisation, especially among the younger generations; to disseminate information on its principles, goals and activities, thus stimulating action by institutions, the civil society and the world of culture, education and science. The Commission also offers consultancy relative to relations between the Government and UNESCO.

In 2011, the Chair appointed by the Ministry of Foreign Affairs was Giovanni Puglisi, while Lucio Alberto Savoia was Secretary General.

In 2011, the National Commission conducted a series of activities (seminars, conferences, school sessions, competitions, exhibitions, workshops, shows) in various Italian cities on the occasion of the International Year of Chemistry, the UN Decade of Education for Sustainable Development 2005-2014, and various United Nations international days. The Commission also activated a number of specific projects in schools, including the *Landscape Competition*, the first national contest designed to enhance cultural appreciation of the landscape. Involving teams of pupils from secondary schools, the competition further reinforced the network of UNESCO-associated schools, bringing the number of associated schools to 103.

In 2011, the Commission organised *UNESCO Thursdays*, a series of sessions devoted to the main themes of UNESCO's mandate in the ambit of celebrations to mark the 150th anniversary of the unification of Italy, and the *High-level Regional Meeting on the Teaching of Philosophy in Europe and North America* (Milan, 14-16 February), in conjunction with UNESCO and the IULM University. The Commission was also represented at the *UNESCO World Forum on Culture and Cultural Industries* (Monza, 6-8 June) and the international forum *Le Vie dei Mercanti: Safeguard of Architectural, Visual, Environmental Heritage* (Second University of Naples, 9-10 June).

On 9 November, the Commission presented a report entitled *The Value of the UNESCO Brand*, a national investigation into the image that public opinion and representatives from the cultural, institutional and business worlds have of the National Commission.

IV. Ministry of Labour and Social Policies

The Ministry of Labour and Social Policies' structure includes several departments and bureaus specifically involved with human rights. Of particular note:

– *DG for the protection of working conditions* (Technical bureau of the national Committee for equality between men and women; Division II – International affairs; Division III – Safety and health at work; Division VI – Law on prevention of work accidents and working conditions; Division VII – Labour disputes in agricultural and service sectors, protection of union rights, strikes in essential public service sectors);

– *DG for social inclusion, social rights and corporate social responsibility* (Division II – Policies for social inclusion and social cohesion; Division III – Policies for children and adolescents; Division IV – Policies for persons with disabilities. Corporate social responsibility);

– *DG for immigration* (Division II – Immigration policies; Division III – Integration policies and international affairs; Division IV – Policies for foreign minors);

– *DG for volunteer work, associations and social groups* (Division I – Social organisations and general affairs; Division II – Associations; Division III – Voluntary work).

A. National Observatory for Children and Adolescents

The Observatory performs a role of coordination among central administrations, local and regional agencies, associations, professional groups and non-governmental organisations dedicated to children's issues.

It was instituted by law 23 December 1997, No. 451, and is currently regulated by decree of the President of the Republic (d.p.r.), No. 103, 14 May 2007, which assigns it joint chairmanship by the Ministry of Labour and Social Policies and the Undersecretary of State to the Presidency of the Council of Ministers mandated of family policies. It is made up of representatives from national and local public administrations, institutions, professional orders, no profit organisation as well as experts in the field of children's rights.

D.p.r. 103/2007 assigns the Observatory the task of preparing three important documents regarding the condition of children and adolescents in Italy:

– The *National plan of action and of measures to safeguard the rights and development of children and adolescents.* Drawn up every two years, the plan contains the fundamental strategic guidelines and concrete commitments that the Government intends to pursue in order to develop a satisfactory policy for children and adolescents in Italy. Before being adopted by a decree of the President of the Republic, the Plan of action must be approved by the Parliamentary Commission for Children and Adolescents. The third action plan (2010-2011) was adopted by presidential decree on 21 January 2011. The plan is organised into four theme-based lines of action: a) *to consolidate the integrated network of services and measures to combat social exclusion*, thereby giving greater continuity to preventative, treatment and recovery programmes; b) *to reinforce the safeguarding of rights*, prevalently in the juridical sphere; c) *to encourage participation in the forging of an intergenerational pact*, gathering together the projects of groups that focus on young citizens as protagonists in society; d) *to promote the integration of immigrants*, a line of action that covers proposals regarding foreign and Roma minors.

– The *Report on the condition of children and adolescents in Italy*, which aims to provide an updated picture of the aspects and phenomena characterising the condition of children and adolescents in Italy, and of the system of social services and measures for promoting and protecting the rights of children and adolescents. The latest report published by the Observatory refers to the two-year period 2008-2009. It presents an analysis of several domains such as social participation; intergenerational relations; condition of Roma, Sinti and Travellers children; intercultural society; the fight against poverty and social exclusion; the machinery for the protection of children's rights and the integrated system of social services.

– The *Periodic report to the United Nations Convention on the Rights of the Child*, pursuant to art. 44 of the Convention. The latest report, merging the 3rd and 4th reports, was sent by Italy in January 2009, and discussed by the Committee in October 2011 (see Part III, The United Nations System, V, F).

In carrying out its various functions, the National Observatory makes use of the National Centre of Documentation and Analysis for Children and Adolescents, which has the task of documenting, analysing, researching, monitoring and training. Since June 2011, the chair of the Centre is Simonetta Matone; the Coordinator of scientific activities, Maria Burani Procaccini.

More specifically, the National Centre of Documentation carries out the following tasks:

– collecting and disseminating regional, national, European and international standards, as well as statistical data and scientific studies;

– creating an annually updated map, based on information provided by regional authorities, of public, private and non-governmental social services, including assistance and health care, and of financial resources dedicated to children on the national, regional and local level;

– analysing the situation of childhood and adolescence in Italy, including the conditions of foreign minors;

– preparing an outline, based on National Observatory directives, of the biennial report on the condition of children in Italy, and of the Government report to the United Nations Committee on the Rights of the Child on the domestic implementation of the Convention on the Rights of the Child;

– formulating proposals, even upon request of local authorities, for the creation of pilot projects aiming to improve children living conditions as well as the assistance to mothers during the prenatal period.

B. National Observatory Monitoring the Condition of Persons with Disabilities

The Observatory is a consultative body giving techno-scientific support in defining and implementing disability-related policies.

It was instituted by law 3 March 2009, No. 18, at the Ministry of Labour, Health and Social Policies. It is chaired by the Ministry of Labour and includes a maximum number of 40 members, who are appointed by ministerial decree and represent central administrations involved in defining and implementing disability-related policies; regional and local authorities; social security institutions; the National Statistics Institute; trade unions; and most representative associations and organisations of persons with disabilities, joined by a maximum number of five experts of proven experience in the field of disabilities.

The strategic and scientific guidance of the Observatory's activities is provided by a Technical and Scientific Committee. In 2011 the composition of the Committee was the following: Matilde Leonardi (Committee coordinator), Raffaele Tangorra (Ministry of Labour and Social Policies), Fiammetta Landoni (Ministry of Health), Raffaele Goretti (Conference of Regions and Autonomous Provinces), Paolo Anibaldi (ANCI), Giovanni Pagano (ANMIC and FAND), Pietro Vittorio Barbieri (FAIP and FISH), Carlo Francescutti (expert), Mario Melazzini (expert).

The Observatory's tasks include the following: to promote the implementation of the United Nations Convention on the Rights of Persons with Disabilities and to prepare, together with CIDU, the national report for the monitoring procedure established by that Convention; to prepare a biennial Plan of action on disability implementing national and international laws; to promote and develop statistic-based studies and research that may contribute to defining priorities and needs.

The Observatory is regulated by the inter-ministerial decree of 6 July 2010, No. 167, which entered into force on 23 October 2010. The Observatory will remain active for three years beginning on that date.

On 6 July 2011 the Observatory held its first plenary meeting at the Ministry of Labour and Social Policies. The meeting was presided over by Minister Maurizio Sacconi, who pinpointed the following thematic priorities for the work of the Observatory: the family, work, and school environments.

C. Committee for Foreign Minors

The Committee for Foreign Minors is an inter-ministerial body instituted by the legislative decree 25 July 1998, No. 286, with the aim to monitor the presence of foreign minors temporarily present on Italian territory, and to coordinate the activities of administrations involved.

Initially instituted under the auspices of the Presidency of the Council of Ministers, it currently operates at the Ministry of Labour and Social Policies. It includes nine representatives, one for each of the following bodies: Ministry of Social Solidarity, Ministry of Foreign Affairs, Ministry of Interior, Ministry of Justice; two representatives from the Association of Italian Municipalities (ANCI), one representative from the Union of Italian Provinces (UPI), two delegates from the most representative associations concerned with issues of the family and unaccompanied minors.

The lgs.d. 25 July 1998, No. 286 (amended by lgs.d. of 13 April 1999, No. 113) and the regulations of the Committee for Foreign Minors (adopted by d.p.c.m. on 9 December 1999, No. 535) define the competencies of this body in relation to two categories of foreign minors: unaccompanied minors present in the territory and minors temporarily admitted.

As regards unaccompanied minors, the Committee monitors accommodation arrangements; ascertains their status; takes initiatives and carries out research in order to identify the family members of minors, even in their Country of origin or in third Countries, seeking collaboration from the competent public administrations and appropriate national and international organisations (in particular, the International Organisation for Migration). It takes a census of unaccompanied minors who are present in Italy. The Committee may then adopt two kinds of measures: the first one is "no repatriation", which amounts to mobilising the integration process of the person into Italian national territory; the second one is an "assisted repatriation" in order to protect the children's right to family unity. As regards the first measure, the local territorial authorities are called upon to manage and monitor intervention. The most frequent choice made for unaccompanied minors is to place them in protected communities in Italy.

As regards temporarily admitted minors, the Committee decides, according to predetermined criteria, upon request of organisations, associations or Italian families concerning the temporarily admission of children in the framework of humanitarian programmes; the Committee then makes decisions for the minors' repatriation. It keeps a register of minors already admitted in the framework of humanitarian programmes and predefines criteria for assessing requests for the admission of other minors.

In 2011, 7,750 unaccompanied foreign minors were referred to the Committee's attention (compared to 4,438 in 2010), including 7,333 males (94.6%) and 417 females (5.4%). The main Countries of origin were Egypt (15%), Afghanistan (14%), Tunisia (13%), Bangladesh (6.6%) and Morocco (6.4%). About 75% of these warnings came from six Regions, namely Sicily (21%), Lazio (19.9%), Lombardy (9.6%), Apulia (8.8%), Emilia-Romagna (7.5%) and Calabria (7.4%).

V. Ministry of Justice

Within the Ministry of Justice there are various departments and bureaus specifically involved with human rights. The most relevant are:

– *Office for studies, research, legislation and international relations* (Office of the Head of Department – Department of penitentiary administration): focused on coordinating activities with international organisations devoted to the protection and promotion of human rights of adult prisoners; it deals with complaints lodged by inmates to the European Court of Human Rights;

– *Office II*: (DG for litigation and human rights – Department of legal affairs): it is actively involved in examining cases pending before the European Court of Human Rights and in procedures relating to compliance with international obligations, and to the incorporation into domestic law of provisions of international instruments;

– *Office III: Protection and support for the rights of minors. Promotion of measures in favour of subjects who risk the greatest degree of social exclusion* (DG for enforcement of judgements – Department of juvenile justice): dedicated to promoting and protecting the rights of unaccompanied foreign minors and of persons at risk of social exclusion.

VI. Judicial Authorities

The judiciary, that is to say the various organs of justice – ordinary, administrative and auditing – constituting judicial power, is the fundamental guarantee of rights and legality in a State that respects the principles of democracy, the division of powers and the rule of law. The Italian courts – the Constitutional Court, which delivers judgements regarding the constitutionality of laws, the Supreme Court, which is the court of last resort, the penal and civil tribunals and trial courts, and those concerned with administrative, audit and military matters – deal in a contentious manner with cases which often affect human rights in the most various ways and according to the most disparate perspectives. Access to a judge to obtain a ruling on a right that a plaintiff claims has been breached is a fundamental human right, linked to which are the many other procedural rights that distinguish the fair trial.

Besides ruling on individual cases, the justice system contributes to the evolution of applicable law, through its own case-law. In recent years, and in relation to the theme of fundamental rights in particular, Italian rulings have been strongly influenced by that of international courts, especially the European Court of Human Rights and the Court of Justice of the European Union. The interaction between national judicial organs and international courts with jurisdiction over human rights stresses the universal nature of the latter. The dialogue with international courts and with those of other Countries called upon to apply the same standards regarding individual human rights does not just concern the supreme courts of a State, but all judges, who can draw on rulings made in foreign or international courts to improve existing guarantees regarding fundamental rights, fully respecting the Constitution and the law. Part IV of this Yearbook is specifically devoted to a summary presentation of cases in the Italian courts on which rulings were delivered in 2011 (with particular reference to those made by the Constitutional and the Supreme Court), and of case-law elaborated by the European Court of Human Rights or the Court of Justice of the European Union which directly concerns Italy, either because the Italian State was the "defendant" or because the intervention of the European judge regarded pleas presented by Italian citizens or related to Italian legal norms.

VII. National Economy and Labour Council (CNEL)

CNEL is a body provided for in art. 99 of the Constitution. Since 2005, the Chair has been Antonio Marzano; he was re-confirmed by the Council of Ministers in July 2010, for the 9th council period (2010-2015).

Its function is essentially consultative. It expresses opinions on request of the Parliament, the Government and the Regions; on its own initiative it prepares comments and recommendations on proposed legislation, reports, studies and in-depth analyses.

The CNEL structure includes an Assembly, a Chair's office and committee, several specialised Commissions (among which a Commission for social policy and a Commission for European and international policies), as well as several committees and bodies: e.g. the Committee on immigration; the Committee on union representation in public employment; the Observatory on social economy; the Socio-economic Observatory on crime; the Coordinated Committee of consultants on the Southern Regions; the National body of coordination for policies of foreign citizens' social integration at the local level.

In the course of 2011, the CNEL produced 27 documents, including:

– fifteen texts containing observations and recommendations; of particular note are the *Contribution to the United Nations Conference on Sustainable Development in Rio de Janeiro 2012*; the *Agenda of Priorities for Adjustment Towards Equitable and Sustainable Development*; the *Establishment of the National Council for Sustainable Development*;

– a government bill regarding the *Self-reform of the National Council of the Economy and Labour*;

– six reports, including *The Arab Spring: Economic and Social Challenges and Opportunities* and *The Labour Market, 2010-2011*;

– two statements, including the *Annual Report to Parliament and the Government on the Level and Quality of Services Provided by Central and Local Government Bodies to Companies and Citizens*;

– two volumes containing the acts of conferences and debates;

– *The Inter-institutional (CNEL – ISTAT) Cooperation Agreement on the Measuring of Progress and Wellbeing.*

VIII. Independent Authorities

Independent authorities include: Communications Regulatory Authority (AGCOM); Data Protection Authority; Committee Guaranteeing the Implementation of the Law on Strikes Affecting Essential Public Services; Authority Protecting Free Competition and the Market (Antitrust Authority); Italian Companies and Stock Exchange Commission (CONSOB); Institute for the Vigilance on Private Insurance and Insurances of Collective Interest (ISVAP); Regulatory Authority for Electricity and Gas; Authority for the Vigilance on Contracts for Public Works, Services and Supplies; National Ombudsperson for children and adolescents. The following section deals with the four independent authorities with the most direct relevance for human rights.

A. Communications Regulatory Authority (AGCOM)

AGCOM was set up by the law 31 July 1997, No. 249. It has a double mandate: to ensure correct competition among market actors and to guarantee the fundamental freedoms of citizens in the area of communications, particularly as regards the protection of minors.

It is composed of the following bodies: *Chair* (in 2011 this was Corrado Calabrò); *Infrastructure and Networks Commission*, made up of four Commissioners (in 2011 these were Michele Lauria, Sebastiano Sortino, Gianluigi Magri and Antonio Martusciello); *Services and Products Commission*, made up of four Commissioners (in 2011 these were Stefano Mannoni, Nicola D'Angelo, Roberto Napoli and Enzo Savarese); *Council*, made up of the Chair and all the Commissioners.

As reported in the 2011 annual report on its work and activities (relative to the period May 2010-April 2011), the Authority devoted particular attention to acting as a watchdog on behalf of children and users, and to punishing improper practices. To this end, in the period considered, a total of 67 cases were opened (compared to 73 in the previous year) against local and national broadcasters, in order to ascertain whether violations had been committed and, if so, to act accordingly. Forty-nine of these cases ended with injunction orders, including: 12 violations of art. 4, para. 1, lett. b) of lgs.d. No. 177 of 31 July 2005 (Adequate coverage of the national territory); 4 for violation of the above-mentioned article and of the Self-regulatory code regarding media and minors; 2 for violation of art. 34, para. 4 of lgs.d. No. 177 (Ban on broadcasting films unsuitable for children under 14 from 7 a.m. to 10.30 p.m.); 10 for violation of the Self-regulatory Code regarding media and minors, in conjunction with art. 34, para. 4 of lgs.d. 177 (Ban on the broadcasting of programmes unsuitable for children under 18 from 7 a.m. to 11.00 p.m. on all broadcasting platforms); 9 for violation of art. 1, para. 26 of law No. 650, dated 23 December 1996 (Ban on audiotex and international services containing erotic, pornographic or obscene forms or content).

From the regulatory point of view, AGCOM worked together with the Committee for the Application of the Self-regulatory Code Regarding Media and Minors in order to draw up criteria for the classification of programmes suitable for adults only included in conditional access programme schedules, as per art. 34, para. 1 and 3 of the Consolidated law on audio-visual and radio services, as modified by lgs.d. No. 44 of 15 March 2010. These criteria were laid down in a document approved by the Media and Minors Committee on 5 July 2010, in agreement with the Authority. The document was then submitted to the Ministry of Economic Development for approval. With resolution 88/10/CSP of 6 May 2010, AGCOM established a board of experts in order to draw up detailed regulations covering appropriate technical measures designed to prevent children having regular access to programmes that are seriously harmful for their physical, mental or moral development, or which contain pornographic scenes or gratuitous, recurrent or brutal violence, as per art. 34, para. 5 and 11 of the Consolidated law on audio-visual and radio services.

Finally, of its various investigative activities, particular mention should be made of AGCOM's work to draw up a *White Paper on the Relationship between the Media and Minors.* Adopting an interdisciplinary approach, the aim of the study is to conduct an in-depth investigation of the synergic relationship between what is on offer in the multimedia world and the social behaviour of minors.

B. Data Protection Authority

The Data Protection Authority (*Autorità garante per la protezione dei dati personali*) was instituted by legislative decree No. 675, 31 December 1996, later substituted by legislative decree 30 June 2003, No. 196 (Personal data protection code), with the aim to ensure protection of the fundamental rights and freedoms and respect for the dignity of persons, in the treatment of personal data.

This joint body is made up of four members elected by Parliament, who remain in office for a seven-year non-renewable mandate. The current joint body entered office on 18 April 2005 and includes Francesco Pizzetti (Chair), Giuseppe Chiaravalloti (Vice Chair), Mauro Paissan and Giuseppe Fortunato.

In 2011, the Authority adopted many *measures* to protect the fundamental rights of individuals with regard to the processing of personal data, with particular reference, amongst others, to the following issues:

– *Sensitive and judicial data.* Greater privacy for people with disabilities who purchase a car (16 February 2011);

– *Journalism and other expressions of thought*. Journalism: the essentiality of information and the diffusion of clinical data (13 January 2011);

– *Labour*. Use of CCTV systems in a company (17 November 2011); use of CCTV systems in a nursing home (10 November 2011);

– *Health*. Epidemiological research on military personnel in Bosnia (19 January 2011);

– *Telemarketing*. Regulations for the processing of personal data for marketing purposes conducted over the telephone by an operator, following the setting up of the public register of citizens who do not wish to be contacted for such purposes (19 January 2011).

In 2011, the Authority also issued *Guidelines for the Processing of Personal Data Contained in Administrative Acts and Documents by Public Subjects for the Purpose of Publishing Data on the Internet* (2 March 2011) and a measure regarding *Vehicle Tracking Systems in the Work Environment* (4 October 2011).

C. Committee Guaranteeing the Implementation of the Law on Strikes Affecting Essential Public Services

The Committee was instituted by law 12 June 1990, No. 146, modified by law 11 April 2000, No. 83. It comprises nine members designated by the Chairs of the Chamber of Deputies and the Senate among experts in matters of constitutional law, labour law and industrial relations, and appointed by decree of the President of the Republic. In 2011 the office of Commissioner was composed of Giovanni Pitruzzella (Chair until November 2011), Roberto Alesse (Chair since November 2011), Pietro Boria, Gaetano Caputi, Alessandro Forlani, Elena Montecchi, Iolanda Piccinini, Nunzio Pinelli and Salvatore Vecchione.

The Commission has the following tasks:

– assessing the capacity of essential services as defined in accords among the social parties and in self-regulatory codes, to guarantee conciliation between exercising the right to strike, and enjoyment of the constitutionally guaranteed human rights;

– expressing views on interpretative or applicative issues regarding the content of self-regulatory agreements or codes, upon joint request by the parties or on its own initiative;

– requesting that those calling the strike delay the date of abstention from work if the Commission intends to attempt conciliation, or if it finds that the abstention violates legal and/or contractual obligations for a strike in essential public services;

– immediately pointing out to potential strikers, any violations of norms that may emerge regarding the giving of notice beforehand, and any other limitation regarding the phase preceding collective abstention;

– notifying the authority competent to order strikers back to work, of situations where a strike or collective abstention from work might give rise to an imminent, probable danger harming constitutionally protected human rights;

– taking note of behaviour by administrations or enterprises that provide essential public services in clear violation of the law;

– assessing behaviour by the parties involved and, if any non-compliance or violation of legal or contractual obligations emerges regarding indispensable services, inflicting penalties pursuant to art. 4 of law 146/1990, as modified from art. 3 of law 83/2000, obliging the employer to apply disciplinary sanctions.

On 7 July 2011, the Committee presented the 2011 annual report to the Chamber of Deputies regarding its activities in 2010. The first significant finding emerging from the report is the increase in conflict. In 2010, there were 2,093 strike calls, an increase of 10% on the previous year. The figure represents a significant peak in a substantial growth trend in the resort to strike action. The announced strikes related to a large degree to company- or local-level disputes, while the amount of strikes at a national level was more limited. The sector of greatest conflict lays in local public transport (346 strikes called), followed by the refuse collection (and related services) sector (270 strikes called, an increase of 75% on the previous year). In this second sector, conflict was prevalently in the southern Regions: as many as 210 (about 78%) of the 270 strikes called related to southern Regions, especially Sicily (94), Campania (65) and Apulia (38). These sectors have jumped ahead of air transport, which for many years was the area with the greatest intensity of conflict. Strike action was revoked following immediate instructions received from the Committee in 81% of cases. As a result, the resort to procedures to evaluate the actions of the parties involved remained at very low levels: 33 procedures were begun in 2010, and penalties were approved in 27 cases.

In 2010, the Committee also held 48 hearings of labour relations parties, of which 34 were with union representatives, 7 with employers' representatives, and 7 were joint.

D. National Ombudsperson for Children and Adolescents

The National Ombudsperson for Children and Adolescents was established with law No. 112 of 12 July 2011, following a long passage through Parliament that began in 2008. A monocratic organ, the holder of the post is appointed by the Presidents of the Chamber of Deputies and of the Senate, who choose a figure of unquestioned morality, independence and professional competence in the field of children's rights. The term of office is four years. On 30 November 2011, the President of the Senate, Renato Schifani, and the President of the Chamber of Deputies, Gianfranco Fini, appointed Vincenzo Spadafora, the former President of UNICEF Italy, to be the Ombudsperson.

The Ombudsperson has, amongst others, the following duties:

– to promote the implementation of the United Nations Convention on the Rights of the Child and other international and European instruments in the field;

– to ensure suitable forms of consultation and collaboration with all national and international bodies, organisations and networks for the promotion and protection of children and adolescents;

– to verify that minors receive equal opportunities in exercising their right to health and education;

– to express his or her opinion on normative acts regarding the protection of the rights of children and adolescents, on the National plan of action and on measures to protect the rights and development of children and adolescents;

– to inform the Government, Regions or the pertinent local and territorial authorities, in their respective areas of responsibility, of all appropriate initiatives for ensuring the full advocacy and safeguarding of the rights of children and adolescents, with particular reference to the right to a family, to education and to health;

– to inform the judicial authorities and all competent bodies, in cases of emergency, of minors in a state of abandonment, so they may be taken into care by the competent authorities;

– to inform the Director of Public Prosecution's Office at the Juvenile Court of situations in which minors are in a state of suffering or there is a risk that their rights may be violated;

– to make observations and recommendations about the pinpointing of the essential levels of services regarding the civil and social rights of minors, as per art. 117, paragraph 2, point m) of the Constitution, and to act as a watchdog to ensure that these levels are respected;

– to promote greater awareness of the rights of children and adolescents, organising, to this end, awareness-raising initiatives and study and research activities.

Article 6 of law 112 states that anyone may turn to the Ombudsperson to report the violation of rights or the risk thereof.

Finally, article 3 states that the Ombudsperson is to establish suitable forms of collaboration with the regional ombudspersons or analogous figures. The National Conference for the Rights of Children and Adolescents was set up for this purpose; coordinated by the National Ombudsperson, it brings together all the other Ombudspersons, where these have been established (see in Part I, Italian Law, IV).

IX. Non-governmental Organisations

In Italy there are numerous non-governmental organisations active in protecting human rights. Some of them, organised in networks on the national and international level, have gained the consultative status before international organisations and actively participate in the organisations activities.

By 31 December 2011 there were 96 non-governmental organisations in Italy having consultative status with the United Nations Economic and Social Council (ECOSOC), including 9 with general status, 69 with special status and 18 with "roster" status. 207 non-governmental organisations with headquarters or representative offices in Italy enjoy consultant status with the Council of Europe (compared to 196 in 2010).

In addition, some of the most important international non-governmental organisations have a local branch in Italy. They include Amnesty International, the International Federation on Human Rights, Save the Children, Médecins sans Frontières, Action Aid. The Italian associations *Nessuno tocchi Caino* and *Non c'è pace senza giustizia* attract great international attention.

Particularly worthy of note, as well, is the *Comitato per la promozione e protezione dei diritti umani*, a network of 83 non-governmental organisations working to promote human rights, created in January 2002 by initiative of the Fondazione Basso (Basso Foundation), with the support of a group of human rights experts. In 2011, Barbara Terenzi acted as coordinator, while Carola Carazzone was the main spokesperson.

The Committee's main goal is to stimulate and support the Italian legislative process in order to create an independent National Institution for Human Rights, in full compliance with the standards promoted by the United Nations General Assembly (resolution 48/134 of 20 December 1993) and the "Paris Principles".

Alongside activities linked to the creation of the national institution for human rights, since 2005 the Committee has systematically monitored the human rights situation in Italy. This supervisory activity, focusing on civil and political, economic, social and cultural rights in an integrated perspective, has as its source of reference the legal framework of the two related international covenants.

In 2011, the Committee published a report entitled *Italy One Year After the Recommendations of the United Nations Human Rights Council: First Report Monitoring Non-governmental and Associative Organisations of the Committee for the Promotion and Protection of Human*

Rights. The report examines the extent to which Italy has implemented the 92 recommendations made in the Universal Periodic Review, with particular reference to the following aspects: civil and political rights and international instruments; national legislation; the National Institution for Human Rights; human rights education; rights of migrants, refugees and asylum seekers; racism and xenophobia; women's rights; discrimination on the basis of sexual orientation; rights of minors; overcrowding in the prisons; torture; human trafficking; independence of the media system; the situation regarding public development aid.

With this report, the Committee asked the Government to prepare, following the example of other European Union nations, a medium-term follow-up report, to make it public by sending it to the Office of the United Nations High Commissioner for Human Rights and to promote wider knowledge of the recommendations and the mechanism of the Universal Periodic Review in Italy.

X. Human Rights Teaching and Research in Italian Universities

In recent years, the Italian academia has shown a growing attention towards research and training in the subject of human rights. Human rights are now part of many teaching programmes and university curricula, ranging from undergraduate and post-graduate courses to research programmes in a number of scientific sectors. A mapping of university institutions and research centres specifically dedicated to human rights is here presented. A list of human rights-oriented courses offered in bachelor, master, postgraduate and doctoral degree, active or started up in 2011, is also presented. In particular, only those courses and structures formally named as involving "human rights" or equivalent denominations (rights of man, fundamental rights) have been mentioned. The outcome is a quite complete presentation of the currents state of affairs in the field of human rights education in the Italian academia.

Data relating to graduate degrees, single courses and doctorate programmes can be found on the website of the Ministry of Education, University and Research (section "teaching programmes" at http://offf.miur.it).

University institutions and research centres

Six were up and running in 2011, compared to five in the previous year.

University	Name	Founding Year
University of Padua	Interdepartmental Centre on Human Rights and the Rights of Peoples	1982
University of Salento	Inter-University Centre on Bioethics and Human Rights	1992
41 European universities in partnership	European Inter-University Centre for Human Rights and Democratisation (EIUC)	2002
University of Naples	Centre for Studies on Human Rights in the Era of Globalisation and Conflicts	2003
University of Ca' Foscari, Venice	Interdepartmental Human Rights Research Centre (CIRDU)	2003
University of Salerno	Department of Individual Rights and Comparison	2011

Bachelor's degree courses

No change with respect to 2010.

University	Name	Scientific Area
University of Padua	Political Science, International Relations, Human Rights	L-36: Political science and international relations

Master's degree courses

No change with respect to 2010.

University	Name	Scientific Area
University of Bergamo	Human Rights and the Ethics of International Cooperation	LM-81: Cooperation development sciences
University of Bologna	International Cooperation, Protection of Human Rights and Ethno-cultural Heritage in the Mediterranean and Eurasia	LM-81: Cooperation development sciences
	International Cooperation, Development and Human Rights	LM-81: Cooperation development sciences
University of Padua	Institutions and Policies of Human Rights and Peace	LM-52: International relations

Teaching programmes

In 2011, a total of 118 human rights teaching programmes were run in 64 faculties (2010: 125 programmes in 66 faculties), subdivided as follows:

– 51 teaching programmes in 19 Faculties of Political Science (2010: 60 programmes in 22 Faculties of Political Science);

– 31 teaching programmes in 20 Faculties of Law (2010: 30 programmes in 21 Faculties of Law);

– 8 teaching programmes in 7 Faculties of Economics (2010: 7 programmes in 5 Faculties of Economics);

– 7 teaching programmes in 3 Faculties of Arts and Philosophy (2010: 5 programmes in 3 Faculties of Arts and Philosophy);

– 6 teaching programmes in 5 Faculties of Education (2010: 6 programmes in 4 Faculties of Education);

– 3 teaching programmes in a Faculty of Political Studies and Advanced European and Mediterranean Study (compared to 2 in 2010);

– 3 teaching programmes in a Faculty of Cultural Heritage Conservation (none in 2010);

– 2 teaching programmes in 2 Faculties of Foreign Languages and Literature (no change with respect to 2010);

– 2 teaching programmes in a Faculty of Sociology (no change with respect to 2010);

– 1 teaching programme in each of the following faculties: Humanistic Sciences; Social Sciences; Human and Social Sciences; Mathematical, Physical and Natural Sciences; Advanced School of Modern Languages for Interpreters and Translators (no change with respect to 2010).

In contrast to 2010, no courses were run in any Faculty of Communication Sciences or Statistics.

As in 2010, the university with the greatest number of human rights courses was Padua (19 programmes), followed by Turin (9), Bologna and Florence (7), and Bari (5).

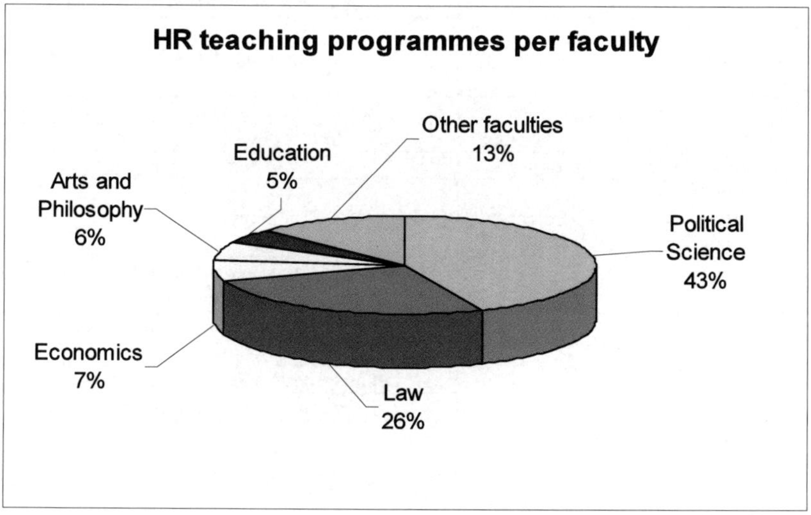

University	Department	Teachings
Aldo Moro University of Bari	Law	Human rights
		Human rights – theory of fundamental rights
		International protection of human rights
		International protection of human rights – human rights protection in the European Convention on Human Rights
	Foreign Languages and Literatures	International protection of human rights
University of Bergamo	Educational Sciences	Teaching on marginalisation and human rights
	Humanities	Teaching on human rights and international cooperation
University of Bologna	Cultural Heritage Conservation	Public law and human rights protection
		Human rights and history of international law
		International human rights law and European law on cooperation
		Public law and protection of fundamental rights
	Law	Fundamental rights
		Tax law and fundamental rights
	Political Science	International protection of human rights (seminar)
		Human rights, constitutions and institutions
University of Cagliari	Law	Constitutional law, governance and human rights protection
University of Calabria	Economics	Human rights theory
		Protection of rights
	Political Science	Institutions and rights in the European Union
		History of human rights and citizenship
University of Cassino and Southern Lazio	Law	Fundamental rights
University of Catania	Economics	Protection of rights in the civil trial
	Political Science	Philosophy of social rights
G. d'Annunzio University of Chieti – Pescara	Economics	Protection of rights
	Social Sciences	Human rights
University of Ferrara	Law	Human rights and humanitarian law in armed conflicts
University of Florence	Economics	International law, human rights and armed conflict
	Law	Legal systems and protection of rights
		Welfare State and human rights
	Educational Sciences	Human rights
	Political Science	Citizenship-related rights and self-Government units

		Civil society and religious rights
		International protection of human rights
University of Foggia	Law	Constitutional rights II – Fundamental rights
University of Genoa	Law	Civil and social rights
University of L'Aquila	Economics	Theory of interpretation and human rights
University of Macerata	Law	Social and citizenship-related rights
	Arts and Philosophy	Philosophy of rights and cultures
		Philosophy of rights and cultures II
University of Messina	Political Science	International organisation and human rights
University of Milan	Law	Rights of religions and human rights
	Political Science	Theories on equality and rights
		Theories on fundamental rights
		International protection of human rights
University of Milan-Bicocca	Law	European constitutional law (fundamental rights)
		International protection of human rights
	Sociology	Cooperation and human rights protection
		Rights and European citizenship
Sacro Cuore University	Law	Human rights
	Political Science	International protection of human rights
University of Modena and Reggio Emilia	Law	Theory and practice of human rights
University of Molise	Economics	Citizenship and citizenship-related rights
	Human and Social Sciences	Human rights and globalisation
Second University of Naples	Law	International protection of human rights
	Political Studies and Jean Monnet Advanced European and Mediterranean Studies	Constitutions and fundamental rights in Arab-Islamic systems
		Protection of rights in multi-cultural States
		Human rights
Federico II University of Naples	Economics	International protection of human rights
	Political Science	International protection of human rights
Suor Orsola Benincasa University – Naples	Educational Sciences	Human rights
University of Padua	Law	Human rights and public ethics
	Educational Sciences	Pedagogy of childhood, adolescence and rights of the child
	Political Science	Economic and social rights
		Fundamental rights and European citizenship
		Human rights

		Human rights and the status of women
		Human rights and international justice
		Sport and human rights in the European Union law
		Human rights in Italian and comparative constitutional law
		Philosophy of human rights
		International organisation for human rights and peace
		Globalisation of human rights and promotion of women
		Human rights, monitoring, electoral observation, peace-keeping
		Public policy and human rights
		Sociology of criminal law, prevention of deviance, prison conditions and rights of detainees
		General sociology and sociology of human rights
		History of human rights politics
		Economic development and human rights
		International human rights protection
University of Palermo	Political Science	Human rights and multi-culturalism
		Philosophy of human rights
University of Pavia	Law	Protection of fundamental rights
	Political Science	Gender studies: history of feminist movements – achievements of rights
University of Perugia	Political Science	Human rights and international crime
Amedeo Avogadro University of Eastern Piemonte-Vercelli	Political Science	Democracy, rights, religions
		European fundamental rights
University of Pisa	Mathematical, Physical and Natural Sciences	Legal and political theories of human rights
La Sapienza University of Rome	Political Science	Communications of rights and active citizenship
		Human rights and international jurisdictions
		Human rights and cooperation strategies
Roma Tre University	Political Science	International organisation and protection of human rights
		Protection and promotion of minors' rights in international and European relations (seminar)
Guido Carli LUISS – Free International University of Social Studies	Political Science	International protection of human rights

University of Salento	Arts and Philosophy	Human rights
		International protection of human rights
University of Salerno	Law	Human rights
		Human rights and biolaw
		International protection of human rights
University of Siena	Political Science	International protection of human rights
University of Turin	Law	International humanitarian law and human rights protection
		Fundamental rights guarantees
		Social order, juridical hermeneutics and protection of fundamental rights
	Political Science	Citizenship, social rights, justice
		Human rights and globalisation
		International organisation and protection of human rights
		Theories of human rights
		Vulnerable groups and human rights protection
		History of human rights
University of Trieste	Political Science	Human rights
	Advanced School of Modern Languages for Interpreters and Translators	Comparative human rights
University of Udine	Law	Human rights theory
Carlo Bo University of Urbino	Law	Human rights
		International protection of human rights
Ca' Foscari University of Venice	Arts and Philosophy	Human rights and policies of citizenship SP.
		Human rights and policies of citizenship SP. I
		Human rights and policies of citizenship SP. II
	Foreign Languages and Literatures	International law and human rights
University of Verona	Educational Sciences	Social and citizenship-related rights
		Protection of fundamental rights

Doctoral programmes (academic years 2010-2011 and 2011-2012)

A total of 11 doctoral programmes were being run or organised in 2011 (compared to 13 in 2010).

University	Name	Area of Scientific Discipline
University of Cassino and Southern Lazio, Department of Public law	Human rights protection in national constitutional courts and other European courts case-law	IUS/08, IUS/09, IUS/10, IUS/13, IUS/14, IUS/21, IUS/12, IUS/20, IUS/16
University of Florence, Department of Comparative and Criminal Law	Theory and history of law – Theory and history of human rights	IUS/18, IUS/19, IUS/20
Federico II University of Naples, Department of Roman Law, History and Theory of Law	Philosophy of law: art and technique of jurisprudence – Hermeneutics of human rights	IUS/19, IUS/20
University of Palermo, Department of Studies on Politics, Law and Society	Human rights: evolution, protection and limits	IUS/01, IUS/09, IUS/12, IUS/20, SPS/02, IUS/13, IUS/19, IUS/10, SPS/09, SECS-P/01, IUS/08
Amedeo Avogadro University of Eastern Piedmont, Department of Law and Economics	Local autonomies, public services and citizenship's rights	IUS/05, IUS/08, IUS/09 IUS/10, IUS/21
Scuola Superiore Sant'Anna in Pisa	Politics, human rights and sustainability	SPS/01, SPS/06, IUS/13, IUS/03, IUS/14, SPS/04, SECS-P/02, SECS-P/06, SECS-P/08
La Sapienza University of Rome, Department of State Theory	International order and human rights	IUS/13, IUS/14, IUS/08, IUS/07, IUS/01
Libera Maria Santissima Assunta University – LUMSA, Department of Law	Fundamental rights and freedoms in contemporary legal systems	IUS/01, IUS/11, IUS/13, IUS/17, IUS/20, IUS/18, IUS/07
	International adoptions: issues on the protection of fundamental human rights	IUS/01, IUS/11, IUS/13
University of Salerno, Department of Law on Civil and Economic Relations in Contemporary Legal Systems	Comparative human rights	IUS/01, IUS/02, IUS/07, IUS/13, IUS/14, IUS/16, IUS/17
University of Teramo, Department of Public Legal Studies	Protection of fundamental rights – Italian and European public law	IUS/08, IUS/09, IUS/10, IUS/21

Sub-national Human Rights Structures

I. Peace Human Rights Offices in Municipalities, Provinces and Regions

On the municipal, provincial and regional levels, by virtue of the inclusion of the "peace human rights norm" in thousands of municipal, provincial and regional statutes, and of the adoption of special regional laws linked to this topic (see Part I, Italian Law, IV), several consultancies, offices, departments and bureaus dedicated to human rights, peace, equal opportunities, development cooperation, fair trade and international solidarity have been established in Italy. A more detailed picture of the spread of these structures within Italian local authorities and Regions is provided in the 2011 edition of the Yearbook.

II. Ombudspersons

The 2010 Budget Act (law No. 191, 23 December 2009) – as modified by l.d. No. 2 of 25 January 2010, converted into law 42/2010 – instructed the Municipalities (article 2, paragraph 186) to close the municipal ombudsperson's offices in order to limit public spending, but granted the possibility to attribute the functions of these offices to the provincial ombudsperson, defined as the "territorial ombudsperson". When this law came into force, hundreds of local ombudspersons' posts were phased out as the mandates ended (see the *2011 Yearbook*, pp. 134-137). In the light of this situation, it is uncertain whether the few provincial ombudspersons that, prior to the abolition of the local ones, had signed agreements with Municipalities (e.g., Padua, Prato, Arezzo), can be described as territorial ombudspersons. The agreements between the Ombudspersons of the Autonomous Provinces of Trent and Bolzano the Municipalities in those Provinces have remained in force. Mention must also be made of the Ombudspersons for the Union of Mountain Municipalities of the Lunigiana (Massa Carrara) in Tuscany and for the Union of the Terre d'Argine Municipalities (Modena) in Emilia-Romagna, who have appointed an associate Ombudsperson.

In 2011 there were 14 incumbent regional Ombudspersons out of a total of 17 Regions and Autonomous Provinces that make provision for such an office in their respective statutes or in special regional laws: Abruzzo, Basilicata, Emilia-Romagna, Lazio, Liguria, Lombardy,

Marche, Molise, Piedmont, Tuscany, Valle d'Aosta and Veneto, plus the Autonomous Provinces of Bolzano and Trento. The post is currently vacant in Campania, Sardinia and Umbria, while no ombudsperson has ever been appointed in Calabria and Apulia. The role is not normatively envisaged by the Regions of Sicily and Trentino-Alto Adige (where, however, the Region has delegated to the Ombudspersons of the Autonomous Provinces full responsibility in their respective territories), while in Friuli Venezia Giulia the law establishing this institution (dating back to 1981) was abrogated with a budget-balancing act in 2008 (regional law No. 9, 14 August 2008).

At the European and international level, 14 provincial and regional Ombudspersons are members of the European Ombudsman Institute (EOI). On 24 September 2011, the general assembly of the EOI nominated the following to be members of the new executive committee: Lucia Franchini, Ombudsperson for the Region of Tuscany; Vittorio Galatro, Ombudsperson for Nocera Inferiore; and Vittorio Gasparrini, Ombudsperson for the Municipalities of Incisa in Val d'Arno and Rignano sull'Arno. Enrico Formento Dojot, Burgi Volgger and Catello Aprea, respectively the Ombudspersons for the Region of Valle d'Aosta, the Autonomous Province of Bolzano, and the Region of Basilicata, are members of the International Ombudsman Institute (IOI).

III. National Coordinating Body of Ombudspersons

The Regions and Autonomous Provinces' Ombudspersons National Coordinating Body is an associative body working to harmonise and enhance the institutional role of the ombudsperson in Italy, and to guarantee every citizen, regardless of where he or she resides, protection in dealing with the public administration at any level, whether State, regional or local.

Besides creating effective liaisons with Parliament and the Italian Government, the Coordination promotes the full application of treaties and of European and international human rights law, in particular the Charter of Fundamental Rights of the European Union. In addition, it develops relations with the European Ombudsman and with the Ombudspersons of EU Member States, even through the European Network of Ombudsmen. Moreover, it fosters coordination initiatives in all Regions with the ombudspersons at every territorial level, in order to widen the scope of their role and to enhance standards for the protection of individual rights and common interests; and it organises pertinent research and study programmes. The Coordination is made up of the incumbent Ombudspersons in the Regions and in the Autonomous Provinces. It operates through the office of an Ombudsperson elected collegially from time to time and has its headquarters in Rome, at the Network of the Presidents of the Assembly, of Regional Councils, and Autonomous Provinces (*Conferenza dei Presidenti dell'Assemblea, dei Consigli regionali e delle Province autonome*) where it normally meets.

Following the meeting of the Coordinating Body on 21 February 2011, the Ombudsperson of the Region of Piedmont, Antonio Caputo, was elected as the Coordinator. The Coordinating Body held five meetings in the course of 2011. Of the main themes discussed, it is important to mention the preparation and presentation of projects to be developed in the ambit of the Italian Ombudsperson Institute (see *2011 Yearbook*, p. 138), and the pursuit of forms of collaboration with the National Association of Italian Municipalities (ANCI) and the Union of Italian Provinces (UPI), in order to foster the territorial presence of the ombudsperson – also by promoting an agreed model for the establishment of a territorial ombudsperson in all the Italian Provinces – and to set up a national network operating in the ambit of the National Coordinating Body, so as to ensure fruitful collaboration between territorial and regional ombudspersons.

With regard to the activities of the Italian Ombudsman Institute, it should be noted that, on 13 April 2011, the Ombudsperson of the Region of Tuscany and the Human Rights Centre of the University of Padua signed a memorandum of understanding, with Vittorio Gasparrini as coordinator of the Institute. The agreement falls within the framework of the implementation of the memorandum of understanding between the National Coordinating Body of Ombudspersons and the Human Rights Centre, signed on 21 June 2010.

IV. Network of Ombudspersons for Children and Adolescents

The Network was formally established on 30 April 2010 by the regional Ombudspersons who had gathered together in Naples for the occasion. The main aim of the body is to promote best practices across the Country. The Ombudsperson of the Region of Lazio, Francesco Alvaro, is the current network coordinator.

During the year, the regional Ombudspersons for children continued to meet periodically to exchange information about the situation on the ground in various areas, about actions pursued by different regional institutions, common issues, the possibility of agreeing to and launching joint cross-cutting initiatives to study and promote children's rights, and possible synergies and areas of cooperation between regional institutions concerned to safeguard the rights of children and adolescents (for example, a research and action project to share best practices and involving various Regions), and finally, about starting to reflect on themes of particular significance (the figure of the National Ombudsperson for Children, listening to minors, essential levels of welfare services [LIVEAS], etc.).

Three coordination sessions were organised in 2011. The first was held in Venice on 1 July, and was coordinated by the Ombudsperson for Children and Adolescents of the Region of Veneto, Aurea Dissegna (see in this Part, Region of Veneto, V); the second, held in Bolzano on 9 September, was organised by Simon Tschager, the Ombudsperson for Children and Adolescents of the Autonomous Province of Bolzano; and the third, held on 10 October in Catanzaro, was organised by the Ombudsperson for Children of the Region of Calabria, Marilina Intrieri.

Following the approval of law No. 112 (Establishment of the National Ombudsperson for Children and Adolescents) of 12 July 2011, the National Network for the protection of Children and Adolescents' rights was formally established. It is presided over by the National Ombudsperson for Children and Adolescents, Vincenzo Spadafora, appointed on 30 November 2011 (see in this Part, National Bodies with Jurisdiction over Human Rights, VIII, D), and is made up of the regional Ombudspersons for children (or similar institutions). The Network has the task of: working towards the adoption of common lines of action by the regional Ombudspersons with regard to the protection of the rights of children and adolescents, to be implemented at the regional and national levels and to be promoted and supported in international settings; and to ensure a constant exchange of data and information on the condition of minors at a national and regional level. In Italy, 19 Regions and Autonomous Provinces have passed laws to establish local Ombudspersons for children or similar (Abruzzo, Apulia, Basilicata, Calabria, Campania, Emilia-Romagna, Friuli Venezia Giulia, Lazio, Liguria, Lombardy, Marche, Molise, Piedmont, Sardinia, Tuscany, Umbria, Veneto, and the Provinces of Bolzano and Trent). Abruzzo, Calabria, Emilia-Romagna, Lazio, Liguria, Marche, Apulia, Tuscany, Veneto and the Autonomous Provinces of Bolzano and Trent have appointed their respective Ombudspersons.

V. National Coordinating Body of Local Authorities for Peace and Human Rights

The National Coordinating Body is an association founded in 1986, including Municipalities, Provinces and Regions committed, in Italy, to promoting peace, human rights, solidarity and international cooperation. More than 700 members among Municipalities, Provinces and Regions have adhered to the Coordinating Body. The Chair of this association is Marco Vinicio Guasticchi, President of the Province of Perugia; the Director is Flavio Lotti.

The Coordinating Body's main activity in 2011 was the organisation, in conjunction with the *Tavola della Pace* ("Peace Roundtable"), of the *Perugia-Assisi March for Peace and Brotherhood among Peoples*. The march was held on 25 September 2011, fifty years after the first Perugia-Assisi march, organised by Aldo Capitini and with the same slogan, on 24 September 1961. Among the fringe events it is worth mentioning the meeting of *1000 Young People for Peace*, which was held in Bastia Umbra (Perugia) on 23 and 24 September 2011, during which young people exchanged ideas and planned new paths on the themes of peace, work and the future. The fiftieth anniversary of the first peace march also marked the culmination of the *Year of Values*, an initiative launched on 21 September 2011 with the 2010-2011 national programme of peace and human rights action/education entitled *My School For Peace.* Also in relation to the initiatives associated with the *Year of Values*, the National Coordinating Body and the *Tavola della Pace* organised, between 4 and 20 May 2011, six themed forums in six different Italian cities (Bari, Matera, Padua, Riccione, Senigallia and Trent). The forums focused on seven values lying at the heart of the Italian Constitution and the Universal Declaration of Human Rights: peace, freedom, human rights, hope, non-violence, justice and responsibility. This initiative involved up to 42,000 pupils from 260 schools throughout Italy, who participated in the project *Every School is a Great Workshop of Values*, in the course of the national programme for peace and human rights education promoted by the coordinating body.

Other initiatives in which the coordinating body participated in 2011 include: *Italy-Lebanon Cooperation. Experiences of Decentralised Cooperation Between Local Authorities*, an international conference organised in Turin on 30-31 March; a national seminar of the *Tavola della Pace*, entitled *Towards Freedom, Human Rights and Democracy*, held in Assisi between 15 and 17 April 2011; a meeting for reflection and collective action called *The Seed and the Tree. Resisting/existing in Italy Today with Aldo Capitini and Giorgio La Pira*, held in Predappio (Forli-Cesena) on 6-7 May 2011; and the national preparatory seminar for the Perugia-Assisi March for Peace and Brotherhood Among Peoples, *Towards 25 September*, in Perugia on 1-2 July.

The Coordinating Body is part of the promoting committee of the campaign for citizenship rights, *I am Italy, too* (L'Italia sono anche io), designed to promote, through two citizens' bills submitted to Parliament, reform of the right of citizenship so that children born in Italy from legally resident foreign citizens are eligible for Italian citizenship, and a new norm granting legal foreign workers who have been present in Italy for five years the right to vote in local elections.

VI. Archives and Other Regional Projects for the Promotion of a Culture of Peace and Human Rights

Besides the Pace Diritti Umani – Peace Human Rights Archive of the Region of Veneto, established with r.l. 18/1988 (see in this Part, Region of Veneto, III), a number of other archives and similar projects have been set up in Italy at regional level to help promote and disseminate a culture of human rights and peace. On 7 April 2000, the Region of Campania approved, with r.l. No. 12 (Promotion and dissemination of a culture of peace and human rights education) the establishment of the Archive for Peace and for Human Rights. The archive was activated following the signing of an agreement between the Regional Education Authority and the Department of the Analysis of Environmental and Territorial Dynamics at the University of Naples Federico II.

The main aims of the Archive are to promote and disseminate, especially in schools and universities, the research results and teaching materials it produces, and to provide institutions, associations and citizens with documentation or information useful for fostering a culture of peace in the community, both by updating its internet site (http://archiviopace.altervista. org) and by organising twinning schemes, non-violent training, peace education activities in schools, seminars, conferences and regional awards. Amongst the activities promoted by the Archive, it is worth noting the publication of the *Agenda della Pace* ("Peace Agenda"), which is brought out periodically and is designed to offer suggestions and ideas for teachers, students, institutions and citizens regarding the themes of peace and human rights; and the awarding of the annual Prize "Pace Campania".

The *Peace and Human Rights* project of the Emilia-Romagna Region was set up by the Regional Council in conjunction with the Office for Social Policies, Immigration, Youth Projects and International Cooperation, and with the Management and Statistical Systems Control Service of the Regional Council. The project draws inspiration from the content of r.l. No. 12 of 24 June 2002 (Regional interventions for cooperation with developing Countries and Countries in transition, for international solidarity and for the promotion of a culture of peace), and its purpose is to support the activities described in the law.

The main functions of the project are to offer regional associations and institutions opportunities to enhance their knowledge, exchange ideas and share information, and to provide information and documentary support services to associations and institutions working locally in the areas envisaged by the regional law, through the updating of the dedicated website (http://www. paceediritti.it/). Activities carried out in the ambit of this project include a mapping of associations and institutions involved in human rights advocacy and active in the region, and the preparation of an educational kit for first-level secondary schools, entitled *Knowing Your Rights is a Duty*.

Other initiatives at the regional and Autonomous Provinces level include:

– the forum *Trentino for Peace and Human Rights*, a permanent body set up in 1991 on initiatives of the Provincial Council of Trent, by p.l. No. 11 of 10 June 1991 (Promotion and spreading of a culture of peace).

The forum has a number of principal goals: to keep a watchful eye on issues relating to peace, human rights, solidarity, active citizenship and responsibility, with a view to developing and rethinking interventions and existing norms; to create a network of bodies active in the Province (associations, institutions, public and private bodies, researchers, teachers and university professors), so as to foster links and dealings; and to monitor the decisions of Council of the Autonomous Province of Trento regarding these themes.

– the Register of Bodies Working for Peace and Human Rights in Abruzzo, which is currently being set up pursuant to regional law No. 29 of 17 October 2005 (Promotion and spreading of a culture of peace and human rights education).

The purpose of the Register is, together with that of the Prize "Abruzzo for Peace and Human Rights", and the activities of the Permanent Committee for Peace and Human Rights, to foster, in the Abruzzo community, cultural sensitivity and concern for social issues relating to the principles of freedom and human solidarity.

Region of Veneto

The Region of Veneto has been operating organically for the promotion of human rights, the culture of peace and international cooperation, ever since 1988, the year when the first specific law on such issues was adopted: regional law 30 March 1988, No. 18 (Regional measures for the promotion of a culture of peace). During the same year, the Regional Council instituted the Ombudsperson (r.l. 28/1988) and the Commissioner for Children and Adolescents (r.l. 42/1988).

In 1999, regional law 18/1988 was replaced by the current r.l. 16 December 1999, No. 55, on "Regional measures for the promotion of human rights, a culture of peace, development cooperation and solidarity".

In the context of the Regional Government, issues concerning human rights pertain to the Councillor on Economy, Development, Research and Innovation Marialuisa Coppola. Measures and activities regarding international relations and development cooperation respond directly to the Regional Governor, Luca Zaia.

In virtue of r.l. 55/1999, the Committee on Human Rights and the Culture of Peace (articles 12-13) and the Committee on Development Cooperation (articles 14-15) operate to fulfil their mandate of formulating *three-year programmes* and *annual plans* of implementation according to their respective areas of competence and intervention. In addition, the law promotes and supports the Regional Archive "Pace Diritti Umani – Peace Human Rights" (article 2), the Venice for Peace Research Foundation (article 17) (both established with r.l. 18/1988), the activities of the European Commission for Democracy through Law (Venice Commission) of the Council of Europe (article 19) and initiatives of decentralised cooperation promoted by the Ministry of Foreign Affairs and by the European Union (article 7).

Finally, every two years, the Regional Government convenes a regional Conference serving as a meeting-point enabling the exchange of experiences among local actors working in the area of cooperation and international solidarity (article 20). The last conference took place in Treviso on 10 and 11 December 2009 in the framework of the celebrations for the tenth anniversary of r.l. 55/1999.

The *Department for international relations* is the central administrative structure dealing with implementation of the law 55/1999.

The regional infrastructure for peace and human rights is completed by the Commission for the Realisation of Equal Opportunities between Men and Women, established with r.l. 30 December 1987, No. 62, the Regional Observatory on Social Policies, set up with Regional Government deliberation

3 August 2010, No. 2077; the Regional Observatory on Immigration, instituted in 2007 pursuant to r.l. 30 January 1990, No. 9. Moreover, by way of r.l. 28 December 1998, No. 33, the Region promotes and supports financially the European Master's degree Programme in Human Rights and Democratisation (E.MA), located in Venice.

With the recent adoption of r.l. 22 January 2010, No. 6, the Region has recognised the social and cultural value of fair trade, proclaiming its support for the organisations which operate in this sector.

In the session of 18 October 2011, the Regional Council approved, on the first reading, the text of the new statute. Paragraph 7 of article 5, devoted to fundamental principles, contains a commitment to promote a culture of peace, and to work for social justice, human rights, and dialogue and cooperation between peoples.

I. Regional Department for International Relations

The Regional Department (until September 2010, Department for International Relations, International Cooperation, Human Rights and Equal Opportunities) is the central administrative structure dealing with implementation of r.l. 55/1999. The Director managing this structure is Diego Vecchiato. The Department has a staff of 30, including personnel, interns and collaborators.

The Regional Department is dedicated to overseeing a good portion of the international activities taken up by the Region, including: the management of international relations, the signature of memoranda of understanding with national and foreign institutions, the participation in international bodies and initiatives, the promotion of international solidarity, and of all sorts of activities concerning human rights, the culture of peace, the promotion of equal opportunities and the protection of linguistic minorities. The Department head office also hosts the Veneto Regional Committee for UNICEF.

Moreover, in the specific area of human rights, the Regional Department provides technical support to the Committee for human rights and the culture of peace; it oversees the organisation of several important events, including the *Biennial Conference for human rights and development cooperation* and the Prize, *Veneto for peace and solidarity among peoples* (in 2011 the Prize was awarded to Ornella Milanesi for the project to fight congenital heart diseases at the Orota Referral Hospital in Asmara, Eritrea). Furthermore, the Department participates in the activities of the Venice Commission of the Council of Europe and fulfils its obligations linked to the Region's participation in the European Master's Programme in Human Rights and Democratisation (E.MA).

The role of the Department in the regional activities realised during the year 2011 has therefore been transversal to the bodies discussed in the following paragraphs.

II. Committee for Human Rights and the Culture of Peace

Established pursuant to article 12 of r.l. 55/1999, the Committee concurs in setting up pertinent triennial programmes and annual plans regarding the initiatives promoted by the Region of Veneto on human rights and a culture of peace (article 13). The Committee comprises representatives from local authorities, civil society, academia, entrepreneurs and social sectors.

The *2011 Annual Plan* regarding the implementation of regional measures to promote human rights and a culture of peace was passed with Regional Government decree No. 1597 of 4 October 2011. The aim of the plan is to pursue and develop the guidelines laid down by the 2010-2012 three-year programme.

The objectives established by the programme adopted by the Regional Council with resolution No. 5 on 12 January 2010 include: the setting up and development of coordination networks concerning the culture of human rights; the establishment and promotion of a culture of human rights based on non-discrimination, respect for the rights of women, children, adolescents, minorities and vulnerable groups; the advocacy of a culture of peace and integration based on intercultural and interreligious dialogue, the peaceful management of conflicts, and reciprocal acceptance of ethnic, religious and language diversities.

Besides reaffirming its commitment, in compliance with regional law 55/1999, regarding the Archive "Peace Human Rights" (Archivio "Pace Diritti Umani"), the Venice for Peace Research Foundation and the Prize "Veneto for Peace and Solidarity between Peoples", in 2011 the Regional Council approved direct initiatives for a total cost of 300,000 euros. This was half the sum made available in the previous year:

– projects in the school system: the *Peace Project 2010-2011* (7th year) of the Fabio Besta Professional Institute in Treviso; *In & Out* (2nd year), organised by the Municipality of Jesolo (Province of Venice); *Music Beyond Borders – The Logic of Conflict, the Culture of Peace*, run by the Liceo Scientifico Statale G.B. Quadri in Vicenza; *School and the City. Active Citizenship and Responsible Education* (2nd year), run by the Municipality of Rovigo; *TAM-TAM: growing up with rights*, run by the Municipality of Maser (Treviso); *Towards an Educative Community*, run by the Liceo Scientifico Statale Leonardo da Vinci in Treviso; *Education for a Global Vision = Knowledge of Human Rights*, run by the Municipality of San Martino Buon Albergo (Verona);

– projects for the training of human rights operators: *The Right to Water: A Human Right, Economic Resource or Common Asset?* (2nd year), run by the Province of Venice; the *Summer School in Applied Anthropology 2011* (4th year), organised by the Municipality of Portogruaro (Venice); *It Works! Educating Self and Others, Evaluation and Assessment in Human Rights Education with Children and Adolescents in the Schools of the Province of Padua* (2nd year), run by the Istituto Comprensivo di Vigodarzere (Padua);

– projects in the field of citizen awareness: *ImmaginAfrica 2011* (4th year), run by the Department of History of the University of Padua; *Development Goals for the Millennium and Childhood: An Inextricable Link in a Spirit of Equity*, run by the Italian Committee for UNICEF; *Rights and Citizenship – Active Minors*, run by the Municipality of Volpago del Montello (Treviso); the activities relating to the information and awareness-raising initiatives promoted by the Regional Department for International Relations.

III. Regional Archive "Peace Human Rights"

The Regional Archive was created pursuant to r.l. 18/1988 and reconfirmed by the successive r.l. 55/1999. The Archive is managed by the Human Rights Centre of the University of Padua according to a special agreement with the Region, in application of article 2 of the forementioned law. The Archive is one of the main instruments by which the Region of Veneto promotes the culture of human rights, peace, development cooperation and solidarity in Italy and in other Countries.

The Archive works to collect, elaborate and make publicly available documents, thematic databases, and informational resources on topics regarding regional law, particularly through the regular updating of the portal "Archivio Pace Diritti Umani" (http://unipd-centrodirittiumani.it/en) and by spreading human rights awareness through multi-media tools and social networks. In addition, it oversees publication of books, teaching aids, in-depth study packets and multi-media cd-roms, and ensures technical and scientific support for persons most closely interested to the promotion and to the realisation of the culture of peace.

During 2011 the number of online databases available from the Archive rose to eight, thanks to the setting up of a specific database bringing together and systematically presenting all the documents cited in the *Italian Yearbook of Human Rights 2011*, and subsequent editions (including the present one).

The other seven databases, optimised during 2011, collect respectively: legal instruments of international human rights, humanitarian, criminal and refugees law, translated into Italian; the publications edited from 1982 to today by the Human Rights Centre of the University of Padua; data on institutional norms concerning the establishment of the ombudsperson in Italian Municipalities (with populations over 5,000 inhabitants), Provinces and Regions; norms on peace, human rights and equal opportunities in Italian Municipalities (with populations over 5,000 inhabitants) Provinces and Regions; the associations and NGOs active in Veneto in matters of human rights and development cooperation; documentation and publications relating to the rights of the persons with disabilities; and the volumes collected at the Piergiorgio Cancellieri library of the Human Rights Centre.

In the course of the year, besides its regular updating and deepening activities on issues relating to human rights and peace (newsletters, theme-based dossiers, multimedia content), the Archive published three numbers of the four-monthly review *Pace diritti umani/Peace human rights*, and organised a series of initiatives, in particular regarding documentary, multimedia and communication activities, in conjunction with regional and international bodies and organisations. Of these, the following are the most noteworthy:

– a meeting between Pavel Nedved, winner of the Football Player of the Year award (Ballon d'Or) in 2003, and students of degree courses in human rights of the University of Padua, which took place on 15 February 2011 in the context of teaching programmes regarding sport and human rights in the European Union law;

– a series of three international workshops organised by the University of Padua's Jean Monnet European Centre of Excellence between March and October 2011, on the themes of: intercultural dialogue education; the participation of civil society in intercultural dialogue; and the cultural and value roots of intercultural dialogue in the context of the European Union;

– two conference events organised to celebrate the Human Rights Day 2011: *Monitoring Human Rights in Prison*, on 12 December 2011, with the participation of the then President of the Council of Europe's Committee for the Prevention of Torture, Mauro Palma; and *Electoral Observation Missions: A Testing Ground for Human Rights and Governance*, on 15 December 2011.

IV. Venice for Peace Research Foundation

Like the Regional Archive, the Foundation was established by r.l. 18/1988 and reconfirmed successively by r.l. 55/1999. The Foundation's main goal is to carry out research, partly in collaboration with national and international institutions, on matters of security, development and peace.

Among the most recent activities of the Foundation it is worth stressing three research projects – *Religions and Memory. Strategies of Memory and Oblivion in Asian Religious Discourse; The Role of Memory in the Construction of Peace and the European Integration Process; Guarantees of Access to Natural Resources* – and the publication of the ninth edition of the Geopolitical Peace Yearbook, entitled *Stati di paura e precarie sicurezze* (Fear Condition and Fragile Security), published by Altraeconomia (Milan).

V. Ombudsperson for Children and Adolescents

The Office of the Ombudsperson for Children and Adolescents (*Ufficio di protezione e tutela pubblica dei minori*) was created by r.l. 9 August 1988, No. 42. The Ombudsperson is elected by the Regional Council, to which he or she presents a detailed yearly report on the activities performed during each year. The Ombudsperson works toward the non-conflictual, non-jurisdictional protection of children's and adolescents' rights, freely and independently with respect to other public institutions. It is a monocratic authority which collaborates with a staff of experts and collaborators from various professions and disciplines; the Ombudsperson for Children operates free of charge. After having been appointed on 7 December 2010 by the President of the Regional Council, Aurea Dissegna took office as the new Regional Ombudsperson for Children and Adolescence at the end of the year.

> Regional law 42/1988, the United Nations International Convention on the Rights of the Child and the Council of Europe Convention on the Exercise of Children's Rights constitute the paradigm which founds and orients action by the Ombudsperson for Children and Adolescents. His or her functions are regulated by article 2 of the above-mentioned regional law. They include: awareness-raising, training and support for volunteer legal guardians for children; promoting a culture fostering children's and adolescents' rights in collaboration with local authorities and in connection with public opinion and the information media; listening to children involved in situations of distress, risk or prejudice, in cases brought to the Office's attention, and undertaking orientation, mediation and consultation measures; vigilance over guardianship given to minors living outside their family of origin; notification to the competent administrative and legal authorities as well as to social services regarding situations of risk or prejudice to minors; collaboration with public administrations in order to foster goal-sharing; support for the assumption of responsibility by individuals, professionals and institutions operating in favour of children and adolescents; network-building among figures dedicated to the protection of minors

Over the years the Office of the Ombudsperson for Children and Adolescents has trained and provided support for over 950 voluntary legal guardians throughout the Region of Veneto, 70% of whom have declared their willingness to carry on occupying this role and to continue working on the project. In 2011 the Office continued its advice, support and training activities, and organised three new basic training courses for different public health care authorities in the Region.

In 2011 the Ombudsperson's Office received 302 requests for a voluntary legal guardian from the judicial authorities (ordinary and juvenile courts), regarding a total of 314 children and adolescents in the Region.

In relation to its institutional listening, mediation and advisory activities, the Office opened 347 case files in 2011, following requests from Municipalities (45%), Local Health Authorities (ULSS) (22%), parents (13%) and private citizens (7%). The most frequent problems concerned: mistreatment (17%), neglect (11%), foster care placements (13%), parental conflict (12%). The principal kind of response adopted by the Office was to refer the cases to social and healthcare services (95%).

To complement its work relating to the provision of guidelines for communication between the school system and social and health care services, in 2011, the Ombudsperson's Office brought out a supplementary volume to the previous publication (*Orientamenti per la comunicazione tra scuola e servizi sociali e sociosanitari – Guidelines for communications between schools and welfare and health care services*). The supplementary material dealt in greater depth with issues that emerged during the training course that was run between April and October 2010 in conjunction with the Regional School Office, the Regional Department of Social Services and the Human Rights Centre of the University of Padua. The course was attended by about 80 people, including school principals, teachers, and social and healthcare workers and managers from around the Region.

As regards the activities of cultural promotion and research begun in 2011, it is particularly worth mentioning the Office's involvement, as a partner of Public Health Authority (ULSS) No. 3, in the European project *Involved by Right*, designed to try out new ways of stimulating the participation and involvement of children and adolescents removed from the care of their family of origin and placed in that of the social services, and the research-action associated with the subject of the legal institution of social service care. This inter-regional research project will be coordinated by the Human Rights Centre of the University of Padua.

VI. Ombudsperson

The Ombudsperson of the Region of Veneto was established with r.l. No. 28 of 6 June 1988, and is a monocratic authority with the freedom to act independently in the defence of citizens' rights and interests, in cases of maladministration or an abuse of powers by public authorities. The Ombudsperson has the support of an office staffed by legal experts with specific competence in the areas covered by the office's activities. The intervention of the Ombudsperson is free of charge. He or she is elected by the Regional Council from among citizens possessing the necessary training and expertise in administrative and legal matters, and remains in office for five years. Every year the Ombudsperson presents a detailed report on his or her work. On 19 October 2011, with resolution No. 74, Regional Council of Veneto adopted the Ombudsperson's report for 2010 and the first quarter of 2011.

The post is currently occupied by Roberto Pellegrini, who was nominated by the President of the Regional Council on 7 December 2010 and took office on 20 January 2011.

> The Ombudsperson has the following tasks: to intervene following complaints of maladministration or an abuse of powers by public authorities; to protect common interests; to ask to be shown any act or document, even secret ones; to encourage the setting up of round tables for discussion and agreement (service conferences); to direct citizens towards appropriate structures and advise them on initiatives or possible solutions; to promote reconciliatory solutions to disputes; to demand action from those responsible for various kinds of proceedings; to demand that disciplinary proceedings be taken against negligent public officials; to stir public authorities into action and make proposals. The Ombudsperson's role is therefore to act as a guarantor in disputes between citizens and public authorities. He or she cannot intervene in civil law issues between private citizens unless a public authority is also involved.

About 6,000 people from all the Provinces of Veneto sought assistance from the Regional Ombudsperson's Office in 2011. The issues concerned covered every sphere of administrative law, especially with regard to the environment and the local authorities (councils, provinces, the Veneto Environmental Protection Agency [ARPAV], the State railway company, superintendencies), tax matters (questions regarding local council property tax, refuse tax, car tax) and issues regarding the legitimacy of acts passed by local authorities. The Regional Ombudsperson intervenes exclusively in cases involving citizens and public authorities or public service providers (for example, the postal service, electricity and phone companies).

The Office also devoted particular attention to cases concerning health and social services (local health authorities, hospitals, social welfare institutes, etc.), and also took official action following issues raised by the press. In these areas, mention must be made of intervention by the Regional Ombudsperson's Office with regard to housing difficulties faced by disabled people, recognition of medical treatment received abroad, waiting lists, access to documents concerning medical records, access to services from health authorities outside an individual's area of residence, the introduction of fees for stays in nursing homes. The Office also took action in many questions regarding access to official documents.

VII. Regional Commission for Equal Opportunities between Men and Women

The Commission was instituted by regional law 30 December 1987, No. 62. It is the regional consultative body on gender policies aimed at the actual implementation of the principle of parity and equal opportunities, set forth by the Constitution and by the Regional Statute. Pursuant to Regional Government deliberation No. 1231 of 30 April 2004, the Commission receives administrative assistance from the Regional Department for International Relations. The new composition of the Commission was decided with decree of the President of the Regional Government No. 118, on 1 July 2011. The Chair of the Commission is Simonetta Tregnago.

The Commission's main function is to carry out inquiries and research on the condition of women in Veneto, with particular reference to issues involving employment, labour and professional training, and to spread information about these spheres. Within this function, the Commission maintains its commitment to be present in the territory and to develop new synergies with all the actors and forces in order to promote and support the realisation of equal opportunities in the social, political and economic reality of the population of Veneto. Moreover, it may formulate opinions on the current status of compliance with laws and on law proposals as well as prepare its own law proposals. The Commission carries out its activities partly in coordination with other Commissions on the local, regional and national level, and actively confronting with all the women's realities in the territory.

Among the activities carried out in the course of 2011, the Commission conducted an inquiry into domestic murders in Veneto in the three-year period 2009-2011. The aim was to learn more about the causes of serious offences such as murder and attempted murder in the domestic environment, where, in the majority of cases, the victims are women. The Commission also published reports detailing the results of two other studies it had promoted, one on the theme of violence in couples and between young people in the family unit (*Violenza sulle donne. I giovani come la pensano? Risultati, esperienze e riflessioni*); and one about girls who are about to drop out of education in order to work (*Ragazze in Veneto fra scuola e lavoro*).

VIII. Regional Observatory on Social Policies

With deliberation No. 2077 of 3 August 2010, the Regional Government operated a reorganisation of the regional observatories in the social sphere, setting up, as of 2011, a single new observatory to replace the three previously existing bodies that formed the *Integrated Network of Regional Observatories on Social Policies* (the Observatory on new generations and the family; the Observatory on the condition of the elderly and of persons with disabilities; and the Observatory on dependency and social marginalisation). The new structure became definitive as of January 2011.

The function of Observatory on Social Policies is to activate an information-gathering, monitoring and evaluation system for interventions and actions relating to regional health and social service policies, in order to support decision-making and planning processes, and to develop a regional social information system capable of ensuring close dealings between local systems, integrating into the wider regional information system and responding to requests for information from the New Health Information System (NSIS). This function is performed through the organisation of events, training activities and consultancy work regarding health and social service issues, the development and management of databases and support activities (in particular, studies and research) for the regional social services office. The Observatory's activities are organised in line with the themes dealt with by the previous Observatories: minors, young people, the family, elderly, people with disabilities, various forms of dependency, social exclusion, voluntary service and European projects.

IX. Regional Observatory on Immigration

The Observatory is overseen by the Project unit on migratory flows (Councillor's office on migratory flows policies) and it is managed by *Veneto Lavoro*. Its establishment was foreseen by the *three-year programme 2007-2009* comprising measures and initiatives in the field of immigration, and confirmed by the adoption of the following programme 2010-2012 pursuant to article 3 of r.l. 9/1990 (Measures for the field of immigration).

The Observatory is defined as a technical-scientific instrument aiming to monitor, analyse and diffuse data and information on migratory movements and integration at the regional and national levels. To this end, it ensures collaboration with other regional observatories interested in various aspects of the migration phenomenon; it ensures the constant operation and data input for databases, the monitoring of immigration dynamics, and in-depth inquiry into specific phenomena. It examines the living conditions and socio-scholastic integration of children as well as education and training. It ensures an updated collection of specialised laws, proposing training sessions in order to facilitate their awareness and correct implementation.

In July 2011, the Observatory published its eighth *Annual Report on Foreign Immigration in Veneto*. The report contains a systematic analysis of data and trends (in comparison to the previous year) regarding crucial issues for the Region in relation to migratory flows, such as demographic dynamics, work and unemployment, education, personal welfare services, policies to encourage foreigners to return to their native Country, and the social and work-related effects of the economic crisis on the immigrant population.

According to the reported data, 505,000 foreigners (480,000 at the end of 2009) were resident in Veneto at the end of 2010, equivalent to 11.1% of the national total (4,562,000). The foreign population amounts to 10.2% of the region's total, making Veneto the Region with the fourth largest foreign population after Emilia-Romagna, Umbria and Lombardy. In 2010, foreigners comprised 22% of all births in Veneto, while children born from a foreign mother were 27% of the total. It is estimated that about 8,500 foreigners were granted Italian citizenship in Veneto in 2010, 13% of the national figure (63,000). The ten main Countries of origin of the foreign population resident in Veneto (based on 2009 figures) are: Romania, Morocco, Albania, Republic of Moldova, China, former Yugoslav Republic of Macedonia, Serbia, Bangladesh, India and Ukraine.

PART III

ITALY IN DIALOGUE WITH INTERNATIONAL HUMAN RIGHTS INSTITUTIONS

The United Nations System

I. General Assembly

The United Nations General Assembly is the main deliberative body of the UN. It is articulated in six main Committees, each made up of all UN Member States. Human rights issues are discussed mainly within the Third Committee (Social, Humanitarian and Cultural Committee). This Committee has competence in dealing with issues such as torture and other degrading, inhuman or cruel punishment or treatment; advancement of women; rights of refugees and displaced persons; promotion and safeguarding of children's rights; rights of indigenous people; elimination of racism, racial discrimination, xenophobia and related intolerance; rights to self-determination; social development.

In December 2011, the 66th session of the General Assembly adopted 66 resolutions on human rights, previously discussed and approved by the Third Committee during the months of October and November 2011. Particularly worth noting are those related to:

– Adoption of the United Nations Declaration on Human Rights Education and Training (A/RES/66/137). The Declaration, drafted between 2008 and 2011 by the United Nations Human Rights Council and its Advisory Committee, affirms the right of everyone to know, seek and receive information about all human rights and fundamental freedoms (art. 1), and invites Member States and relevant institutions to include human rights, humanitarian law, democracy and the rule of law in the *curricula* of all institutions of learning;

– Adoption of the Optional Protocol to the Convention on the Rights of the Child to establish an individual communication procedure (A/RES/66/138). The Protocol will allow the United Nations Committee on the Rights of the Child to receive individual communications from minors, and to conduct field visits to investigate cases of serious and systematic violations of the rights of children. The GA recommends starting the process of ratification by Member States in 2012, stating that the Protocol will enter into force after having reached the number of ten ratifications;

– Promotion of the Declaration on the Right and Responsibility of Individuals, Groups and Organs of Society to Promote and Protect Universally Recognised Human Rights and Fundamental Freedoms (A/RES/66/164). The GA invites Member States to promote and fully implement the Declaration, and to ensure that human rights defenders can carry out their important role in the context of peaceful demonstrations, in accordance with the national legislation that must be consistent with the Charter of the United Nations and international human rights law. Finally, States should work to ensure that no one is subjected to excessive and indiscriminate use of force, arbitrary arrests and detentions, torture or other forms of punishment or inhuman and degrading treatment, enforced disappearances, or the threat of such actions;

– National institutions for the promotion and protection of human rights (A/RES/66/169). The resolution encourages Member States to establish or strengthen national institutions for human rights, and that they be independent, pluralistic, and effective, as stated in the Paris Principles.

The GA has also adopted four resolutions on the human rights situation in the following Countries: Democratic People's Republic of Korea, Myanmar, Iran and Syria.

In 2011, Italy's Permanent Representative at United Nations headquarters in New York is Cesare Maria Ragaglini; Luca Zelioli is responsible for monitoring the Third Committee's human rights activities. The following chart shows the most important interventions by the Italian delegation, President of the Republic and Government representatives in General Assembly meetings in 2011.

Date	Event	Statements
2 March 2011	Informal Meeting of the GA on the Security Council reform	Statement by Amb. Ragaglini
28 March 2011	65th Plenary session of the GA	Statement by the President of the Republic Napolitano
19 May 2011	Informal Meeting of the GA on international migrations and development	Statement by the Deputy Permanent Representative, Amb. Bernardini, on "The contribution of migrants to development"
10 June 2011	High-level meeting on the comprehensive review of the progress achieved in realising the Declaration of commitment on HIV/AIDS and the Political declaration on HIV/AIDS	Statement by Amb. Ragaglini
23 June 2011	Launch of the "World drug report 2011" of UNODC, United Nations Office on Drugs and Crime	Statement by Amb. Ragaglini
27 July 2011	Plenary meeting of the GA on "The revitalisation of the Conference on disarmament and taking forward multilateral disarmament negotiations"	Statement by Amb. Ragaglini
19 September 2011	Panel "Strengthening law enforcement and capacity building efforts"	Statement by the Minister of Foreign Affairs Frattini
22 September 2011	Global counterterrorism forum	Statement by the Minister of Foreign Affairs Frattini

23 September 2011	Ministerial meeting on Somalia	Statement by the Minister of Foreign Affairs Frattini
24 September 2011	66th Plenary session of the GA	Statement by the Minister of Foreign Affairs Frattini on "The role of mediation in the peaceful settlement of disputes"
13 October 2011	16th Meeting of the Third Committee of the GA	Statement by Stefano Mogini, legal advisor of the Permanent mission of Italy to the UN, introducing the draft resolution "Strengthening the United Nations crime prevention and criminal justice program, in particular its technical cooperation capacity"
8 November 2011	66th Plenary session of the GA	Statement by Amb. Ragaglini on the occasion of the introduction of the Security Council's activities annual report
28 November 2011	66th Plenary session of the GA	Statement by Amb. Ragaglini on equitable representation on and increase in the membership of the Security Council
5 December 2011	Follow-up to the International Year of Volunteers and the commemoration of its tenth anniversary	Statement by the Deputy Permanent Representative of Italy to the UN, Amb. Bernardini
7 December 2011	Fifth High-level dialogue on financing for development	Statement by Amb. Ragaglini

Source: Permanent Italian Representative's Office at the United Nations, New York.

A. Resolutions on Human Rights: Italy's Voting Behaviour

As in the past, again in 2011, Italian action in support of human rights has given precedence primarily to the following themes: promotion of the rule of law and strengthening of democracy; the fight against torture, xenophobia, racism and all forms of discrimination, with special attention on religious discrimination and intolerance; children's rights and protection; abolition of the death penalty; combating violence against women and female genital mutilation.

More in detail, Italy presented the resolution *Strengthening the United Nations Crime Prevention and Criminal Justice Programme, in particular its technical cooperation capacity*, adopted by consensus by the General Assembly (A/RES/66/177). Italy also sponsored 36 resolutions (+7 compared to 2011) and was asked to pass an open vote on 15 resolutions, the outcome of which is shown below.

Subject	Resolution	Resolution's main sponsor	Information regarding Italy	Results of the voting process in plenary session
Social development	A/RES/66/67 Tenth anniversary of the International Year of Volunteers	Brazil and Japan	Co-sponsor of the resolution	Adopted without a vote
	A/RES/66/121 Policies and programmes involving youth	Republic of Moldova	Co-sponsor of the resolution	Adopted without a vote
	A/RES/66/122 Promoting social integration through social inclusion	Peru	Co-sponsor of the resolution	Adopted without a vote
	A/RES/66/123 Cooperatives in social development	Mongolia	Co-sponsor of the resolution	Adopted without a vote
	A/RES/66/127 Follow-up to the Second World Assembly on Ageing	Argentina	Co-sponsor of the resolution	Adopted without a vote
Advancement of women	A/RES/66/129 Improvement of the situation of women in rural areas	Mongolia	Co-sponsor of the resolution	Adopted without a vote
	A/RES/66/130 Women and political participation	United States	Co-sponsor of the resolution	Adopted without a vote
	A/RES/66/131 Convention on the Elimination of All Forms of Discrimination against Women	Sweden	Co-sponsor of the resolution	Adopted without a vote
Refugees, returnees, displaced persons and humanitarian questions	A/RES/66/133 Office of the United Nations High Commissioner for Refugees	Denmark	Co-sponsor of the resolution	Adopted without a vote
	A/RES/66/135 Assistance to refugees, returnees and displaced persons in Africa	Sierra Leone	Co-sponsor of the resolution	Adopted without a vote

Report of the Human Rights Council	A/RES/66/136 Report of the Human Rights Council	Tanzania	Abstention	122 in favour, 3 against, 59 abstentions
	A/RES/66/137 United Nations Declaration on Human Rights Education and Training	Morocco	Co-sponsor of the resolution	Adopted without a vote
	A/RES/66/138 Optional Protocol to the Convention on the Rights of the Child on a Communications Procedure	Slovakia	Co-sponsor of the resolution	Adopted without a vote
Promotion and protection of the rights of children	A/RES/66/140 The girl child	Angola	Co-sponsor of the resolution	Adopted without a vote
	A/RES/66/141 Rights of the child	Poland	Co-sponsor of the resolution	Adopted without a vote
Elimination of racism, racial discrimination, xenophobia and related intolerance	A/RES/66/143 Inadmissibility of certain practices that contribute to fuelling contemporary forms of racism, racial discrimination, xenophobia and related intolerance	Russian Federation	Abstention	134 in favour, 24 against, 32 abstentions
	A/RES/66/144 Global efforts for the total elimination of racism, racial discrimination, xenophobia and related intolerance and the comprehensive implementation of and follow-up to the Durban Declaration and Programme of Action	Argentina	Abstention	138 in favour, 3 against, 46 abstentions
Right of peoples to self-determination	A/RES/66/146 The right of the Palestinian people to self-determination	Egypt	Co-sponsor of the resolution In favour	187 in favour, 7 against, 3 abstentions
	A/RES/66/147 Use of mercenaries as a means of violating human rights and	Cuba	Against	130 in favour, 53 against, 6 abstentions

	impeding the exercise of the right of peoples to self-determination			
Implementation of human rights instruments	A/RES/66/148 International Covenants on Human Rights	Sweden	Co-sponsor of the resolution	Adopted without a vote
	A/RES/66/149 World Down Syndrome Day	Brazil	Co-sponsor of the resolution	Adopted without a vote
	A/RES/66/150 Torture and other cruel, inhuman or degrading treatment or punishment	Denmark	Co-sponsor of the resolution	Adopted without a vote
	A/RES/66/229 Convention on the Rights of Persons with Disabilities and the Optional Protocol thereto	Mexico	Co-sponsor of the resolution	Adopted without a vote
Human rights questions, including alternative approaches for improving the effective enjoyment of human rights and fundamental freedoms	A/RES/66/153 Promotion of equitable geographical distribution in the membership of the human rights treaty bodies	Cuba	Against	135 in favour, 54 against, 1 abstentions
	A/RES/66/154 Human rights and cultural diversity	Cuba	Against	136 in favour, 53 against, 2 abstentions
	A/RES/66/155 The right to development	Cuba	Abstention	154 in favour, 6 against, 29 abstentions
	A/RES/66/156 Human rights and unilateral coercive measures	Cuba	Against	137 in favour, 54 against, 0 abstentions
	A/RES/66/158 The right to food	Cuba	Co-sponsor of the resolution	Adopted without a vote
	A/RES/66/159 Promotion of a democratic and equitable international order	Cuba	Against	130 in favour, 54 against, 6 abstentions
	A/RES/66/160 International Convention for the	France	Co-sponsor of the resolution	Adopted without a vote

	Protection of All Persons from Enforced Disappearance			
	A/RES/66/161 Globalization and its impact on the full enjoyment of all human rights	Egypt	Against	137 in favour, 54 against, 0 abstentions
	A/RES/66/162 Sub-regional Centre for Human Rights and Democracy in Central Africa	Burundi	Co-sponsor of the resolution	Adopted without a vote
	A/RES/66/163 Strengthening the role of the United Nations in enhancing periodic and genuine elections and the promotion of democratisation	United States	Co-sponsor of the resolution	Adopted without a vote
	A/RES/66/164 Promotion of the Declaration on the Right and Responsibility of Individuals, Groups and Organs of Society to Promote and Protect Universally Recognised Human Rights and Fundamental Freedoms	Norway	Co-sponsor of the resolution	Adopted without a vote
	A/RES/66/165 Protection of and assistance to internally displaced persons	Norway	Co-sponsor of the resolution	Adopted without a vote
	A/RES/66/166 Effective promotion of the Declaration on the Rights of Persons Belonging to National or Ethnic, Religious and Linguistic Minorities	Austria	Co-sponsor of the resolution	Adopted without a vote
	A/RES/66/168 Elimination of all forms of intolerance and of discrimination based on religion or belief	Poland	Co-sponsor of the resolution	Adopted without a vote

	A/RES/66/169 National institutions for the promotion and protection of human rights	Germany	Co-sponsor of the resolution	Adopted without a vote
	A/RES/66/170 International Day of the Girl Child	Canada	Co-sponsor of the resolution	Adopted without a vote
	A/RES/66/171 Protection of human rights and fundamental freedoms while countering terrorism	Mexico	Co-sponsor of the resolution	Adopted without a vote
	A/RES/66/173 Follow-up to the International Year of Human Rights Learning	Benin	Co-sponsor of the resolution	Adopted without a vote
Human rights situations and reports of Special Rapporteurs and Representatives	A/RES/66/174 Situation of human rights in the Democratic People's Republic of Korea	Poland	Co-sponsor of the resolution In favour	123 in favour, 16 against, 51 abstentions
	A/RES/66/230 Situation of human rights in Myanmar	Poland	Co-sponsor of the resolution In favour	83 in favour, 21 against, 39 abstentions
	A/RES/66/175 Situation of human rights in Iran	Canada	Co-sponsor of the resolution In favour	89 in favour, 30 against, 64 abstentions
	A/RES/66/176 Situation of human rights in Syria	Germany	Co-sponsor of the resolution In favour	133 in favour, 11 against, 43 abstentions
International drug control	A/RES/66/183 International cooperation against the world drug problem	Mexico	Co-sponsor of the resolution	Adopted without a vote

Source: United Nations, General Assembly

II. Human Rights Council

The Human Rights Council is the subsidiary body of the General Assembly with the mandate to promote universal respect for the protection of all human rights and fundamental freedoms for all, without distinction of any kind. Established in 2006 with resolution 60/251, the Council is an intergovernmental body composed of 47 Member States of the UN General Assembly, elected for an initial period of three years, renewable for no more than two consecutive terms. It usually meets in Geneva in three sessions per year, for a total period of at least ten working weeks. Furthermore, although it is a body of government representatives, the Council is open to the contribution of non-governmental organisations that have advisory status with the ECOSOC (United Nations Economic and Social Council), which may participate in the meetings and submit written documents.

For the monitoring of human rights, the Council has established several "mechanisms" (resolution A/HRC/RES/5/1 of June 2007), including: the Universal Periodic Review (UPR), the Special Procedures (that include mandates by Country and thematic mandates), the Advisory Committee and a Complaints Procedure.

During 2011, the Council held:

– Three ordinary sessions: 16th (28 February-25 March 25), 17th (30 May-17 June); 18th (12-30 September);

– Four Special Sessions, one devoted to the human rights situation in Libya (15th session, 25 February), and three devoted to the situation in Syria (16th, 17th and 18th session, respectively, 29 April, 22 August and 2 December 2011);

– Three sessions of the UPR: 10th (24 January-4 February), 11th (2-13 May), 12th (3-14 October).

On 20 May 2011, Italy was elected for the second time to the Human Rights Council (the first term covered the 2007-2010 period). Italy's candidacy was accompanied by a statement prepared by the Government (A/65/733) containing voluntary commitments undertaken by Italy to promote the strengthening of human rights both domestically and internationally.

Italy's international commitments, according to the letter of candidacy, primarily regard support for the work of United Nations mechanisms dealing with human rights, including the Special Procedures of the Human Rights Council and the Secretary General's Special Adviser on the Prevention of Genocide.

Other priorities include: the fight against impunity (promoting, in particular, the ratification of the Statute of the International Criminal Court); implementation of initiatives for education and training in human rights, under the Global Programme for education in human rights; combating all forms of discrimination (with a special reference to racial discrimination and those forms based on religion or belief); combating forms of violence against women, promotion of the rights of children and persons with disabilities, promotion of legality and democracy (in particular by participating in election observation missions and in *capacity-building* programmes); combating the trafficking of human beings.

At the national level, the letter of candidacy commits Italy to strengthening dialogue with civil society in formulating and implementing programmes and policies on human rights, as well as implementing, in a precise and timely way, the 78 accepted recommendations of the 92 received during the 2010 Universal Periodic Review (UPR), in areas such as the situation of migrants and asylum seekers, the treatment of the Roma and Sinti minorities, the independence of the judiciary system and the administration of justice, and the commitment to establish appropriate national institutions for human rights in conformity with the Paris Principles.

Italy provided a significant contribution to the preparation of the Declaration on Human Rights Education and Training, creating, along with France, Morocco, Costa Rica, the Philippines, Senegal, Slovenia and Switzerland (members of the Human Rights Council), the *Platform for Human Rights Education and Training*, an informal grouping of States whose precise role was to facilitate the drafting of the text of the Declaration and accelerate its adoption.

The Declaration was adopted by the General Assembly on 19 December 2011 by resolution A/RES/66/137.

Particularly significant was the speech made to the Human Rights Council by the President of the Republic, Giorgio Napolitano, during his visit to Geneva on 4 March 2011.

In 2011, Italy was represented at the Human Rights Council by Ambassador Laura Mirachian, Permanent Representative to the International Organisations in Geneva, by Counsellor Paolo Cuculi and by Chief Secretary Roberto Nocella. The following chart shows the main instances of intervention by the Italian delegation to the Human Rights Council during 2011.

Date	Event	Statements
24 January-4 February 2011	10th session of the UPR	Statements with reference to the review of the human rights situation in the following States: Nauru, Santa Lucia, Nepal, Oman, Myanmar, Georgia, Namibia, Niger, Mozambique
7 February 2011	Seminar on the fight against female genital mutilation, organised by the Inter-African Committee on traditional practices affecting the health of women and children, in collaboration with UNFPA, UNICEF and UNHCR	Intervention of Amb. Mirachian on "Building bridges between Europe and Africa: Engaging the Media"

25 February 2011	15th Special Session of the Council on the "Situation of human rights in the Libyan Arab Jamahiriya"	Statement by Amb. Mirachian
28 February 2011	16th session of the Human Rights Council	Statement by the Minister of Foreign Affairs Frattini during the High Level Segment
4 March 2011	16th session of the Human Rights Council	Statement by the President of the Republic Napolitano
8 March 2011	16th session of the Human Rights Council	Statement by First Secretary Nocella on female genital mutilations during a side event on traditional practices harmful to human rights, organised by the NGOs Defence for Children International, Franciscans International and World Vision
10 March 2011	16th session of the Human Rights Council	Statement by Counsellor Cuculi during the debate on freedom of religion or belief
11 March 2011	16th session of the Human Rights Council	Statement by Counsellor Cuculi during a side event on "Restoring the dignity of children living and/or working on the Street", organised by the NGOs Associazione Papa Giovanni XXIII and the Bureau International Catholique de l'Enfance
14 March 2011	16th session of the Human Rights Council	Statement by Amb. Mirachian on the human rights situation in Libya
15 March 2011	16th session of the Human Rights Council	Statement by Counsellor Cuculi on the issue of minority rights
29 April 2011	16th Special Session of the Council on the "Situation of human Rights in the Syrian Arab Republic"	Statement by Amb. Mirachian
2-13 May 2011	11th session of the UPR	Statements with reference to the review of the human rights situation in the following States: Denmark, Somalia, Sierra Leone, Latvia, Greece, Sudan, Hungary
31 May 2011	17th session of the Human Rights Council	Statement by Counsellor Cuculi on the issue of human rights of migrants
9 June 2011	17th session of the Human Rights Council	Statement by Amb. Mirachian on the occasion of the presentation of the report of the International Commission of Inquiry on Libya
14 June 2011	17th session of the Human Rights Council	Statement by First Secretary Nocella on the human rights situation of Roma population
14 June 2011	17th session of the Human Rights Council	Statement by Counsellor Cuculi during the debate on religious tolerance

22 August 2011	17th Special Session of the Council on the "Situation of human Rights in the Syrian Arab Republic"	Statement by Amb. Mirachian
12 September 2011	18th session of the Human Rights Council	Statement by Amb. Mirachian on the occasion of the opening of the session
13 September 2011	18th session of the Human Rights Council	Statement by First Secretary Nocella on children and armed conflicts
14 September 2011	18th session of the Human Rights Council	Statement by First Secretary Nocella on the right to development
26 September 2011	18th session of the Human Rights Council	Statement by Amb. Mirachian on the Israeli-Palestinian situation
30 September 2011	18th session of the Human Rights Council	Statement by Amb. Mirachian after the adoption of the resolution on human rights of migrants, proposed by Mexico
30 September 2011	18th session of the Human Rights Council	Statement by Amb. Mirachian on the so-called "Durban process"
10 October 2011	12th session of the UPR	Statements with reference to the review of the human rights situation in Zimbabwe
2 December 2011	18th Special Session of the Council on the "Situation of human Rights in the Syrian Arab Republic"	Statement by Amb. Mirachian

Source: Permanent Italian Representative's Office at the United Nations, Geneva

A. Italy's Voting Behaviour

During 2011, Italy participated in three regular Council sessions, including two – the 16th and 17th – as observer (without the right to vote), and one (the 18th) as a full Member State. During the 16th ordinary session of the Council (28 February-25 March), 36 resolutions were adopted: Italy co-sponsored 16, as follows.

Resolution	**State presenting the resolution**	**Outcome of the voting process**
A/HRC/RES/16/1 United Nations Declaration on Human Rights Education and Training	Morocco	Adopted without a vote
A/HRC/RES/16/2 The human right to safe drinking water and sanitation	Germany and Spain	Adopted without a vote

A/HRC/RES/16/4 Freedom of opinion and expression: mandate of the Special Rapporteur on the promotion and protection of the rights to freedom of opinion and expression	Egypt and United States of America	Adopted without a vote
A/HRC/RES/16/5 Mandate of the Special Rapporteur on the situation of human rights defenders	Norway	Adopted without a vote
A/HRC/RES/16/6 Mandate of the Independent Expert on minority issues	Austria	Adopted without a vote
A/HRC/RES/16/7 Mandate of the Special Rapporteur on violence against women, its causes and consequences	Canada	Adopted without a vote
A/HRC/RES/16/8 Situation of human rights in the Democratic People's Republic of Korea	Hungary and Japan	30 in favour, 3 against, 11 abstentions
A/HRC/RES/16/9 Situation of human rights in the Islamic Republic of Iran	Sweden and United States of America	22 in favour, 7 against, 14 abstentions
A/HRC/RES/16/11 Human rights and the environment	Costa Rica and Maldives	Adopted without a vote
A/HRC/RES/16/12 Rights of the child: a holistic approach to the protection and promotion of the rights of children working and/or living on the street	Hungary and Uruguay	Adopted without a vote
A/HRC/RES/16/13 Freedom of religion or belief	Hungary	Adopted without a vote
A/HRC/RES/16/15 The role of international cooperation in support of national efforts for the realisation of the right of persons with disabilities	Mexico and New Zealand	Adopted without a vote
A/HRC/RES/16/19 Cooperation between Tunisia and the Office of the High Commissioner for Human Rights	Hungary	Adopted without a vote
A/HRC/RES/16/23 Torture and other cruel, inhuman or degrading treatment or punishment: mandate of the Special Rapporteur	Denmark	Adopted without a vote
A/HRC/RES/16/24 Situation of human rights in Myanmar	Hungary	Adopted without a vote
A/HRC/RES/16/25 Situation of human rights in Cote d'Ivoire	Nigeria	Adopted without a vote

Source: United Nations, Human Rights Council

During the 17th ordinary session of the Council (30 May-17 June 2011), Italy co-sponsored 14 of the 25 resolutions adopted and promoted a side event on the issue of human trafficking, entitled *Deported without justice: barriers to trafficked persons accessing justice*, organised by Franciscans International and the Global Alliance Against Traffic in Women.

Resolution	State presenting the resolution	Outcome of the voting process
A/HRC/RES/17/1 Mandate of the Special Rapporteur on trafficking in persons, especially in women and children	Germany and Philippines	Adopted without a vote
A/HRC/RES/17/2 Independence of judges and lawyers	Hungary	Adopted without a vote
A/HRC/RES/17/3 The right to education: follow-up to resolution 8/4	Portugal	Adopted without a vote
A/HRC/RES/17/4 Human rights and transnational corporations and other business enterprises	Norway and Argentina	Adopted without a vote
A/HRC/RES/17/5 Mandate of the Special Rapporteur on extrajudicial, summary and arbitrary executions	Sweden	Adopted without a vote
A/HRC/RES/17/8 Proclamation of 19 August as the International Day of Remembrance of and Tribute to the Victims of Terrorism	Afghanistan	Adopted without a vote
A/HRC/RES/17/11 Accelerating efforts to eliminate all forms of violence against women	Canada	Adopted without a vote
A/HRC/RES/17/13 Extreme poverty and human rights	France	Adopted without a vote
A/HRC/RES/17/17 Situation of human rights in Libya	Jordan	Adopted without a vote
A/HRC/RES/17/19 Human rights, sexual orientation and gender identity	South Africa and Brazil	23 in favour, 19 against, 3 abstentions
A/HRC/RES/17/20 Technical assistance and cooperation on human rights for Kyrgyzstan	Kyrgyzstan and United States of America	Adopted without a vote
A/HRC/RES/17/21 Technical assistance and cooperation on human rights for Cote d'Ivoire	Nigeria	Adopted without a vote
A/HRC/RES/17/24 Situation of human rights in Belarus	Hungary	21 in favour, 5 against, 19 abstentions
A/HRC/RES/17/25 Technical assistance and cooperation on human rights for Somalia	Nigeria	Adopted without a vote

Source: United Nations, Human Rights Council

During the 18th ordinary session of the Council (12-30 September 2011), 28 resolutions were adopted: Italy co-sponsored 10, and participated to six voting procedures. They appear as follows:

Resolution	State presenting the resolution	Information regarding Italy	Outcome of the voting process
A/HRC/RES/18/1 The human right to safe drinking water	Germany and Spain	Co-sponsor of the resolution	Adopted without a vote
A/HRC/RES/18/2 Preventable maternal mortality and morbidity	Burkina Faso, Colombia and New Zealand	Co-sponsor of the resolution	Adopted without a vote
A/HRC/RES/18/3 Panel to commemorate the 20th anniversary of the adoption of the Declaration on the Rights of Persons Belonging to National or Ethnic, Religious and Linguistic Minorities	Austria	Co-sponsor of the resolution	Adopted without a vote
A/HRC/RES/18/4 The use of mercenaries as a means of violating human rights and impeding the exercise of the right of people to self-determination	Cuba	Against	31 in favour, 11 against, 4 abstentions
A/HRC/RES/18/5 Human rights and international solidarity	Cuba	Against	33 in favour, 12 against, 1 abstention
A/HRC/RES/18/6 Promotion of a democratic and equitable international order	Cuba	Against	29 in favour, 12 against, 5 abstentions
A/HRC/RES/18/7 Special Rapporteur on the promotion of truth, justice, reparations and guarantees of non-recurrence	Argentina, Morocco and Switzerland	Co-sponsor of the resolution	Adopted without a vote
A/HRC/RES/18/12 Human rights in the administration of justice, in particular juvenile justice	Austria	Co-sponsor of the resolution	Adopted without a vote
A/HRC/RES/18/13 The role of prevention in the promotion and protection of human rights	Ukraine	Co-sponsor of the resolution	Adopted without a vote
A/HRC/RES/18/18 Enhancement of technical cooperation and capacity-building in the field of human rights	Brazil, Morocco, Norway and Thailand	Co-sponsor of the resolution	Adopted without a vote

A/HRC/RES/18/19 Technical assistance and capacity-building in the Republic of Yemen in the field of human rights	Yemen	Co-sponsor of the resolution	Adopted without a vote
A/HRC/RES/18/20 Panel on the promotion and protection of human rights in a multicultural context including through combating xenophobia, discrimination and intolerance	Egypt	In favour	37 in favour, 1 against, 8 abstentions
A/HRC/RES/18/23 Promoting awareness, understanding and application of the Universal Declaration of Human Rights through Sport and the Olympic Ideal	Brazil and United Kingdom	Co-sponsor of the resolution	Adopted without a vote
A/HRC/RES/18/25 Advisory services and technical assistance for Cambodia	Japan	Co-sponsor of the resolution	Adopted without a vote
A/HRC/RES/18/26 The right to development	Egypt	In favour	45 in favour, 1 abstention
A/HRC/RES/18/27 From rhetoric to reality: global call for concrete action against racism, racial discrimination, xenophobia and related intolerance	South Africa	Abstention	35 in favour, 1 against, 10 abstentions

Source: United Nations, Human Rights Council

Italy participated as an observer in the 15th and 16th Special Sessions on the situation of human rights, respectively, in Libya and Syria; it took part in the 17th and 18th Special Sessions, both on the situation in Syria, as a Member State of the Council. In all these cases, Italy is one of the Countries that supported the request to convene such sessions.

During the 15th Special Session on Libya (25 February 2011), Italy sponsored the final resolution A/HRC/RES/S-15/1, adopted by consensus by the Council.

During the 16th Special Session on Syria (29 April 2011), Italy sponsored the final resolution A/HRC/RES/S-16/1, adopted with 26 votes in favour, 9 against and 7 abstentions (Italy did not vote as a non-Member of the Council).

During the 17th Special Session on Syria (22 August 2011), Italy sponsored the final resolution A/HRC/RES/S-17/1, adopted with 33 votes in favour, 4 against and 9 abstentions.

Finally, during the 18th Special Session on Syria (2 December 2011), Italy sponsored the final resolution A/HRC/RES/S-18/1, adopted with 37 votes in favour, 4 against and 6 abstentions.

Overall, the Human Rights Council in the three ordinary sessions of 2011 adopted 89 resolutions, 40 of which were co-sponsored by Italy (45%).

B. Universal Periodic Review

With the 12th session of the UPR, which ended on 14 October 2011, the Human Rights Council completed the first cycle of review of all 193 UN Member States, respecting the deadline that was given at the time of the inauguration of the process in 2008. Subject to review, every State was represented by delegations of government officials, and about 80% of these delegations were headed by Ministers. There was also active participation on the part of local, national and international non-governmental organisations.

Each State is required to report on the implementation of the recommendations received. The second round of the UPR (2012-2016) will primarily focus on checking the status of the implementation of these recommendations, and the development of the overall human rights situation in the Countries under review.

Italy underwent review in 2010 (7th session) and will be reviewed again in 2014, during the 20th session of the UPR. During the previous examination, Italy received 92 recommendations. It fully accepted 78, partially rejected 2 and fully rejected 12. Detailed information on the outcome of the first Universal Periodic Review of Italy is contained in the 2011 edition of the *Italian Yearbook of Human Rights* (pp. 169-173).

C. Special Procedures

During 2011, the Human Rights Council activated three new thematic Special Procedures (Independent Expert on the promotion of a democratic and equitable international order; Special Rapporteur on the promotion of truth, justice, reparation and guarantees of non-recurrence; Working group on the issue of human rights and transnational corporations and other business enterprises) and three new Country mandates (Ivory Coast, Iran and Syria). In total, therefore, 45 Special procedure (35 thematic and 10 Country mandates) were employed in the Council in 2011.

Each Special Rapporteur, within their mandate, submits an annual report to the Council containing the summary of communications sent to Governments on individual cases of alleged violations of human rights, together with the responses of the Governments and any comments by the Special Rapporteur.

During 2011, Italy was included in five reports of this nature, including four on the same themes addressed by the Special Rapporteurs in 2010 (adequate housing, human rights defenders, contemporary forms of racism, right to freedom of opinion and expression), when the reports concerning Italy numbered seven. Compared to 2010, in 2011 Italy was included in the Special Rapporteur's report on torture, but not referred to in the Special Rapporteurs' reports on, respectively, the human rights of migrants, the right to education and arbitrary executions.

Council Session	Date	Symbol	Title
16	14/02/2011	A/HRC/16/42/Add.1	Report of the Special Rapporteur on adequate housing as a component of the right to an adequate standard of living, and on the right to non-discrimination in this context, Raquel Rolnik – Addendum – Summary of communications sent and replies received from Governments and other actors
16	28/02/2011	A/HRC/16/44/Add.1	Report of the Special Rapporteur on the situation of human rights defenders, Margaret Sekaggya – Addendum – Summary of cases transmitted to Governments and replies received
16	01/03/2011	A/HRC/16/52/Add.1	Report of the Special Rapporteur on torture and other cruel, inhuman or degrading treatment or punishment, Juan E. Méndez – Addendum – Summary of information, including individual cases, transmitted to Governments and replies received
17	13/05/2011	A/HRC/17/40/Add.1	Report of the Special Rapporteur on contemporary forms of racism, racial discrimination, xenophobia and related intolerance, Githu Muigai – Addendum – Summary of cases transmitted to Governments and replies received
17	27/05/2011	A/HRC/17/27/Add.1	Report of the Special Rapporteur on the promotion and protection of the right to freedom of opinion and expression, Frank La Rue – Addendum – Summary of cases transmitted to Governments and replies received

Source: United Nations, Human Rights Council

– 14 February 2011: *Report of the Special Rapporteur on the right to adequate housing as a component of the right to an adequate standard of living, and on the right to non-discrimination in this context*, Raquel Rolnik. The report contains an urgent appeal sent on 19 March 2010 to the Italian Government by the Rapporteur on the right to adequate housing, the Independent Expert on minority issues and the Special Rapporteur on contemporary forms of racism, regarding the "nomad plan" implemented by the Municipality and the Prefecture of Rome between July 2009 and June 2010. According to information received by the Special Rapporteurs, before implementation of the plan about 7,200 Roma people lived in Rome, 2,200 of whom lived in 7 "authorised camps", 2,750 in 14 "tolerated camps", and 2,200 in 80 "non-authorised camps".

The nomad plan provides for the relocation of some 6,000 Roma to 13 camps called "villages", and provides for the dismantling of the other camps. The reports received express concern over the fate of 1,200 people for whom no room in the villages was found, especially given the fact that the official documents do not clarify the eligibility criteria for obtaining housing. The concern expressed in the report is that "evictions" can be used as a punitive measure to force these people to leave the Country. Furthermore, the nomad plan, the report says, was drafted and implemented without consulting any of the stakeholders or groups that work with people of Roma origin. The nomad plan, therefore, negatively affects the private and family life of the Roma community, in terms of access to work and essential services (since many villages are located in isolated places lacking transport services) as well as access of Roma children to education.

On 23 June 2010, the Government responded to the appeal of the Special Rapporteurs, stating that the nomad plan could not be compared to a "forced eviction" operation, that it was actually an extraordinary measure to deal with particularly degraded sanitary, social and environmental conditions, carried out in full compliance with all procedural safeguards: adequate notice, consultation at various levels and in every phase of the operation, and the provision of alternative accommodation subject to availability by the city of Rome. Moreover, the Government argues that the Roma communities themselves were aware of the deteriorating conditions in which they lived, and had expressed willingness to relocate. According to the Government, the so-called solidarity villages have facilities to ensure the safety of the persons residing there, and carry out programmes of social inclusion, through training and career guidance, and the educational integration of the children. The management of these villages requires the full involvement of representatives of the Roma community. As an alternative to the villages, there are several regional projects aimed at including Roma people in other Municipalities of Lazio, while for citizens of other EU Countries there is the possibility of joining the voluntary repatriation programme, which covers travel expenses. The Government insists that only people with serious criminal records were excluded from the relocation plan. At the time the response was submitted, there were no cases of complaint or negative reports by or on behalf of people affected by relocation, nor were any judicial investigations under way related to the implementation of the nomad plan.

The report also contains a letter sent to the Government on 26 April 2010 by the Rapporteur on the right to adequate housing, and the Special Rapporteur on contemporary forms of racism in relation to two alleged cases of "forced evictions" that took place in Milan, respectively, 21 January 2010 in Via Sant'Arialdo and 9 April 2010 in Via Siccoli, Via Guglielmo Pepe and Ponte delle Milizie, which involved a total of about 250 Roma people. In addition to the destruction of their settlements, there is a concern that 95 Romanians of Roma origin, accused of illegal occupation of public land, may be subject to collective expulsion. The Special Rapporteurs therefore invite the Government to provide explanations for such actions and to clarify whether there are ongoing appeals or complaints against the "evictions"; whether there are investigative proceedings pending and prosecution of the cases in question; whether a proper consultation process with those involved in the "evictions" was observed; what steps have been taken to prevent these people from remaining homeless; what forms of compensation were offered.

At the date of the report's submission, the Italian Government had not provided any response in this respect.

– 28 February 2011: *Report of the Special Rapporteur on the situation of human rights defenders*, Margaret Sekaggya. The report contains a letter dated 1 March 2010 to the Italian Government to seek clarification on the prison sentence, later commuted to a fine, for interruption of public services, delivered against Roberto Malini and Dario Picciau, co-presidents of EveryOne Group, a non-governmental organisation that works to promote and protect the rights of minorities in Italy, including the Roma population. The Government replied on 20 May 2010, stating that the conviction on a criminal offence was issued in full compliance with the guarantees of due process and the International Covenant on Civil and Political Rights, and that the two defendants were able to contest the conviction on 22 February 2010.

– 1 March 2011: *Report of the Special Rapporteur on torture and other cruel, inhuman or degrading treatment or punishment*, Juan E. Méndez. The report contains the letter sent 12 February 2010 to the Italian Government by the Rapporteur on torture and the Rapporteur on arbitrary executions, to request information about the progress of investigations relating to deaths in prison custody of seven men (Stefano Cucchi, Aldo Bianzino, Federico Aldrovandi, Marcello Lonzi and 3 other men held, respectively, in the prisons of Velletri, Imperia and Lecce, whose names were not reported) between 2003 and 2009. These deaths may be attributable to torture, neglect, excessive use of force or detention conditions deemed hazardous to the lives of prisoners. The Government replied on 12 May 2010, providing information on the progress of legal proceedings relating to each of the cases cited.

– 13 May 2011: *Report of the Special Rapporteur on contemporary forms of racism, racial discrimination, xenophobia and related intolerance*, Githu Muigai. The report contains the urgent appeal of 19 March 2010 and the letter of 26 April 2010 sent to the Italian Government, with the joint signature of the Rapporteur on the right to adequate housing (see above).

– 27 May 2011: *Report of the Special Rapporteur on the promotion and protection of the right to freedom of opinion and expression*, Frank La Rue. The report contains a letter sent 6 July 2010 to the Italian Government, in which the Special Rapporteur expresses concern about the compatibility of bill 1415 (Standards on the subject of telephone, data transmission and environmental interceptions), with the laws regulating the right to freedom of expression. According to the bill, in fact, anyone not accredited as a professional journalist may be sentenced to imprisonment for a period of up to four years for recording any kind of communication or conversation without the consent of the person involved, and making it public. The Special Rapporteur maintains that such a severe penalty would seriously impair the right of everyone to seek and distribute information, in violation of the International Covenant on Civil and Political Rights, which Italy ratified. The reference, in particular, is art. 19 of the Covenant, which stipulates that: "Everyone has the right to freedom of expression; this right includes freedom to seek, receive and distribute information and ideas of all kinds, regardless of the limits, whether oral, written or printed, or by any means of communication." La Rue also expressed concern about the introduction of penalties for journalists and editors who publish the content of material leaked from interceptions or wiretapping before the start of a trial, which incur imprisonment of up to thirty days and a fine of up to 10,000 euros for journalists, and as much as 450,000 euros for publishers. The Special Rapporteur emphasises that these measures, as well as being disproportionate to the offence, may hinder the work of those who work in investigative journalism on matters of public interest, such as corruption, given the excessive length of legal proceedings in Italy. The Special Rapporteur therefore recommends that the Chamber of Deputies not adopt the bill in its current form and engage in a fruitful dialogue with all parties, especially journalists and the media, to ensure that their concerns are taken into account, also declaring himself available to provide technical assistance to ensure that the bill becomes compliant with international standards on human rights and the right to freedom of expression.

The Government replied on 3 September 2010, stressing that the bill in question was still being debated by Parliament, and that several amendments had been proposed: therefore, the Government considered it premature to discuss specific aspects of the provision in its current phase, reserving the right to analyse the impact on human rights in due course. Furthermore, appealing to the Parliament not to exercise its legislative function appears to denote an attitude which does not respect parliamentary sovereignty. The Government underlined the fact that the purpose of the law is to achieve a satisfying balance between the security interests of society (in this specific case the interest of criminal investigations) and basic human rights, in particular, the right to respect for private and family life and the right to freedom of expression and information. All these principles, recognised in the Italian Constitution, have equal status on the international stage and cannot be considered separately. The measure, therefore, complies with art. 10, para. 2, of the European Convention on Human Rights, which states that the exercise of freedom of expression/information "may be subject to such formalities, conditions, restrictions or penalties as are prescribed by law and are necessary in a democratic society, [...] the protection of the reputation or rights of others, for preventing the disclosure of confidential information, or for maintaining the authority and impartiality of the judiciary."

During 2011, no Special Rapporteur made visits to Italy. The table below shows the visits made in recent years, those agreed (but not yet scheduled) and those merely requested by Special Rapporteurs.

Visits carried out and reports	**Agreed visits**	**Requested visits**
Special Rapporteur on the independence of judges and lawyers (11-14/3/2002). Report: E/CN.4/2002/72/Add.3	Special Rapporteur on contemporary forms of slavery (agreed in December 2008, dates to be confirmed)	Special Rapporteur on the right to freedom of opinion and expression (requested in September 2009)
Special Rapporteur on the human rights of migrants (7-18 June 2004). Report: E/CN.4/2005/85/Add.3	Independent expert on extreme poverty and human rights (dates to agreed)	
Special Rapporteur on the right to freedom of opinion and expression (20-29 October 2004). Report: E/CN.4/2005/64/Add.1		

Special Rapporteur on contemporary forms of racism (9-13 October 2006). Report: A/HRC/4/19/Add.4		
Working Group on arbitrary detention (12-14 November 2008). Report: A/HRC/10/21/Add.5		

Source: United Nations, Human Rights Council

III. High Commissioner for Human Rights (OHCHR)

The Office of the High Commissioner for Human Rights was created by the General Assembly in 1993 with resolution 48/141, following explicit recommendation formulated in the final Declaration of the World Conference on Human Rights held in Vienna in June 1993.

The Commissioner's task is to coordinate, strengthen and streamline the United Nations system in the field of human rights. In 2011 the High Commissioner for Human Rights is Navanethem Pillay (South Africa), elected in 2008.

In 2011, the High Commissioner did not visit Italy: the last visit was on March 2010 (see *2011 Yearbook*, p. 178). According to the data reported by the Office of the High Commissioner, updated to 30 June 2011, for the second consecutive year, Italy is not listed as one of the voluntary donors.

Voluntary contributions to OHCHR from EU Member States, 2006-2010 (US $)

	Donor	2006	2007	2008	2009	2010	Total (2006-2010)
1	Netherlands	7,986,194	7,698,918	11,646,972	12,771,703	10,279,253	50,383,040
2	Spain	7,804,014	5,846,774	10,673,854	13,900,952	6,855,401	45,080,995
3	Sweden	6,301,105	5,931,726	8,687,174	6,531,532	8,421,862	35,873,399
4	United Kingdom	6,002,052	6,988,119	7,087,518	5,145,128	5,429,354	30,652,171
5	Germany	1,522,727	1,635,946	4,367,405	7,632,262	6,378,447	21,536,787
6	Ireland	3,909,953	5,191,257	6,074,130	2,808,989	2,621,232	20,605,561
7	Denmark	3,818,592	4,734,312	4,232,505	3,593,071	2,764,261	19,142,741
8	Finland	2,226,082	2,828,585	3,441,350	4,013,917	3,779,143	16,289,077
9	France	2,168,142	2,473,746	2,836,865	2,273,913	2,774,133	12,526,799
10	Belgium	1,531,975	1,569,932	1,842,939	1,534,527	1,082,251	7,561,624
11	Italy	145,103	2,180,267	2,379,520	272,109	0	4,976,999
12	Austria	174,877	570,880	543,833	564,596	836,862	2,691,048
13	Luxembourg	181,222	155,643	371,940	216,535	201,389	1,126,729
14	Greece	144,928	170,998	178,827	249,370	131,062	875,185

15	Portugal	160,000	80,000	80,000	80,000	100,000	500,000
16	Poland	100,000	100,240	99,379	100,752	0	400,371
17	Slovenia	30,000	50,000	70,000	101,492	301,492	50,000
18	Romania	5,000	294,985	0	0	0	299,985
19	Hungary	46,312	42,602	74,405	27,855	0	191,174
20	Estonia	16,841	26,229	49,697	26,962	24,361	144,090
21	Cyprus	7,377	17,420	40,707	3,631	28,178	97,313
22	Czech Republic	13,198	17,042	22,804	20,000	20,543	93,587
23	Latvia	14,925	30,738	32,000	0	0	77,663
24	Slovakia	0	0	9,569	9,990	9,990	29,549
25	Lithuania	12,096	16,106	0	0	0	28,202
26	Bulgaria	0	5,500	11,000	0	0	16,500
27	Malta	0	0	985	0	0	985
	Total	**44,322,713**	**48,657,971**	**64,855,379**	**61,879,287**	**51,787,723**	**271,503,073**

Source: Office of the High Commissioner for Human Rights. Data as per 30 June 2011

IV. High Commissioner for Refugees (UNHCR)

The Office of the United Nations High Commissioner for Refugees was set up by the United Nations General Assembly on 14 December 1950 with resolution A/RES/428(V). The UNHCR is mandated to coordinate international action to protect refugees and to resolve refugee problems worldwide. Its main purpose is to safeguard the rights and wellbeing of refugees, ensuring that everyone can exercise the right to seek asylum and find refuge in another State, with the option to return home voluntarily, integrate locally or to resettle in a third Country. The UNHCR is also mandated to assist stateless people. In 2011, the High Commissioner for Refugees is António Guterres (Portugal), appointed in 2005.

Since 1953 UNCHR has been present in Italy with its own office in Rome. The Italian Office in particular participates in the procedure for determining refugee status in the Country, carries out activity involving international protection, training and communication concerning refugees and asylum-seekers both Italy and in various crisis areas around the globe. It is also dedicated to raising awareness in public opinion and to soliciting funds from Governments, companies and private citizens. Since 2006 the Italian Office has worked as regional Office, responsible not only for Italy but also for Cyprus, Greece, Malta, Portugal, San Marino and the Holy See; and since 2009, for Albania as well. The spokesperson for the UNHCR in Italy in 2011 was Laura Boldrini.

According to figures provided by UNHCR, as of January 2011, there were 61,327 persons of concern to the agency domiciled in Italy, 56,397 of whom were refugees, 4,076 asylum seekers and 854 stateless persons.

In 2011 in Italy 34,100 asylum applications were registered (+240% compared to 2010), by far the highest number ever recorded, which places Italy in fourth place among the 44 industrialised Countries with the most asylum applications (about 8% of total requests), behind the U.S. (17%), Germany (12%) and France (10%). Tunisia is the leading Country of origin of asylum seekers in Italy (3,500 registered applications), followed by Nigeria (2,900 applications), Ghana (1,300) and Pakistan (1,200).

Already in 2008, Italy held fifth place among the industrialised Countries for the number of asylum applications (30,300, equal to 8% of total requests). However, in 2009, following an agreement signed with Libya, that number was almost halved (17,600 requests), decreasing further in 2010, with only 10,400 applications, (about 3% of total requests), which placed Italy in 14th place among the industrialised nations. Following the so-called "Arab Spring" in the Countries of North Africa, the number of asylum applications in 2011 tripled compared to the previous year.

Ranking of the top-10 receiving Countries in 2011 (reference period 2007-2011)

Country	2007	2008	2009	2010	2011	Total	Annual change '11-'10	Share		Rank		Per 1,000 inhabitants						Per 1 USD/ GDP per capita (PPP)	
												Total		Rank		Total		Rank	
								'11	'07-'11	'11	'07-'11	'11	'07-'11	'11	'07-'11	'11	'07-'11	'11	'07-'11
USA	50,720	49,560	49,020	55,530	74,020	278,850	33%	17	15	1	1	0.2	0.9	24	24	1.6	5.9	1	2
France	29,390	35,400	42,120	48,070	51,910	206,890	8%	12	11	2	2	0.8	3.3	10	14	1.5	6.1	2	1
Germany	19,160	22,090	27,650	41,330	45,740	155,970	11%	10	8	3	3	0.6	1.9	17	18	1.3	4.4	3	3
Italy	14,050	30,320	17,600	10,050	34,120	106,140	240%	8	6	4	7	0.6	1.8	16	20	1.2	3.6	5	8
Sweden	36,370	24,350	24,190	31,820	29,650	146,380	-7%	7	8	5	5	3.2	15.6	3	3	0.8	3.9	6	6
Belgium	11,120	12,250	17,190	21,760	25,980	88,300	19%	6	5	6	8	2.4	8.2	5	8	0.7	2.4	8	10
UK	28,300	31,320	30,670	22,640	25,420	138,350	12%	6	7	7	6	0.4	2.2	19	17	0.7	4.0	7	5
Canada	28,340	36,900	33,250	23,160	25,350	147,000	9%	6	8	8	4	0.7	4.3	12	11	0.6	3.8	9	7
Switzerland	10,840	16,610	14,490	13,520	19,440	74,900	44%	4	4	9	10	2.5	9.8	4	6	0.5	1.8	10	12
Turkey	7,650	12,980	7,830	9,230	16,020	53,710	74%	4	3	10	14	0.2	0.7	25	26	1.2	4.1	4	4

Source: UNHCR – Asylum Levels and Trends in Industrialised Countries 2011

Two more statistics are needed to better understand the ability of each Country to accommodate asylum seekers: the number of asylum applications in relation to the breadth of the population and national wealth, expressed in terms of GDP per capita.

In relation to the first indicator, between 2007 and 2011, Malta and Cyprus received, on average, the highest number of asylum applications relative to their population: respectively 20.1 and 17.1 applications per 1,000 inhabitants. Italy, however, occupies 16th place, with 1.8 applications per 1,000 inhabitants. In relation to the second indicator, between 2007 and 2011, France and the United States were the Countries that, on average, received the highest number of asylum applications: respectively 6.1 and 5.9 for every dollar of GDP per capita. Italy occupies 8th place, with 3.6 applications for every dollar of GDP per capita (see table above).

In addition to ordinary protection and assistance for these people (including the registration of refugees, counselling for documentation, collection of biographical data from asylum seekers, the localisation of refugees/asylum seekers in the territory to supply protection and other lasting solutions to the needs arising from their status as refugees, as well as training for all sector operators, governmental and otherwise), in 2011, some of the activities carried out by the UNHCR were:

– 19 June 2011: visit to Lampedusa by the United Nations High Commissioner for Refugees, António Guterres and UNHCR Goodwill Ambassador, Angelina Jolie, on the eve of World Refugee Day.

– 11 July 2011: submission of recommendations by the UNHCR to the Chamber of Deputies (UNHCR Italy: press release of 11 July 2011) marking the start of the parliamentary debate on the conversion of the law-decree for transposition of the directive on common standards and procedures for returning illegally staying third-Country nationals (the so-called "Return directive"). In the context of the transposition of the Return directive, the UNHCR particularly welcomed the introduction into the Italian system of assisted voluntary repatriation which can also be accessed by illegal immigrants and people affected by refusal of entry or expulsion. Of great concern however is the extension of the maximum period of detention in Identification and Expulsion Centres (CIE) to 18 months, without provisions for strengthening the guarantees and rights of those detained, or an improvement to CIE conditions and their services. Therefore, UNHCR recommended limiting the maximum duration of the detention period and, in any case, providing better guarantees for the people detained. As required by the directive, it called for immediate release if detention is not justified in the absence of reasonable prospects for carrying out the expulsion. In addition, the Office of the High Commissioner strongly supported the introduction of an explicit reference to the principle of *non-refoulement*, invoked by the directive in several points. As regards the prohibition of re-entry into the Country, applied at the time of expulsion, the Return directive states that this should not affect the future possibility of seeking asylum. Consequently, the UNHCR considers it essential that measures be provided to ensure asylum seekers access to the Country and the related recognition procedure, especially when an individual needs international protection because of changes occurring in their personal situation or the Country of origin. Finally, UNHCR recommends that the regulatory principles and the safeguards introduced by the Return directive are complied with for any expulsion from the Country, including those within the procedures for expulsion at the border.

– 9 September 2011: Meeting in Lampedusa between the High Commissioner for Refugees and the Undersecretary of State for the Ministry of Interior, Sonia Viale (UNHCR Italy: press release dated 9 September 2011). During the meeting, the High Commissioner expressed concern about prolonged detention and reception conditions, and the growing climate of tension in the Contrada Imbriacola centre. The High Commissioner then urged the authorities to implement adequate measures to provide for the timely transfer of migrants to appropriate structures, so that the Lampedusa centre could remain a transit point dedicated to first aid and the activation of subsequent procedures. The High Commissioner particularly urged the authorities to give top priority to transferring the children in Lampedusa to reception structures in other parts of the Country to ensure their protection and appropriate support.

Italy's contributions to UNHCR, 2000-2011

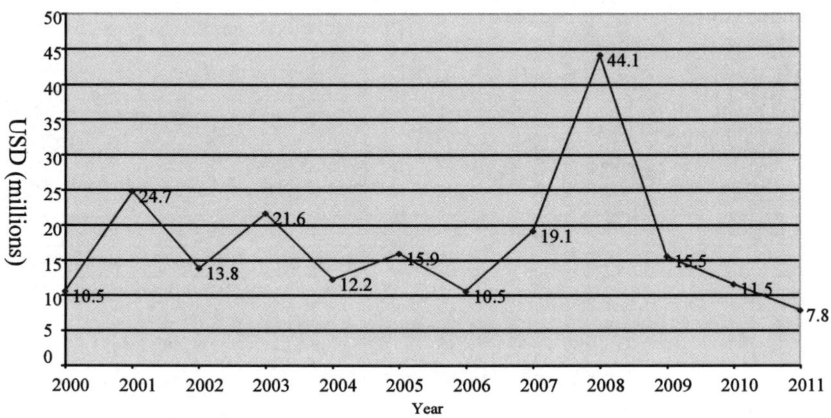

In 2011, Italy contributed to the UNHCR budget allocating about 7.8 million dollars (25th place among UNHCR donors), with a decrease of approximately 4 million dollars over the previous year (see chart above).

V. Human Rights Treaty Bodies

The core international human rights instruments adopted by the United Nations are: the Convention for the Elimination of All Forms of Racial Discrimination (ICERD, 1965); the Covenant on Civil and Political Rights (ICCPR, 1966); the Covenant on Economic, Social and Cultural Rights (ICESCR, 1966); the Convention on the Elimination of All Forms of Discrimination against Women (CEDAW, 1969); the Convention against Torture and other Cruel, Inhuman or Degrading Treatment or Punishment (CAT, 1984); the Convention on the Rights of the Child (CRC, 1989); the Convention on the Protection of the Rights of all Migrant Workers and Members of Their Families (ICRMW, 1990); the Convention on the Rights of Persons with Disabilities (CRPD, 2006); the Convention for the Protection of All Persons from Enforced Disappearance (CPED, 2006).

Italy has ratified seven conventions and their related optional protocols (see chart below) while it has signed the CPED (2007), the Optional Protocol to CAT (2003) and the Optional Protocol to ICESCR (2009). It has not yet signed the ICRMW. The situation has not changed since 2010.

Convention		Deposit date of ratification instrument	Declarations/ Reservations	Recognition of specific Committee competencies
ICERD		05/01/1976	Yes (art. 4)	Individual communications (art. 14): Yes
ICESCR		15/09/1978	No	-
ICCPR		15/09/1978	Yes (art. 15.1 and 19.3)	Inter-State communications (art. 41): Yes
	OP – 1	15/09/1978	Yes (art. 5.2)	-
	OP – 2	14/02/1995	No	-
CEDAW		10/06/1985	Yes (general)	-
	OP	22/09/2000	No	Inquiry procedure (art. 8 and 9): Yes
CAT		12/01/1989	No	Individual communications (art. 22): Yes Inter-State communications (art. 21): Yes Inquiry procedure (art. 20): Yes
CRC		05/09/1991	No	-

	OP-AC	09/05/2002	Binding declaration in accordance with art. 3: 17 years old	-
	OP-SC	09/05/2002	No	-
CRPD		15/05/2009	No	-
OP		15/05/2009	No	Inquiry procedure (art. 6 and 7): No

Legend: OP = Optional Protocol; OP-AC = Optional Protocol to the Convention on the Rights of the Child on the Involvement of Children in Armed Conflict; OP-SC = Optional Protocol to the Convention on the Rights of the Child on the Sale of Children, Child Prostitution and Child Pornography.

Each of these conventions has established a Committee of experts to monitor the implementation of the treaty provisions by its States Parties, the so-called treaty bodies. Each committee is composed from 10 to 23 independent experts, selected according to their recognised experience in human rights issues. In 2011 Alessio Bruni is member of the Committee against Torture.

First of all, the Committees examine periodical reports submitted by contracting States (usually once every 4 or 5 years) on the status of implementation of the internationally agreed rights. The Committees also publish their interpretation of the content of human rights provisions (the so-called "General comments").

Italy is subject to monitoring by seven Committees, as indicated in the following table. In 2011, Italy presented the XVI, XVII and XVIII joint report to the Committee on the Elimination of Racial Discrimination, and discussed two reports, before the Committee on the Elimination of Discrimination against Women and the Committee on the Rights of the Child respectively.

Italy's cooperation with United Nations Treaty Bodies

Committee	**Total number of reports**	**Latest report**	**Latest concluding observations**	**Reporting status**
Committee on the Elimination of Racial Discrimination	18	July 2011	-	XVI, XVII and XVIII submitted and awaiting for discussion (scheduled for March 2012)
Committee on Economic, Social and Cultural Rights	4	April 2003	November 2004	V report: overdue, since June 2009
Human Rights Committee	5	March 2004	April 2006	VI report: overdue, since October 2009

Committee on the Elimination of Discrimination against Women	6	December 2009	August 2011	VII report: to be submitted in July 2015
Committee against Torture	4	May 2004	July 2007	VI report: to be submitted in June 2011
Committee on the Rights of the Child	4	January 2009	October 2011	V and VI report: to be submitted in April 2017
OP – AC	2	January 2009	October 2011	Information about the implementation of the Protocol to be included in the V and VI combined report
OP – SC	2	January 2009	October 2011	Information about the implementation of the Protocol to be included in the V and VI combined report
Committee on the Rights of Persons with Disabilities	-	-	-	I report: overdue, since June 2011

A. Committee on Economic, Social and Cultural Rights

In 2011 the Committee held two sessions: the 46th (2-20 May) and the 47th (14 November-2 December). During the 46th session, reports on Germany, Republic of Moldova, Russian Federation, Turkey and Yemen were analysed; in the 47th, those of Argentina, Cameroon, Estonia, Israel and Turkmenistan. During the year, no General comments were adopted.

The last periodic report on Italy was discussed by the Committee in November 2004, during its 33rd session (for a discussion of the report refer to *2011 Yearbook*, pp. 182-184). Italy should have submitted its fifth report in June 2009 but as of 31 December 2011, it had not yet complied with that commitment.

B. Human Rights Committee (civil and political rights)

In 2011, the Committee held three sessions: 101st (14 March-1 April), 102nd (11-19 July) and 103rd (17 October-4 November). During the 101st session, reports on Mongolia, Serbia, Seychelles, Slovakia, and Togo were analysed, in the 102nd, the reports on Ethiopia, Kazakhstan, Bulgaria and Dominica, and in the 103rd, reports on Jamaica, Kuwait, Norway, Iran and Malawi.

Moreover, during the 102nd session, the Committee adopted General comment No. 34 relative to art. 19 of the International Covenant on Civil and Political Rights (Freedom of opinion and expression).

The last periodic report on Italy was discussed by the Committee in October 2005, during its 85th session (for a discussion of the report refer to *2011 Yearbook*, pp. 184-186). Italy should have submitted its sixth report in October 2009, but as of 31 December 2011, it had not yet complied with that commitment.

C. Committee against Torture

In 2011, the Committee held two sessions: 46th (9 May-31 June) and 47th (31 October-25 November). During the 46th session, reports on Finland, Ghana, Ireland, Kuwait, Mauritius, Monaco, Slovenia and Turkmenistan were analysed, in the 47th, those of Belarus, Bulgaria, Djibouti, Germany, Greece, Madagascar, Morocco, Paraguay and Sri Lanka. During the year, no General comments were adopted.

The last periodic report on Italy was discussed by the Committee in May 2007, during its 38th session (for a discussion of the report refer to *2011 Yearbook*, pp. 187-188). Italy should have submitted its sixth report in July 2011, but as of 31 December, it had not yet complied with that commitment.

D. Committee on the Elimination of Racial Discrimination

In 2011, the Committee held two sessions: the 78th (14 February-11 March) and 79th (8 August-2 September). During the 78th session, reports on Armenia, Bolivia, Cuba, Ireland, Lithuania, Republic of Moldova, Norway, Rwanda, Serbia, Spain, Uruguay and Yemen were analysed, in the 79th, those of Albania, Czech Republic, Georgia, Kenya, Maldives, Malta, Paraguay, Ukraine and the United Kingdom. During the year, General recommendation No. 34 on racial discrimination against people of African descent was also adopted.

Italy submitted (but has not yet discussed) its latest report in July 2011.

Latest report presented by Italy

Reporting round	XVI, XVII and XVIII periodic report (combined)
Scheduled date for the submission of the report	18/02/2011
Actual date of submission of the report	05/07/2011
Report	CERD/C/ITA/16-18

In the report, Italy sets out the main legislative, administrative and legal principles put in place between 2006 and 2010 to give effect to the Convention on the Elimination of Racial Discrimination.

– In *Italian law*, the principle of non-discrimination is enshrined in art. 3 of the Constitution. Italy has implemented two recent European directives in this regard: directive 2000/43/EC on equal treatment between persons irrespective of racial or ethnic origin (with lgs.d. of 9 July 2003, No. 215, with which, among other things, the UNAR – National Office against Racial Discrimination – at the Department for Equal Opportunities of the Presidency of the Council of Ministers was established) and directive 2000/78/EC on equal treatment in employment and working conditions (with lgs.d. 9 July 2003, No. 216). In 2006, it adopted a National action plan against racism, while in 2010 it established a working group made up of representatives of central and local government and other significant actors, with the support of the Presidency of the Council of Ministers – UNAR and the Ministry of Foreign Affairs – CIDU (Inter-Ministerial Committee for Human Rights), with a mandate to prepare a new National action plan against all forms of racial discrimination.

– At the *institutional level*, Italy continues to be engaged in the process of establishing the Independent National Commission for the Promotion and Protection of Human Rights and Fundamental Freedoms, in line with the Paris Principles. To this end, an inter-ministerial working group is preparing a draft resolution which will be sent to Parliament as soon as the necessary funding is available. UNAR is also undergoing a reorganisation phase that provides for, among other things, the establishment of a technical committee for making recommendations and giving opinions on inspection activity, and a *contact centre* to which other national institutions can refer, including the Office of the National Equality Advisor, the National Network of Equality Advisors (regional and provincial), and the Observatory for Protection against Discriminatory Acts, established within the Department of Public Safety of the Ministry of the Interior. Again in this area, between 2009 and 2010, the UNAR has begun an extensive programme of measures that includes guidelines, training courses and strategic proposals aimed at promoting effective coordination between the regional anti-discrimination observatories. The objective is to strengthen the monitoring and legal assistance in these regional centres and to establish a "network of regional anti-discrimination antennas" capable of covering at least 50% of the Country by 2012. To this end, a series of *memoranda of understanding* have already been signed between the UNAR and different Regions (including Emilia-Romagna, Liguria, Piedmont, Sicily and Apulia), some Provinces (Pistoia and Messina) and Municipalities (including Rome).

– *Incitement to hatred and racial discrimination.* Italian law sets out specific rules against racist and xenophobic acts: particularly worth noting is the law of 13 October 1975, No. 654, ratifying and implementing the International Convention on the Elimination of All Forms of Racial Discrimination, as amended by the law of 25 June 1993, No. 205 (known as the "Mancino law") and the law of 24 February 2006, No. 85. These laws punish the formation of organisations, associations, movements or groups whose purpose is incitement to discrimination or violence for racial, ethnic, national or religious motives, and they make specific provisions for aggravating circumstances for all crimes committed with the aim of discrimination or racial hatred. Regarding recourse to racist and xenophobic language in political discourse, which may be contained in written documents, public speeches or political programmes, it is up to the relevant judiciary to ascertain any malice and consequent responsibility. In this regard, two judgements were issued in 2009 in relation to incidents of intolerance attributable to two well-known Italian politicians. The Venice Court, by judgement of 26 October 2009, considered the deputy Mayor of Treviso, Giancarlo Gentilini, guilty of inciting racial hatred and sentenced him to a fine of 4,000 euros and prohibited him from participating in public meetings for a period of three years, on account of the insulting words and tones used towards immigrants during a Lega Nord party rally held in Venice in 2008. Gentilini's lawyer announced his intention to appeal. In July 2009, the Supreme Court definitively confirmed the sentence of two months' imprisonment against Flavio Tosi, the Mayor of Verona, for the dissemination of racist ideas (the actions date back to 2001 when Tosi, as a Regional Councillor, organised a petition for the removal of a "nomad camp" in the city of Verona and was sued by seven citizens of Sinti origin and by the national organisation *Opera Nomadi*).

– *Right to personal security.* Education in human rights is a central element in the training of Italian law enforcement agencies to prevent incidents of abuse or excessive use of force. In particular, the Ministry of the Interior has included human rights law in the training *curricula* of police staff at all levels. Furthermore, the investigation of possible personal liability is guaranteed by appropriate disciplinary measures that, by law, always follow criminal proceedings. Despite some delays, the effectiveness of these mechanisms is confirmed by the recent guilty verdicts against police officers involved in the events surrounding the G8 in Genoa and the Global Forum in Naples (2001)

– *Political rights.* According to the constitutional framework, in Italy two different systems of political representation for foreigners have been introduced at the local level: advisory organisations for foreigners and the Adjunct Council Member. The former are collegiate bodies composed of a number of foreigners directly elected by the foreign residents; they have advisory powers, and the President may be invited to attend sessions of Council meetings. The adjunct councillors are also directly elected and, unlike the advisory bodies, have the right to participate in all sessions of the council meetings but without voting rights.

– The *right to nationality*. The main requirement for obtaining Italian citizenship is continuous residence in Italy for at least ten years. It is also important to remember that foreigners born in Italy may acquire Italian citizenship on reaching the age of eighteen, provided they have maintained a residence in Italy on an ongoing basis. The report speculates that because immigration is relatively recent in Italy, most of the second generation of immigrants are still minors.

– *Right to freedom of thought, conscience and religion*. The practice of public and private worship is fully guaranteed by art. 19 of the Constitution and includes two aspects: the opening of places of worship (churches, mosques, synagogues, etc.) and the simultaneous exercise of the right to freedom of assembly, guaranteed by art. 17 of the Constitution. According to Italian law, places of worship are subject to ordinary legislation, to the exclusion of provisions arising from bilateral agreements (so-called "*intese*"). At the institutional level, the Observatory on religious policy in the Ministry of the Interior is responsible for studying and evaluating the religious phenomenon in all its components. Furthermore, specialised training courses and workshops are regularly organised by the Ministry of Education, Universities and Research to prepare the various actors to face the challenges posed by a complex multicultural social environment and the growing presence of foreign students.

– *Right to freedom of opinion and expression*. Art. 21 of the Constitution guarantees this right. With particular regard to radio and television, the relevant legislation, dating back to 2004, states that the system must be guided by the principles of pluralism, impartiality and freedom of opinion and expression. To ensure compliance with these principles, an *ad hoc* parliamentary commission was established. In addition, a specific independent regulatory Authority has the task of monitoring compliance with the rules and regulations which enshrine the right to non-discrimination in the media, and can impose penalties for violations of these regulations.

– *Right to work*. The Italian legal system provides for the possibility of using civil and administrative measures in order to legitimise access to employment or to ensure the protection of foreign workers from discriminatory practices. In terms of positive actions, UNAR has decided to implement a strategy that is capable of going beyond the provision of legal assistance to victims of discrimination and to have an impact on the structural causes of discrimination. To this end, UNAR has created a number of opportunities for businesses to help two categories of disadvantaged people who often suffer discrimination in the workplace: people with disabilities and foreigners.

– The *right to housing*. Although Italian law guarantees equal access to basic goods and services (see, in particular, art. 43, para. 2, letter c of lgs.d. 25 July 1998, No. 286 (Consolidated immigration act), often there are cases of discrimination in respect to housing rights, especially regarding property rental, loan applications and applications for public housing units. To combat such practices, in June 2010 the Ministry of Labour and Social Policies and the Ministry of Education, University and Research adopted the *Integration Plan: Security, Identity and Engagement*, which offers some solutions to facilitate access to housing by immigrants living and working in Italy.

– *Refugees and asylum seekers*. Over the years, specific reception centres (CARA) were created with a capacity of 2,083 beds. These centres are home to people without documents, those who violate the procedures of entry and residence in Italy (whose identification may not take longer than 20 days) and asylum seekers. In the case of the latter, generally, the decision on granting asylum is made within 35 days. At the end of that period, if no decision has yet been made, the asylum seekers are issued with a temporary renewable residency permit, so they can leave the centre during the day. In order to expedite the process, the ten regional committees for the recognition of refugee status (Gorizia, Milan, Rome, Foggia, Siracusa, Crotone, Trapani, Turin, Bari and Caserta) have recently added some additional sections both within the original committees (Milan, Bari and Trapani) and the more distant regional headquarters (Verona from Gorizia, Florence from Rome). Transparency is ensured by the presence of UNHCR representatives in each of these committees. If still no decision has been made within six months, the applicant is issued a residence permit that allows him/her to seek work. To this end, the Protection System for Asylum Seekers and Refugees (SPRAR), which consists of networks of local institutions and the private sector, operating in most Regions, provides around 6,000 jobs a year to facilitate the integration of asylum seekers and refugees.

– *Foreign nationals*. In terms of reception, the initial phase includes health services, cultural mediation, legal assistance, identification, processing of applications and, possibly, repatriation, but only for those who are not entitled to remain in Italy. To this end, reception centres (CDA) can accommodate up to 3,400 people. Then there are the Initial Assistance and Reception Centres (CPSA), with a capacity of 1,200 people, and located in the places most affected by arrivals by sea (such as, for example, the island of Lampedusa). Finally there are 13 Identification and Expulsion Centres (CIE) across the Country, which can accommodate 1,806 people. The Government also claims to be interested in combating illegal immigration, because of its potential connections with organised crime and the negative effects it produces on the whole society, including on immigrants who arrive legally in Italy. To this end, payment of a minimum tax was introduced as well as an Italian language test for the issuance or renewal of residence permits. Regarding the extension of the stay in CIE for up to 18 months, this measure, in line with the European directive on repatriation, was adopted to enable the identification of immigrants without documents. It is important to emphasise that it is the judicial authority, and not the administration, that periodically evaluates (every 30/60 days) the necessity and legitimacy of the extension of stay in the Identification and Expulsion Centres. Finally, the Government declared that the so-called "security package" did not introduce any restriction on the right to education and health care, because it does not require medical staff or head teacher to report irregular migrants.

– *The rights of minorities.* Law 482/1999 recognises the rights of linguistic minorities that have a historical link with a specific territory: for this reason, the Roma, Sinti and Travellers communities are not included as protected minorities. However, the inclusion of these populations has been promoted at various levels, both through institutional mechanisms (see, for example, the regular meetings organised by the Ministry of the Interior or UNAR between representatives of the Roma and Sinti communities, organisations dealing with the rights of these communities and representatives of ANCI, National Association of Italian Municipalities and UPI, Union of Italian Provinces), both fostering access to financial resources for the implementation of affirmative action and through information and awareness-raising campaigns. An important step toward recognising the needs of the Roma community came with art. 1, para. 1267 of law 27 December 2006, No. 269 (Budget Act 2007), establishing the Fund for social inclusion of migrants in the Ministry for Social Solidarity. Among the priorities of the Fund are measures to promote access to housing for members of the Roma, Sinti and Travellers communities.

E. Committee on the Elimination of Discrimination against Women

In 2011, the Committee held three sessions: the 48th (17 January-4 February), 49th (11-29 July) and 50th (3-21 October). During the 48th session, reports on Bangladesh, Belarus, Israel, Kenya, Liechtenstein, Sri Lanka and South Africa were analysed. In the 49th session, reports on Costa Rica, Djibouti, Ethiopia, Italy, Nepal, Republic of Korea, Singapore and Zambia were analysed; and in the 50th, Chad,

Ivory Coast, Kuwait, Lesotho, Mauritius, Montenegro, Oman and Paraguay. During the year, no General recommendations were adopted.

Latest report presented by Italy

Reporting round	VI periodic report
Scheduled date for the submission of the report	10/07/2006
Actual date of submission of the report	16/12/2009
Report	CEDAW/C/ITA/6
List of issues	CEDAW/C/ITA/Q/6
Reply of the Government to list of issues	CEDAW/C/ITA/Q/6/Add.1
Summary of the discussion	CEDAW/C/SR. 982 e 983
Concluding observations	CEDAW/C/ITA/CO/6
Date of discussion of the report	14 July 2011, during the 49th session of the Committee (11-29 July 2011)

The Committee examined the sixth periodic report from Italy (discussed in *2011 Yearbook*, pp. 190-193) during the 49th session (11-29 July 2011), after which the following concluding observations and recommendations were adopted.

Regarding positive aspects, the Committee welcomes the adoption of numerous legislative bills, programmes and plans of action to combat discrimination and violence against women, including: law 7/2006 on the prevention and prohibition of the practice of female genital mutilation; law 11/2009 which introduced the offence of stalking and mandatory detention for those responsible for acts of sexual violence; lgs.d. 198/2006 and 5/2010 which, respectively, adopt and amend the code of equal opportunities between men and women; law 120/2011 which introduces a number of principles concerning gender equality in relation to access to the administration and control of companies listed on regulated markets; the Action plan on women, peace and security, adopted in December 2010; the National action plan to combat violence against women and stalking, adopted in October 2010. The Committee also notes with satisfaction the ratification by Italy of the Protocol to Prevent, Suppress and Punish Trafficking in Persons, especially Women and Children, supplementing the UN Convention against Transnational Organized Crime (in 2006); the Convention on the Rights of Persons with Disabilities (in 2009), the Council of Europe Convention on Action against Trafficking in Human Beings (in 2010).

The Committee nevertheless expresses *concerns* and made its own *recommendations* in the following areas:

– *Temporary special measures.* The Committee is concerned that the interpretation of the concept of temporary special measures contained in the Government report appears to be inconsistent with the interpretation that the Committee gave it in its General recommendation No. 25 of 2004, and that such measures are not routinely taken as part of a necessary strategy to accelerate *de facto* equality between men and women. The Committee therefore urges Italy: to ensure that all officials have adequate knowledge of the concept of temporary special measures under art. 4 (1) of the Convention on the Elimination of All Forms of Discrimination against Women[1] and the Committee's interpretation; to consider the fact that definitive and long-term measures, by themselves, may not be sufficient for promoting the right of women to non-discrimination, and that the temporary special measures are appropriate tools for achieving gender equality, especially in the workplace; to apply temporary special measures in areas where women are under-represented, such as in legislative, executive, administrative and political bodies, or for disadvantaged women, such as rural, migrant, elderly, Roma and Sinti women and women with disabilities.

– *Stereotypes and harmful practices.* The Committee recommends that Italy develop comprehensive and coordinated policies targeted at men, women, boys and girls, in order to combat the spread of the image of women as sex objects, as well as stereotypes regarding the role of women in society and in the family, pursuant to art. 2 letter f of the Convention. Such policies should include legal and administrative measures, as well as education and information campaigns directed at public officials, civil society and the entire population. Special attention should be paid to the existence of gender stereotypes in the media and advertising. On this issue, Italy is invited to provide the Committee with written information about implementing these recommendations, within two years.

– *Violence against women.* In addition to adopting general measures to address the problem of violence against women in family and society, with particular reference to the most vulnerable situations (migrant women, the elderly, women belonging to the Roma and Sinti communities, women with disabilities), Italy should ensure that women who are victims of violence have immediate protection, including measures such as the removal from the family of the party responsible for the violence, the hosting of victims in well-protected and well-funded shelters, free and fast access to forms of legal, medical and psychological support, and adequate compensation.

---

1 Art 4(1): "The adoption, by the Member States, of temporary special measures aimed at accelerating the process of de facto equality between men and women is not considered discrimination, according to the definition in this Convention, but must absolutely not lead to the persistence of unequal or separate regulations. Such measures shall be discontinued when the objectives of equal opportunity and treatment have been achieved."

Public officials, particularly members of the police, judiciary, health, welfare and educational systems, should receive appropriate training in these areas. Furthermore, a broad awareness campaign should be developed through the media and national education programmes in order to make violence against women a socially unacceptable phenomenon. Finally, Italy should ratify without delay the Council of Europe Convention on Preventing and Combating Violence against Women and Domestic Violence. On this issue, Italy is invited to provide the Committee, within two years, with written information about implementing these recommendations.

– *Trafficking and exploitation of prostitution.* The Committee expresses concern regarding the application of art. 18 of lgs.d. 286/1998 granting a special residence permit for providing victims of trafficking and exploitation with social protection. According to the Committee, however, if it is strictly interpreted, art. 18 might deny adequate protection to women who are victims of trafficking in another Country and subsequently brought to Italy for the purpose of exploitation.

Moreover, the "security package" adopted by the Government in 2010, seriously limits the ability of law enforcement officials to identify potential victims of trafficking and exploitation. The Committee therefore calls on Italy to expedite the adoption of the National action plan against trafficking; to ensure that a strict interpretation of art. 18 of lgs.d. 286/1998 does not involve the lack of an adequate level of protection for women who are victims of trafficking in other Countries; to conduct an assessment of the impact of the measures (under discussion) that criminalise prostitution in public places, in order to highlight potential risks in terms of exploitation of women who leave the street prostitution circuits to enter indoor prostitution that, as recognised by the Government, remains hidden and unknown; to continue to formulate strategies and programmes to prevent the entry of women into prostitution circuits and to provide support and rehabilitation to women who wish to leave prostitution.

– *Participation in public life and politics.* Italy is urged to intensify its efforts, including adopting temporary special measures in order to strengthen the representation of women in the highest decision-making roles of political bodies, including Parliament and regional councils, public administration, the diplomatic service, and the private sector.

– *Education.* The Committee, concerned over the high school drop-out rate of girls from the Roma and Sinti communities, urges the Government to take appropriate action in this matter, particularly under the Decade of Roma Inclusion 2005-2015.

– *Right to work.* The labour market in Italy continues to be characterised by a high rate of female unemployment, despite the high level of education of women. The Committee draws the Government's attention to the problems faced by women who interrupt their careers for family reasons, the concentration of women in low paid sectors of employment, and the gap between salaries of men and women for equal work. The Committee, therefore, taking note of the Government's intention to adopt a national reform plan that includes, by 2020, a 12% increase in the female employment rate and the introduction of incentives to stabilise employment, invites Italy to take concrete action to address this situation and to ensure the reconciliation of private and family life and professional responsibilities. The Government is also urged to take prompt action to abolish the practice of "blank resignations" and to address the complex problems of discrimination which may particularly affect migrant women and women with disabilities.

– *Health.* While acknowledging the achievements of the 2010-2012 National action plan on prevention and organisation of screening programmes to prevent breast cancer, the Committee is concerned that this disease still represents the most common cause of cancer deaths among women in Italy, and that over 60% of women living in the southern part of the Country have no access to mammograms. The Committee therefore urges Italy to ensure equal access to screening services throughout the Italian territory, including Regions in the south.

– *Vulnerable groups of women.* Italy is urged to intensify efforts to eliminate discrimination against Roma and Sinti women, female immigrants, female asylum seekers and older women, in relation to access to education, health and employment, and to combat all forms of violence against these women, both within the community and society in general, also promoting their awareness of the availability of adequate social services and legal solutions. The Government should also sponsor information and awareness campaigns involving the heads of health services, religious leaders and heads of women's organisations. Finally, the Government should fully and immediately implement the law prohibiting female genital mutilation and to prosecute those responsible for these practices.

– *Ratification of other treaties.* The Committee urges Italy to consider ratifying the Convention on the Protection of the Rights of All Migrant Workers and Members of Their Families and the Convention for the Protection of All Persons from Enforced Disappearance.

F. Committee on the Rights of the Child

In 2011 the Committee held three sessions: the 56th (17 January-4 February), 57th (30 May-17 June) and 58th (19 September-7 October). During the 56th session, reports on Denmark, Afghanistan, Belarus, Democratic People's Republic of Laos, New Zealand, Ukraine and Singapore were analysed; in the 57th session, reports on Bahrain, Cambodia, Costa Rica, Cuba, Czech Republic, Egypt and Finland were analysed; in the 58th session, reports on Iceland, Italy, Panama, Republic of Korea, Seychelles and Syria were analysed. During the year General comment No. 13 on the child's right to freedom from all forms of violence was adopted.

Latest report presented by Italy

Reporting round	III and IV periodic report (combined)
Scheduled date for the submission of the report	04/10/2008
Actual date of the submission of the report	30/01/2009
Report	CRC/C/ITA/3-4
List of issues	CRC/C/ITA/Q/3-4
Reply of the Government to list of issues	CRC/C/ITA/Q/3-4/Add.1
Summary of the discussion	CRC/C/SR.1642 and 1643
Concluding observations	CRC/C/ITA/CO/3-4
Date of discussion of the report	20 September 2011, during the 58th session of the Committee (19 September-7 October 2011)

The Committee examined the third and fourth periodic reports on Italy (presented in *2011 Yearbook*, pp. 193-199) during its 58th session (19 September to 7 October 2011), after which the following concluding observations and recommendations were made.

Regarding positive aspects, the Committee welcomes the adoption of numerous legislative bills, programmes and action plans to promote and protect the rights of children and adolescents, including: law 62/2011 on the protection of the relations between detained mothers and children who are minors; law 112/2011 on the establishment of the National Ombudsperson for Children and Adolescents; law 38/2006 on combating the sexual exploitation of children and child pornography, including through the internet; law 54/2006 on separation of parents and joint custody of their children; law 296/2006, which makes education compulsory for at least 10 years and raises the limit of the working age from 15 to 16 years of age; law 7/2006 on the prevention and prohibition of female genital mutilation; National plan of action and intervention for the protection of rights and the development of subjects of a developmental age 2010-2011; Special Plan of action for the development of the national system of social and educational services for early childhood (2007-2009), National action plan against poverty and social exclusion (2006-2008); establishment of the Coordinating Committee for Government activities against trafficking in human beings (2007), the Inter-Ministerial Commission for the support of victims of trafficking, violence and serious exploitation (2007) and the Observatory on trafficking in human beings (2007).

The Committee also notes with satisfaction the ratification by Italy of the Council of Europe Convention on Combating Trafficking in Human Beings (in 2010); the Convention on the Rights of Persons with Disabilities and its Optional Protocol (in 2009); the Protocol to Prevent, Suppress and Punish Trafficking in Persons, especially Women and Children, supplementing the United Nations Convention against Transnational Organized Crime (in 2006); the Council of Europe Convention for the Protection of Children against Exploitation and Sexual Abuse (in 2007).

The Committee however expresses *concerns* and makes its *recommendations* in the following areas:

– *Coordination.* The Committee urges Italy to reconsider and clarify the role of the National Observatory on Children and Adolescents with regard to the coordination of various institutions involved in the implementation of policies and programmes related to the promotion of children's rights, and to equip the Observatory with the human and financial resources required for that purpose. In addition, the Government should ensure the consistent application of the Convention throughout the Country, by adopting, for this purpose, national standards such as the basic levels of social benefits.

– *National plan of action.* The Committee is concerned that the National plan of action and intervention for the protection of rights and development of subjects of developmental age (children and adolescents) 2010-2011 has not yet been implemented, that the necessary funds have not yet been allocated and there is no provision for a specific monitoring system. Therefore, Italy is invited to allocate the necessary funds without further delay and modify the Plan of action to include an appropriate monitoring mechanism.

– *Independent monitoring.* The Committee, under General comment No. 2 of 2002, recommends that Italy make the new office of the National Ombudsperson for Children and Adolescents operational as soon as possible and provide it with the human, technical and financial resources to fulfil its mandate in an independent and effective way. It also calls on Italy to expedite the process of establishing independent national institutions on human rights, in line with the Paris Principles.

– *Non-discrimination.* The Committee, deeply concerned about certain policies, laws and practices that discriminate against children who are in disadvantaged situations, recommended that Italy take all necessary measures to effectively eliminate all forms of discrimination against Roma and Sinti children, particularly in education and in access to essential services; establish an effective National action plan on the prevention of racism, racial discrimination, xenophobia and related intolerance; strengthen the mandate of UNAR (Office for the Promotion of Equal Treatment and the Fight against Racial Discrimination); incorporate the aggravating circumstance of the motivations of hatred into art. 61 of the criminal code, and adopt appropriate legislative measures to eliminate any residual discrimination between children born within and those born out of wedlock; speed up the ratification of the Convention of the Council of Europe on the Legal Status of Children Born out of Wedlock.

– *Respect the opinion of children.* In this context, Italy should adopt a general legislative measure that upholds the right of children to be heard in courts, administrative bodies, institutions, school and family in all matters that affect them, and for this purpose establish appropriate mechanisms and procedures to ensure that child participation is effective. Italy, moreover, should, as soon as possible, adopt guidelines for the appointment of special curators for children in adoption cases.

– *Registration and nationality.* The Committee expresses concern about the legal restrictions and practices in relation to the right of children of foreign origin to be registered, with particular reference to law 94/2009 on public safety, that makes it mandatory for non-Italian citizens to show their residence permits to obtain civil records. Therefore, the Committee invites Italy to enshrine in law the obligation to register births for all children who are born and live in Italy, and facilitate its implementation; launch awareness campaigns on the right of children to be registered at birth regardless of ethnic or social origin and the residential status of parents; facilitate access to citizenship for those children who would otherwise be stateless.

– *Access to appropriate information.* The Committee recommends that Italy promote the development of a code on media and children that fully incorporates the provision of art. 17 of the Convention on the Rights of the Child, including the disclosure of information and material of social and cultural benefit to the child, and re-establish the Committee to monitor the code on internet and minors, whose mandate expired in 2007 and has not been renewed.

– *Corporal punishment.* In line with the General comments 8/2006, on the child's right to protection from corporal punishment, and 13/2011, on the child's right to freedom from all forms of violence, Italy should reform the national legislation in order to make explicit the prohibition of all forms of corporal punishment in all spheres, beginning with the family.

– *Children deprived of the family environment.* The Committee welcomes the progress made towards de-institutionalisation of care for children deprived of family environment, pursuant to law 149/2001, and urges the Government to effectively and fairly apply the laws throughout the national territory. Moreover, Italy is expected to adopt minimum standards and criteria agreed upon at the national level in relation to the institutions for alternative care for children deprived of the family environment, including residential structures, such as community family or group homes, and ensure independent monitoring of these institutions and identify criteria for receiving public funds in order to accommodate these children; ensure appropriate selection, training and supervision of adoptive families, as well as adequate financial support.

– *Adoption.* The Committee invites Italy to introduce the principle of the best interest of the child as a primary consideration in all legislation concerning adoption, including laws 184/1983 and 149/2001; to conclude bilateral agreements with all Countries of origin that have not yet ratified the 1993 Hague Convention on Protection of Children and Cooperation in Respect of Intercountry Adoption; ensure effective and systematic monitoring of private adoption agencies, pursuant to art. 21 letter d of the Hague Convention, also in limiting the number of adoptions, and ensuring that the adoption processes do not result in economic benefits to either party.

– *Children with disabilities.* Italy is called upon to reconsider existing policies in order to adopt a human rights-based approach in relation to children with disabilities, and develop training initiatives aimed at Government officials and any other relevant actor in relation to this approach. The Government should also ensure a sufficient number of specialised support teachers in all schools, so that all children with disabilities have access to the highest educational standards.

– *The right to education.* The Government should refrain from further cuts to the education sector and ensure that schools are equipped with adequate human, technical and financial resources to provide quality education to all children. In addition, the Government should deal effectively with violence and bullying in schools through social and educational measures, such as the establishment of student councils and other forums for dialogue, information and awareness campaigns on the status of students, rather than simply employing punitive and disciplinary measures; implement the lgs.d. of 9 April 2008, No. 81 concerning the protection of health and safety in the workplace, with reference to schools; develop programmes to improve the integration of foreign students.

– *Migrant children, asylum seekers and refugees.* The Committee recommends that Italy ensure that every child who tries to enter the Country and comes to be under its jurisdiction, both on the high seas or within the national territory, is entitled to an individual assessment of their case and immediate access to asylum procedures and other forms of national and international protection. Italy should also amend its legislation to prohibit the expulsion of minors, even on grounds of public order or national security risks, wherever there is valid reason to believe that there is a real risk of irreparable damage to the child. The Committee, finally, reminds Italy that the rights enshrined in the Convention on the Rights of the Child should not be considered limited to children who are nationals of a State Party, but should extend to all children regardless of their migrant status; therefore, it invites Italy to amend the law on immigration in order to secure for migrant children equal rights to education, health and other social services.

– *Children belonging to minorities.* Italy should put an end to the state of emergency in relation to nomad community settlements and related ordinances adopted in 2008. The Committee also recommends adopting, with the participation of all communities involved, a National action plan to promote a real integration of the Roma and Sinti communities into Italian society, and adopt measures to address harmful practices such as, for example, early marriage; ratify the European Charter for Regional or Minority Languages.

– *Children in armed conflicts.* The Committee calls on Italy to amend the criminal code in order to expressly prohibit and criminalise the recruitment and employment of persons under 18 years during armed conflict by armed forces or armed groups; adopt legislation that prohibits and criminalises the sale of light weapons and small arms to Countries where children are employed in the armed forces; include the recruitment and use of children in armed conflict as a cause for obtaining refugee status.

– *Sexual exploitation.* Italy is called upon to fully harmonise its legislation with the Optional Protocol to the Convention on the Rights of the Child relating to Child Trafficking, Child Prostitution and Child Pornography, in particular by introducing the definition of child pornography into the criminal code, and develop and implement appropriate strategies for prevention and protection of victims of sexual abuse and exploitation.

– *Ratification of other treaties.* The Committee urges Italy to consider ratifying the Convention on the Protection of the Rights of All Migrant Workers and Members of Their Families and the Convention for the Protection of All Persons from Enforced Disappearance, the Optional Protocol to the International Covenant on Economic, Social and Cultural Rights, the Optional Protocol to the Convention against Torture and the Convention on the Reduction of Statelessness of 1961.

G. Committee on the Rights of Persons with Disabilities

In 2011, the Committee held two sessions, the 5th (11-15 April) and 6th (19-23 September), during which concluding observations were made regarding Tunisia (5th session) and Spain (6th). During the year, General comments were not adopted.

Italy should have submitted its first periodic report in June 2011, but as of 31 December, it has not yet complied with that commitment.

H. Committee on Migrant Workers

In 2011, the Committee held two sessions, the 14th (4-8 April) and the 15th (12-23 September), during which concluding observations were adopted on Mexico (14th session), Argentina, Chile and Guatemala (15th session). During the year, General comments were not adopted.

Italy has not ratified the Convention on the Protection of the Rights of All Migrant Workers and Members of Their Families and, therefore, is not subject to monitoring by the Committee.

I. Committee on Enforced Disappearances

In 2011, the Committee held two sessions, the 14th (4-8 April) and 15th (12-23 September), during which concluding observations were adopted regarding Mexico (14th session), Argentina, Chile and Guatemala (15th session). During the year, General comments were not adopted.

Italy has not ratified the Convention for the Protection of All Persons from Enforced Disappearance, and therefore is not subject to monitoring by the Committee.

VI. Specialised United Nations Agencies, Programmes and Funds

A. International Labour Organisation (ILO)

The International Labour Organisation is the international organisation responsible for drawing up and overseeing international labour standards. Instituted in 1919 with the Treaty of Versailles, the ILO was the first specialised agency of the United Nations in 1946 (see the Agreement between the United Nations and the International Labour Organisation, New York, 30 May 1946).

Since its institution, the ILO has adopted 189 conventions covering a vast array of issues: freedom to associate and right to collective bargaining; equal opportunities and treatment; abolition of forced labour and child labour; promotion of employment; professional training; social security; working conditions; labour administration and inspection; prevention of work accidents; protection of maternity care; protection of migrants and specific categories of workers such as maritime labourers, medical assistants, plantation labourers. Among the conventions, ILO considers 8 to be "fundamental": No. 29, on Forced Labour (1930); No. 87, on Freedom of Association and the Right to Organise (1948); No. 98, on the Right to Organise and Collective Bargaining (1949); No. 100, on Equal Remuneration for Men and Women Workers for Work of Equal Value (1951); No. 105, on the Abolition of Forced Labour (1957); No. 111, on Discrimination in respect of Employment and Occupation (1958); No. 138, on the Minimum Age for Admission to Employment (1973); No. 182, on the Prohibition and Immediate Action for the Elimination of the Worst Forms of Child Labour (1999).

Italy has been a Member of the ILO since 1919 (it is one of the founding members); in 1937 it withdrew and then joined again, becoming a permanent Member in 1945. The ILO has its own office in Rome, Italy, operating since 1920, and the International Training Centre, established in Turin in 1965.

Italy has ratified 111 conventions adopted by the ILO, including all those defined as fundamental.

Fundamental

Convention	**Date of deposit of instrument of ratification**	**Status**
C029 – Forced Labour Convention, 1930 (No. 29)	18 Jun 1934	In Force
C087 – Freedom of Association and Protection of the Right to Organise Convention, 1948 (No. 87)	13 May 1958	In Force
C098 – Right to Organise and Collective Bargaining Convention, 1949 (No. 98)	13 May 1958	In Force
C100 – Equal Remuneration Convention, 1951 (No. 100)	08 Jun 1956	In Force
C105 – Abolition of Forced Labour Convention, 1957 (No. 105)	15 Mar 1968	In Force
C111 – Discrimination (Employment and Occupation) Convention, 1958 (No. 111)	12 Aug 1963	In Force
C138 – Minimum Age Convention, 1973 (No. 138) Minimum age specified: 15 years	28 Jul 1981	In Force
C182 – Worst Forms of Child Labour Convention, 1999 (No. 182)	07 Jun 2000	In Force

Governance (Priority)

Convention	Date of deposit of instrument of ratification	Status
C081 – Labour Inspection Convention, 1947 (No. 81)	22 Oct 1952	In Force
C122 – Employment Policy Convention, 1964 (No. 122)	05 May 1971	In Force
C129 – Labour Inspection (Agriculture) Convention, 1969 (No. 129)	23 Jun 1981	In Force
C144 – Tripartite Consultation (International Labour Standards) Convention, 1976	18 Oct 1979	In Force

Technical

Convention	Date of deposit of instrument of ratification	Status
C001 – Hours of Work (Industry) Convention, 1919 (No. 1)	06 Oct 1924	Conditional Ratification
C002 – Unemployment Convention, 1919 (No. 2)	10 Apr 1923	In Force
C003 – Maternity Protection Convention, 1919 (No. 3)	22 Oct 1952	In Force
C004 – Night Work (Women) Convention, 1919 (No. 4)	10 Apr 1923	Denunciation 06 Aug 2001
C006 – Night Work of Young Persons (Industry) Convention, 1919 (No. 6)	10 Apr 1923	In Force
C007 – Minimum Age (Sea) Convention, 1920 (No. 7)	14 Jul 1932	Automatic Denunciation 28 Jul 1981 by C138
C008 – Unemployment Indemnity (Shipwreck) Convention, 1920 (No. 8)	08 Sep 1924	In Force
C009 – Placing of Seamen Convention, 1920 (No. 9)	08 Sep 1924	In Force
C010 – Minimum Age (Agriculture) Convention, 1921 (No. 10)	08 Sep 1924	Automatic Denunciation 28 Jul 1981 by C138
C011 – Right of Association (Agriculture) Convention, 1921 (No. 11)	08 Sep 1924	In Force
C012 – Workmen's Compensation (Agriculture) Convention, 1921 (No. 12)	01 Sep 1930	In Force
C013 – White Lead (Painting) Convention, 1921 (No. 13)	22 Oct 1952	In Force
C014 – Weekly Rest (Industry) Convention, 1921 (No. 14)	08 Sep 1924	In Force
C015 – Minimum Age (Trimmers and Stokers) Convention, 1921 (No. 15)	08 Sep 1924	Automatic Denunciation 28 Jul 1981 by C138

C016 – Medical Examination of Young Persons (Sea) Convention, 1921 (No. 16)	08 Sep 1924	In Force
C018 – Workmen's Compensation (Occupational Diseases) Convention, 1925 (No. 18)	22 Jan 1934	In Force
C019 – Equality of Treatment (Accident Compensation) Convention, 1925 (No. 19)	15 Mar 1928	In Force
C022 – Seamen's Articles of Agreement Convention, 1926 (No. 22)	10 Oct 1929	In Force
C023 – Repatriation of Seamen Convention, 1926 (No. 23)	10 Oct 1929	In Force
C026 – Minimum Wage-Fixing Machinery Convention, 1928 (No. 26)	09 Sep 1930	In Force
C027 – Marking of Weight (Packages Transported by Vessels) Convention, 1929	18 Jul 1933	In Force
C032 – Protection against Accidents (Dockers) Convention (revised), 1932 (No. 32)	30 Oct 1933	Automatic Denunciation 07 Jun 2000 by C152
C035 – Old-Age Insurance (Industry, etc.) Convention, 1933 (No. 35)	22 Oct 1947	Shelved Conventions
C036 – Old-Age Insurance (Agriculture) Convention, 1933 (No. 36)	22 Oct 1947	Shelved Conventions
C037 – Invalidity Insurance (Industry, etc.) Convention, 1933 (No. 37)	22 Oct 1947	Shelved Conventions
C038 – Invalidity Insurance (Agriculture) Convention, 1933 (No. 38)	22 Oct 1947	Shelved Conventions
C039 – Survivors' Insurance (Industry, etc.) Convention, 1933 (No. 39)	22 Oct 1952	Shelved Conventions
C040 – Survivors' Insurance (Agriculture) Convention, 1933 (No. 40)	22 Oct 1952	Shelved Conventions
C042 – Workmen's Compensation (Occupational Diseases) Convention (revised), 1934 (No. 42)	22 Oct 1952	In Force
C044 – Unemployment Provision Convention, 1934 (No. 44)	22 Oct 1952	Shelved Conventions
C045 – Underground Work (Women) Convention, 1935 (No. 45)	22 Oct 1952	Denunciation 29 May 2008
C048 – Maintenance of Migrants' Pension Rights Convention, 1935 (No. 48)	22 Oct 1952	Shelved Conventions
C052 – Holidays with Pay Convention, 1936 (No. 52)	22 Oct 1952	Automatic Denunciation 28 Jul 1981 by C132
C053 – Officers' Competency Certificates Convention, 1936 (No. 53)	22 Oct 1952	In Force
C055 – Shipowners' Liability (Sick and Injured Seamen) Convention, 1936 (No. 55)	22 Oct 1952	In Force
C058 – Minimum Age (Sea) Convention (revised), 1936 (No. 58)	22 Oct 1952	Automatic Denunciation 28 Jul 1981 by C138

C059 – Minimum Age (Industry) Convention (revised), 1937 (No. 59)	22 Oct 1952	Automatic Denunciation 28 Jul 1981 by C138
C060 – Minimum Age (Non-Industrial Employment) Convention (revised), 1937 (No. 60)	22 Oct 1952	Automatic Denunciation 28 Jul 1981 by C138
C068 – Food and Catering (Ships' Crews) Convention, 1946 (No. 68)	22 Oct 1952	In Force
C069 – Certification of Ships' Cooks Convention, 1946 (No. 69)	22 Oct 1952	In Force
C071 – Seafarers' Pensions Convention, 1946 (No. 71)	10 Apr 1962	In Force
C073 – Medical Examination (Seafarers) Convention, 1946 (No. 73)	22 Oct 1952	In Force
C074 – Certification of Able Seamen Convention, 1946 (No. 74)	23 Jun 1981	In Force
C077 – Medical Examination of Young Persons (Industry) Convention, 1946 (No. 77)	22 Oct 1952	In Force
C078 – Medical Examination of Young Persons (Non-Industrial Occupations) Convention, 1946 (No. 78)	22 Oct 1952	In Force
C079 – Night Work of Young Persons (Non-Industrial Occupations) Convention, 1946 (No. 79)	22 Oct 1952	In Force
C080 – Final Articles Revision Convention, 1946 (No. 80)	11 Dec 1947	In Force
C088 – Employment Service Convention, 1948 (No. 88)	22 Oct 1952	Denunciation 09 Aug 1971
C089 – Night Work (Women) Convention (revised), 1948 (No. 89)	22 Oct 1952	Denunciation 27 Feb 1992
C090 – Night Work of Young Persons (Industry) Convention (revised), 1948 (No. 90)	22 Oct 1952	In Force
C091 – Paid Vacations (Seafarers) Convention (revised), 1949 (No. 91)	05 May 1971	Automatic Denunciation 28 Jul 1981 by C146
C092 – Accommodation of Crews Convention (revised), 1949 (No. 92)	23 Jun 1981	In Force
C094 – Labour Clauses (Public Contracts) Convention, 1949 (No. 94)	22 Oct 1952	In Force
C095 – Protection of Wages Convention, 1949 (No. 95)	22 Oct 1952	In Force
C096 – Fee-Charging Employment Agencies Convention (revised), 1949 (No. 96)	09 Jan 1953	Automatic Denunciation 01 Feb 2000 by C181
C097 – Migration for Employment Convention (revised), 1949 (No. 97)	22 Oct 1952	In Force
C099 – Minimum Wage Fixing Machinery (Agriculture) Convention, 1951 (No. 99)	05 May 1971	In Force

C101 – Holidays with Pay (Agriculture) Convention, 1952 (No. 101)	08 Jun 1956	Automatic Denunciation 28 Jul 1981 by C132
C102 – Social Security (Minimum Standards) Convention, 1952 (No. 102)	08 Jun 1956	In Force
C103 – Maternity Protection Convention (revised), 1952 (No. 103)	05 May 1971	Automatic Denunciation 07 Feb 2001 by C183
C106 – Weekly Rest (Commerce and Offices) Convention, 1957 (No. 106)	12 Aug 1963	In Force
C108 – Seafarers' Identity Documents Convention, 1958 (No. 108)	12 Aug 1963	In Force
C109 – Wages, Hours of Work and Manning (Sea) Convention (revised), 1958	23 Jun 1981	Convention not in force
C112 – Minimum Age (Fishermen) Convention, 1959 (No. 112)	05 May 1971	Automatic Denunciation 28 Jul 1981 by C138
C114 – Fishermen's Articles of Agreement Convention, 1959 (No. 114)	10 Apr 1962	In Force
C115 – Radiation Protection Convention, 1960 (No. 115)	05 May 1971	In Force
C117 – Social Policy (Basic Aims and Standards) Convention, 1962 (No. 117)	27 Dec 1966	In Force
C118 – Equality of Treatment (Social Security) Convention, 1962 (No. 118)	05 May 1967	In Force
C119 – Guarding of Machinery Convention, 1963 (No. 119)	05 May 1971	In Force
C120 – Hygiene (Commerce and Offices) Convention, 1964 (No. 120)	05 May 1971	In Force
C123 – Minimum Age (Underground Work) Convention, 1965 (No. 123)	05 May 1971	Automatic Denunciation 28 Jul 1981 by C138
C124 – Medical Examination of Young Persons (Underground Work) Convention, 1965 (No. 124)	05 May 1971	In Force
C127 – Maximum Weight Convention, 1967 (No. 127)	05 May 1971	In Force
C132 – Holidays with Pay Convention (revised), 1970 (No. 132)	28 Jul 1981	In Force
C133 – Accommodation of Crews (Supplementary Provisions) Convention, 1970	23 Jun 1981	In Force
C134 – Prevention of Accidents (Seafarers) Convention, 1970 (No. 134)	23 Jun 1981	In Force
C135 – Workers' Representatives Convention, 1971 (No. 135)	23 Jun 1981	In Force
C136 – Benzene Convention, 1971 (No. 136)	23 Jun 1981	In Force
C137 – Dock Work Convention, 1973 (No. 137)	23 Jun 1981	In Force
C139 – Occupational Cancer Convention, 1974 (No. 139)	23 Jun 1981	In Force

C141 – Rural Workers' Organisations Convention, 1975 (No. 141)	18 Oct 1979	In Force
C142 – Human Resources Development Convention, 1975 (No. 142)	18 Oct 1979	In Force
C143 – Migrant Workers (Supplementary Provisions) Convention, 1975 (No. 143)	23 Jun 1981	In Force
C145 – Continuity of Employment (Seafarers) Convention, 1976 (No. 145)	23 Jun 1981	In Force
C146 – Seafarers' Annual Leave with Pay Convention, 1976 (No. 146)	28 Jul 1981	In Force
C147 – Merchant Shipping (Minimum Standards) Convention, 1976 (No. 147)	23 Jun 1981	In Force
C148 – Working Environment (Air Pollution, Noise and Vibration) Convention, 1977	28 Feb 1985	In Force
C149 – Nursing Personnel Convention, 1977 (No. 149)	28 Feb 1985	In Force
C150 – Labour Administration Convention, 1978 (No. 150)	28 Feb 1985	In Force
C151 – Labour Relations (Public Service) Convention, 1978 (No. 151)	28 Feb 1985	In Force
C152 – Occupational Safety and Health (Dock Work) Convention, 1979 (No. 152)	07 Jun 2000	In Force
C159 – Vocational Rehabilitation and Employment (Disabled Persons) Convention, 1983 (No. 159)	07 Jun 2000	In Force
C160 – Labour Statistics Convention, 1985 (No. 160)	08 Nov 1989	In Force
C164 – Health Protection and Medical Care (Seafarers) Convention, 1987 (No. 164)	07 Nov 2002	In Force
C167 – Safety and Health in Construction Convention, 1988 (No. 167)	12 Feb 2003	In Force
C170 – Chemicals Convention, 1990 (No. 170)	03 Jul 2002	In Force
C175 – Part-Time Work Convention, 1994 (No. 175)	13 Apr 2000	In Force
C181 – Private Employment Agencies Convention, 1997 (No. 181)	01 Feb 2000	In Force
C183 – Maternity Protection Convention, 2000 (No. 183)	07 Feb 2001	In Force

In order to monitor the application of conventions ratified by States, in 1926 the ILO created the Committee of Experts on the Application of Conventions and Recommendations, a body made up of 20 eminent specialists in social and legal areas, independent of Governments and appointed individually. The monitoring mechanism requires every Member State to present a periodical report on measures adopted, in law and in practice, in the application of each ratified convention. At the same time, it must send a copy of the report to employers' and workers' organisations, who have the right to provide further information. The Government reports are first examined by the Committee of Experts, which may adopt two different types of measures: *observations* and *direct requests.* The observations contain comments on fundamental issues emerging with the application of a particular convention by a State, and are published in the Committee's annual report. The direct requests, instead, refer to issues of an essentially technical nature, or else aim to request information; they are not published in the annual report, but are directly transmitted to the Governments involved.

After the examination, the Committee submits to the International Labour Conference – the most highly representative body of the ILO, with representation from all ILO Member States – an annual report containing its observations and recommendations. The report is closely examined by the Committee of the Conference on the Application of Standards, a tripartite body composed of representatives from the Government, employers and workers. The Committee selects a certain number of observations from the report for in-depth discussion. The Governments called upon in such observations are urged to present their own comments before the Conference Committee. In many cases, the Conference Committee adopts conclusions urging States to take specific measures in order to remedy a problem, to ask the ILO to carry out missions in their territory, or to request technical assistance.

During 2011, Italy received 21 direct requests (+5 compared to 2010) and 6 observations (+2 compared to 2010) from the Committee of Experts on the Application of Conventions and Recommendations.

With the direct requests, the Committee sought to obtain more information on legislative, administrative and political tools relating to the implementation of the following conventions (the date by which Italy was bound to reply is indicated in brackets):

No. 26 – Methods for establishing minimum wages (2016), No. 29 – Forced labour (2012), No. 71 – Seafarers' pensions (2014), No. 74 – Certificates for qualified seafarers (2014), No. 77 – Medical examination of adolescents (Industrial) (2016), No. 78 – Medical examination of adolescents (Non-industrial) (2016), No. 79 – Night work for adolescents (Non-industrial) (2016), No. 90 – Night work for young girls (Industry) (revised) 2016), No. 94 – Labour Clauses (Public Contracts) (2016), No. 95 – Salary Protection (2016), No. 99 – Methods for establishing minimum wages (Agriculture) (2016), No. 102 – Social Security (Minimum Standards) (2016), No. 105 – Abolition of forced labour (2012), No. 115 – Protection against Radiation (2015), No. 118 – Equal Treatment (Social Security) (2016), No. 119 – Machine guarding standards (2015), No. 143 – Migrant workers (Supplementary Provisions) (2012), No. 145 – Continuity of employment (Seafarers) (2014), No. 167 – Health and safety in the Construction business (2015), No. 170 – Chemical products (2015)

The observations focused on the following conventions (the date by which Italy was bound to reply is indicated in brackets): No. 81 – Labour Inspection (2014), No. 129 – Labour Inspection (Agriculture) (2014), No. 139 – Occupational Cancer (2015), No. 143 – Migrant Workers (Supplementary Provisions) (2012), No. 159 – Vocational Rehabilitation and Employment (Disabled Persons) (2013), No. 181 – Private Employment Agencies (2013).

Convention No. 81 Labour Inspection

– In relation to art. 3, para. 1 and 2 of the Convention, the Committee reiterates the recommendations already made in 2010 on the need to distinguish, with sufficient clarity, the powers and working methods of labour inspectors from those of officials of other agencies responsible for the opposing illegal forms of labour and immigration (see *2011 Yearbook*, pp. 202-203).

– In relation to art. 4, the Committee asks Italy to indicate the criteria used for determining the performance of an inspection and for assessing the results of such inspections.

– In relation to art. 11, the Committee asks Italy to provide detailed information on financial resources allocated to the labour inspectorate.

– In relation to articles 5, 20 and 21, the Committee asks that the Government clarify whether the annual report on labour inspection, the compilation of which is an obligation under the Convention, is published by a central authority, and to include in that report details of each of the following: laws and regulations governing the jurisdiction of labour inspection, personnel of the labour inspection service; statistics of establishments under the control of inspection and number of workers employed in these establishments; statistics on inspection visits; statistics of violations and sanctions imposed; statistics on accidents in the workplace; statistics on occupational diseases.

Similar observations were made under *Convention No. 129 concerning Labour Inspection in Agriculture.*

Convention No. 139 on Occupational Cancer

– The Committee notes with satisfaction the adoption of the lgs.d. 9 April 2008, No. 81 concerning the protection of health and safety in the workplace, establishing a general framework of protection for workers exposed to carcinogens and mutagens. In particular, the Committee appreciates that articles 234 and 245 establish a definition and a list of carcinogens and mutagens in line with art. 1 of the Convention, and that art. 243 ensures compliance with the Italian law with art. 3 of the Convention, through the establishment of a health surveillance system, based on a register of exposure and medical records, which sets forth, for each employee, his employment, the carcinogen or mutagen used and, if known, the degree of exposure to that agent. As for health surveillance, the Committee notes the information provided by the Government on medical examinations conducted before and during the employment activity at risk, but reminds the Government that, pursuant to art. 5 of the Convention, such tests must be conducted even after the employment period, and therefore calls on the Government to take appropriate measures to comply with this requirement.

Convention No. 143 on Migrant Workers (Supplementary Provisions)

– In relation to articles 2, 3 and 6 of the Convention, the Committee asks that the Government provide information on the legislation adopted to transpose it into Italian law directive 2009/52/EC of the European Parliament and Council of 18 June 2009 providing for minimum standards on sanctions and measures against employers who employ third-Country nationals whose stay is illegal, and the measures to identify and suppress human trafficking and to prosecute those responsible for this crime in any Country in which they operate.

– In relation to articles 1 and 9 (minimum standards of protection), the Committee emphasises the vulnerable position of migrant workers in irregular situations of exploitation and violation of their fundamental human rights. Particularly worrisome are the conditions of exploitation of irregular migrants from Asia, Africa and Eastern Europe, working mainly in construction and agriculture. In this regard, the Committee recalls the concerns already expressed in the past in relation to the fact that art. 10-*bis* of lgs.d. 286/1998, which introduces the crime of illegal entry or presence, can lead to further marginalisation and stigmatisation of undocumented migrants, as well as increased vulnerability to exploitation and violation of their human rights. Furthermore, art. 10(a), in connection with art. 331 of the code of criminal procedure (mandatory reporting of crime reports by public officials), may also prevent violations of the rights of illegal immigrants from being reported. While acknowledging the difficulties encountered by Italy in the management of a large influx of migrants and the Government's efforts to address the problem of irregular immigration, the Committee recalls that the Convention provides that all migrant workers are entitled to a basic level of protection, regardless of their irregular status. Therefore, emphasising the fact that access to justice is a fundamental human right that must be guaranteed to all migrant workers, in principle and in practice, the Committee asks that the Government indicate the mechanisms that actually exist, capable of facilitating complaints from irregular migrant workers. The Government should also provide information on the number of irregular migrants, employed mainly in agricultural and construction sectors, who have filed a complaint for violation of their fundamental rights or for reasons of remuneration and access to social security benefits, and the results of these complaints. Finally, the Committee requests that the Government provide information on activities to detect the illegal employment of migrants and the employment of migrants in abusive work conditions.

– In relation to articles 10 and 12 (national policies on equality of opportunity and treatment of migrant workers legally residing in the Country), the Committee urges the Government to communicate the outcomes of specific programmes and initiatives aimed at promoting equality of opportunity and treatment among migrant workers legally resident in Italy and Italian citizens, with particular reference to the *Integration Plan: Security, Identity and Engagement*, adopted in June 2010 by the Ministry of Labour and Social Affairs and the Ministry of Education, University and Research.

Convention No. 159 on Vocational Rehabilitation and Employment of People with Disabilities

According to Government data, as a result of the application of law 68/1999 on employment rights of people with disabilities, in 2008 about 28,000 were employed of the 99,500 persons with disabilities registered on the mandatory hiring lists; in 2009, the number of people with disabilities employed was 20,830 against 83,148 of these in the registers. The Committee urges the Government to strengthen its efforts to promote employment opportunities for people with disabilities and to ensure that these persons obtain and maintain jobs and manage to move forward in them. The Government should also provide, by 2013, information on the impact of national policy on vocational rehabilitation and employment of people with disabilities, as well as detailed statistics on the number of persons employed, the type and duration of their contracts, and the opportunities for education and training offered to people with disabilities.

Convention No. 181 on Private Employment Agencies

– The Committee reiterates that Convention No. 181 recognises the role that can be played by private employment agencies for the purpose of a well functioning labour market, but also emphasises the need to protect workers from abuses. A full and productive job and decent working conditions are fundamental to responding to the crisis. However, there is a concern, shared by some of the social partners, that the private employment agencies do not fully guarantee a fair treatment in terms of employment and working conditions. Therefore, the Committee urges the Government to prepare a report on measures taken under the Budget Act 2010 and subsequent legislation to ensure adequate protection for workers employed by private employment agencies, under articles 11 and 12 of the Convention, and the number and type of abuses and fraudulent practices concerning the activities of these agencies (articles 10 and 14).

None of these observations was selected for a more detailed discussion in 2011 by the Conference Committee on the Application of the Regulations.

The ILO's general budget is structured on three lines of funding: the regular budget, voluntary contributions in addition to the regular budget (so-called *Regular Budget Supplementary Account*) and the resources for technical cooperation. In 2011, Italy contributed about 5% of the ILO's regular budget, a sum equal to about 19.4 million Swiss francs (unchanged from 2010).

In 2010-2011, Italy granted an additional voluntary contribution to its annual budget of 300,000 dollars (in 2008-2009 the contribution was approximately 1.5 million dollars), and is one of the six donor Countries, along with the Netherlands, Denmark, Norway, Belgium and Germany.

In 2011 (as in 2010), Italy did not contribute to the ILO technical cooperation resources. In the period 2006-2009, however, this contribution came to a total of 32.9 million dollars (see the following graph). Through these funds, Italy financed ILO technical assistance activities in the Mediterranean (Egypt, Algeria, Lebanon, Morocco and Tunisia), in the Balkans (Serbia, Albania) and in Latin America (Uruguay and Argentina).

Italy's contributions to ILO extra-budgetary resources for technical cooperation, 2006-2011

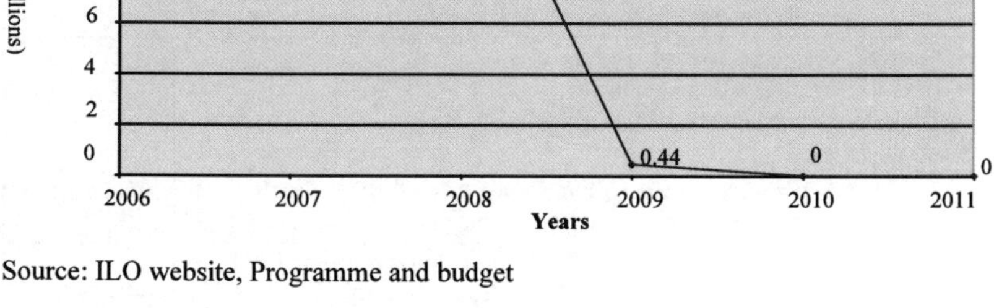

Source: ILO website, Programme and budget

B. United Nations Educational, Scientific and Cultural Organisation (UNESCO)

The human rights that fall under the responsibility of UNESCO include the right to education, the right to benefit from scientific progress, the right to participate freely in cultural life, and the right to information, including freedom of opinion and expression. In connection with these, also relevant are the right to freedom of thought, conscience and religion, the right to seek, receive and impart information and ideas through any instrument and across borders, the right to protection of the moral and material interests resulting from any scientific, literary or artistic work, the right to freedom of assembly and association, the right to education, the right to benefit from scientific progress, the right to participate freely in cultural life, the right to information, including freedom of opinion and expression.

Italy has been a Member State of UNESCO since 1948. Since its inception, UNESCO has adopted 27 conventions and Italy has ratified 20 of them (see table).

Convention		**Date of deposit of instrument of ratification**
Universal Copyright Convention, with Appendix Declaration relating to art. XVII and resolution concerning art. XI, 1952.		24/10/1956
	Protocol 2 annexed to the Universal Copyright Convention concerning the Application of that Convention to the Works of Certain International Organisations, 1952	24/10/1956
	Protocol 3 annexed to the Universal Copyright Convention concerning the Effective Date of Instruments of Ratification or Acceptance of or Accession to that Convention, 1952.	24/10/1956
	Protocol 1 annexed to the Universal Copyright Convention concerning the Application of that Convention to the Works of Stateless Persons and Refugees 1952	19/12/1966
Convention for the Protection of Cultural Property in the Event of Armed Conflict with Regulations for the Execution of the Convention, 1954		09/05/1958
	Protocol to the Convention for the Protection of Cultural Property in the Event of Armed Conflict 1954	09/05/1958
	Second Protocol to the Hague Convention of 1954 for the Protection of Cultural Property in the Event of Armed Conflict, 1999.	10/07/2009
Convention concerning the International Exchange of Publications, 1958		02/08/1961
Convention concerning the Exchange of Official Publications and Government Documents between States, 1958		02/08/1961

Agreement on the Importation of Educational, Scientific and Cultural Materials, with Annexes A to E and Protocol annexed, 1950		26/11/1962
	Protocol to the Agreement on the Importation of Educational, Scientific or Cultural Materials, with Annexes A to H, 1976.	02/07/1981
Convention against Discrimination in Education, 1960.		06/10/1966
	Protocol Instituting a Conciliation and Good offices Commission to be Responsible for Seeking the settlement of any Disputes which may Arise between States Parties to the Convention against Discrimination in Education, 1962	06/10/1966
International Convention for the Protection of Performers, Producers of Phonograms and Broadcasting Organisations, 1961		08/01/1975
Convention on Wetlands of International Importance especially as Waterfowl Habitat, 1971		14/12/1976
	Protocol to amend the Convention on Wetlands of International Importance especially as Waterfowl Habitat, 1982	27/07/1987
Convention for the Protection of Producers of Phonograms against Unauthorised Duplication of their Phonograms, 1971		20/12/1976
Convention concerning the Protection of the World Cultural and Natural Heritage, 1972		23/06/1978
Convention on the Means of Prohibiting and Preventing the Illicit Import, Export and Transfer of Ownership of Cultural Property, 1970		02/10/1978
Universal Copyright Convention as revised at Paris on 24 July 1971, with Appendix Declaration relating to article XVII and resolution concerning article XI, 1971		25/10/1979
	Protocol 1 annexed for Universal Copyright Convention as revised at Paris on 24 July 1971 concerning the application of that Convention to works of Stateless persons and refugees, 1971	25/10/1979
	Protocol 2 annexed for the Universal Copyright Convention as revised at Paris on 24 July 1971 concerning the application of that Convention to the works of certain international organisations, 1971	25/10/1979
Convention relating to the Distribution of Programme-Carrying Signals Transmitted by Satellite, 1974		07/04/1981
Convention on the Recognition of Studies, Diplomas and Degrees in Higher Education in the Arab and European States Bordering on the Mediterranean, 1976		14/04/1981

Convention on the Recognition of Studies, Diplomas and Degrees concerning Higher Education in the States belonging to the Europe Region, 1979		20/01/1983
Convention on the Protection and Promotion of the Diversity of Cultural Expressions, 2005		19/02/2007
Convention for the Safeguarding of the Intangible Cultural Heritage, 2003		30/10/2007
International Convention against Doping in Sport, 2005		27/02/2008
Convention on the Protection of the Underwater Cultural Heritage, 2001		08/01/2010
Convention on the Recognition of Qualifications concerning Higher Education in the European Region, 1997		01/10/2010

Italy has not ratified the Protocol amending articles 6 and 7 of the Convention on Wetlands of International Importance, and particularly as Waterfowl Habitats, (1978), nor the following three agreements: Agreement for Facilitating the Circulation of Educational, Scientific and Cultural Audio-Visual Materials (1948); Convention on Technical and Vocational Education (1989); Multilateral Convention for Avoidance of Double Taxation of Copyright Royalties (1979).

On the other hand, Italy is not required to ratify, the four regional conventions regarding the recognition of studies and qualifications in higher education in the States, respectively, the African, Asian, Latin American and Arab regions.

Italy, as a Member of UNESCO, is bound to the principles enshrined in the declarations and recommendations adopted by its bodies.

The Permanent Representative of Italy to UNESCO in 2011 is Maurizio Enrico Serra. Besides being a Member of the Executive Council, in 2011, Italy was represented in the Intergovernmental Oceanographic Commission, the International Committee for the Safeguarding of Intangible Cultural Heritage, the Committee for the Protection of Cultural Property in the Event of Armed Conflict, as well as at the following advisory bodies of the General Conference: International Coordination Council of Man and the Biosphere Programme; Intergovernmental Committee for Promoting the Return of Cultural Property to the Country of Origin or its Restitution in Case of Misappropriation; Intergovernmental Council of the International Programme for the Development of Communication; Intergovernmental Council on the International Hydrological Programme; the Legal Committee; Commission for Conciliation and Good Offices Responsible for Resolving Disputes that may Arise

Between States Parties of the Convention against Discrimination in Education (Member: Francesco Margiotta-Broglio).

On the subject of bioethics, at UNESCO there are two committees: the International Bioethics Committee (IBC) and Intergovernmental Bioethics Committee (IGBC).

The IBC was established in 1993, largely through the efforts of the then Director General of UNESCO, Federico Mayor, and is composed of 36 independent experts from different geographical areas working in different disciplines. Its mandate is to oversee the progress of science and its applications in order to ensure respect for human dignity and human rights and to stimulate reflection on the ethical and legal aspects raised by research in life sciences and its applications. In this perspective, over the years it has prepared numerous recommendations and other documents, the most important of which is the Universal Declaration on Bioethics and Human Rights, adopted by the General Conference of UNESCO in 2005. The Committee meets once a year upon convocation by the Director General of UNESCO. The 2011 session was held in Baku (Azerbaijan), 31 May-2 June. During the session three main topics were discussed: the adoption of the report on the principle of respect for human vulnerability and personal integrity under art. 8 of the Universal Declaration on Bioethics and Human Rights, the issue of human cloning and international governance, and the theme of traditional medicine and its ethical implications. At the end of the session, in addition, the Committee elected as its President for the biennium 2012-2013 Stefano Semplice, Professor of Moral Philosophy at the "Tor Vergata" University of Rome, who has been a Board Member since 2008.

The IGBC was created in 1998 pursuant to art. 11 of the IBC Statutes. It is composed of 36 Member States elected by the General Conference of UNESCO, whose representatives meet at least once every two years to discuss the IBC proposals and recommendations, and to disseminate such proposals, together with their opinions, between UNESCO Member States. The seventh session of the IGBC was held in Paris from 5 to 6 September 2011, and was mainly devoted to the analysis of the IBC's work in 2010-2011. In 2011, Italy was not part of the IGBC.

In terms of education, it is reported that in 1991, the 26th General Conference of UNESCO established the International Programme for University Cooperation (*IUC – International University Cooperation*), in order to make UNESCO a laboratory of ideas and a catalyst for international cooperation between universities and educational and scientific institutions around the world. To this end, the programme seeks to encourage the creation of a network of centres of excellence (*UNESCO Chairs*) capable of implementing programmes for education and advanced research in fields related to UNESCO's policies, with special reference to issues of peace, human rights, democracy and intercultural dialogue.

There are over 650 UNESCO Chairs created throughout the world; in Italy there are 13 Chairs, 3 of which deal specifically with human rights, bearing the wording: Chair in "Human rights, democracy and peace", established in 1999 at the University of Padua (Chair: Antonio Papisca); Chair in "Human rights and ethics of international cooperation", established in 2003 at the University of Bergamo (Chair: Felice Rizzi); Chair in "Bioethics and human rights", established in 2009 at the "Regina Apostolorum" Pontifical Athenaeum, European University of Rome (Chair: Alberto Garcia).

In regard to the protection of the world cultural heritage, on 29 November 2011 an agreement was signed between UNESCO (signed by the Assistant Director General for Culture, Francesco Bandarin) and the Italian Ministry of Cultural Heritage and Activities, by which the Organisation is committed to providing the Italian Government an adequate technical support to improve the conservation of World Heritage in Pompei, Herculaneum and Torre Annunziata. The agreement is part of numerous expert missions sent by UNESCO to Italy between 2010 and 2011, following the initial collapse of the *Schola Armaturarum* (6 November 2010), and subsequent collapses of other structures belonging to this Heritage.

In 2011, Italy contributed 5% of the regular UNESCO budget (which covers the recurrent expenditure for the maintenance staff and the main activities of the Organisation), a sum equal to about 15.3 million dollars, placing it at the sixth place among the main contributors to the Organisation. Moreover, again in 2011, Italy was in third place (after Japan and the European Commission) in terms of voluntary contributions (which are used to fund multi-annual cooperation programmes managed by UNESCO), with a contribution of approximately 11.5 million dollars (+2 million dollars compared to 2010).

UNESCO Machinery

The UNESCO machinery responsible for monitoring the implementation of conventions and recommendations is made up of the General Conference, the Executive Council and the Committee on Conventions and Recommendations, a subsidiary body of the Council consisting of 30 members (representatives of States).

The Committee meets twice a year, usually during the sessions of the Executive Council. The main function of the Committee is to examine both the periodic reports on the States on the implementation of a selected number of conventions and recommendations as well as the individual communications (complaints) of alleged violations of human rights presented by teachers, students, researchers, artists, writers, journalists (this procedure is strictly confidential).

As for the first function, the Committee monitors the implementation of three conventions (Convention against Discrimination in Education, 1960; Convention on the Means of Prohibiting and Preventing the Illicit Import, Export and Transfer of Ownership of Cultural Property, 1970; Convention on Technical and Vocational Education, 1989) and eleven recommendations (Recommendation against Discrimination in Education, 1960; Recommendation concerning the Status of Teachers, 1966; Recommendation concerning Education for Understanding, Cooperation and International Peace and Education relating to Human Rights and Fundamental Freedoms, 1974; Recommendation concerning the Status of Scientific Researchers, 1974; Recommendation on the Development of Adult Education, 1976; revised Recommendation concerning the International Standardisation of Educational Statistics, 1978; Recommendation concerning the Status of Artists, 1980; Recommendation on the Recognition of Studies and Qualifications in Higher Education, 1993; Recommendation concerning the Status of the Teaching Staff of Higher Education, 1997; revised version of the Recommendation concerning Technical and Vocational Education, 2001; Recommendation concerning the Promotion and Use of Multilingualism and Universal Access to Cyberspace, 2003), generally adopted on a schedule with a five-year basis.

In 2007, the Executive Council adopted a specific procedure for the monitoring of these conventions and recommendations, under which the States must submit their reports to the Secretariat of UNESCO, at regular four years intervals. The Secretariat draws up summary reports based on information received, to be submitted to the Committee. The Committee, therefore, does not directly analyse the reports submitted by the States, nor does it have the possibility of a dialogue with them, as with other United Nations mechanisms. Since, moreover, in the reports by the Secretariat the information on individual Countries is grouped by theme, the monitoring process involves a significant loss of information. At the end of the monitoring phase, the Committee invites the Executive Council to adopt the recommendations, of a rather general nature, with respect to the States.

In 2011, the Committee held two sessions. At its meeting of 4-6 May, it monitored the implementation of the Recommendation concerning the status of the teaching staff of higher education and the Recommendation concerning the promotion and use of multilingualism and universal access to cyberspace.

At the session of 21-26 September, the Committee monitored the implementation of the Recommendation on the Recognition of Studies and Qualifications in Higher Education, the Convention on the Means of Prohibiting and Preventing the Illicit Import, Export and Transfer of Ownership of Cultural Property, the Convention on Technical and Vocational Training, the Recommendation on the Development of Adult Learning and the Recommendation concerning the Status of Artists.

With regard to the Convention on the means of Prohibiting and Preventing the Illicit Import, Export and Transfer of Ownership of Cultural Property, on 30 June 2011, the Secretariat received periodic reports from 45 Countries, including Italy. The information provided by Italy on the implementation of the Convention includes the following:

– *Inventory and identification.* Italy has established an inventory of public and private property and church property;

– *Actions taken to prevent illicit excavations.* Italy considers that the ownership of objects that have not yet been discovered or that have been extracted from archaeological excavations should revert to the public authorities;

– *Actions taken to control the export and import of cultural property.* In Italy special police units have been established and trained with the task of identifying and protecting imported and exported cultural property, with special reference to archaeological and museum property;

– *Systems for exchange, acquisition and transfer of ownership of cultural property.* Art market professionals in Italy are licensed and are required to keep a register to specify the nature of transactions and provide, where appropriate, certification of authenticity. A register of stolen goods has also been established.

– *Bilateral agreements.* Cooperation for the return of cultural property is favoured by the loan of the property, by joint archaeological excavations and the organisation of joint exhibitions.

As regards the examination of individual complaints of alleged violations of human rights, from 1978 to 2011 the Committee considered 566 communications. Of these, 360 were declared eligible and covered the following categories of victims: persons released before the end of a sentence (211 cases); persons released following the conclusion of a sentence (14 cases); persons authorised to leave their Country for study or teaching (21 cases); persons authorised to return to their own Country (35 cases); persons able to resume their employment or their own activities falling within UNESCO jurisdiction (29 cases); persons who are able to resume a previously banned publication or broadcast (14 cases); persons who are able to resume a normal life following the cessation of threats (45 cases); beneficiaries of changes in education laws that were discriminatory against ethnic or religious minorities (10 cases); persons able to obtain passports, grants or diplomas (12 cases); persons able to resume their studies (9 cases).

An Intergovernmental Committee (24 members) operates in the field of application of the Convention on the Protection and Promotion of the Diversity of Cultural Expressions, with the task of examining the quadrennial reports on States to be transmitted, with comments, to the Conference of States Parties to the Convention. The first cycle of monitoring of these reports will begin in 2012, when the Committee will receive the initial report by 94 States. Italy is required to submit its report by 30 April 2012.

Finally, the International Bureau of Education, UNESCO's specialised institute, organises the International Conference on Education, a forum for dialogue between the Ministers of Education of Member States of UNESCO, which also involves researchers, teachers, experts, and representatives of non-governmental organisations. At each conference, each State must submit a national report on the development of education.

The last conference was held in Geneva in 2008: Italy submitted its report relating to issues of higher education, the right to education and inclusion policies.

C. The Food and Agriculture Organisation of the United Nations (FAO)

The FAO was established in 1945 in Ville de Quebec, Canada. Since 1951, its main headquarters have been located in Rome. The organisation currently involves 191 States, in addition to 2 associate Countries and the European Union. The FAO is present in 130 Countries.

As well as playing a leading role in the global fight against hunger, FAO promotes the adoption of international standards, contributing to the signing of conventions and agreements on issues related to food and agriculture, and also hosting conferences and meetings (World Food Summit of 1996 and 2002).

The governing bodies of the FAO are the Conference, composed of all States Parties, with the task of formulating policies and approving the budget of the Organisation; the Council, consisting of 49 States elected on a rotating basis by the Conference for a period of 3 years, with the task of supervising the implementation of programmes and policies; the Director General, also elected by the Conference for a renewable term of 4 years, with the task of managing the Organisation's activities. The Director-General, until 31 December 2011, was Jacques Diouf (Senegal), while from 1 January 2012, José Graziano da Silva (Brazil) will take office.

The FAO is composed of seven Departments, of which the most relevant to the issue of human rights are those dedicated to agriculture and consumer protection, and social and economic development. Italy is currently appointed to the Council, with a three-year term that started on 1 December 2011. The 37th Session of the FAO Conference was held in Rome from 25 June to 2 July 2011. One of the three Vice-Presidents of the Conference is Pietro Sebastiani.

Historically, Italy is one of the major funders of the FAO. It contributes to the Organisation's regular budget with 5% (9,578,584.74 dollars), and is a major supporter of the technical cooperation activities. In particular, Italy participates in the FAO/Italy Cooperation Programme and the FAO programme devoted to decentralised cooperation, launched in 2002, involving local authorities, universities, foundations, NGOs and the private sector. To date, it has sponsored 17 projects totalling approximately 10 million dollars. In the period 2002-2011 it contributed to the Trust Fund for Food Security with 100 million euros and is committed to ensuring an annual allocation to the Emergency and Rehabilitation Division of FAO. In the period 2002-2010, Italy provided voluntary contributions amounting to about 110 million euros.

The FAO, indicated by the Secretary-General Ban Ki Moon as a reference organisation for the management of relations between Expo 2015 and the United Nations, has signed a collaboration agreement with Expo 2015, an event that will be hosted by the city of Milan and will have the theme *Feeding the Planet, Energy for Life.*

D. The World Health Organisation (WHO)

The primary objective of the Organisation, established in 1948, is the attainment by all peoples of the highest possible level of health, understood not as the absence of disease but as a state of complete physical, mental and social wellbeing.

> It is the global Organisation that provides direction and coordination in health issues. Among other activities, the WHO provides guidance on global health issues; it addresses health research, and develops international standards; it contributes to drafting health policies and providing technical assistance to Member States; it monitors trends in health care; it provides financial support for medical research and provides emergency aid in cases of crisis or natural disaster.
>
> Governing bodies of the WHO are the Secretariat, the World Health Assembly and the Executive Council. It is also divided into 6 regional offices, which are flanked by offices across the Member States and collaborating centres that support its activities in the field.

In Italy there are two offices of the WHO (Rome and Venice) and currently 26 accredited collaborating centres. The latter, specialised institutions which receive no funding from the WHO, are identified by the Director General of the WHO and are part of a worldwide network to support the Organisation in various medical and scientific fields. In Italy their activity is coordinated by the Ministry of Health.

E. The United Nations Development Programme (UNDP)

The United Nations Development Programme (UNDP) was established by the General Assembly in 1965, and has the role of central agency for the coordination and funding of development cooperation of the United Nations system. It has offices and activities in 177 Countries.

UNDP action pursues the general objective of "human development", understood as not only economic growth but also as social development, based on gender equality and respect for human rights. Its functions are divided into four main areas: poverty reduction and achievement of the Millennium Development Goals; democratic governance; conflict prevention and post conflict reconstruction; environment and sustainable development. All UNDP activities and programmes follow an approach centred on human rights (Human rights-based Approach to development programming – HRBA) which provides that all stages of planning, from initial planning to final evaluation, are oriented and aimed at the progressive realisation of human rights. In this context, the United Nations Declaration on the Right to Development, which in 2011 saw the celebration of the twenty-fifth anniversary of its adoption, is a primary point of reference for the idea of *people-centred* development, oriented toward the person, and therefore human development.

UNDP conducts research and analysis, preparing studies and reports. Of the most significant, worth noting is the *Annual Report on Human Development* and the report on the state of the achievement of the Millennium Development Goals. The first study, as well as periodically delving more deeply into issues related to human development (in 2011 the report was entitled *Environmental Sustainability and Equity*), performs a census of the living conditions in 187 Countries. Through the human development index (HDI), an indicator that takes into account life expectancy at birth, the level of schooling and GDP per capita, the UNDP offers an alternative to purely economic indicators to assess the degree of development of each Country. The ranking for Italy, which in 2011 was in 24th place, remains unchanged from the previous year, while it appears to have worsened by 3 ranking positions in comparison to 2006. Italy then loses two more positions if the human development index is adjusted with parameters that take into account inequalities, while in the rankings that refer to the gender gap, it is ranked 15th place.

The other particularly important report is on the state of achievement of the Millennium Development Goals, and analyses the successes and challenges ahead as the deadline for their achievement is set for the end of 2015. In the 2011 report, Italy's position emerged in relation to Objective No. 8, namely the goal to develop a global partnership for development. Italy in particular has not fulfilled the commitments made in 2005 under the OECD with regard to the percentage of GDP to be allocated for Official Development Assistance (0.15% instead of 0.515%).

F. The United Nations Environment Programme (UNEP)

The United Nations Environment Programme (UNEP) based in Nairobi, Kenya, was established in 1972 at the conclusion of the World Conference on Human Environment held in Stockholm that year. The UNEP's mission is to coordinate and facilitate the realisation of a global partnership for development projects and environmental protection activities so that nations and peoples may improve their quality of life without jeopardising that of future generations.

In performing its functions, UNEP works closely with other UN agencies, other international organisations, national governments and civil society organisations. Its activities include producing studies and research in environmental and sustainable development; the development of tools for the protection of natural resources; the coordination and promotion of international standards on the environment; the transfer of technologies for knowledge in the field of the environment. The Permanent Representative to the UNEP and also head of the Italian Embassy mission in Nairobi is Ambassador Paola Imperiale.

The governing bodies of UNEP are the Steering Committee, composed of 58 Governments elected by the UN General Assembly for a period of four years; the Committee of Permanent Representatives; the Committee of Ministers and Officials. It is organised into six regional offices, six field offices, seven liaison offices, and eight sectoral divisions. The current Director General is Achim Steiner.

In the debate that in recent years, and especially in view of the Rio +20 Conference on the Environment, has focused on strengthening international environmental governance, the reform of the UNEP from programme to specialised United Nations agency has taken a prominent role.

Italy too, in line with the position adopted by the European Union, supports the creation of a United Nations Organisation (UNEO) that makes it possible, firstly, to overcome the fragmented nature of the international environmental protection system, and secondly, to respond effectively to the increasingly urgent need to incorporate the environmental dimension into all economic and development policies.

In 2011, the UNEP submitted a report for a global green economy, entitled *Towards a Green Economy – Pathways to Sustainable Development and Poverty Reduction* in which the green economy is defined as an improvement of human welfare and social equity, capable at the same time of ensuring a significant reduction of environmental and ecological risk.

G. The United Nations Human Settlements Programme (UN-HABITAT)

UN-HABITAT, the United Nations Human Settlements Programme, was created in 1978 by a resolution of the General Assembly with the mission of promoting sustainable urbanisation in social and environmental terms, for the ultimate purpose of guaranteeing everyone the right to decent housing. It is based in Nairobi and the current Director General is Joan Clos (Spain). The Permanent Representative to UN-HABITAT and also the head of the Italian Embassy mission in Nairobi is Amb. Paola Imperiale.

> Taking into account the fact that almost half the world's population lives in cities, UN-HABITAT plays a particularly important role. These centres of production, consumption and welfare, often become places of social exclusion, poverty and marginalisation.
>
> In many developing Countries, 50% of city dwellers live in slums and are therefore denied any access to safe drinking water, sanitation and other basic services. The work of UN-HABITAT is closely linked to the Millennium Development Goals and in particular with the Objective No. 7 (Ensure environmental sustainability).
>
> It also works closely with local authorities, including Municipalities, Provinces and Regions, mainly due to the special relationship formed with UNACLA, the United Nations Advisory Committee on the Local Authorities. The latter consists of mayors and representatives of umbrella organisations of local authorities chosen by the Director General of UN-HABITAT on the basis of their expertise and commitment in implementing the UN agenda on human settlements. The main task of UNACLA, as well as providing guidance and making suggestions to the Director-General of UN-HABITAT on all issues related to the governance of cities, is to interact with governments, local authorities and other international partners to promote the activities and programmes of UN-HABITAT. During 2011, in particular, the focus of the UNACLA activities was urban mobility.

In 2011, the University "La Sapienza" in Rome, in collaboration with UN-HABITAT, began an interdisciplinary course of advanced training on *Sustainable development and the MDGs* with the aim of training technicians and researchers from Europe and Africa. In 2011, UN-HABITAT accepted the nomination of the city of Naples as the location for the next *World Urban Forum*, whose theme will be the urban future, to be held in September 2012.

H. The United Nations Children's Fund (UNICEF)

UNICEF was created as an emergency fund set up by the General Assembly on 11 December 1946 to provide assistance to children of European Countries after World War II. In 1953, after several years of activity, it became a permanent fund whose mandate is aimed at children of Africa, Asia and Latin America. Having a mission to protect and promote the rights of boys, girls and adolescents with the aim of improving their living conditions, UNICEF could do no less than use the principles and provisions of the Convention on the Rights of the Child and the Millennium Development Goals.

UNICEF's international structure is composed of regional offices, field offices and international branches, including the headquarters in New York and Geneva, the logistics centre in Copenhagen and the Research Centre – Istituto degli Innocenti in Florence. It is present in over 190 Countries, both with programmes of direct assistance (developing and emerging Countries) and with National Committees (industrialised Countries). The latter are engaged in fundraising and public awareness-raising campaigns. In 2010, Italy was ranked in 15th place among the donor Countries, two positions less than in 2009.

UNICEF's governing bodies are: the Board of Directors, made up of 36 Member States, which identifies the strategies of the organisation, supervises programmes and approves its budgets; the Executive Director (from 1 May 2010 it is the American Anthony Lake), appointed by UN Secretary General in consultation with the Board, is responsible for managing the administration and represents the organisation abroad. Italy, in the period 2009-2011 was a Member of the UNICEF Board of Directors.

Since 1980, UNICEF has published the annual report on *The State of the World's Children*, a document that aims to take stock of all major issues affecting the situation of children and adolescents worldwide. In 2011, it was dedicated to the theme of *Adolescence. An Age of Opportunity*.

In Italy there is the Italian Committee for UNICEF, a non-governmental organisation established in 1974 whose activity is regulated by a cooperation agreement signed with UNICEF International. It operates through a professional organisation based in Rome and a dense network of volunteers who carry out their activities at the regional and provincial committees for UNICEF. The current President of UNICEF Italy is Giacomo Guerrera, who succeeded Vincenzo Spadafora. In November 2011, the latter was appointed Ombudsperson for Children and Adolescents (see Part II, National Bodies with Jurisdictions over Human Rights, VIII, D).

The main objectives of the Italian Committee for UNICEF are to promote, throughout Italy, protection and the protection of the rights of every child and adolescent.

Driven by an integrated approach, it sponsors awareness campaigns to promote social change and improve the quality of life for children in situations of hardship and marginalisation as well as numerous programmes aimed at building a world fit for children.

VII. International Organisations with Permanent Observer Status at the General Assembly

Of the 69 intergovernmental organisations of a universal or regional nature with the status of permanent observer at the UN General Assembly, 19 maintain permanent representation offices at the United Nations headquarters in New York. They participate in the work and the annual sessions of the Assembly and have access to all related documentation.

One of the most active organisations in issues related to human rights, with particular attention to migration issues, is the International Organisation for Migration.

A. The International Organisation for Migration (IOM)

The IOM currently has 146 Member States. A further 13 States and 85 international organisations and non-governmental organisations enjoy observer status.

The IOM is a highly decentralised structure. It consists of eight regional offices whose key function is to formulate strategies and regional action plans; two special liaison offices (New York and Addis Ababa) engaged in strengthening relations with the diplomatic missions, non-governmental and multilateral institutions; two administrative centres and more than 240 national and local offices around the world.

Among the latter, six perform coordination roles (Nairobi, Canberra, Bangkok, Rome, Astana, Guyana).

The primary mission of IOM is to promote orderly migration based on respect for human dignity. To this end, it collaborates with Governments and civil society to promote economic and social development through migration; to defend the dignity and welfare of migrants; to support international solidarity through humanitarian assistance to individuals in need; to improve understanding of migration issues; to facilitate international dialogue on migration issues and provide operational advice in the field of migration management.

Annually, the IOM publishes the report on migration in the world, which in 2011 was focused on the need to engage in an open and constructive debate on migration. Indeed, the report emphasises how distorted communication on migration contributes to spreading anti-migrant sentiments and drastically affects the public perception of migration.

Since 1951, the year in which the IOM was established, Italy has hosted the Coordination Centre for the Mediterranean Countries in Rome. The IOM is also present in Lampedusa, centre for initial assistance and reception on the island, and in Sicily, at the centres in Trapani, Caltanissetta and Siracusa. The main activities of the IOM offices in Italy are: information services relating to migration; approach to migration for work and social integration; combating trafficking in human beings and providing assistance to victims; reuniting families through DNA tests; projects designed to foster preventing the spread of HIV and to promote the consideration of the health implications of migration.

Among the many projects implemented by the IOM in Italy, worth mentioning is the awareness campaign on migration aimed at the media and addressed to the Italian population, launched with the aim of overturning clichés on migration and aimed at highlighting the positive role played by migrants in the Italian socio-economic context; the programme for assisted voluntary return for foreigners arriving in Italy after 1 January 2011 following the events in North Africa and the project *Return to start*, providing practical support and a grant for the reintegration of foreigners holding a residence permit or another permit of a temporary nature who wish to return to their Country of origin. Also noteworthy is the role played by the IOM in the humanitarian effort for the reception of migrants who arrived in Italy following the events in Tunisia and the conflict in Libya.

In December 2011, the IOM, with support from the research centre IDOS, published the research work *1951 to 2011 – Migration in Italy, past and future.*

The research, produced for the 60th anniversary of the IOM, tells how the evolution of the IOM in Italy goes hand in hand with the changes in migratory flows that brought Italy to be first a Country of emigrants and then of immigration. According to the data provided, the foreign population in Italy, expected to increase in the coming years, is now almost 4 million, and the Italians living abroad are estimated to be around the same number. Although they appeared in 2010, two other publications worthy of note for Italy published by the IOM are the report on the situation of migrants in the Province of Caserta and the Castelvolturno area, and the report *Stagione amara* (*Bitter Season*) about the seasonal work system and the conditions of migrant workers in agriculture in Campania, Apulia and Sicily.

Council of Europe

Founded on 5 May 1949, the Council of Europe (CoE, 47 Member States) is the first and most advanced system of promotion and protection of human rights at the regional level. Major bodies of the Council of Europe are the Committee of Ministers and the Parliamentary Assembly. In 1994 the Congress of Local and Regional Authorities was established as an advisory body. The European Court of Human Rights works organically within the institutional framework of the Council of Europe.

The main legal instrument adopted by the CoE is the European Convention for the Protection of Human Rights and Fundamental Freedoms (ECHR, 1950), which established the European Court of Human Rights in Strasbourg (ECtHR); the Convention has been accompanied over the years by 14 protocols. Other essential legal tools are the European Social Charter (1961, revised version of 1996), the European Convention for the Prevention of Torture and Inhuman or Degrading Treatment or Punishment (1987), the Framework Convention for the Protection of National Minorities (1995), the European Convention on the Rights of the Child (1996), the Convention on Human Rights and Biomedicine (Oviedo Convention, 1997) and the Convention on Action against Trafficking in Human Beings (2005). For each of these conventions a system has been put in place for the monitoring of the current state of their implementation by the States that ratified them, generally focused on the activities of a committee of independent experts. Within the General Secretariat of the CoE, the *Directorate-General for Human Rights and Rule of Law* oversees the dynamic application of various treaties and its follow-up mechanisms, providing assistance and support to the bodies of the Council of Europe and the Member States and organises programmes, and training and awareness initiatives.

In September 2011, the Secretariat of the Council of Europe set up a branch office in Venice, in order to increase visibility for the policies and priorities of the Organisation on issues such as social innovation, intercultural dialogue and sustainable development, with particular attention to the Balkans and the Mediterranean. Among the activities organised by the Office, worth noting is the organisation, in collaboration with the Human Rights Centre of the University of Padua, of a training course for Italian lawyers engaged in the protection of the rights of Roma and Sinti, which was held in Venice, on 13 and 14 October 2011.

The Permanent Representative of Italy to the Council of Europe is Amb. Sergio Busetto. In 2011, Italy contributed to the budget of the Council of Europe for a total of 24,654,554 euros.

The pages that follow will illustrate, with reference to Italy's role, the activities of the Parliamentary Assembly and the Committee of Ministers; the five bodies set up under the Treaty: the European Court of Human Rights, the Committee for the Prevention of Torture, the European Committee of Social Rights, the Advisory Committee on the Framework Convention for the Protection of National Minorities, the Group of Experts on Action against Trafficking in Human Beings; four bodies established by the Committee of Ministers: Commissioner for Human Rights, the European Commission against Racism and Intolerance, the European Commission for Democracy through Law, the Group of States against Corruption.

Those not taken into consideration are: the Steering Committee on Bioethics, since Italy has not yet deposited the instrument of ratification of the Oviedo Convention and its Protocols (see Part I, International Human Rights Law, III), and the Standing Committee of the Convention for the Exercise of the Rights of Children, as there is no recent activity by the body.

I. Parliamentary Assembly

In the Parliamentary Assembly of the Council of Europe (PACE), made up of delegations from the national Parliaments of the Member States of the CoE, 18 members of the Senate and the Chamber of Deputies sit for Italy; there are an equal number of alternate members. The President of the Italian delegation is Luigi Vitali, who is also one of the 20 Vice-Presidents. The President of the Committee for Political Affairs and Democracy is Pietro Marcenaro, while Giuseppe Santini is the President of the Committee on Migration, Refugees and Displaced Persons (in 2011: Committee on Migration, Refugees and Population) and President *ex officio* of the three related Subcommittees (detention, integration and cooperation with the non-European Countries of origin and transition).

The Assembly is a forum for discussion on the main issues underlying the mandate of the Council of Europe and has an advisory role in relation to all international conventions developed in this context. It elects the judges of the European Court of Human Rights, the High Commissioner for Human Rights, the Secretary-General and his Deputy.

In 2011, the PACE adopted a number of documents (resolutions and recommendations) on issues that are particularly sensitive for Italy, with particular reference to the problematic management of migration flows as a result of large-scale arrivals of irregular migrants, asylum seekers and refugees caused by the uprisings in Tunisia, Egypt and Libya.

Resolution 1805 on large-scale arrivals of irregular migrants, asylum seekers and refugees off the coast of southern Europe (see also recommendation to the Committee of Ministers No. 1967), was adopted on 14 April 2011 on the basis of a report submitted to the Committee on Migration, Refugees and Population (*rapporteur*: Strik). In it, the Parliamentary Assembly stresses the need to respond giving priority to humanitarian needs and the international protection of migrants arriving on Italian and Maltese shores and recognises the pressure experienced by the coastal Countries of Europe, accepting their efforts and asking them to continue to provide aid and assistance to migrants in difficulty. The Assembly, recognising that the events in North Africa are of common concern to all Member States of the CoE, asks them to: recognise the joint responsibility and the need to find common solutions for the management of these migratory events; urgently provide humanitarian assistance and reception of migrants and avoid automatic recourse to custodial measures against them and, in particular, to ensure that persons belonging to vulnerable groups are not detained, guaranteeing the right of asylum (analysing the applications for international protection in a timely fashion) and respecting the principle of *non-refoulement*, to support the activities of the UNHCR, the IOM and the International Committee of the Red Cross and to show solidarity with the coastal European Countries, sharing the responsibility with them.

With reference to the measures needed to tackle the causes of these migrations, the Assembly urges the Member States to provide support for economic, social, democratic and legal reforms in the Countries of origin, provide opportunities to facilitate legal migration opportunities and be prepared to provide the necessary assistance to Libya, when the conflict is finished.

Resolution 1820, on the subject of *Asylum seekers and refugees: sharing responsibilities in Europe* (also see recommendation 1973), was adopted on 21 June 2011 on the basis of a report submitted to the Committee on Migration, Refugees and Population (*rapporteur*: Chope). In it, the PACE emphasises the need to take further measures to ensure that responsibilities towards refugees and asylum seekers, particularly those from the southern shore of the Mediterranean Sea, are shared in a reasonable way in Europe and that asylum seekers have access to fair and effective examination systems for their demands. Specifically, the Assembly calls on Member States to: encourage the reform of the Dublin system, in particular with reference to the criterion that the determination of refugee status must be taken into account by the first Country of entry; provide assistance to coastal Countries, including Malta and Italy, which receive mixed flows of migrants on a large scale; rely more on reports of interceptions at sea in order to coordinate the response against the traffickers of human beings. At the same time, the PACE recognises that such a sharing of responsibility involves a special commitment by the Countries that are at the forefront in receiving these flows, in particular: to ensure access in that Country to any person who may require international protection, to provide appropriate reception conditions and fair and prompt high-quality asylum procedures and to ensure the integrity of its borders and monitoring of irregular migration flows.

Recognising the role and responsibility of the European Union in this field, finally, the Parliamentary Assembly asks UE institutions to adopt a series of measures, in particular to ensure that, as part of the Dublin system and the mandate of FRONTEX, it is fully consistent with respect for the human rights of the persons concerned.

Resolution 1821, on the issues of interception and rescue at sea of irregular migrants, refugees and asylum seekers (see also recommendation 1974), was adopted on 21 June 2011 on the basis of a report submitted to the Committee on migration (*rapporteur*: Tejera). In this paper, the PACE identifies a number of issues related to differences in interpretation and application of the measures adopted by the various Member Countries for the management of the arrival of illegal immigrants and requires them a series of measures to be applied during patrol operations, whatever their nature. These include: to fulfil, without exceptions and delays, their obligation to rescue persons in distress at sea; to ensure that the patrol activities recognise the mixed composition of the flow of people trying to cross the maritime borders; to ensure human treatment and the systematic implementation of human rights for all persons who are intercepted at sea and to refrain from any practice that could amount to a breach of the principle of *non-refoulement*; to ensure fair access to prompt and adequate measures of protection for asylum seekers and victims of trafficking (or potential victims); to ensure that the choice to detain the intercepted people in detention facilities excludes vulnerable groups and takes place only when absolutely necessary, with the approval of the courts; to suspend all bilateral agreements with third Countries which may not provide the protection of human rights of the persons concerned; to sign and ratify the main international legal instruments regarding the rights of refugees and human trafficking, as well as to ensure that the patrol and boundary control operations do not interfere with the specific protection provided to vulnerable groups under international law. With reference to the challenges posed to coastal States sustaining arrivals of irregular migrants, PACE calls on the international community to provide these Countries with any assistance necessary to ensure a consistent and harmonised approach to maritime law and to establish an "interagency" group to solve the main problems in the field of interception at sea.

Again with reference to these issues, as a result of a motion for a resolution (doc. 12617) filed on 23 May 2011 on *Responsibility for loss of life in the Mediterranean*, the Committee on Migration, Refugees and Population instructed *rapporteur* Tineke Strik (Netherlands) to carry out an investigation into the circumstances that led, in April 2011, to the death of 61 illegal migrants fleeing Libya and, according to some sources, abandoned to their fate by the Italian armed forces operating in the area, despite repeated requests for help. In this context, the Dutch member of Parliament made a visit to Rome on 6 and 7 September 2011 during which she met with people who had survived the sinking, the Italian coastguard officials and NGO representatives. The report on this investigation, which also included missions to Malta and France, is being prepared.

Another motion, this time for a recommendation (doc. 12557), was presented to the same Committee on the same theme of arrivals of irregular migrants in the Italian coastal areas as a result of tensions in the Countries of the southern Mediterranean, with the aim of supporting European cooperation in this field and to invite international organisations and Member States to give priority to the management of the crisis and its consequences. The report on this subject (*rapporteur*: Chope) is being prepared.

During the year under review, the Assembly also addressed other relevant issues with reference to the human rights situation in Italy.

Resolution 1787 (also see recommendation 1955) on the execution of judgements of the ECtHR, was adopted on 26 January 2011 on the basis of a report submitted to the Committee on Legal Affairs and Human Rights (*rapporteur*: Pourgourides). In the document, Italy is identified along with Bulgaria, Cyprus, Greece, Republic of Moldova, Poland, Romania, Russia, Turkey and Ukraine, among the Countries that are the furthest behind in this area.

According to the PACE, Italy must therefore take immediate steps to address the structural problems related to the excessive length of judicial proceedings, in line with the numerous interim resolutions adopted by the Committee of Ministers in this regard (see *2011 Yearbook*, p. 212), and to avoid violations of the provisional measures ordered by the Court, as has happened in a number of cases involving foreign nationals.

Resolution 1808 (also see recommendation 1968) on the strengthening of the mechanisms for the prevention of torture in Europe, was adopted 14 April 2011 on the basis of a report submitted to the Committee on Legal Affairs and Human Rights (*rapporteur*: Gardetto). Among the requests contained in this document, the PACE calls on Member States that have not yet done so (one of which is also Italy) to ratify the Optional Protocol to the United Nations Convention against Torture, and to designate an independent and adequately funded national preventive mechanism in this regard; States Parties to the Convention on the Prevention of Torture of the CoE are meanwhile invited to amend the text (through the CM) in order to allow for the election of members of the CPT by the PACE and the automatic publication of the reports of the Committee as soon as they have received the comments by the Government concerned.

Resolution 1811 (also see recommendation 1970) on the protection of migrant women in the labour market, was adopted on 15 April 2011, on the basis of a report submitted to the Committee on Migration, Refugees and Population (*rapporteur*: Frahm) which, in its explanatory part, contains numerous references to the situation of female migrant workers in Italy. In the resolution's text, the Assembly recognises the need for host Countries to develop and implement specific measures for the protection of members of this social group, regardless of their immigration status and type of employment. Requested measures include: the increase in legal migration opportunities for women and the adoption of human rights-based migration policies which are sensitive to gender issues, greater protection of human rights and the promotion of equal opportunities; the prevention and combating of exploitative practices in the labour market. Some of the recommendations contained in the document are aimed at achieving recognition by Member States of the important productive role and social value of domestic work.

Resolution 1827 on the progress of the monitoring procedures of the Assembly during the period June 2010-May 2011, was adopted on 24 June on the basis of a report submitted to the Committee on monitoring the fulfilment of obligations and commitments by Member States of the CoE (*rapporteur*: Marty). Although not included in the list of Countries subject to the current monitoring cycle, the Committee includes recommendations on Italy derived from observations by other monitoring bodies of the CoE. Among these, the PACE asks Italy to ratify the European Charter for Regional or Minority Languages, Protocol XII to the ECHR on the Fight against Discrimination, the Criminal Law Convention and the Civil Law Convention on Corruption. It also asks national Parliaments (including Italian Parliament) to promote progress in the execution of judgements of the ECtHR and begin the necessary legislative changes designed to eliminate the structural problems that lead to repeated violations of the ECHR.

In addition to these resolutions, it is worth noticing that a motion for a recommendation on *Strengthening the institution of the Ombudsman in Europe* (doc. 12639), presented on 15 June 2011 to the Committee on Legal Affairs and Human Rights, refers to the need to provide ombudspersons with adequate resources to carry out their duties in a fully independent manner. In terms of negative trends, the motion refers to the elimination of the municipal ombudspersons in Italy, as set out in the financial law for 2010 (see Part II, Sub-national Human Rights Structures, II).

With regard to the activities of the Italian Parliament in 2011, the reports to be noted are those by: Pietro Marcenaro on reconciliation and political dialogue between the Countries of the former Yugoslavia (7 January 2011, Committee on Legal Affairs and Human Rights), Giacomo Santini on guaranteed access to health care for migrants and foreign nationals (1 February 2011, the Committee on Migration, Refugees and Population), and Luca Volonté on violence against Christians in the Middle East (25 January, 2011, Political Affairs Committee) and on the request for the status of "Partner for democracy" of the Parliamentary Assembly submitted by the Parliament of Morocco. In addition, some Italian parliamentarians participated in election observation missions sent by the PACE with regards to the parliamentary elections in Turkey on 12 June 2011 (Giuseppe Saro, Giacomo Santini, Pietro Marcenaro and Andrea Rigoni), the presidential elections in Bulgaria on 23 and 30 October 2011 (Luca Volonté), and the elections of Tunisia's Constituent Assembly on 23 October 2011 (Pietro Marcernaro).

II. Committee of Ministers

On the subject of human rights, the Committee of Ministers (CM) relies on the work of the Steering Committee for Human Rights, an intergovernmental body composed of representatives of the 47 Member States which performs, among others things, standard-setting and follow-up.

The CM adopts recommendations regarding the Member States and on matters for which a common policy is agreed upon – in accordance with its role in the implementation of the European Social Charter (art. 29) – with the aim of asking some States to adapt their laws and public policies with the provisions contained in the Charter. In addition, it is ultimately responsible for monitoring the Framework Convention on National Minorities (art. 26). In this context, it adopts specific resolutions by Country based on the opinions of the Advisory Committee of the Framework Convention.

With regard to its role in relation to the European Court of Human Rights, the CM has the function of supervising the execution of judgements of the Court, ensuring that Member States act in accordance with the rulings issued by the same. The Committee terminates each case by adopting a final resolution. Finally, the CM may apply to the Court for a ruling on issues related to difficulties of interpretation of the judgements of the Court itself which would impede their implementation and, if it believes that a Member State is refusing to comply with a final judgement, it may refer the issue to the Court.

In 2011, the CM adopted eight conclusive resolutions on the implementation of judgements of the ECtHR for Italy: CM/ResDH(2011)13 on the Cordova case and six other cases; CM/ResDH(2011)14 on the Grava case and six other cases; CM/ResDH(2011)66 on the Scoppola case; CM/ResDH(2011)120 on the Lombardi Vallauri case; CM/ResDH (2011)13 on the Zagaria case and ten other cases; CM/ResDH(2011)122 on the F. C. B. case and 4 other cases, CM/ResDH(2011)123 on the Bocellari and Rizza case and 3 other cases; CM/ResDH(2011)124 on the Chizzotti case and 6 other cases. On 11 March 2011, during its 1108th Session, the CM also adopted two decisions on a number of judgements concerning Italy. In the first decision (CM/Del/Dec(2011) 1108/17E), with reference to the case of *Saadi and ten other cases against Italy*, the Committee notes that the ECtHR held that the enforcement of expulsion measures against some of the applicants would have been a breach of art. 3 of the ECHR (prohibition of torture). It therefore asks that Italian authorities provide information on the status of expulsion measures against the applicants and, in the case that they had not been waived, to revoke them. In the subsequent decision (CM/Del/Dec(2011)1108/18E) for cases *Ben Khemais v. Italy* (judgement of 24 February 2009) and *Trabelsi v. Italy* (judgement of 13 April 2010), the CM points out that the case-law of the Court requires States to comply with the provisional measures indicated by the same, pursuant to art. 39 of its rules, invites the Italian Government to provide detailed information about the applicants' situation in Tunisia and reiterates its request to the Italian authorities to provide evidence to demonstrate the effective compliance with the provisional measures ordered by the Court. In addition, the CM asks that information be provided on the requested comment to the appeal courts by the Ministry of Justice on the application of the requirements of the Convention and on the steps taken to create a mechanism to ensure that all relevant authorities are rapidly informed when a temporary measure is prescribed by the ECtHR.

Among other documents adopted by the CM with reference to Italy, it is worth mentioning the resolution CM/ResCSS(2011)9, adopted on 6 July 2011, on the application of the European Code of Social Security (1964). After having established that the Italian situation gives full effect to the parts of the Code accepted by Italy, the Committee decides to invite the Italian Government to provide more detailed information on the administration and organisation of social security and measures aimed at combating tax evasion and fraud in the field of social security.

III. European Court of Human Rights

The European Court of Human Rights (ECtHR), having its structure and functioning reformed with the entry into force of the Additional Protocol XIV on 1 June 2010, is the first international court specifically designed for the protection of human rights in a particular region of world. The Italian judge who now sits at the Court is Guido Raimondi, elected by the PACE in January 2010. Of the 640 members of the Registry, which provides legal and administrative support to the Court in the exercise of its functions, 19 are Italian.

In the course of its activities, the ECtHR has issued a total of 2,166 judgements with reference to Italy, 1,651 of which have highlighted the violation of at least one of the articles of the ECHR. In fact, after Turkey, Italy is the Country with the highest number of judgements by the ECtHR. In recent years, however, Russia, Turkey, Romania, Poland and Ukraine outweigh Italy for the number of complaints. The cases referred to the Court in Strasbourg concerning Italy, are mostly relative to art. 6(1) ECHR (trial within a reasonable time), art. 6 ECHR (fair trial),

1 Protocol I ECHR (peaceful enjoyment of property), and 8 ECHR (private and family life).

The statistical data provided by the Court and updated in December 2011 reported that the total number of complaints pending against Italy amounts to about 13,750. In 2011, the Court received 4,733 valid applications by individuals who complain of a violation of the rights enshrined in the ECHR by Italy (3,624 in 2009 and 3,852 in 2010). In the same period, 556 applications were declared inadmissible or struck off from the register, while 84 led to the delivery of a decision on the merits; 214 were communicated to the State in view of a hearing on their merits. The 668 judgements in 2010 were an exception; in 2009 there were 70 rulings on the merits regarding Italy. Also received by the ECtHR were 31 requests for temporary measures pursuant to art. 39 of the rules of Court, regarding the suspension of deportation proceedings for as many applicants; 5 were granted by the ECtHR, 7 were rejected, while 19 were deemed outside the scope.

The ECtHR judgements that had most resonance during 2011 were those adopted by the Grand Chamber in the cases *Giuliani and Gaggio* v. *Italy* (application 23458/02, judgement of 24 March 2011) and *Lautsi and others v. Italy* (application 30814/06, judgement of 18 March 2011). An analysis of judgements of the Court in relation to Italy in the year 2011 is presented in Part IV, Italy in the Case-law of the European Court of Human Rights.

IV. Committee for the Prevention of Torture

The European Committee for the Prevention of Torture and Inhuman or Degrading Treatment or Punishment (CPT) was established by the 1987 Convention of the same name, conceived as complementary to the regulations under art. 3 ECHR. The CPT is a body composed of independent experts and has one member for each State Party to the Convention for the Prevention of Torture (ratified today by all the Member States of the Council of Europe) and the members of the Committee are elected by the Committee of Ministers. The independent expert and President of the Italian CPT up to 19 December 2011 was Mauro Palma. On 7 December 2011, the Committee of Ministers elected in his stead, Andreana Esposito (resolution CM/ResCPT(2011)5), who will serve until December 2015. The first President of the CPT, in 1989, was Antonio Cassese.

The CPT, up to today, has led nine visits to Italy, the last on 14 to 18 June 2010. Under the principle of confidentiality, the most recent report available is related to the visit in 2009 (CPT/Inf (2010)14), published on 28 April 2010 together with the relevant observations of the Italian Government (see *2011 Yearbook*, pp. 214-216). The report on the visit of 2010 was not yet publicly available when this publication was being prepared. From press releases issued by the CPT in relation to the last visit, it shows that the delegation addressed three main issues: the provisions relating to health care in prisons as a result of the transfer of powers from Prison Administration to the National Health Service; policies and measures to reduce the incidence of suicide and self-harm in prison; the current system of investigation into the alleged ill-treatment of persons detained or arrested.

On 7 December 2011, the CPT announced the list of the ten Countries in which, as part of its programme of periodic visits, it intends to examine the treatment of persons deprived of their liberty. Italy is one of these Countries alongside Croatia, Estonia, Iceland, Lithuania, Monaco, Portugal, Russian Federation, Slovenia and the United Kingdom.

V. European Committee of Social Rights

The European Committee of Social Rights (ECSR) was established pursuant to art. 25 of the European Social Charter of 1961 in order to determine whether the legislation and practice of States parties comply with the provisions of the European Social Charter, its Protocols and the European Social Charter (revised) (ESC-R). Currently, the Committee is composed of 15 independent experts elected by the Committee of Ministers for a period of six years, renewable only once. Since 10 November 2010 Giuseppe Palmisano has been a part of it, and will remain in office until 31 December 2016.

> Italy ratified the European Social Charter in 1965 and the revised European Social Charter in 1999, accepting 97 of its 98 numbered paragraphs. The only provision not accepted regards art. 25 ESC-R, which protects the right of workers in the event of the insolvency of their employer. As of 2011, it appears that Italy has not presented the Committee with the first report on this provision of the revised Charter. Between 1967 and 2011, the Government submitted 20 reports on the application of the Charter of 1961 and 10 on the application of the revised Charter.

The latest *conclusions* on Italy were adopted by the Committee at its 254th session (5-9 December 2011) and published 31 January 2012. The document refers to the tenth report which was presented, as per the provisions of the Committee, by 31 October 2010, in parts, between 29 October 2010 and 7 July 2011. *Conclusions 2011* relates to the provisions of the Charter accepted by Italy in relation to the thematic group on the rights of children, families and migrants (articles 7, 8, 16, 17, 19, 27 and 31 ESC-R). Specifically, the reference period goes from 1 January 2003 to 31 December 2009 for articles 8, 17, 27 and 31, and from 1 January 2005 to 31 December 2009 for the remaining items.

Overall, the final document of the Committee refers to the Italian situation in relation to 36 articles and numbered paragraphs of the revised Charter, providing 17 conclusions on compliance (occasionally asking for the submission of additional information) and 16 in regard to non-compliance. In relation to three provisions (articles 7.5, 17.1 and 27.1), the Committee postpones its assessment to the next report, asking the Italian Government for the specific data needed to assess the status of implementation of the articles in question. In conjunction with art. 16, 19 and 31, the ECSR underlines how these were also the subject of collective complaint lodged by the *Centre on Housing Rights and Evictions* (COHRE) against Italy (complaint 58/2009, decision of 25 July 2010), in which the Committee found a violation of all the contested provisions, read in conjunction with art. E (non-discrimination) (see *2011 Yearbook*, pp. 218-220). Since this decision was taken beyond the period covered by the report, the conclusions of the Committee do not refer to the later developments after this decision; however the facts highlighted in the collective complaint are taken into account in the way in which they occurred during the reporting period. Conversely, in these conclusions, the Committee presents the follow-up to another decision, *European Roma Rights Centre (ERRC) v. Italy* (complaint 27/2004, decision of 7 December 2005), in which a violation of art. 31 was found, again read in conjunction with art. E.

Article of the ESC-R	**Conclusions of conformity**	**Conclusions of non-conformity**	**Request for further information**
Art. 7 ESC-R (right of children and young persons to protection)	para. 6 (Inclusion of time spent on vocational training in the normal working time) 7 (Paid annual holidays) 8 (Prohibition of night work) 9 (Regular medical examination) 10 (Special protection against physical and moral dangers)	para. 1 (Prohibition of employment under the age of 15) 2 (Prohibition of employment under the age of 18 for dangerous or unhealthy activities) 3 (Prohibition of employment of children subject to compulsory education) 4 (Working time for young persons under 18)	para. 5 (Fair pay)
Art. 8 ESC-R (right of employed women to protection of maternity)	para. 1 (Maternity leave) 2 (Illegality of dismissal) 4 (Regulation of night work)	para. 3 (Time off for nursing mothers)	

	5 (Prohibition of dangerous, unhealthy or arduous work)		
Art. 16 ESC-R (right of the family to social, legal and economic protection)		Whole article (composed just by one paragraph)	
Art. 17 ESC-R (right of mothers and children to social and economic protection)		para. 2 (Free primary and secondary education – regular attendance at school)	para. 1 (Assistance, education and training)
Art. 19 ESC-R (right of migrant workers and their families to protection and assistance)	para. 2 (Departure, journey and reception) 3 (Co-operation between social services of emigration and immigration States) 5 (Equality regarding taxes and contributions) 7 (Equality regarding legal proceedings) 9 (Transfer of earnings and savings) 11 (Teaching language of host State)	para. 1 (Assistance and information on migration) 4 (Equality regarding employment, right to organise and accommodation) 6 (Family reunion) 8 (Guarantees concerning deportation) 10 (Equal treatment for the self-employed)	
Art. 27 ESC-R (right of workers with family responsibilities to equal opportunity and treatment)	para. 2 (Parental leave) 3 (Illegality of dismissal on the ground of family responsibilities)		para. 1 (Participation in working life)
Art. 31 ESC-R (right to housing)	para. 1 (Adequate housing) 2 (Reduction of homelessness) 3 (Affordable housing)		

In relation to *art. 7 ESC-R* (right of children and adolescents to protection), the Committee, although requesting more detailed information and updated information on the subject under consideration where necessary, concludes that the situation in Italy is in compliance with para. 6 (inclusion of time devoted to training during normal working hours), para. 7 (paid annual leave), para. 8 (prohibition of night work), para. 9 (regular medical checks) and para. 10 (special protection against physical and moral dangers). On the contrary, the Italian situation is deemed to be in non-compliance with para. 1 (prohibition of employment of children under 15 years) because the data provided does not prove that the existing provisions prohibiting the employment of children below this age (law 27 December 2006, No. 296) are effectively enforced. A similar evaluation is made with reference to para. 2 (prohibiting the employment of persons under 18 in dangerous or unhealthy activities) because there is no evidence that the labour inspectorate conducts inspections in places of vocational training where some tasks undertaken by persons under 18 years could be considered dangerous or unhealthy, although they have not been declared as such. According to the Committee, the implementation of art. 7 includes monitoring the application of the legislation in question, although in point of fact it bans this type of activity for young people under the age of 18 years. The Committee's conclusions are also critical in relation to para. 3 (prohibition of employing children below the school-leaving age) since the effective enjoyment of the right to education does not appear to be guaranteed, given that there is no evidence that the legislation on the prohibition of employment under the age of 15 (law 296/2006) is actually followed. In relation to para. 4 (maximum working hours for workers under the age of 18 years) the ECSR notes a contradiction between the lgs.d. No. 45/1999, which sets a maximum limit of working hours for children under 18 years (including aged between 15 and 16 years), and the aforementioned law No. 296 of December 27, 2006, raising the age limit for compulsory education to 16 years. While awaiting information on the contradiction outlined above, the Committee states that the situation in Italy is not in compliance with the provision of the Charter, since it has not been established whether the length of working hours for young people between 15 and 16 years is reasonable.

In relation to para. 5 (equal pay), as previously mentioned, the Committee is postponing its conclusions until it has received more detailed information on the level of remuneration for young workers, with particular reference to minimum wages net of taxes and contributions, and data that illustrate the average net remuneration of apprentices in comparison with the starting salaries of adult workers.

With reference to *art. 8 ESC-R* (right of employed women to protection), the Committee concludes that the situation in Italy is in compliance with para. 1 (leave), para. 2 (illegal dismissal), para. 4 (regulation of night work) and para. 5 (prohibition of dangerous, unhealthy or arduous work). On the contrary, the Committee considers that the situation related to para. 3 (sufficient breaks for breastfeeding) is not in compliance, since neither domestic workers nor those who work from home are entitled to paid breaks for breastfeeding their very young babies.

In relation to *art. 16 ESC-R* (the right of the family to social, legal and economic protection), the Committee concludes that the situation in Italy is not compliant.

In particular, it is emphasised that in the complex national system of family benefits, there is no indication of equal treatment of foreigners. In addition, with specific reference to the operations of identification and census implemented to address the so-called "nomad emergency" (d.p.c.m. of 21 May 2008) to deal with the Roma and Sinti families since the adoption of the "security pacts" in November 2006, the ECSR stresses that the conditions under which such operations were carried out are an obstacle to proper protection against arbitrariness, in breach of art. 16. Also in this context, the Committee notes that, on 16 November 2011 (outside the period of reference), the Council of State ruled that such identity checks were disproportionate for a democratic society (see Part IV, Human Rights in Italian Case-law, V, B). The set of motivations that led the Committee to maintain that the situation in Italy does not comply with art. 16 ESC-R is the same that motivated the decision on violation of the article at issue in the complaint *COHRE v. Italy*.

With regard to the first paragraph (assistance, education and training) of *art. 17 ESC-R* (right of children and adolescents to social, legal and economic protection), the Committee decides to postpone its conclusions while waiting for more detailed information. In particular, the Italian Government is requested to provide statistics on the number of children in the new shelters set up following the progressive closure of institutions for minors (formally starting with law 149/2001) and the number of children in foster care.

Concerning juvenile delinquency, the ECSR requests more detailed information on the condition of juvenile delinquents in relation to the maximum duration of the period prior to trial, the possibility that they may be detained and sentenced together with adults, and the effective enjoyment of the right to education. In relation to the second paragraph (free primary and secondary education – regular attendance at schools), the Committee assesses the Italian situation as non-compliant, stressing that the measures taken by the Government, in particular the programmes and initiatives undertaken by the Ministry of Education to improve access to education by Roma and Sinti communities during the reference period, are insufficient.

With reference to *art. 19 ESC-R* (right of migrant workers and their families to protection and assistance), the Committee found that the situation in Italy complies with para. 2 (departure, journey and reception), 3 (co-operation between social services of emigration and immigration Countries), 5 (equality in relation to taxes and contributions), 7 (equality in relation to legal proceedings), 9 (transfer of earnings and savings) and 11 (teaching of the national language of the host Country). On the contrary, the ECSR concludes that the Italian situation does not comply with para. 1 (assistance and information on migration), mainly because of the misleading and racist propaganda against migrants of Roma and Sinti origins indirectly permitted or coming directly from Italian public authorities, as found in the decision on the complaint *COHRE v. Italy*.

In this context, the ECSR stresses that Italy does not appear to be meeting its obligation to take appropriate measures against these forms of propaganda and asks the Government to provide more specific information on the measures taken to combat it, with special reference to Roma and Sinti. Also in relation to para. 4 (equality in conditions of employment, the right to membership in trade unions and housing), the Committee concludes with an assessment of non-compliance: complaining about the lack of specific information that had already been requested in previous conclusions relating to art. 19 ESC-R (*2006 Conclusions*), the ECSR finds that there is no evidence that migrant workers enjoy a treatment that is equally favourable to that of Italian citizens with regard to enjoyment of the benefits of collective bargaining and access to housing. As already noted in the decision on the complaint of COHRE, the Committee adds that forced "evictions" carried out against the Roma and Sinti from 2006 were made without due respect for the necessary procedural safeguards which, with regard to housing, guarantee these people treatment that is equally favourable to that of other Italian citizens. Furthermore, the Committee points out that, although not within the reference period, on 16 November 2011 the Council of State ruled that the so-called state of "nomad emergency", underlying the disputed "eviction" operations, was not justified and therefore the State's actions based on that reasoning are illegal (see Part IV, Human Rights in Italian Case-law, V, B). The Italian situation is also considered to be non-compliant in relation to para. 6 (family reunification); in this context, the Committee believes that the requirements related to income – applicants must demonstrate annual income from legitimate sources equal to the minimum annual amount, increased by half for each person involved in the procedure for family reunification – tend to hinder family reunification rather than facilitate it.

With regard to para. 8 (guarantees concerning expulsion) the situation of non-compliance is based on the fact that, during the reference period, the "security measures" ("security pacts" and decree on the so-called "nomad emergency") established a discriminatory legal framework against Roma and Sinti communities, making it very difficult for them to obtain the identity documents needed to legalise their residency status, thus allowing the expulsion of Italian citizens as well citizens of other European Union Member States to take place. In relation to para. 10 (equal treatment for the self-employed), the Committee estimates that while the information provided by Italy shows no discrimination between migrant employees and self-employed migrants, in the case of equal treatment between employees and self-employed migrants and between self-employed migrants and Italians, an assessment of non-compliance under one of the numbered paragraphs of art. 19 ESC-R also leads to a similar conclusion for the paragraph in question, since the same reasons of non-compliance described in other sections apply to self-employed workers. Therefore, the Committee, having found a situation of non-compliance with regard to paras. 1, 4, 6, 8 and 12 of art. 19 ESC-R, adopts the same conclusion for para. 10 too. With regard to para. 12 (teaching of the migrant's native language), the Committee's reasons for its assessment of non-compliance are on the grounds that it was not proved that Italy promotes and facilitates the teaching of the migrant workers' native language to their children.

With reference to *art. 27 ESC-R* (right of workers with family responsibilities to equal opportunities and equal treatment), the ECSR identifies a situation of compliance with respect to para. 2 (family leave) and 3 (illegitimacy of dismissal based on family responsibilities), while with reference to para. 1 (participation in working life), it postpones its conclusions while waiting for more detailed information. In particular, the Committee requests that the Italian Government specify: whether there are instruments for information, counselling and placement for workers with family responsibilities, in order to assist in the advancement of their professional lives; whether workers are entitled to the relevant security social benefits (especially in terms of health care) during periods of family leave and whether such periods are taken into account for the award of a pension and to calculate the amount of pension; the manner in which both the level of expertise of the staff in nurseries and, in general, childcare services are monitored, as well as which forms of financial assistance are made available to parents of children using these services.

Finally, the conclusions of the Committee in relation to *art. 31 ESC-R* (right to housing) have identified a situation of non-compliance with respect to all its numbered paragraphs. In relation to para. 1 (adequate housing), the measures taken by public authorities to improve housing conditions, currently sub-standard, for the majority of people of Roma origin, are considered inadequate by the Committee, which therefore reiterates what has already been said in the two decisions on complaints submitted by ERRC and COHRE. With regard to para. 2 (reduction of the status of "homelessness"), the Committee justifies its conclusions on a number of reasons: the steps taken by the Italian Government to reduce the number of homeless people are considered to be insufficient in terms of quantity (while an assessment from the point of view of quality required additional data and information); the forced "eviction" of Roma and Sinti communities continues to be carried out in non-compliance with the necessary procedural safeguards aimed at ensuring full respect for the human dignity of every individual and without providing any alternative accommodation; actions by the police in Roma and Sinti settlements were not respectful of the dignity of their inhabitants and those responsible for the destruction of the personal effects of the inhabitants of these settlements have often not been investigated or, if identified, not punished for their acts. The Committee adds that the second reason is the same one that led to decisions of violation in the ERRC and COHRE complaints (along with the third reason). In relation to the third and last paragraph (price of accessible housing), the Committee, noting that the right to housing may not be subject to any discrimination (art. E ESC-R), provides that, in certain Italian Regions and Municipalities, citizens of other States Parties to the European Social Charter and to its revised version, legally residing and working in Italy, are not entitled to equal treatment with respect to suitability for subsidised housing and access to benefits related to housing.

The ECSR adds that the data presented in the report does not show that resources have been invested with the effect of improving the practical experience of Roma access to subsidised housing without discrimination. In this case, too, the second reason is the same one that led to the decision that a breach had been committed in the two collective complaints mentioned above. Moreover, in the general analysis of the Italian situation with respect to art. 31 ESC-R, the Committee presented follow-up information on the decision issued on the 2004 ERRC complaint, indicating that for each of the numbered paragraphs, the Italian situation continues to be in non-compliance with what was decided on the merits in 2005.

The eleventh report on the implementation of the Social Charter (revised), which the Committee is scheduled to present by 31 October 2011, refers to the provisions accepted by Italy in relation to the thematic group "Employment, training and equal opportunities." It will therefore regard articles 1 ESC-R (right to work), 9 ESC-R (right to vocational guidance), 10 ESC-R (right to vocational training) 15 ESC-R (right of persons with disabilities to independence, social integration and participation in community life), art. 18 ESC-R (right to exercise an activity for profit on the territory of the other party), art. 20 ESC-R (right to equality of opportunity and treatment in employment and occupation without discrimination based on gender) and art. 24 ESC-R (right to protection in cases of dismissal) for a total of 19 numbered paragraphs (except for art. 25 ESC-R which would be part of this thematic group). Observations of the ECSR in relation to this report will be published at the end of December, in the *Conclusions 2012*.

In relation to the Additional Protocol of 1995, Italy has not yet submitted a declaration allowing national NGOs to submit collective complaints to the ECSR. In addition to the two collective complaints mentioned several times above, since the entry into force of the Protocol for Italy (1997), to date, two further complaints have been presented by international NGOs in which the Committee did not find violations: *European Federation of Employees in Public Services (EUROFEDOP) v. Italy* (4/1999), *World Organisation Against Torture (OMCT) v. Italy* (19/2003).

VI. Group of Experts on Action against Trafficking in Human Beings

The Group of Experts (GRETA) was formed in line with art. 36 of the Council of Europe Convention on Action against Trafficking in Human Beings (the Convention) and is charged, together with a Committee made up of the representatives in the CM of the States Parties to the Convention, with monitoring the implementation of the obligations contained in the aforementioned Convention.

The Group is made up of 15 independent experts known for their recognised competence in the fields of human rights, assistance and protection of victims of trafficking in human beings or having professional experience in the areas covered by the Convention.

The monitoring procedure is divided into 4-year rounds. The Group of Experts starts the dialogue with the Party under evaluation by sending out a questionnaire, which may be followed by requests for further information. If the Group of Experts deems it necessary, additional information may be requested to civil society organisations or gathered by organising a visit to the Country concerned. The draft report is sent to the relevant Government for comments. On receiving them, GRETA prepares its final report and conclusions and transmits it to the Party concerned and to the Committee of the Parties, which can adopt recommendations on the basis of the contents of the document. Each Party to the Convention appoints a contact person to co-operate with GRETA, distributing the questionnaire to the different national bodies concerned, co-ordinating their replies and submitting a consolidated version of the replies to the questionnaire to GRETA.

The first evaluation round covers the period 2010-2013 and was initiated by analysing the first ten Countries which ratified the Convention. During 2011, the Group of Experts adopted and published its first evaluation reports on the state of implementation of the Convention in: Albania, Austria, Bulgaria, Croatia, Cyprus, Denmark and the Slovak Republic.

According to the current schedule, Italy is part of the fourth group of Parties and will be included in the monitoring round together with Andorra, San Marino and Ukraine. The questionnaire is expected to be sent to the Italian contact person in the second half of 2012.

VII. Commissioner for Human Rights

The Commissioner for Human Rights of the Council of Europe is an independent non-judicial institution created by the Committee of Ministers' resolution (99)50 of 7 May 1999. From 1 April 2006 to 1 April 2012 this office has been held by Thomas Hammarberg (Sweden).

In 2011 the Commissioner visited eight Council of Europe Member States: Albania, the Czech Republic, Bosnia and Herzegovina, Armenia, Malta, Turkey, Russia, Italy, the Republic of Ireland, Serbia and the Slovak Republic.

The visit to Italy took place on 26 and 27 May 2011. The purpose of the visit was to re-examine a series of critical issues relating to the human rights situation in the Country, with particular reference to the protection of the rights of Roma, Sinti, migrants and asylum-seekers. During the visit, the Commissioner met representatives of national Italian authorities, the Chair of the Senate Special Commission for the Protection and Promotion of Human Rights, Pietro Marcenaro, as well as delegates from the ANCI (National Association of Italian Municipalities) and a number of intergovernmental and non-governmental organisations which defend the rights of the social groups targeted by the visit. The subsequent report was published on 7 September 2011 (CommDH (2011)26), together with the observations presented by the Italian Government on 5 September. The visit was the fourth to Italy by this institution. The previous ones took place: from 10 to 17 June 2005 (report published on 14 December 2005 – CommDH (2005)9); from 19 to 20 June 2008 (report published on 28 July 2008 – CommDH (2008)18) and from 13 to 15 January 2009 (report published on 16 April 2009 – CommDH (2009)16).

The 2011 report is divided into two parts. *Part I* explores the question of the protection of the human rights of Roma and Sinti, examining the following issues in detail: anti-gypsyism in political discourse; the right to housing and the practice of evictions; violent hate crimes; statelessness; overall strategies for the inclusion of Roma and Sinti in society. *Part II* focuses on the protection of the human rights of migrants, including asylum-seekers. In this section, the Commissioner analysed the following aspects: rescue operations and interceptions at sea; reception of migrants and asylum-seekers; integration of refugees and other beneficiaries of international protection. For each of these subjects, the report presents a summary of the actual situation in Italy and a number of recommendations, often referring back to the conclusions reached at the end of previous visits.

Concerning the *presence of racist and xenophobic speech, targeting notably Roma and Sinti, in political discourse in Italy*, the Commissioner noted that there were no indications that the situation had improved compared to previous observations in 2008 and 2009. In particular, he was shocked by the election posters he saw in Milan for the May 2011 local elections which contained warnings against the risk of the city turning into a "Gypsytown" (*zingaropoli*) if the candidate for the centre-left coalition, Giuliano Pisapia, were to win. In reiterating his own position against this type of political discourse, the Commissioner writes that such discourse effectively offsets the good work towards social inclusion that is carried out by civil society organisations throughout the Country, as it legitimises prejudice and discrimination towards Roma and Sinti. Hammarberg then mentions several other monitoring mechanisms of the Council of Europe which have expressed conclusions sharing his position, such as the *opinion* of the Advisory Committee on the Framework Convention for the Protection of National Minorities (see in this Part, Council of Europe, IX) and the previously-mentioned *decision* of the European Committee of Social Rights in the case *COHRE v. Italy*. In order to respond effectively to this situation, the Commissioner then calls upon Italy to take urgent action and to adopt a series of measures presented by the European Commission against Racism and Intolerance (ECRI, *The use of racist, anti-semitic and xenophobic elements in political discourse*, 2005), including: self-regulatory measures for political parties; signing the Charter of European Political Parties for a Non-Racist Society; the adoption and implementation of provisions penalising the leadership of any group that promotes racism; the establishment of an obligation to suppress public financing of organisations which promote racism, including public financing of political parties; and the effective implementation of criminal law provisions against racist offences and racial discrimination. Moreover, the Commissioner calls on Italy to commit to promoting knowledge of Roma culture and history among the general public, also through a wide dissemination and use in schools, of the Council of Europe's specially prepared factsheets.

On the issue of *the right to housing and on "evictions"*, the Commissioner refers back to the observations he presented in the previous reports in 2008 and 2009 and highlights the fact that the legal instruments adopted by the Government to manage the situation of Roma and Sinti in Italy, in particular the declaration of a "state of emergency" on nomads (d.p.c.m. 21 May 2008), has provided the bedrock for widespread evictions, often in manners that are at variance with human rights standards, as claimed in the aforementioned *decision* by the ECSR. The report also points out that the extension up to the end of 2011 of the "nomad emergency" in some Regions (by d.p.c.m. 17 December 2010) appears to have had a spill-over effect even on other Regions where it has never been formally declared. The visit dedicated special attention to the situation in Milan, which registered an unprecedented number of systematic evictions in recent times (100 just from January to May 2011). The Commissioner visited one unauthorised and one regular settlement to gain a better picture of the practical implementation of these policies and their impact on the persons concerned. The Commissioner expresses serious concern over the reported practices concerning evictions of Roma and Sinti in Italy and over the impact that these practices have on the right to housing and other human rights of the persons concerned. He urges the Italian authorities to bring the situation fully into line with the revised European Social Charter, as requested in the above-mentioned *decision* of the Committee of Social Rights. Hammarberg also recalls that the right to adequate housing includes the right to be protected against forced eviction and is guaranteed in several international human rights treaties, which are binding on Italy. Italy is under an obligation, therefore, to ensure that evictions are only carried out as a last resort and with appropriate procedural safeguards. The report adds that adequate alternative housing and compensation for all losses must be made available to those affected, that evictions must not render individuals homeless and that Italy is under the obligation to ensure that there is no discrimination against particular groups or segregation in housing. In this respect, the Commissioner draws the attention of the Italian authorities to the recommendations, general principles and legal frameworks contained in the Committee of Ministers of the Council of Europe's recommendation on Improving the housing conditions of Roma and Travellers in Europe (Rec(2005)4) and encourages them to strengthen the social inclusion element of their policies in the field of housing of Roma and Sinti, also exploiting to the full the potential offered by civil society organisations.

On the question of *violent hate crimes*, the Commissioner, with particular reference to a Human Rights Watch report on racist and xenophobic violence in Italy (HRW, *Everyday Intolerance. Racist and Xenophobic Violence in Italy*, 2011) notes how people belonging to the Roma community suffer violence at the hands of both private individuals and of law enforcement officials. In the latter case violence tends to take place during forced evictions, raids, or when Roma are in the company or custody of law enforcement officials for different reasons, including administrative procedures. In this area, prosecutions for racist and xenophobic violence are rare in Italy, and officials are reported to often downplay the extent of the problem and fail to condemn attacks. Incomplete data collection also compounds the problem, although the report notes with interest the establishing of an Observatory for the Protection of Minority Victims of Discrimination (OSCAD) within the State Police, tasked with monitoring progress on hate-motivated crimes. The Commissioner then asks Italian authorities to improve their response to racially-motivated violence, as this is a long-standing major concern of human rights monitoring bodies in Italy. He also suggests that Italy should devote attention to ECRI's General Policy Recommendation No. 11, which provides extensive guidance both on improving the response of the police to racist offences and on combating racially-motivated misconduct by the police force itself. More generally, the Commissioner considers that efforts are needed at all levels of the criminal justice system, from the police to the prosecuting authorities and the courts. The Commissioner therefore feels that action is required from the political leadership to make all those involved in this system fully aware of the need to actively and thoroughly counter all manifestations of racism and racial discrimination.

Concerning the issue of *statelessness* and, in particular, the situation of over 15,000 Roma born in Italy from stateless parents and therefore *de facto* stateless themselves, the Commissioner notes that their situation is even more precarious today as a result of two measures: the "security package" which criminalised irregular entry to Italy and staying without a valid residence permit, and the previously-mentioned "nomad emergency" legislation, which allowed the carrying out of censuses of the population of Roma settlements. In practice, the Commissioner observes, this has resulted in many Roma and Sinti living in Italy, including Italy-born stateless persons, being liable to criminal prosecution and expulsion. Among the recommendations for improving the situation, the report urges the Italian authorities to address the situation of thousands of people who are life-long or long-term residents of Italy and live there without Italian or any other nationality; it draws their attention to the recommendation of the Committee of Ministers on the nationality of children (CM/Rec(2009)13); and it reiterates the Commissioner's request for Italy to ratify the European Convention on Nationality without reservations, as the intention had indeed been indicated in the Italian Government's observations on the previous report.

On the issue of *overall strategies for the inclusion of Roma and Sinti in society*, the Commissioner notes that no progress whatsoever has been achieved since he highlighted this need in his Memorandum of 2008. This situation has been repeatedly highlighted by both international and national bodies dealing with the protection of human rights, particularly the Advisory Committee on the Framework Convention for the Protection of National Minorities (see above). On this point, the Commissioner reiterates his call on the Italian authorities to adopt and implement a national strategy for the social inclusion of Roma and Sinti. This must be drawn up in consultation with representatives and organisations from these communities, with maximum respect for the diversity of situations which exist at the local level. To this end, the establishment of a task force at the national level is suggested, which would support a network of stakeholders active in the social inclusion of Roma and Sinti at the regional and local level. In general, for such a strategy to yield long-term results, the report recommends a paradigm shift, focusing on social inclusion, non-discrimination and combating anti-gypsyism rather than on coercive measures.

Part II of the report, on *protection of the human rights of migrants, including asylum-seekers*, starts by recognising the magnitude of the challenges to human rights that the increase in the number of migrants and asylum-seekers, caused by the unrest in Tunisia and the armed conflict in Libya have created, and confirms that these challenges have a European dimension. The Commissioner reiterates his call for the situation currently faced by Italy to be met with more solidarity and cooperation at the European level. At the same time, the report stresses that Italy must abide by its human rights obligations towards all migrants, including asylum-seekers, who are subject to Italian jurisdiction. In fact, despite the commitment often shown by the Italian authorities in protecting the human rights of such people, concerns remain in some areas.

As concerns *rescue operations and interceptions at sea*, the Commissioner recognises the essential role of the Coastguard and the Border Police in saving the lives of many migrants who had tried to reach Europe on unseaworthy boats; yet he notes that over 1,500 people lost their lives while trying to cross the Mediterranean and that the responsibility for these deaths remains to be ascertained. The report refers to the investigation carried out by PACE (see in this Part, Council of Europe, I) in 2011, as well as to the widespread practice of returning migrants to the port of departure, repeatedly criticised because it contravenes international human rights law (see Part IV, Italy in the Case-law of the European Court of Human Rights).

And so the Commissioner welcomes the efforts of the Italian authorities to rescue migrants and encourages them to maintain this precious long-standing tradition. Yet at the same time he appeals to them to ensure that in all cases where migrants are in distress at sea, rescue operations enjoy absolute priority over all other considerations, as instructed by the PACE resolution 1821(2011) (see in this Part, Council of Europe, I). Still in this connection, the Commissioner urges the Italian authorities to discontinue any practices in connection with interceptions at sea which may result in migrants being sent to Countries where they are at risk of ill-treatment. Finally, Hammarberg strongly encourages the Italian Government to continue to keep the Country's borders open for people who are forced to flee from Libya and are in need of international protection.

On the subject of *the reception of migrants, including asylum-seekers*, the Commissioner encourages the Italian Government to ensure that the reception capacity in Italy for migrants is able to respond to the fluctuating trends of arrivals and variations in the number of asylum applications, particularly by expanding the accommodation capacity of the Protection System for Asylum-seekers and Refugees (SPRAR). The report also calls on the Italian authorities to ensure that asylum-seekers enjoy conditions, in all centres in which they are accommodated, which meet national and international standards, such as access to free legal aid or psycho-social assistance, so as to ensure that the currently good levels of protection are maintained even in a context of increasing asylum applications. In this context, the importance of effectively implementing special measures to identify and cater for the special needs of vulnerable people is also highlighted. Moreover, the Commissioner calls on the Italian authorities to ensure that all migrants are adequately screened in order to assess potential international protection needs. The report also reaffirms the prohibition of collective expulsion of foreigners contained in art. 4 of Protocol 4 of the ECHR, and asks the Italian authorities to ensure that all returns of non-citizens, including in the framework of the current migration flows, are fully in line with this provision.

Concerning the *integration of refugees and other beneficiaries of international protection*, the Commissioner points out that the lack of a reliable system to support their integration is one of the main long-standing concerns voiced by organisations dealing with the rights of refugees and asylum-seekers in Italy: although they are entitled, on a par with Italian nationals, to numerous social and economic rights, the lack of social networks, together with a series of shortcomings in Italian legislation and administrative practice, often pose insurmountable obstacles to their efforts to achieve self-reliance. Consequently, the Commissioner calls on Italy to devote more attention and resources to the integration of refugees and other beneficiaries of international protection, in particular by considerably strengthening the capacity of SPRAR to provide them with accommodation and services. Finally, he suggests a comprehensive review of laws and regulations that impact refugee integration, the introduction of positive action measures, and more effort to address the problems encountered by refugees who obtain Italian nationality and the excessive delays they experience in obtaining family reunification.

Among other activities of the Commissioner for Human Rights, it is worth mentioning the publication of the updated collection of all the *Viewpoints* published between 2006 and 2010. These publications were recently replaced by a new communications tool, *Human Rights Comment*, a sort of blog in which the Commissioner examines and comments briefly on the human rights situation in Europe. Over the year in question, Hammarberg published 27 *Comments*, some of which contain specific references to the situation in Italy:

– *African migrants are drowning in the Mediterranean* (8 June 2011): the Commissioner highlights the rescue activities carried out by the Coastguard and fishing boats from Italy and other Countries for the migrants fleeing Libya; at the same time, he criticises the deterrents, in particular that of returning migrants, used by European Governments to discourage their arrival. According to Hammarberg, Europe has a responsibility, which it has not yet deployed, to aid these migrants, both in emergencies and through aerial surveillance of the Libyan coast so as to prepare in advance for rescue operations.

– *Politicians using anti-Roma rhetoric are spreading hate* (28 June 2011): this comment, published following the Commissioner's visit to Italy, was inspired by the anti-Roma electoral posters on show in Milan for the May 2011 administrative elections (see above), considered an extreme manifestation of xenophobia and racism towards Roma by politicians. While pointing out that such behaviour is common to several European Countries, the Commissioner highlights the special responsibility of politicians to fight discrimination and build bridges between different parts of society, and warns that in the absence of efforts to promote the social inclusion of Roma, situations of discrimination of this type will not decrease.

– *European media and anti-Gypsy stereotypes* (7 July 2011): in this analysis, the Commissioner criticises the biased and sensationalist behaviour of certain European media towards Roma and Sinti, and voices the need to promote an ethical form of journalism and the diffusion of a code of conduct to put an end to the negative stereotyping of Roma and Sinti in the media. The aggressive language and negative stereotypes used against Roma by the Italian media, which contributed to the acceptance by public opinion of an intensification in the number of "evictions" and expulsions, are mentioned as examples of the anti-Gypsy rhetoric in Europe.

– *Judgements issued by the European Court cannot be ignored* (19 July 2011): the Commissioner stresses the importance of prompt execution of judgements issued by the Strasbourg Court to strengthen the protection of human rights in Europe and deplores the delays accumulated by some Member States; among the States most frequently criticised by the Parliamentary Assembly of the CoE on this count are Bulgaria, Greece, Italy, Republic of Moldova, Poland, Romania, Russia, Turkey and Ukraine.

– *Penalising women who wear the burqa does not liberate them* (20 July 2011): this comment addresses the general subject of Islamophobia and prejudice against Muslims in Europe, examining the ongoing debate in some European Countries about prohibiting wearing burqas and niqabs in public. According to the Commissioner, this imposition goes against European human rights standards and tends to penalise women rather than defending their best interest, and to distract attention from deeper intercultural tensions. In listing the measures currently valid in some European Countries on this issue, mention is made of the recourse made by some local administrators in northern Italy to an old anti-terrorism law in order to punish women who wear veils which cover them completely (law 22 May 1975, No. 152, which forbids the partial or total covering of one's face during public events, for security reasons).

– *Clear laws needed to protect trans persons from discrimination and hatred* (27 July 2011): the Commissioner addresses the need to afford trans persons specific forms of protection from gender-based discrimination, calling on the Member States of the CoE to implement legal reforms (including mention of transphobia in the criminal code) and measures to monitor progress in this area. When describing the prejudice and hate crimes which trans persons suffer in Europe, Hammarberg quotes a report by Transgender Europe which reported 41 transphobic murders since 2008; Italy is one of the 10 Countries in which they occurred.

– *Several hundred thousand people in Europe are stateless – They need extra protection* (2 August 2011): in his analysis of the conditions of vulnerability and marginalisation of stateless persons in Europe (approximately 589,000, according to UNHCR data), the Commissioner also mentions the approximately 15,000 *de facto* stateless ethnic Roma living in Italy (see above). From the Commissioner's viewpoint, Governments, ombudspersons, domestic human rights institutions and NGOs must act to protect the rights of these people.

– *Ten years of "global war on terror" undermined human rights – Also in Europe* (1 September 2011): on the tenth anniversary of the 11 September 2001 attacks, the Commissioner presents a critical reflection on the official responses to the attack, including those provided in Europe. Tackling the issue of extraordinary renditions, Italy is one of the Countries mentioned (together with Germany and the United Kingdom) which used diplomatic or judicial shields to keep unwanted revelations out of the public domain.

– *Public service media needed to strengthen pluralism* (6 December 2011): the Commissioner identifies the two main threats to freedom of expression and pluralism of the media in Europe in the attempts by State authorities to dominate the media market and the trend towards commercialisation and monopoly. The case of Italy, where Silvio Berlusconi was simultaneously Prime Minister and owner of the largest private television company, with consequent governmental interference in the media, is cited as an example of the problems that can derive from the concentration of media ownership in the private sector.

Finally, in 2011 the Commissioner's Office published a collection of essays on the relationship between human rights and communication and information media (*Human Rights and a Changing Media Landscape*). In the chapter on human rights and pluralism of the media, written by the former OSCE Representative on Freedom of the Media, Miklós Haraszti, the "anomaly" of the Italian radio and TV market, already examined in a 2004 report by the OSCE Representative (*Visit to Italy: the Gasparri law*, see *2011 Yearbook*, pp. 244-246) is presented as a case in point.

VIII. European Commission against Racism and Intolerance

The European Commission against Racism and Intolerance (ECRI), established in 1993, is a monitoring body of the Council of Europe specialised in combating any form of racism, xenophobia, anti-semitism and intolerance in a human rights perspective.

The members of the ECRI remain in office for five years. They are selected for their moral authority and their recognised experience in the field of combating racism, xenophobia, anti-semitism and intolerance; they act on an individual basis and independently. The Commission is composed by a member and, if a Government so wishes, a deputy member for each State of the Council of Europe.

The experts in respect of Italy are Vitaliano Esposito (actual member) and Antonio Mura (deputy member). Both will remain in office until January 2013. The External Relations Officers of the Commission Secretariat, part of the Directorate-General Human Rights and the Rule of Law of the Council of Europe, is Stefano Valenti.

In the course of 2011, the Commission published the reports relative to the fourth monitoring cycle relative to Armenia, Bosnia and Herzegovina, the Principality of Monaco, Spain, Turkey, Azerbaijan, Cyprus, Serbia and Lithuania and made visits to Montenegro, Luxembourg, Iceland, Lithuania, Ukraine, Sweden, Andorra, Denmark and Croatia.

The fourth report on Italy (CRI(2012)2) was adopted on 6 December 2011 and published on 21 February 2012. The visit to which the report refers was carried out in November 2010. As is the practice, the delegation interacted with both public officials and representatives of NGOs and from academia. Official meetings were organised by the Inter-Ministerial Committee for Human Rights in Rome, Venice and Naples; at the request of the ECRI Secretariat, an advisory meeting was held with the civil society organisations operating in Veneto, at the Human Rights Centre of the University of Padua. The previous three reports the Commission prepared on Italy are the following: report on the first monitoring cycle (CRI(98)48), adopted and published on 15 June 1998; report on the second monitoring cycle (CRI(2002)4), adopted on 21 June 2001 and published on 23 April 2002; report on the third monitoring cycle (CRI(2006)19), adopted on 16 December 2005 and published on 16 May 2006.

The fourth report covers the situation in Italy up to 22 June 2011 and takes into account the observations made by the Government in response to the provisional draft previously presented to the Italian authorities by the ECRI. These comments are published as an Appendix to the report.

In general, the Commission highlights a series of encouraging developments since the previous monitoring cycle, particularly remarking on the strengthening of anti-discrimination legislation and the progressive increase in the activities and role of the UNAR; at the same time, concern is expressed over a series of particularly critical issues such as, for example, the use of racist and xenophobic discourse in politics and in the media, acts of racist violence, legislative measures which impact foreigners and the treatment of certain social groups, especially Roma, Sinti, migrants, refugees and asylum-seekers.

The report is divided into 11 thematic sections.

Section I – Existence and application of legal provisions. As concerns the *implementation status of the main international legal instruments*, the Commission recommends, as it did in the previous report, that Italy ratify without delay Protocol No. 12 to the ECHR, the European Charter for Regional or Minority Languages, the European Convention on Nationality, the International Convention on the Protection of the Rights of All Migrant Workers and Members of Their Families, as well as the Additional Protocol to the Convention on Cybercrime concerning the criminalisation of acts of a racist and xenophobic nature committed through computer systems. In addition, remarking that the recognition of the right to vote in and stand for local elections would be a factor for integration into Italian society of foreign citizens residing in the Country on a long-term basis, the ECRI encourages the Government to extend the application of the Convention on the Participation of Foreigners in Public Life at Local Level to Chapter C of this Convention.

As concerns *constitutional provisions and other basic provisions*, the Commission asks the Italian authorities to relax the legislation on naturalisation in order to make it easier for persons who are lawfully and habitually resident in the Country to acquire Italian citizenship, in accordance with the provisions of the European Convention on Nationality. Furthermore, the ECRI reiterates its recommendation that the provisions on naturalisation be applied in all cases in a non-discriminatory manner.

As concerns the *content of the relevant criminal law provisions*, the Commission dwells on the changes to the legal framework relative to countering declarations and acts of a racist nature introduced by law 85/2006 (Changes to the criminal code in relation to crimes of opinion) which, compared to the previous law 205/1993, reduces the penalties for offences relating to the dissemination of ideas based on racial superiority, hate or discrimination and reduces its scope, in practice reducing its field of application. In relation to these changes, the ECRI recommends that the Italian authorities look closely at how the courts interpret these provisions in order to assess their effectiveness; moreover, it recommends they should amend these provisions, if necessary, in order to ensure effective protection against the dissemination of racist ideas and incitement to commit discriminatory acts motivated by hatred.

With reference to *application of the relevant criminal law provisions*, the Commission encourages the authorities to continue their efforts to improve the collection of data on the application of these provisions in order to combat racism and xenophobia, taking into account any racist dimension of an act in every stage of the procedure. The ECRI recommends the adoption of measures designed to encourage victims and witnesses of racist incidents to report the offenders, in accordance with its General Policy Recommendation No. 11. ECRI also suggests a stepping-up of efforts to educate all those involved in the criminal justice system (police, prosecutors and judges) and giving lawyers specific training in these provisions.

As concerns the content of significant *civil and administrative law provisions*, on one hand the report welcomes amendments (such as law 6 June 2008, No. 101, which provides for reversal of the burden of proof against the defendant in discrimination cases), which have reinforced the anti-discrimination provisions in areas other than criminal law; on the other hand, the Commission recommends that the Italian authorities further strengthen this legislation. ECRI also suggests that they make it easier for victims of racial discrimination to obtain access to civil and administrative law remedies by ensuring that all organisations active in this area are able to bring cases on behalf of alleged victims of these phenomena.

With reference to the *application of anti-racial discrimination provisions*, the Commission recommends that the Italian authorities step up their efforts to inform the victims of racial discrimination as to the possibility of bringing cases before the civil and administrative courts. It also requests further effort to provide initial and in-service training for members of the justice system and to give lawyers specific training on these provisions.

On the issue of *anti-discrimination bodies and other institutions*, the ECRI dedicates particular attention to the role and the activities of the UNAR and welcomes the growing number of activities and greater visibility achieved by the Office. Specific recommendations are to formally extend UNAR's powers, so that the relevant legislation clearly covers discrimination based not only on ethnic origin and race but also on colour, language, nationality and national origin; to grant the Office the right to bring legal proceedings and to ensure its total independence is secured both in law and in fact; and to increase the human and financial resources for carrying out awareness-raising activities. Moreover, ECRI highlighted the need to continue extending the network of regional centres for monitoring racial discrimination and supply the necessary resources to enable them to function effectively. The report also mentions the *Observatory on Xenophobia and Racism*, set up in the Chamber of Deputies in 2009, welcoming its desire to work in a way that is receptive to civil society, although it remarks on the lack of public awareness of the existence of this body.

Section II – Racism in public discourse. As concerns the *use of racist and xenophobic discourse in politics*, the Commission expressed its grave concern over the widespread attitude in Italy which sees migrants routinely equated with insecurity and leaves members of minority groups increasingly the subject of virulent rhetoric, also from politicians at local and regional level, who exploit this climate of hostility. These acts reflect discriminatory policies and measures which in their turn fuel intolerance, racial discrimination, xenophobia and racism within the population at large and tend to give legitimacy to these phenomena. Accordingly, ECRI urges the Italian authorities to adopt firm measures to tackle the use of such discourse in politics, as well as legal provisions enabling public funding to be withdrawn from parties which promote racism or xenophobia, in line with its General Policy Recommendation No. 7.

As concerns *racism in mass media*, the Commission stresses the importance of impressing on the media, without encroaching on their editorial independence, the need to ensure that reporting does not contribute to creating an atmosphere of hostility and rejection towards members of minority groups and that they should play a proactive role in preventing such an atmosphere from developing. On the question of the code of conduct, ECRI welcomes the 2008 adoption (by the Order of Journalists and the National Federation of the Italian Press, with the support of the UNHCR) of the *Code of Conduct concerning Asylum-seekers, Refugees, Victims of Trafficking and Migrants* (Charter of

Rome), although it expresses disappointment over the limited reach of the Charter, which only covers certain specific minority groups. The *Web and Media Observatory* set up by UNAR is also welcomed. With reference to the provisions on racial and religious discrimination in the 1993 journalists' code of conduct, the Commission notes with regret that breach of these rules is rarely punished and therefore recommends that the Government should encourage the media to systematically apply these provisions and to reword the text so that it clearly covers all forms of discrimination. Moreover, provision of special training on the role of journalism in a multicultural society is requested for media professionals, together with increased representation of migrants and people belonging to ethnic minorities in mass media-related professions.

On the subject of *racism in internet*, ECRI merely highlights the need to combat the dissemination of racist and xenophobic ideas via the internet, suggesting reference to its General Policy Recommendation No. 6 which contains some useful measures to this end.

Section III – Racist violence. In this area, the Commission recommends that Italian authorities intensify their efforts to monitor racist, xenophobic and anti-semitic incidents in Italy, considering that, as many victims are reluctant to file complaints, the real number of incidents is likely to be significantly higher than those officially registered. A specific request is made for the racist, xenophobic or anti-semitic dimension of all offences be systematically taken into account by the criminal justice system. Moreover, ECRI recommends adopting a broader definition of "racist incident", so that it is not up to the evaluation of the police, but covers any incident which is perceived to be racist by the victim or by any other person. Referring to recent violent attacks launched against Roma settlements and groups of migrants of various origins, the Commission expresses its concern over the fact that many of these incidents seem to be of a collective nature, based on the colour or ethnic origin of the victims and, sometimes, as reprisals for offending behaviour for which the victims were not responsible. Consequently, ECRI calls on the Italian authorities to unambiguously condemn all acts of racist violence and strongly recommends that they step up their efforts to prevent racist violence, also by conducting campaigns to raise awareness of the seriousness of racist offences and the fact that the perpetrators will be prosecuted and punished.

Section IV – Racism in sport. The Commission notes with interest the legislation Italian authorities have adopted over time aimed at preventing racially-motivated acts of violence at sports events, introducing stronger penalties in the event of such behaviour and setting up the *National Observatory on Sports Events*. Consequently it recommends the Italian authorities pursue and intensify their efforts, drawing their attention to its General Policy Recommendation No. 12.

Section V – "Pacchetto sicurezza" (Security package) and other measures targeting foreigners. The ECRI notes that some of the measures introduced in 2008 with the adoption of the "security package" have led to an unacceptable increase in the insecurity of foreigners without legal status and stresses its serious concern over the recent ever-increasing tendency to target foreigners with so-called "security measures", further exacerbated by xenophobic political discourse. Despite noting with satisfaction that some particularly questionable proposals have finally been dropped, the Commission strongly recommends that the Italian authorities abolish the requirement that all foreigners wishing to register the birth of a child present a residence permit, which can result in the child being deprived of official papers and at risk of remaining without legal status or, in some cases, stateless. The ECRI also recommends repealing the provision by which the act of letting accommodation to migrants without legal status is punishable with a prison sentence and seizure of the accommodation, and that the authorities make it clear that applicants for family reunion cannot be required to take DNA tests at their own expense in cases where they bear no responsibility for any doubt as to their identity.

Section VI – Vulnerable/Target groups. As concerns the *situation of the Roma people*, concern is immediately expressed over the discriminatory dimension of the "emergency measures" introduced by Italy since the publication of the third Country report ("security pacts" and the declarations of a "state of emergency" in some Regions of Italy). The Commission therefore urges the Italian authorities to ensure that all measures taken with regard to Roma strictly uphold the right and the principle of non-discrimination. Moreover, it recommends the adoption of legislative provisions at national level aimed at affording the Roma and Sinti global protection along the same lines as the measures concerning historical and linguistic minorities, following the latest recommendations of the Advisory Committee on the Framework Convention for the Protection of National Minorities (see in this Part, Council of Europe, IX). On the situation of *de facto statelessness* experienced by many Roma coming from the Balkans (see in this Part, Council of Europe, VII), ECRI urges the Italian authorities to take all measures necessary, without further delay, to allow these people to obtain identity documents enabling them to accede at least to the same rights as stateless persons, although Italy has not yet ratified the Council of Europe Convention on the Avoidance of Statelessness in relation to State Succession. Particular attention is given to the condition of the Roma and the right to housing, which has worsened in recent years. In this area the

Commission recommends that the Italian authorities firmly combat the segregation suffered by the Roma, notably by ensuring that the housing solutions proposed to them do not cut them off from the rest of society but on the contrary, promote their integration. In addition to fully guaranteeing the right to adequate housing for the Roma under Italy's jurisdiction, urgent remedies must be implemented to the health problems reported in this area by international monitoring organisations and NGOs. Furthermore, ECRI urges the Italian authorities to ensure that all Roma who may be evicted from their homes enjoy the full protection of the guarantees of international law on such matters. The Commission also focuses on the right to education of all Roma children and strongly recommends that the authorities ensure that they are enrolled in school and invites them to take all necessary measures to promote regular school attendance by these children. The Italian Government is therefore encouraged to pursue the measures already in place and is invited to strengthen its efforts to counter school drop-outs and interruptions in the schooling of Roma children, as well as facilitating their participation in secondary education. In the areas of work and health, after welcoming recent efforts to improve social inclusion, ECRI strongly encourages the Italian authorities to pursue and intensify their efforts to combat discrimination against Roma, incorporating these efforts into a comprehensive national policy and establishing an effective mechanism to coordinate these efforts at all levels of governance.

With reference to *migrants with legal status*, the Commission, noting with concern how the authorities continue to link integration with security, encourages the Italian authorities to continue their efforts to promote integration of migrants with legal status and reduce the disparity between citizens and non-citizens in the labour market with programmes such as the *Identity and Encounter* plan adopted by the Italian Cabinet on 10 June 2010.

As concerns *refugees and asylum-seekers*, the Commission reiterates its general request for the Italian authorities to codify legislation relative to the right to asylum. ECRI analyses the conditions of these groups in Italy over two different periods: *up to the end of 2010* and *following the uprisings in North Africa in early 2011.* For the former period, it strongly recommends that the Italian authorities take all necessary steps to ensure that the principle of *non-refoulement* is fully respected, and therefore they put an immediate and permanent end to the policy of pushback (*respingimento*) which they began putting in practice in May 2009. According to the Commission, access to asylum procedures must be guaranteed, in full accordance with the 1951 Geneva Convention, the European Convention on Human Rights and the relevant European Union directives. More specifically, the provisions for access to the asylum procedure need strengthening and the authorities must ensure that no decisions to return persons seeking international protection are taken without those persons having had access to assistance from lawyers and interpreters throughout the procedure. Asylum-seekers must not be deported before rulings have been made on their appeals and the exceptions provided for in Italian law to the suspensive effect of an appeal against rejection of an asylum application should be reviewed. The report considers the conditions in which asylum-seekers and migrants without legal status are kept in the three types of reception and holding centres which exist in Italy (CDAs, CARAs and CIEs) and again recommends that asylum-seekers should be detained in these centres only when it is absolutely necessary, for short periods of time and following an examination of the circumstances of the individual's case. In this area, the ECRI recommends that the Italian authorities review reception conditions in CDAs and CARAs to ensure that they meet all the needs of their occupants, both medically and socially and in terms of legal assistance. The Commission also reiterates the necessity of ensuring that asylum-seekers are not left destitute pending examination of their claims.

On the issue of *integration of people belonging to these vulnerable groups*, ECRI recommends that the authorities strengthen the SPRAR so that all potential beneficiaries of this programme are actually covered, and to strengthen its nation-wide reach.

In connection with the situation *following the uprisings in North Africa in early 2011*, the Commission notes that these events concern all European States and hence require a sharing of responsibilities. However, this does not relieve Italy of the obligation to ensure full respect for the rights of individuals coming under its jurisdiction, and so the ECRI reiterates the need to respect the principle of *non-refoulement* systematically and to take all further steps necessary to ensure that all ships under Italian jurisdiction fully respect the principles laid down by international law with respect to rescue at sea, as well as continuing and stepping up their efforts to provide adequate reception for these people.

As regards *migrants without legal status*, the ECRI recommends that the Government consider alterations to Identification and Expulsion Centres (CIEs) and the living conditions there, in particular to ensure that they are suitable for periods of detention lasting up to six months; the authorities must also ensure that all persons held in CIEs have access to the medical care they need and they should investigate all allegations of ill-treatment in these centres and punish those responsible. Greater transparency can be achieved by facilitating access to these centres by NGOs dealing with migrants and asylum-seekers.

As for *deportations under counter-terrorism provisions*, the Commission expresses regret that since the publishing of its third report, Italy has on several occasions proceeded to deport non-citizens from its territory – including under domestic counter-terrorism legislation –, despite the interim measures indicated by the ECtHR under article 39 of its rules. Often, such people were deported to Countries where torture and inhuman or degrading treatment are practised. Consequently, the ECRI urges the Italian authorities to take effective steps to prevent any deportations from Italy that might be in breach of article 3 of the ECHR (prohibition of torture) and suggests that the authorities should refer to its General Policy Recommendation No. 8 on combating racism while fighting terrorism.

As concerns the *conditions of Muslim communities*, the Commission notes with regret that anti-Muslim prejudice still exists in Italy. Drawing their attention to ECRI General Policy Recommendation No. 5, it recommends the Italian authorities intensify their efforts to combat and effectively prevent racism and discrimination against Muslims and encourages them to pursue a regular, constructive dialogue with the representatives of these communities in Italy and to reinforce the structures already established to permit such dialogue.

Section VII – Anti-semitism. The Commission notes that anti-semitic prejudice still exists in Italy, especially at times of increased tensions in the Middle East and encourages the Government to reinforce their efforts to combat anti-semitism and invites them to draw inspiration from its General Policy Recommendation No. 9 which proposes measures in this field.

Section VIII – Discrimination in various fields. In the field of education, the Commission encourages the Italian authorities to continue their efforts to ensure that no pupils suffer any disadvantage in the school system on account of an insufficient command of Italian and recommends ensuring that substitute classes for Catholic religion classes are provided in response to all requests made in accordance with the applicable rules, to ensure that no pupils suffer indirect discrimination, particularly with regard to award of credits.

As concerns *employment*, the ECRI recommends that the authorities step up their efforts to reduce the disparity between citizens and non-EU citizens in the labour market, ensuring in particular that existing anti-discrimination legislation in the field of employment is properly and fully applied, and that an awareness-raising campaign be conducted focusing on the obligations and responsibilities of employers on the one hand and the positive aspects of diversity in the workplace on the other.

On the question of *housing*, the Commission recommends that the authorities ensure that legislation against direct and indirect racial discrimination in the housing field is rigorously applied, both in the private and in the public sector, and strongly encourages them to identify best practices at local level with the aim of eliminating all forms of discrimination in this area.

In the *health* field, the ECRI encourages the authorities to continue and step up their efforts to ensure better provision of health care and better access to health care for groups coming under the ECRI remit, not only with regard to reception of patients and access to care, but also as concerns providing care appropriate to their specific situations.

Section IX – Conduct of law enforcement officials. The Commission invites the authorities to denounce publicly and unambiguously all manifestations of racist behaviours or racial discrimination by members of the police and to ensure that public statements are made that such acts will not be tolerated and will be punished, after conducting a prompt and thorough investigation. In this connection, the ECRI reiterates its recommendation that a body which is independent of the police and the prosecution services be established, charged with investigating allegations of human rights violations and racial discrimination by the police.

Section X – Monitoring racism and racial discrimination. The ECRI reiterates its recommendation that the Italian authorities improve their system for monitoring the situation of minority groups; it stresses the need to ensure that the system put in place is compliant with European standards in matters of data protection and protection of privacy. The system for collecting data on racism and racial discrimination should also take into consideration the gender dimension, particularly from the point of view of possible double or multiple discrimination.

Section XI – Education and awareness-raising. The ECRI, referring to the fact that in 2009 the new subject of "Citizenship and Constitution" was introduced to school curricula, strongly encourages the authorities to pursue and strengthen their efforts aiming to: impress on pupils the need to respect the principles of non-discrimination and of promoting equal opportunities; providing teachers with full training in these fields; bolstering the skills of teaching and auxiliary staff in schools in promoting integration and respect for diversity.

Out of all the recommendations listed in full in this section, there are three for which the Commission requests *priority implementation*: taking steps to enhance the role of the UNAR; ensuring that all Roma who may be "evicted" from their homes enjoy the full protection of the guarantees of international human rights laws; and to respect the principle of *non-refoulement*, bringing push-back (*respingimento*) operations to an immediate and permanent end. The ECRI will conduct an interim follow-up on these three recommendations within two years from the publication of this report.

One of the most significant activities of the Commission in 2011 to be highlighted is the adoption, on 24 June 2011, of the General Policy Recommendation No. 13 (CRI(2011)37). In this document, the ECRI lists a series of provisions and initiatives that they recommend Governments of Council of Europe Member States adopt to combat anti-gypsyism and discrimination against Roma. Specifically, the Commission recommends they: ratify Protocol No. XII to the ECHR and the Framework Convention for the Protection of National Minorities; deploy a national plan with a comprehensive multidisciplinary approach to issues concerning Roma, with the involvement of their representatives; enhancing mutual trust between Roma and public authorities, by training mediators from, among others, the Roma community; combat anti-gypsyism in the fields of education, employment, housing and health care; combat racist violence and crimes against Roma; adopt measures to combat manifestations of anti-gypsyism from the police and those expressed in the media, while recognising the principle of the editorial independence of the latter; combat anti-gypsyism as regards access to places open to the public, to public services and to goods and services, in particular in the banking and insurance sectors; collect statistical data on Roma while respecting their right to confidentiality and informed consent, in order to combat their problems more effectively; condemn all public discourse which explicitly incites discrimination, hatred or violence against these populations; encourage a monitoring system of expressions of anti-gypsyism on the internet and other measures such as the promotion and protection of their culture, the registration of all their children at birth and the advancement of the rights of ethnic Roma women.

IX. Advisory Committee on the Framework Convention for the Protection of National Minorities

The Committee is a monitoring body instituted pursuant to art. 26 of the Council of Europe Framework Convention for the Protection of National Minorities. It is composed of 18 independent experts with recognised expertise in the field of the protection of national minorities. They shall serve on the Committee in their individual capacity, for a period of four years.

Having ratified the Convention in 1998, Italy participated in the first monitoring cycle and presented its report (ACFC/SR(1999)007) on 3 May 1999; the opinion of the Committee (ACFC/IF/OP/I(2002)007) was adopted on 14 September 2001 and the resolution by the Committee of Ministers (ResCMN(2002)10) on 3 July 2002. The second cycle opened with the presentation of the Italian report (ACFC/INF/OPII (2004)006) on 14 May 2004; the relative opinion (ACFC/INF/OP/II

(2005)003) dates back to 24 February 2005, and the consequent resolution by the CM (ResCMN(2006)5) to 14 June 2006.

The third monitoring cycle, yet under way, opened with presentation of the Italian Government report (ACFC/SR/III(2009)011) on 21 December 2009 (see *2011 Yearbook*, pp. 227-228). The Advisory Committee's opinion (ACFC/OP/III(2010)008) was adopted on 15 October 2010 and published on 30 May 2011, after having received related comments by the Italian Government (GVT/COM/III(2011)004) on the issues highlighted in the opinion itself. The conclusive resolution of the Committee of Ministers does not appear to have been adopted yet.

The reflections in the third opinion are drawn from the information presented by Italy in its report and from other written sources and on information obtained through governmental and non-governmental contacts during a visit by the Committee to Trieste, Udine, Gorizia and Rome from 21 to 24 June 2010. The Committee found the Italian authorities maintained a constructive approach, although the State report was presented six months after the due date and no follow-up meeting was organised at the end of the second monitoring cycle. More in detail, the Committee heartily welcomed the cooperation shown by the regional and local authorities during the visit. Among the *positive developments* highlighted as compared to the two previous monitoring cycles, the Committee observes that the authorities, at all levels, have continued to support the preservation and development of minority languages and of the historical and cultural heritage of the linguistic minorities, particularly through commendable initiatives undertaken at the local level. The legislative framework for minority protection has been broadened by the adoption of regional laws which manage the protection of minorities living in their territory (for example, the regional laws of Friuli Venezia Giulia No. 26/2007, 29/2007 and 20/2009 on the protection of the Slovenian, Friulian and German linguistic minorities respectively, and the regional law No. 11/2009 of Piedmont on the protection, valorisation and promotion of the regional linguistic heritage). The process of decentralisation and the various systems of territorial autonomy established in Italy, despite some difficulties encountered, have proven advantageous for people belonging to recognised minority groups, bringing about a multifaceted and advanced level of protection in several Italian Regions and Provinces. The Committee also notes the general atmosphere of frank and constructive dialogue in the relations between linguistic minorities and the authorities, particularly at the regional level. As concerns the Slovenian-speaking minority in Friuli Venezia Giulia, progress in many areas is noted, particularly progress in the demarcation of Municipalities traditionally inhabited by the members of this minority. The Committee welcomes the *positive steps with regard to the functioning of institutional structures* set up to combat discrimination and strengthen measures for preventing and combating racism, as well as the broad range of provisions and programmes implemented by the authorities and NGOs, dedicated especially to the promotion of cultural diversity, respect for human rights, tolerance and intercultural dialogue. *Access to the media in their own language* for people belonging to linguistic minorities, especially the German and French-speaking ones, also appears amply guaranteed.

The Committee notes a series of efforts have been made, particularly at the local and regional level, to promote and increase the public use of minority languages and, although problems remain, it highlights the positive developments in the use of minority languages, particularly Friulian and Slovenian, for topographical indications and other types of bilingual signs. In the field of *teaching*, the report highlights both the existence of networks of schools distributed over several Italian Regions and Provinces, which provide children belonging to minority groups teaching of or in the minority language and the continuing efforts by the Italian Government towards bilateral cooperation with the Countries of origin in order to protect young people from minority groups through the course of their schooling. The Committee also welcomes the efforts made to promote *access to education for Roma and Sinti children* and, in this area, the implementation of programmes aiming to help reduce the absenteeism and drop-out rate of children from these minorities and systematically improve their integration into the school system. However, despite this progress, the situation of these children continues to be a cause of concern, particularly as regards the high drop-out rate after primary school and the large numbers of children still remaining outside the Italian education system. Finally, the report highlights the wide range of mechanisms available in Italy to facilitate the participation by persons belonging to minorities in decision-taking, particularly at the regional and local level.

Among the *negative aspects*, the Committee considers it quite deplorable that, although several draft bills have been submitted to Parliament, *Italy still has no legislative framework at national level for the protection of the Roma and Sinti living in Italy.* Shortcomings are also found in the application of the current legal framework for the protection of minorities; namely, the Committee finds a gap between the needs of these groups and the resources provided by the central authorities and notes that financial cuts and delays in transferring funds, in addition to the recent budgetary austerity measures, have resulted in problems in implementing the legal guarantees relating to the rights of minorities and the activation of programmes promoted by and for these communities, particularly the numerically-smaller ones. As concerns the application of the principles of equality and non-discrimination, serious shortcomings are found, with particular reference to the increasing number of cases reported to the Office for the Promotion of Equal Treatment and the Fight against Racial Discrimination (UNAR), especially towards Roma, Sinti, migrants, refugees and asylum-seekers. Still on the subject of UNAR, the Committee highlights its relatively limited reach and the need to increase the impact of its activities by providing appropriate financial and human resources for its proper functioning. As concerns infrastructures, moreover, the Committee regretfully points out the fact that Italy still does not have a national institution for the protection and promotion of human rights.

In common with other European monitoring bodies, the Advisory Committee notes with deep concern the *serious increase in racist and xenophobic behaviour in Italian society towards certain social groups*, and particularly the behaviour of institutional figures and that seen in the media and on the internet. Strong regret is expressed over the significant increase in manifestations of intolerance, accompanied by hostile and sometimes violent acts against Roma, Sinti and migrants, and the incidents of abuse and violence committed by law enforcement officers against these same people. Still focusing their attention on the situation of these groups, the Committee also expresses concern over the measures adopted as of 2006 ("security packages", decrees on the nomad emergency, censuses in the Roma settlements) and emphasises that the approach taken by the authorities is clearly at odds with the commitments undertaken by Italy with its ratification of the Framework Convention. Some of the *main concerns expressed over the Roma and Sinti* are: the absence of a comprehensive strategy at the national level for their protection, the continuous worsening of their living conditions and the degree of their marginalisation and social exclusion; the continuing placement of these people in "nomad camps" (despite the fact that few of them actually live a nomadic lifestyle), the hostility and violence shown towards them by those belonging to the majority population, and the frequent recourse to forced evictions, usually without any sort of prior consultation or information and without providing adequate alternative housing. The absence of a national body and of local mechanisms for consulting with the representatives of these communities on the provisions and policies which concern them is also highlighted. The Committee further points out *delays in the application of the law 23 February 2001, No. 38* (Provisions for the protection of the Slovenian linguistic minority in the Friuli Venezia Giulia Region). Substantial room for improvement is seen as concerns greater use of Slovenian in public, access to mass media in the minority language for all members of this community and, especially, financial support for the cultural activities and preserving adequate educational opportunities for the members of this minority. Delays and shortcomings are also found in the legal protection available for those belonging to minority groups in the mass media field, especially for the numerically-smaller groups, which experience difficulty in achieving a satisfactory presence in the media. Despite some progress, to the representatives of these groups, the use of minority languages in public life appears under-developed and insufficient as compared to their needs. Linguistic help desks have yet to be opened in some Municipalities, whereas in others, more resources are required to ensure their functioning.

On the educational front, the Committee recognises *limited progress in the promotion of intercultural dialogue and reciprocal understanding* and notes that the presence of information on the culture of minorities in school curricula is still limited. In this area, shortcomings are also recorded as to the availability of the necessary financial resources to develop teaching in the or on the minority languages and of qualified teachers and high quality teaching aids for minority education in the numerically-smaller groups. Finally, the Committee notes that the participation in decision-making at the national level by people belonging to minority groups is still too limited, even in Parliament.

In relation to these and other critical aspects identified in this opinion, the Committee lists a series of detailed recommendations for each subject examined. Among them, the following require *immediate action* by the authorities:

– adopt and effectively implement, after due consultation with the representatives of their communities, a specific legislative framework and a comprehensive strategy for the integration and protection of Roma and Sinti, which also takes into account the differences existing within these communities;

– ensure, through the adoption of urgent measures, decent living conditions for the Roma and Sinti who live in camps, guarantee them equal access to housing, employment, education and health care and bring an end to the inappropriate use of urgent security measures to address their issues;

– prevent, combat and punish in an exemplary manner all forms of discrimination, intolerance, racism and xenophobia, including that encountered at the institutional level and in political discourse; prevent and combat the dissemination of prejudice and racist expressions during sporting events, through the media and on the internet, while respecting the editorial independence of mass media;

– ensure that the current economic crisis and the consequent budget cuts do not have a disproportionate impact on the measures to support minorities living in Italy.

In addition to the most urgent issues just listed above, the Committee recommends that the Italian Government:

– continue its efforts to gather reliable statistical data on the people who belong to linguistic minorities, including Roma and Sinti, while respecting international standards on personal data protection;

– give their full support to the UNAR, allocating greater financial and human resources to enable this institution to perform more effectively and independently and establish without further delay a national institution for the protection of human rights, in line with the Paris Principles;

– raise awareness among public authorities, law enforcement agencies, the judiciary and the media on the respect of human rights and existing legislative safeguards protecting against discrimination, as well as the remedies available; promote reciprocal understanding and respect, particularly towards the most vulnerable groups and ensure that any infringement of human rights by law enforcement officers is investigated effectively and leads to prosecution and appropriate punishments;

– correct existing shortcomings to ensure access to radio and television broadcasts in their own language for those belonging to linguistic minorities, with particular attention to the needs of those belonging to the numerically-smaller minorities;

– make effective corrections to the shortcomings in the public use of minority languages, with particular reference to services provided by local authorities and bilingual topographical indications;

– adopt more effective measures to increase the availability of teachers and teaching aids for minority schooling, continue to develop the teaching of or in the minority languages, raise public awareness on minority languages and cultures including that of Roma, through educational material;

– adopt urgent measures to ensure equal access to education and significantly improve the education levels of Roma and Sinti children;

– work to make the participation of people belonging to minority groups more effective at all levels of public life and effectively promote the presence of these people in the public administration, in elected bodies and in socio-economic planning bodies;

– establish one sole coordinating body for the protection of minorities at the central Government level;

– adopt the necessary measures to ensure the effective participation of Roma and Sinti in public affairs, also establishing a body for consulting their representatives on issues which concern them directly.

In addition to the monitoring activities on Italy in 2011, the Advisory Committee on the Framework Convention adopted and published its opinions on the situation of national minorities in Austria, Denmark, Estonia, Norway, the United Kingdom, the former Yugoslav Republic of Macedonia and Slovenia; it adopted but has not yet published, in line with the principle of confidentiality, its *opinions* on Albania, the Russian Federation and the Czech Republic and published its *opinions* on Armenia, Finland and the Slovak Republic, adopted during the previous year. In the course of their respective monitoring cycles, the Committee also carried out visits to Austria, the Russian Federation, the United Kingdom, the Czech Republic and Romania.

X. European Commission for Democracy through Law

The Commission, also known as the *Venice Commission*, is the Council of Europe's advisory body on constitutional issues; it was established in 1990 and receives financial support by a law of the Region of Veneto.

Since 2009, Gianni Buquicchio has been the President of the *Venice Commission.* There are two further substitute members for Italy in the Commission: Sergio Bartole and Guido Neppi Modona.

One of the Commission's activities is the production of reports on topics within its area of responsibility and promoting seminars on specific Countries and issues. Moreover, on request from the Parliamentary Assembly of the Council of Europe, it can adopt opinions on specific issues. In relation to Italy, it is worth recalling the opinion it adopted in 2005 in the course of its 63rd plenary session (CDL-AD(2005)017) on the compatibility of the so-called "Gasparri law" (law 3 May 2004, No. 112) and the so-called "Frattini law" (law 20 July 2004, No. 215) with the Council of Europe standards on freedom of expression and pluralism of the media (see *2011 Yearbook*, pp. 229-231).

In the course of 2011, the *Venice Commission* adopted 43 opinions: 42 relating to the adoption of laws or draft bills of constitutional importance in the following Countries: Turkey, Armenia, Hungary, Bolivia, Belarus, Georgia, Ukraine, Serbia, Kyrgystan, Montenegro, Republic of Moldova, Kazakhstan, Azerbaijan, Peru, former Yugoslav Republic of Macedonia, Albania, Bosnia and Herzegovina and Russia; and one opinion on the measures necessary to improve the democratic nature of elections in Council of Europe Member States (CDL-AD(2012)005).

In addition, the Commission organised a series of seminars coming under the Campus UniDem (University for Democracy) project, which was created in 1999 in order to foster the efficiency of civil service, good governance, democratisation, the respect of human rights, the application of laws and the development of institutions. The titles of these seminars, held in Trieste with the financial support of the Region Friuli Venezia Giulia, were the following: "The independence of judges and prosecutors: perspectives and challenges" (28 February-3 March 2011); "Information, (social) media and the civil service" (2-5 May 2011) and "The Council of Europe and the European Union: shared values and standards (20-23 June 2011).

XI. Group of States against Corruption

The Group of States against Corruption (GRECO) was established in 1999 in order to monitor the compliance of CoE Member States with the anti-corruption standards and rules of the Organisation.

> The Group comprises 49 States (47 Member States of the CoE plus Belarus and the United States). GRECO's main objective is to improve the capacity of its members to fight corruption by monitoring their compliance with Council of Europe anti-corruption standards through a dynamic process of mutual evaluation and peer pressure. It helps to identify shortcomings in national anti-corruption policies, prompting the necessary legislative, institutional and practical reforms. GRECO also provides a platform for the sharing of best practices in the prevention and detection of corruption.
>
> The monitoring system in GRECO takes place in periodical cycles and involves: a "horizontal" evaluation procedure in which all members are active and ends with the preparation of recommendations on the legislative and institutional reforms required; there is then a separate "compliance" procedure to assess the measures taken by the Member States to implement these recommendations.

Italy became a Member of GRECO on 30 June 2007, after the conclusion of the second periodic monitoring cycle and was therefore subjected to a joint evaluation procedure on the provisions examined in previous years: independence, specialisation and means at the disposal of national bodies involved in combating corruption, breadth and purpose of existing immunity provisions, proceeds of corruption, public administration and corruption, corporations and corruption.

The evaluation report on these issues (Greco Eval I/II Rep (2008) 2E) was adopted on 2 July 2009.

Following the Italian authorities' forwarding of a situation report (31 January 2011) detailing the measures taken to implement the 22 recommendations contained in the evaluation document, the first compliance report on Italy was adopted on 27 May 2011 (Greco RC-I/II (2011) 1E).

According to the analysis carried out by GRECO, the conclusion is that Italy has implemented satisfactorily or dealt with in a satisfactory manner less than half of the recommendations contained in the evaluation report. Progress has been made in the following areas: enhancing transparency and efficiency of public administration, fighting money-laundering, training on corruption detection and investigation and sharing of knowledge and information between law enforcement officials.

Among the critical comments, the need to improve the level of implementation of anti-corruption measures is emphasised, especially through the ratification of the Council of Europe anti-corruption instruments (the Civil Law Convention on Corruption, the Criminal Law Convention on Corruption and its Additional Protocol). With reference to the measures planned by the Government through the adoption of an anti-corruption framework law, GRECO notes with regret the delays in the adoption of this legal instrument and the fact that the attention to certain areas (adoption of codes of conduct for members of Government, the prevention of conflicts of interest, the protection of whistleblowers and the strengthening of anti-corruption provisions in the private sector) is still insufficient.

In 2011, Italy received the third monitoring round by GRECO on the following themes: incriminations; transparency of party funding. The relative evaluation report will be published in 2012.

European Union

I. European Parliament

The European Parliament (EP), together with the Commission and the Council of the European Union, exercises a fundamental role in the promotion and implementation of the Union's human rights policies.

Among the permanent EP Committees closely concerned with human rights issues, figures the Sub-Committee on Human Rights (Italian member: Pino Arlacchi) within the Committee on Foreign Affairs (Vice Chairmen: Fiorello Provera, other Italian members: Pino Arlacchi, Luigi Ciriaco De Mita, Mario Mauro, Pier Antonio Panzeri).

The Committee on Civil Liberties, Justice and Legal Affairs (Vice Chairman, Salvatore Iacolino; other Italian members: Sonia Alfano, Roberta Angelilli, Rita Borsellino, Maro Borghezio, Rosario Crocetta, Clemente Mastella) is dedicated mainly to human rights issues within the European Union.

Other Committees closely related to human rights issues are the Juridical Committee (Vice Chairmen: Raffaele Baldassarre; other Italian members: Luigi Berlinguer, Giuseppe Gargani, Francesco Enrico Speroni); the Committee on Employment and Social Affairs (Italian members: Mara Bizzotto, Andrea Cozzolino, Licia Ronzulli, Andrea Zanoni); the Committee on the Environment, Public Health and Food Safety (Italian members: Paolo Bartolozzi, Sergio Berlato, Elisabetta Gardini, Mario Pirillo, Oreste Rossi, Salvatore Tatarella); the Committee on Development (Vice Chair: Iva Zanicchi); the Committee on Women's Rights and Gender Equality (Vice Chair: Barbara Matera; other Italian member: Roberta Angelilli) that in 2011 prepared a report on women's situation in war; and the Committee on Petitions, which is presented below.

Through reports and resolutions containing critical appraisals and recommendations, the EP dedicates thorough and systematic attention to the key human rights issues. Particularly important are the annual reports of a general nature on the situation of human rights and democracy in the world, normally adopted following the presentation of the annual report on the very same issues drawn up by the European External Action Service (for more details on the 2010 report, see in this Part, European Union, V).

In 2011, the Subcommittee on Human Rights of the European Parliament held hearings on development education (30 August 2011), freedom of the press, including the protection of journalists in armed conflict situations (2 May 2011), caste-based discrimination in south Asia (28 February 2011). It also organised two workshops, one on the role of women in the democratisation process in North Africa and Middle Eastern societies (20 June 2011) and one on "Torture and secret detentions: the UN perspective and the role of the EU" (25 January 2011). In addition, the Subcommittee published several studies in 2011, among which is worth mentioning that on Human Rights in Eastern Partnership Countries; on the Effect of Migration Policies on Human Rights in the European Neighbourhood; EU Human Rights Policy towards Russia and the European Union and the Review of the Human Rights Council.

Worth to mention is also the role of the Committee for Constitutional Affairs (the President is Carlo Casini and the other Italian members are Alfredo Antoniozzi and Roberto Gualtieri) for the part it played in the discussion of European Union accession to the European Convention for the Protection of Human Rights and Fundamental Freedoms (ECHR).

Another event to highlight is that on 21 December 2011 the Bureau of the European Parliament instituted a Directorate for Democracy Support within the Directorate-General for External Policies of the EU (DG ExPo) to streamline and give coherence to Parliament's work on promoting democracy.

In 2011, the Sakharov Prize for Freedom of Thought was awarded to five representatives of the "Arab Spring": Asmaa Mahfouz (Egypt), Ahmed al-Sanusi (Libya), Razan Zaitouneh (Syria), Ali Farzat (Syria) and Mohamed Bouazizi (Tunisia, deceased).

At the end of 2011, the process for the final approval of the annual report on human rights in the world prepared by the European Parliament Committee on Foreign Affairs had not been completed. The draft of the report contains implications for the European Union's strategic policy on human rights and places particular emphasis on aspects such as: EU participation in the activities of the United Nations, especially the General Assembly and the Human Rights Council; the fight against impunity and relationship with the International Criminal Court; promotion of democracy and free elections; dialogue and human rights clauses with third Countries; European neighbourhood policy. The draft report focuses on a series of issues that Parliament considers essential: a worldwide moratorium on the death penalty; arms control; fight against torture and other cruel, inhuman or degrading treatments; protection of human rights defenders; gender issues, with particular reference to violence against women; discrimination in all its forms; freedom of expression and social media; business and human rights.

In the course of 2011, the European Parliament adopted numerous resolutions on questions related to human rights in the EU. Among others, it is worth recalling those on: prison conditions in the EU; the EU response to HIV/AIDS in the Union and neighbouring Countries; the EU anti-terrorism policy; an EU strategic framework to help developing Countries to meet the challenges relating to food security; EU support for the International Criminal Court; the European platform against poverty and social exclusion; mobility and the integration of persons with disabilities and the European strategy on disabilities 2010-2020; the determination of a common position of the EU in preparation for the United Nations Conference on sustainable development (Rio+20); a global approach to the protection of personal data in the EU; strengthening the impact of EU development policy; the priorities and the definition of a new EU political framework on the issue of combating violence against women; the migratory flows caused by instability; the EU strategy for the inclusion of Roma; the face of female poverty in the EU; the revised Hungarian Constitution and the new media law of this same Country.

There were several resolutions concerning the violation of human rights in third Countries and certain regions of the world, referring both to general situations of violence and to violence against single individuals, human rights defenders in particular. Most significant are the resolutions on the situation in Egypt, Tunisia, Libya, Ivory Coast, Syria, Yemen and Bahrain. Attention was also devoted to more transversal issues such as the famine in eastern Africa; the use of rape as a weapon in the conflicts in North Africa and the Middle East; the situation of Christians in relation to freedom of religion; the situation in Haiti one year after the earthquake; progress in the campaign to ban anti-personnel landmines; EU foreign policy in support of democratisation.

Committee on Petitions

The right to petition the European Parliament, enshrined in the CFREU (art. 44, as well as in articles 24 and 227 TFEU) is a fundamental right inextricably linked to the European Union citizenship. The Committee on Petitions' task is to examine petitions presented by citizens and to work to resolve possible infringements of the rights conferred to them by EU law. Chair of the Committee is Erminia Mazzoni.

The report on the Committee's activities in 2010 was published in June 2011. It notes that in 2010 the European Parliament received 1,655 petitions (a drop of 14% compared with the previous year), of which 653 (39.55%) considered inadmissible. The petitions focused mainly on the environment, fundamental rights, the internal market and justice. The Countries specifically mentioned in the greatest number of petitions were first, Spain, Germany third, followed by Italy, Romania and Poland, whereas petitions referring to European Union institutions as a whole came in second place.

In 2011, the Committee on Petitions published a note on the issue *Waste Management in Europe: main problems and best practices* in which the situation in Italy, and particularly in Calabria, is taken as a case study to illustrate the shortcomings of the waste management systems. In April of the same year, the Committee launched a new tool for communicating with the public, a monthly newsletter called "PETI Journal".

II. European Commission

The European Commission has a central role in the development and implementation of European Union policies, including human rights policies, both within the Union and in relation to third Countries.

Of the 27 Commissioners, particularly important to the issue of human rights are the Vice-President and Commissioner for Justice, Fundamental Rights and Citizenship, Viviane Reding; Vice-President Catherine Ashton, who is also the High Representative of the European Union for Foreign Affairs and Security Policy; the Commissioner for Home Affairs, Cecilia Malmstrom; the Commissioner for Employment, Social Affairs and Inclusion, Làszlò Andor and the Commissioner for International Cooperation, Humanitarian Aid and Crisis Response, Kristalina Georgieva.

A vital financial resource for European Union human rights activities worldwide is the European Instrument for the Promotion of Democracy and Human Rights (EIDHR – which had a budget of 1.1 billion euros for the period 2007-2012) and which, among other things, supports the activities of the European Inter-university Centre for Human Rights and Democratisation (EIUC), in particular for the European Master in Human Rights and Democratisation. Particularly significant sources of funding for human rights are the programmes *Fundamental Rights and Citizenship* (with a budget of almost 14 million euros in 2011) and *Daphne* (over 18 million euros in 2011).

Following up on the communication from the Commission on 19 October 2010 (COM(2010)573 final) on a *Strategy for the effective implementation of the Charter of Fundamental Rights by the European Union*, since 2010 the Commission has started producing an annual report on the implementation of the Charter. The first of these, covering calendar year 2010, was published by the Commission (COM(2011)573 final) on 30 March 2011. The report on one hand gives an overview of how the Charter is being applied in the different areas of intervention of the EU and on the other, of the means and the instruments at the disposal of individuals enabling them to proceed against any violations of the Charter. The main objective of the report is two-fold: to make the safeguards and protection provided for in the Charter more effective and accessible for individuals from the practical point of view, and to identify any shortcomings in information and communications which could in the long run hinder the full development of the potential of the Charter. The report provides examples of how the Charter has been applied by the European institutions in defining policies and legislative instruments, for each of the areas of application of the Charter (dignity, freedoms, equality, solidarity, citizens' rights and justice). The most significant issues on this front were those concerning the protection of personal data, access to justice, inclusion of Roma communities and the promotion of equality.

In December 2011, the Commission and the High Representative of the European Union for Foreign Affairs and Security Policy adopted a joint communication addressed to the EP and the Council (COM(2011)886 final) on the EU approach to human rights and democracy. The objective of the communication was to open a discussion with the other European institutions on how to make the EU's external policy on human rights and democracy more active, more coherent and more effective, concentrating on four areas in particular: delivery mechanisms, integrating policies, building partnerships and speaking with one voice. The joint document from the Commission and the High Representative calls for a common reflection on the role of the EU as a world actor in the field of human rights, in the light of the many challenges which have emerged in recent years and the perception that the declarations of the EU on human rights and democracy have not always been matched by its internal and external policies.

In the context of the measures undertaken by the European Commission in response to the exceptional migratory flows from North Africa following the "Arab spring", and with particular reference to Italy, FRONTEX's operation *Hermes* is mentioned, a mission to assist the Italian authorities in managing the inflow, particularly arrivals from Tunisia, on the island of Lampedusa. The mission, which started on 20 February 2011 and was extended until the end of August 2011, covered the supply of human resources and naval and aerial support for the surveillance of the sea borders. On the basis of the operational plan drafted with the agreement of the Italian Government, FRONTEX experts assisted in the debriefing and interviewing of migrants in order to identify those entitled to international protection.

Further details on the Commission's actions are included in the section on EU law in 2011 (see Part I, International Human Rights Law, IV, B).

III. Council of the European Union

Within the Council there are the Human Rights Working Group (COHOM), the Working Party on Fundamental Rights, Citizens' Rights and Free Movement of Persons (FREMP) and the Working Group on Public International Law (COJUR), within which a sub-group devoted to the International Criminal Court operates (COJUR-ICC).

In the course of 2011, the Council of the European Union, in its various configurations, discussed many issues relating to human rights and adopted numerous conclusions. Some of the more interesting ones are mentioned below, with no claim to the list being comprehensive: the conclusions in February 2011 (6387/11) on the role played by the Council in ensuring an effective application of the CFREU; that on the management of migration from Countries in the southern Mediterranean (8909/11) in April 2011 and on immigration and asylum in the EU (10772/11). Regarding the fight against impunity and following the commitments made by the European Union at the Review Conference of the Rome Statute of the International Criminal Court (ICC) in Kampala, Uganda, in 2010, in July 2011 the Council undertook to review the Action plan relative to decision 2011/168/CFSP on EU-ICC strategy. The Action plan, prepared by COJUR-ICC, identifies five main areas for action: coordination of EU activities to implement the objectives of the above-mentioned decision; advancing the universality and integrity of the Rome Statute; supporting the independence of the ICC and its effective and efficient functioning; increasing cooperation with the ICC; working to implement the principle of complementarity. A further important area in which the Council was involved in 2011 was that of the negotiations for the completion of the Common European Asylum System, committed to be concluded by the end of 2012.

IV. Court of Justice of the European Union

For a long time, the Court of Justice played an essential role in consistently holding that human rights constitute an integral part of the Union's legal order. With the entry into force of the Lisbon Treaty, which made the Charter of Nice legally binding, the Court of Justice has taken on an even more important role in the promotion of human rights as related to the application of EU law.

Italian members of the Court currently include Antonio Tizzano as a judge and Paolo Mengozzi as an advocate-general. Up to 15 November 2011, Enzo Moavero Milanesi was a judge in the General Court, but then resigned to take up a Government position. Judge Moavero's position is currently vacant.

For the case-law of the CJEU in 2011, see Part IV, Italy in the Case-law of the Court of Justice of the European Union.

V. European External Action Service

The European External Action Service (EEAS) assists the High Representative of the Union for Foreign Affairs and Security Policy in upholding the CFSP/CSDP and ensuring the consistency of EU external actions in her functions both as President of the Foreign Affairs Council and as Vice-President of the Commission. Pursuant to art. 27 TEU, the

European External Action Service comprises officials from relevant departments of the General Secretariat of the Council and of the Commission as well as staff seconded from national diplomatic services of the Member States. The European Union is represented in the international system by a network of 136 delegations whose functions are very similar to those of embassies.

The structure of the EEAS, headed by the High Representative of the Union for Foreign Affairs and Security Policy, is structured under a series of Managing Directors (MD). Within the MD Global and Multilateral Issues is the Human Rights and Democracy Unit, directed by Véronique Arnault, which is responsible for policies and scheduling on issues concerning human rights, democracy and election observation. The Focal Point of the European Union for EU-ICC cooperation is also housed within the EEAS. It coordinates activities with the national Focal Points on the same subject and supplies them all useful and relevant information in anticipation of the full application of the Council's decision 2011/168/CFSP on the ICC.

On 26 September 2011 the EEAS published its report on *Human Rights and Democracy in the World*, which presents all human rights activities promoted by the EU in 2010 in a comprehensive and analytical manner, both as concerns its relations with third Countries and in the context of working in multilateral forums. The report also details all Union actions adopted in 2010 on specific issues and in relation to specific geographical areas/Countries.

VI. Fundamental Rights Agency

The European Union Agency for Fundamental Rights (FRA), an advisory body set up in 2007, is the main technical instrument for the EU, charged with supporting European and national institutions in the promotion and protection of human rights. The FRA achieves its mission by carrying out studies, research and surveys on a range of issues concerning fundamental rights in the EU. Director of the Agency is Morten Kjaerum (Denmark). Since July 2010 Italy has been represented in the Management Board of the FRA by Daniela Bas (member) and Lorenza Violini (alternate). Stefano Rodotà is a member of the Scientific Committee.

The FRA's research work is done mainly by collecting and making comparative analyses of data on the situation of fundamental rights in the 27 Member States of the EU, including Italy. In this respect, the FRA published several reports and surveys in 2011 in which the situation in Italy was compared with that in other EU Countries, or where it was used to build up an overall picture on a certain issue. Of these, worth to mentioning are: *Fundamental rights of migrants in an irregular situation in the European Union; The legal protection of persons with mental health problems under non-discrimination law; Migrants in an irregular situation: access to health-care in 10 European Union Member States; Respect for and protection of persons belonging to minorities 2008-2010; Migrants, minorities and employment – Exclusion and discrimination in the 27 Member States of the European Union (update 2003-2008); Migrants in an irregular situation employed in domestic work: Fundamental rights challenges for the European Union and its Member States; Multiple Discrimination report (EU-MIDIS); Handbook on European non-discrimination law; Access to justice in Europe: an overview of challenges and opportunities.*

Below is a summary of some of the reports issued by the FRA during 2011. After an introduction to each report, there are some remarks on the most significant data which emerged concerning Italy:

– *Access to justice in Europe: an overview of challenges and opportunities (March 2011).* Taking EU non-discrimination law as the reference point, the report makes a comparative analysis of the effectiveness of access to justice across the EU Member States. The chief difficulties the report found in this area were: excessive duration of the proceedings; high costs (lawyers' fees and legal expenses); restrictions on who is entitled to have recourse to the courts; highly disparate levels of remedy, sometimes so low as to dissuade the plaintiff from acting or insufficient to compensate the harm done to victims.

Concerning Italy, the report noted that out of all the cases regarding Italy deliberated on by the ECtHR (from 1959 to 2009), 70% were about the excessive duration of judicial proceedings. As regards the actors allowed to sue for redress, the report highlights the fact that in Italy NGOs can initiate legal action in the name or on behalf of the victims. Moreover, still in this area, Italy is one of the few Countries, together with Bulgaria, Hungary and Slovakia, which, under some circumstances, allows citizens and associations to present class actions. Finally, the report notes that in the Italian legal system, in proven cases of discrimination, the most widely-used form of redress is of a non-financial nature.

– *Migrants in an irregular situation employed in domestic work: Fundamental rights challenges for the European Union and its Member States (July 2011).* Based on a survey which interviewed immigrants and civil society organisations in ten EU Countries, including Italy, the report highlights some of the problems suffered by migrants in an irregular situation employed in domestic work in relation to enjoyment of their fundamental rights. Although the obstacles to actual enjoyment of fundamental rights affects all workers in this sector, the risk of falling victim to infringement of rights is exacerbated for workers in an irregular situation, who are in general not very aware of their rights and have few chances to access justice. In general, the report shows that the protection of irregular migrant workers employed in the domestic sector varies considerably from one Country to another, as do the roles played by civil society and the judiciary.

As concerns Italy, it is noted that a high proportion of the annual quota assigned for non-EU immigrant workers is reserved for domestic workers (with a high percentage of females). However, a significant number of the latter are in an irregular situation and precisely for this reason, over recent years Italy has adopted a series of initiatives to allow the regularisation of their status. According to the report, in Italy as in other EU Countries, many migrant workers are victims, because of their irregular status, of infringements of their right to a fair salary and working conditions (hours worked, time off for holidays and illness, work accident protection and minimum standards for their board and lodging). Moreover, the criminalisation of irregular migrant status, introduced in Italy's 2009 "security package", would appear to discourage the victims of ill-treatment and abuse in the workplace from having recourse to the authorities.

– *Respect for and protection of persons belonging to minorities 2008-2010 (September 2011).* The report supplies information on the situation of persons belonging to a minority in the EU, with particular reference to the risk that they run of being discriminated against in relation to employment, housing, healthcare and education. Referring to the timeframe 2008-2010, the report examines the most recent developments at the national level on the protection of minorities, giving due consideration to the impact of the entry into force of the Lisbon Treaty. Aspects such as freedom of worship, the right to participate in public life and the right to use the minority language are reference points for the analysis the report carries out.

The situation in Italy stands out in relation to the issues connected to the Roma and Sinti communities and some incidents of discrimination (subsequently declared unlawful by the judiciary) in housing (measures by local authorities designed to privilege those resident in the area for over ten years, or Italian citizens, in the allocation of council houses) and in education (a memorandum issued by the Municipality of Milan forbidding the registration in municipal day care centres of children under 5 whose parents do not have a regular residence permit). As concerns participation in politics of the members of minorities, Italy is listed among the Countries which have ratified the Council of Europe 1992 Convention on the Participation of Foreigners in Public Life at the Local Level, whereas it has not ratified the European Charter for Regional or Minority Languages.

– *The legal protection of persons with mental health problems under non-discrimination law (October 2011).* The report illustrates international and European law on fundamental rights connected with disabilities, with particular reference to non-discrimination law. It examines the different ways in which domestic law of the 27 EU Countries protects and safeguards individuals with mental disabilities or intellectual deficits from discriminatory treatment, particularly in the areas of employment and the workplace.

In relation to Italy, the report mentions law 104/2004, art. 3 of which gives a definition of disability which is sufficiently broad to also encompass mental disability. In terms of equal treatment in employment and working conditions, the report points out that Italy has not introduced the obligation for employers to identify reasonable solutions and appropriate measures so as to allow people with disabilities to have access to and perform a job, in line with the provisions of art. 5 of the Council directive 2000/78/EC. This failure, the report reminds, has led to the European Commission launching infringement proceedings against Italy and in 2011 referring the case to the CJEU.

– *Migrants in an irregular situation: access to healthcare in 10 European Union Member States (October 2011).* The report examines the regulations and practice concerning access to healthcare for irregular migrants in 10 EU Member States, including Italy. The FRA document particularly highlights the obstacles of a legal, economic and practical nature which irregular migrants encounter when they need to receive healthcare.

In Italy, immigrants in an irregular situation have the right to urgent or essential outpatient and hospital care (due to illness, accidents or maternity) in public institutions or private institutions operating within the National Health Service. In order to access this service, a card called "STP – *Stranieri temporaneamente presenti* – temporarily present foreigners" must be requested, even anonymously, at a local health authority (ASL). The card is valid for six months and can be extended. Irregular migrants, if destitute, can have access to medical treatment and medicines at special rates, on condition they present a declaration of absolute poverty. However the report found a certain disparity as concerns access to healthcare because of the different measures adopted at the regional level in different parts of Italy.

– *Fundamental rights of migrants in an irregular situation in the European Union (November 2011).* The report, based on a comparative survey of the fundamental rights situation of migrants in an irregular situation in EU Member States, illustrates the main obstacles of a juridical and administrative nature which this social group encounters as concerns access to basic services such as healthcare, education and justice. Analysing the regulations and the practice in EU States, the report shows how irregular migrants, precisely because of their juridical status, are particularly vulnerable to multiple forms of exploitation and abuse in the workplace and are also subject to discriminatory behaviour as concerns housing, health and private and family life.

In the part of the report devoted to the situation of irregular migrants who for various reasons cannot be removed from the territory of a Member State, the case of Italy stands out because of the provisions of the Consolidated law on immigration, which allows a foreigner who cannot, for practical reasons, be deported immediately, to be held in Identification and Expulsion Centres (art. 14, lgs.d. 286/1998). On the other hand, for those who cannot be deported for humanitarian reasons, Italy is one of the EU Countries which has provisions, as per art. 20 of the lgs.d. 286/1998, by which special measures of temporary protection can be extended in the event of exceptional events such as armed conflict, natural disasters or other particularly serious events. As regards access to basic services, the report reminds the reader that, although illegal immigration is considered a crime in Italy, there is no obligation for medical or educational staff to report the presence of such people.

VII. European Ombudsman

The European Ombudsman, an institution established in 1992 by the Treaty of Maastricht and provided for in art. 24 and 228 TFEU, examines the complaints lodged by European citizens about maladministration in the institutions and bodies of the European Union. Elected by the EP, the Ombudsman performs his duties with complete independence. His activities, which cannot relate to cases pertaining to national, regional or local administrations, even when they are implementing Union law, are carried out in close connection with the European Network of Ombudsmen. This is made up of the national and regional Ombudspersons of Member and Candidate States, as well as of Norway and Iceland and the national committees for petitions. The holder of this position since April 2003 has been Nikiforos P. Dimandouros, previously the national Ombudsperson of Greece.

According to the European Ombudsman's report on his activities in 2010, published in February 2011, over the time frame in question, the Ombudsman's office received 774 complaints, of which 132 from Italy (17%). In addition, according to the early information collected in 2011, it opened 176 investigations and closed 160 of them. In that same year, the Ombudsman opened 4 enquiries on his own initiative. In November 2011 a report was published on the actions taken by EU institutions following the European Ombudsman's recommendations made in 2010. Distinguishing between "critical remarks" and "further remarks", where the former are indicative of cases of maladministration and the latter of potential for improvements, the report shows that in 78% of the cases, the institutions concerned responded in a satisfactory, and in some cases even in an exemplary manner. In just one case, following a response which was not such as to resolve the structural shortcoming highlighted by the complaint, did the Ombudsman start a further investigation on his own initiative. Overall, despite some situations in which the institution object of critical remarks from the Ombudsman reacted with diffidence and limited cooperation, following the Ombudsman's work, achievements were reported in promoting and progressively reinforcing a European administrative culture at the citizens' service.

According to a survey in March 2011 commissioned by the Ombudsman and the European Parliament, the right to lodge a complaint with the Ombudsman, enshrined in art. 43 CFREU, is perceived by the majority of European citizens interviewed as one of the most important rights of European citizens, ranked immediately after the right to move freely and settle to reside in the EU and the right to a good administration.

Organisation for Security and Cooperation in Europe

Through a multi-dimensional approach to security, the OSCE (56 participating States) operates in the fields of conflict prevention, crisis management and post-conflict rehabilitation. Among its specific bodies and mechanism, is to be highlighted the Office for Democratic Institutions and Human Rights (ODIHR), the High Commissioner on National Minorities, the Representative on Freedom of the Media and the Special Representative and Co-ordinator for Combating Trafficking in Human Beings. On 1 July 2011, Lamberto Zannier from the Italian diplomatic service succeeded Marc Perrin de Brichambaut as Secretary General of the OSCE.

The permanent representative of Italy to the OSCE is Ambassador Giulio Tonini. 13 members of the Italian Chamber of Deputies and Senate also sit in the OSCE Parliamentary Assembly. The head of the Italian parliamentary delegation, Riccardo Migliori, was elected Vice-President of the Parliamentary Assembly on 10 July 2010, while Marco Mecacci chairs its Committee on Democracy, Human Rights and Humanitarian Questions.

I. Office for Democratic Institutions and Human Rights (ODIHR)

The ODIHR is the OSCE's main body charged with assisting Member States in the implementation of their human dimension commitments. Based in Warsaw and founded in 1991, the ODIHR celebrated its twentieth anniversary in 2011. Director of the Office since 2008 has been Ambassador Janez Lenarčič (Slovenia).

ODIHR activities are grouped into five macro-areas: elections, democratisation, human rights, tolerance and non-discrimination, issues concerning Roma and Sinti. One of the linchpins of ODIHR action is all the work relating to observation of election processes and it deploys election observation missions managed on a consensual basis and with characteristics which vary according to the circumstances. Upon conclusion of the missions, the ODIHR expresses its assessment through public reports. In the course of 2011, the ODIHR undertook election activities in the following Countries: Estonia, Kazakhstan, Finland, Kyrgyzstan, Albania, Cyprus, former Yugoslav Republic of Macedonia, Republic of Moldova, Turkey, Norway, Latvia, Poland, Switzerland, Bulgaria, Spain, Slovenia, Russian

Federation and Croatia. The election assessment mission for the parliamentary elections in Estonia in March 2011 was led by Cayetana de Zulueta, a former member of the Italian Parliament.

The ODIHR produced several publications in 2011, of which worth to recalling are: *Handbook on Monitoring Freedom of Peaceful Assembly; Guidelines on Political Party Regulation; The Death Penalty in the OSCE Area: Background Paper 2011*, aiming to highlight any significant changes in the situation over the period July 2010-June 2011; *Guidelines for Educators on Countering Intolerance and Discrimination against Muslims: Addressing Islamophobia through Education.* Particularly significant is the *Hate Crimes in the OSCE Region – Incidents and Responses: Annual Report for 2010.* This report, compiled from data and information supplied to the ODIHR by the Governments of the Member States, by civil society and by other international organisations, shows how this issue is still a serious problem in the OSCE region, both considering the large number of incidents and their gravity. As concerns Italy in 2010, there were 63 cases reported to the police (against 142 in 2009). Of these, 23 were classified as racist, 10 xenophobic and 20 as anti-semitic.

II. High Commissioner on National Minorities

The Office of the High Commissioner on National Minorities is the OSCE institution which is charged with identifying and seeking to resolve situations of ethnic tension in the OSCE region. In addition to serving as an instrument for preventing conflict, it can also promote rapid solutions such as to halt processes of escalation of violence. The position of High Commissioner has been held by Knut Vollebaeck (Norway) since July 2007.

Among the High Commissioner's activities in 2011, particularly noteworthy was his participation in the conference organised by the United Nations Secretary General in New York on "*The role of regional and sub-regional arrangements in implementing the responsibility to protect (R2P)*", during which the role of the High Commissioner and the OSCE as a whole acquired special importance in relation to one of the three pillars of the notion of the R2P, namely prevention. In this area, the multidimensional approach to security which characterises OSCE action, combining the concepts of prevention, human rights and security in an innovative fashion, was presented by the High Commissioner as an example of positive involvement of a regional intergovernmental organisation in R2P issues.

Highly important, too, was the October 2011 conference organised by the High Commissioner together with the UNHCR on *The provision of civil status registration for stateless persons in south eastern Europe*. On the occasion of the 50th anniversary of the United Nations Convention on the

Reduction of Statelessness, the High Commissioner on National Minorities drew attention to the situation of thousands of individuals who, having fled the conflicts of the 1990s which followed the break-up of the Soviet Union and Former Yugoslavia, have lost their birth citizenship yet are devoid of any kind of recognition in their new Country of residence. The conference produced the Zagreb Declaration, in which the participants committed to reducing the problem of statelessness and eliminating the obstacles which prevent stateless people from gaining access to civil status registration in their new Country of residence.

Over the course of 2011, the High Commissioner focused particular attention on the situations in Kyrgyzstan, Georgia, Serbia/Kosovo, Bulgaria, and Bosnia and Herzegovina. He also visited the Republic of Moldova, Estonia, Latvia, Romania, Ukraine, Tajikistan, Turkmenistan and Kazakhstan.

III. OSCE Representative on Freedom of the Media

The function of the Representative is to ensure a high level of compliance with the rules and standards on freedom of expression and freedom of the media accepted by the OSCE participating States. Similarly to the High Commissioner on National Minorities, the Representative on Freedom of the Media acts as an early warning instrument in cases of violation of freedom of expression, with particular attention to any obstacles or impediments to the activities of journalists. This position has been held since March 2010 by Dunja Mijatovic (Bosnia and Herzegovina).

As concerns Italy, in May 2011 the OSCE Representative presented a legal analysis on the bill C.1415 relating to "Standards on the subject of telephone, data transmission and environmental interceptions", already the object of an observation by the United Nations Special Representative on freedom of expression in 2010 (see Part III, The United Nations System, II, C) and a previous public declaration by the same Representative in June 2010. In this analysis, the most controversial points of the draft law are examined, considering four main fronts: 1) restrictions on reporting the content of court-ordered electronic surveillance prior to the start of proceedings; 2) limitations on the use of environmental interceptions by journalists in the exercise of their profession; 3) limitations on the publication of the contents of enquiry files, including wiretapping, prior to the opening of a trial, including documents which are not covered by secrecy during the preliminary court proceedings; 4) extending the duty of corrections to websites. Secondly, some recommendations are made to Italy, which can be summarised as follows: there should be no general restriction on publishing non-secret information of public interest obtained through electronic surveillance or relating to judicial proceedings; journalists should not face prison sentences for publishing information that is of public interest; journalists should not be required to join the National Order of Journalists in order to qualify for protections within the law should they publish communications recorded without the consent of the party; there should be no restrictions on publishing non-secret information related to court proceedings; no-one should be punished for the mere "possession" of secret information; the requirement to publish corrections that applies to print media should not be generally extended to internet sites. In a further communication from the Representative in October 2011, it was confirmed that without further changes, the draft law on wiretapping constitutes a measure which is potentially harmful for investigative journalism in Italy.

Again with reference to Italy, in a press release of 14 March 2011, the Representative on Freedom of the Media condemned the attacks and intimidation against some journalists in Italy and called upon the Government to carry out swift and thorough investigations into all the cases. Referring to the brutal beating of Fabio Cosma Colomba, a journalist for Metropolis, and the letter containing death threats sent to the headquarters of the public service broadcaster RAI in Rome, addressed to the journalists Michele Santoro, the host of the political show *AnnoZero*, Marco Travaglio, co-founder of the independent newspaper *Il Fatto Quotidiano* and a regular guest of *AnnoZero*, Gianni Barbacetto, a well-known journalist investigating corruption cases and Peter Gomez, editor of the online daily ilfattoquotidiano.it, the OSCE Representative expressed her deep concern over the climate of violence and intimidation against Italian journalists, all the more alarming in the light of the fact that these acts appear to take place in an atmosphere of impunity.

IV. Special Representative and Co-ordinator for Combating Trafficking in Human Beings

The OSCE Office of the Special Representative and Co-ordinator for Combating Trafficking in Human Beings was set up with the purpose of assisting States in the implementation of commitments and in the full usage of recommendations proposed by the 2003 OSCE Action plan. It has also the mandate to ensure co-ordination of OSCE efforts in combating trafficking in human beings. The position of Special Representative has since January 2009 been held by Maria Grazia Giammarinaro.

During 2011 the Special Representative introduced the practice of making official visits to some OSCE States, following which a constructive dialogue on the most urgent and important issues related to trafficking is opened with the authorities of the Country visited. At the end of this process of exchange and sharing of ideas, a summary report is published, if the Country in question agrees to it, containing the remarks and recommendations of the Special Representative in relation to the implementation of the Country's OSCE commitments in this field. The first Countries which have been visited in relation to this new activity of the Special Representative were the United Kingdom and Canada, in March and August 2011 respectively.

In 2011 the Special Representative published her annual report entitled *An Agenda for Prevention: Activities and Challenges in 2011*, also containing an in-depth study on the trafficking of human beings for labour exploitation.

International Humanitarian and Criminal Law

I. Adapting to International Humanitarian and Criminal Law

Italy is party to all the main international conventions on the law of armed conflict and international criminal law. With law 14 June 2011, No. 95, Italy ratified the Oslo Convention banning Cluster Munitions, adopted in Dublin on 30 May 2008. The text of the law of ratification, which gives full and complete execution to the Convention, designates the Ministry of Defence as the authority responsible for the destruction of the stockpiles of cluster munitions still held by the Armed Forces, while the Ministry of Foreign Affairs is the national authority responsible for presenting the initial report (due by 28 August 2012) to the Secretary General of the United Nations and the periodical reports as per art. 7 of the Convention, as well as receiving and presenting any requests for clarification as per art. 8 of the same. Moreover, as per art. 9 of the Convention, which obliges States Party to take all measures necessary to implement the Convention, including establishing penal sanctions to punish any activities forbidden by the Convention, law 14 June 2011, No. 95 punishes anyone who uses, develops, produces, or otherwise acquires, stockpiles, retains or transfers, directly or indirectly, cluster munitions or parts of the same, or assists, including financial assistance, encourages or induces others to engage in such activities, with imprisonment from three to twelve years and fines from euros 258,228 to euros 516,456. This same law allocates part of the Fund for humanitarian mine clearance, set up by law 7 March 2001, No. 58, to carrying out programmes for clearing areas with residual cluster munitions and to offering assistance programmes for cluster munitions victims. The funding for the munitions disposal was set at 500,000 euros for 2011, 2,006,400 euros for 2012 and 2,000,000 euros for each year from 2013 to 2015.

It should be remembered that at the end of 2011, in the context of the IV Review Conference on the United Nations Convention on Prohibitions or Restrictions on the Use of Certain Conventional Weapons Which May be Deemed to be Excessively Injurious or to Have Indiscriminate Effects (1980), the negotiations as to the possibility of adopting a sixth Additional Protocol on the use of cluster munitions were definitively closed. After four years of debate, the negotiation was definitively closed due to the opposition expressed by the majority of the States present at the Review Conference. It should be pointed out that the Protocol, sponsored by the largest producers and users of cluster munitions who remained non-signatories to the Oslo Convention, received the support of 12 States, including Italy, despite their having ratified the Convention banning Cluster Munitions.

2011 saw the continuation of the parliamentary process introducing provisions for the adaptation of the domestic legal order to the Statute establishing the International Criminal Court. On 8 June 2011 the Chamber of Deputies approved the consolidated draft bill (C.1439-A), then passed to the Senate for examination. The legislative proposal, an amalgam of several parliamentary initiatives presented in 2008-2009, ignoring the part relative to substantial criminal law, is limited to considering the procedural aspects relative to the relationship between Italian jurisdiction and that of the Court. Indeed all the bill does is regulate the judicial cooperation and the domestic implementation of the decision of the international court. Specifically, it regulates the procedure for the handing over to the ICC of people present on Italian soil, after the issue by the Court of an arrest warrant or a prison sentence, and also considers the implementation of criminal fines and the applicable procedure should Italy be identified by the International Criminal Court as the Country where a prison sentence should be served. It is interesting to note how the need to accelerate the legislative process of the bill derived from the deterioration of the situation in Libya in 2011 and the arrest warrants issued by the Court at that time at the request of the Prosecutor Luis Moreno-Ocampo. Indeed, in the absence of the necessary legal provisions, Italy's capacity to satisfy requests for cooperation from the Court could have proven somewhat problematic.

In order to follow up on the developments of an important issue involving Italy which is thematically close to the subject considered here, it is useful to recall that in September 2011 hearings were held before the International Court of Justice (ICJ) on the case which Germany brought against Italy for infringement of the jurisdictional immunity of States, after Italian judges had issued enforcement measures against German State property to pay damages to some Italians deported to Germany during World War II. In July of the same year the ICJ had authorised the Greek State to intervene in the case, in accordance with art. 62 of the Statute of the Court. Greece's legal interest in intervening in the case derived from the fact that the complaints made by Germany against Italy included the execution by Italian courts of sentences issued by Greek courts, which could not be implemented in the home Country, aiming to secure compensation to Greek citizens in relation to violations suffered at the hands of the Third Reich in the Hellenic Republic.

II. The Italian Contribution to Peace-keeping and Other International Missions

In 2011, with two law-decrees converted into law by Parliament (l.d. 20 December 2010, No. 228 converted by law 22 February 2011 No. 9 and l.d. 12 July 2011, No. 107, converted by law 2 August 2011, No. 130), Italy financed the extension of the participation of Italian military and civilian personnel in international missions. Whereas the first decree, predating the start of hostilities and the intervention of the international community in Libya, still refers to the participation of the *Guardia di Finanza* (Italy's military corps specialising in customs, excise and tax issues) in the mission planned under the Italian cooperation agreement with Libya on combating illegal immigration and people-trafficking, in the second, the Italian State makes the necessary provisions for the implementation of resolutions 1970 (2011) and 1973 (2011) of the United Nations Security Council.

It seems important to remember here that the intervention of the international community in Libya was marked by two separate stages. The first stage of the intervention, which started on 19 March 2011 and was codenamed *Operation Odyssey Dawn*, saw the participation of a coalition of States including France, the United Kingdom, the United States, Denmark, Norway, Canada, Belgium and Italy. Italy mobilised men and equipment from the Air Force and the Navy, supplying the coalition with the logistics and strategic support of seven air bases (namely Trapani, Gioia del Colle, Sigonella, Decimomannu, Aviano, Amendola and Pantelleria). In addition to giving air support and the naval complement, Italy hosted the command and control centre of coalition operations at Naples Capodichino airport. The second stage of the intervention, which began on 23 March 2011, saw NATO take command of the mission which until then had been managed by the international coalition. On 30 March 2011 *Operation Unified Protector* began, and command passed to the Canadian General Charles Bouchard. From the Joint Force Command (JFC) in Naples, he took control of the air and sea missions, while the units of the SNMG2 (*Standing NATO Maritime Group 2*), under Rear Admiral Gualtiero Mattesi, were charged with ensuring the respect of the naval arms embargo. *Operation Unified Protector*, which lasted about seven months, ended, in line with the North Atlantic Council mandate, at midnight on 31 October 2011.

As concerns Italy's operational contribution to the international mission in Libya, Italian aeroplanes flew 1,182 missions for reconnaissance, aerial defence and supply, deploying a broad range of equipment and planes. The Navy, in addition to contributing to air missions, participated with numerous different types of vessels, in the naval embargo and the patrol and supply operations. The Ministry of Defence also contributed to 11 missions transporting medical supplies and evacuating the wounded. In accordance with l.d. 12 July 2011, No. 107, the cost of Italy's participation in the Libyan mission for the period July-December 2011 was 58 million euros.

The same law-decree also contains measures for combating piracy (art. 5), including the possibility of the Ministry of Defence stipulating conventions with Italian shipping companies for the protection of Italian ships in transit in international waters at risk from piracy (areas subsequently defined in a Ministry of Defence decree dated 1 September 2011), and which would see the presence on board the vessels, on request and at the expense of the shipowners, of Navy Military Protection Units (NMP). These units are made up of 6 trained and specially-equipped navy personnel whose duty it is to guarantee, in full autonomy, the direct protection of the ships from acts of piracy or armed plundering. As concerns the fight against crimes of piracy described in the shipping code, provision is made for the Commander of each unit and relative subordinates to be considered officers and agents of criminal police investigation departments. Moreover, as is the case with other international missions, the applicable legislation is that of the peacetime military criminal code. Following the memorandum of understanding signed on 11 October 2011 between the Ministry of Defence and the Italian Shipowners' Confederation (CONFITARMA) and the subsequent requests from some shipowners, the first NMP, out of the total of 10 planned for, have begun duties on Italian merchant navy ships.

As concerns the presence of women in international peace-keeping and cooperation missions, reference should be made to Italy's National action plan on "Women, Peace and Security" 2010-2013 adopted by the Ministry for Foreign Affairs in December 2010. The Action plan, adopted in accordance with the United Nations Security Council resolution 1325 (2000) of the same name, in addition to introducing actions aiming to promote the inclusion of the gender dimension in all sectors of peace policies, commits Italy to giving more value to the presence of women in the national armed forces, thus consolidating the inclusion of the female quota in peace-keeping missions and in the related decision-making bodies. The most recent data available from the Ministry of Defence show that the number of women in the Army make up 6.5% of the forces (6,942 out of 106,785), 3.95% in the Navy (1,076 out of 43,910), 1.97% in the Air Force (809 out of 43,148) and 0.97% in the *Carabinieri* (military police) (1,067 out of 109,597).

The following list shows the military and police missions in which Italy participated with its own forces in the course of 2011. The largest mission, that in Afghanistan, had a budget of over 780 million euros and saw 4,200 staff present.

Country/Geographic Area of Intervention	Italy's Mission and Activities
Afghanistan	International Security Assistance Force (ISAF) (military and police component)
	EUPOL AFGHANISTAN (military and police component)
Lebanon	United Nations Interim Force in Lebanon (UNIFIL), which includes the use of naval units in the UNIFIL Maritime Task Force
Kosovo/Balkans	Multinational Specialised Unit (MSU) of KFOR (NATO), in support of the European Union Rule of Law Mission in Kosovo (EULEX Kosovo)
	Operation Joint Enterprise (NATO) Security Force Training Plan in Kosovo
	Cooperation programmes of Italian police forces in Albania and in the Countries of the Balkan area
	Participation of State Police officers, judges, prison police and administration officers to the mission EULEX Kosovo
	Participation of State Police officers to the United Nations Mission in Kosovo (UNMIK)
Bosnia-Herzegovina	Integrated Police Unit (IPU) in the framework of the European Union ALTHEA operation
	Participation of officers from the *Arma dei Carabinieri*, the State Police and the Judiciary in the European Union Police Mission (EUPM)
Eastern Mediterranean	Mission Active Endeavour in the Mediterranean (NATO)
Occupied Palestinian territories	Temporary International Presence in Hebron (TIPH2);
	Participation of State Police officers and of a judge to the European Union Police Mission for the Palestinian Territories (EUPOL COPPS)
Occupied Palestinian territories/Egypt	European Union Border Assistance Mission in Rafah (EUBAM Rafah)
Sudan	United Nations/African Union Mission in Darfur (UNAMID)
Democratic Republic of the Congo	Mission EUPOL RD CONGO
Cyprus	United Nations Peacekeeping Force in Cyprus (UNFICYP)
Albania	Italian Delegation of Experts – activity in support of the Albanian armed forces
Georgia	European Union Monitoring Mission in Georgia – EUMM Georgia (extended until 30 September 2011)
Somalia/Indian Ocean	European Union ATALANTA military mission
	NATO operation to combat piracy
Iraq	Consulting, education and training activities for Iraqi armed and police forces

United Arab Emirates	Air Task Force in support of the operations in Afghanistan and Iraq (Abu Dhabi, Bahrain and Tampa – USA)
Haiti	Participation of officers from the *Arma dei Carabinieri* to the United Nations Stabilisation Mission in Haiti (MINUSTAH)
Somalia-Uganda	Participation to the European Union Training Mission to contribute to the training of Somali security forces (EUTM SOMALIA) (activities in Uganda and Kenya)
Libya	Participation of officers from the *Guardia di Finanza* (Financial Police) to the mission in Libya, in order to guarantee the ordinary maintenance and the efficiency of the naval units given by the Italian Government to the Libyan Government, implementing the cooperation agreements signed by the Italian Republic and the Great Socialist People's Libyan Arab Jamahiriya, in order to face the phenomena of illegal immigration and of trafficking in human beings (extended until 30 June 2011 but then suspended after the break out of the war) Military operation implementing measures to protect civilians and civilian populated areas under threat of attack in the Libyan Arab Jamahiriya as well as to enforce compliance with the ban on flights in the airspace of the Libyan Arab Jamahiriya and the arms embargo established by the UN Security Council resolutions 1970 (2011) and 1973 (2011) (until 30 September 2011)
Afghanistan and other States	Participation of officers from the *Guardia di Finanza* (Financial Police) to the Joint Multimodal Operational Units (JMOUs) established in Afghanistan, United Arab Emirates and Kosovo

Part IV

National and International Case-law

Human Rights in Italian Case-law

Part IV presents a selection of the case-law of the Constitutional Court, the Court of Cassation and the Administrative Courts (Council of State and the regional administrative courts [TARs]), as well as a selection of judgements of ordinary courts, published during 2011. This Part also presents the cases ruled by the European Court of Human Rights (ECtHR) in which Italy was the defendant, and some other cases directly related to Italy decided by the Court of Justice of the European Union (ECJ).

Continuing the approach taken in the *2011 Yearbook*, the selection of issues and related law cases handled by the Italian courts does not purport to be exhaustive. It mainly focuses on decisions in which explicit reference is made to international human rights law and in particular to the European Convention on Human Rights (ECHR). Accordingly this section is divided into three parts – one devoted to Italian case-law, one devoted to Italy before the Strasbourg Court and a third part devoted to the ECJ. All three parts are closely related to one another.

In 2011 too the positive trend continued in domestic courts, starting with the Constitutional Court, to resort extensively and expressly to sources of international human rights law. International norms are applied, both independently and as "intermediate rules" integrating the parameter of constitutionality under which to verify the legitimacy of domestic piece of legislation. As for the so called "communitarisation" of international standards on human rights, that is their integration into European Union law as a result of the entry into force of the Lisbon Treaty, the situation did not seem different from that described in the *2011 Yearbook*. It is established case-law in Italy that the dispositions of the ECHR and of other international instruments are well suited to supplement the content of domestic laws. In case of inconsistency, the international rule overrides the domestic one by virtue of art. 117 (1) of the Constitution. The Constitutional Court declares unconstitutional a domestic law provision on grounds of breach of art. 117(1) only if it finds it impossible to reach an interpretation of the domestic rule consistent with the international norms. Here the international rule functions as an "intermediary" rule in judging the constitutionality of the domestic norm. On the other hand an ordinary court is not allowed, at present, to disapply a domestic rule that directly contradicts the norm of an international treaty on human rights, asserting its virtual incorporation into EU law. To have the domestic law removed, the court has to raise the question of constitutionality.

In this first section, after a summary of recent Italian case-law on the "communitarisation" of international rules on human rights, this Part the following issues will be dealt with: legislation interpreting retroactively and *in pejus* norms in spite of settled case-law and international standards; human dignity and issues of bio-law, asylum and international protection; discrimination; the right to work as a human right; immigrants' human rights; issues relating to criminal law and detention; rights of children and adolescents; rights of persons with disabilities and non-autonomous individuals; property rights and rules governing expropriation; reasonable duration of trials and mediation in civil disputes; mayors' power to issue ordinances and the principle of legality; foreign States' immunity from Italian jurisdiction and binding principles of international law.

I. The "Communitarisation" of International Human Rights Standards: Issues Concerning Public Hearings and Statute of Limitations

Concerning the relationship between Italian law and international human rights law, once the Lisbon Treaty entered into force and the provisions of the Charter of Fundamental Rights (CFREU) became legally binding, the case-law of the Court of Cassation and of the Constitutional Court continued in 2011 on the same course that they had already entered the previous year (see *2011 Yearbook*, pp. 256-261). Particularly interesting in this regard is judgement 80/2011. The Court's decision harmonises with the earlier judgement 93/2010, which had already found unconstitutional, in light of art. 6 ECHR and related ECtHR case-law, the rules which required that certain interim measures directed against members of mafia gangs and their assets, should be adopted without any public hearing. Having found those provisions allowing for an *in camera* procedure at trial and on the appeals level unconstitutional, the Constitutional Court must now decide whether this principle should also apply to proceedings held before the Court of Cassation. In its reasoning, the Constitutional Court reconstructs briefly the role of "intermediate rules" of the ECHR provision in relation to art. 117 (1) of the Constitution ("Legislative power shall be vested in the State and the Regions in compliance with the Constitution and the constraints deriving from EU legislation and international obligations"). According to the Constitutional Court, "the safeguarding of fundamental rights within the EU arises (or will arise) from three distinct sources: firstly from the CFREU [...] secondly, from the ECHR, as a result of the European Union's accession thereto, and finally from 'general principles', which [...] include the rights enshrined in the ECHR itself and those emanating from the constitutional traditions common to the Member States". It follows that the ECHR is not directly applicable as EU law within each domestic legal system, because the EU has not yet acceded to the ECHR. Moreover, CFREU rules that match those of the ECHR – and the rules of the latter, once the EU shall have acceded to that international instrument – cannot affect the division of competences between Member States and EU institutions. "The precondition for the applicability of the Nice Charter is, therefore, that the facts of the case submitted to the court's scrutiny be governed by European law [...] and not only by domestic laws unconnected to European law." Finally, concerning the relevance of "general principles" regarding human rights that can validly be concluded from the ECHR and from the various legal traditions of the Member States, their close relevance to the matters covered by EU law is explicitly set forth in art. 6 of the Treaty on European Union (TEU). Accordingly, they cannot govern – as provisions of EU law – situations exclusively governed by domestic law. In conclusion, the Constitutional Court holds that the provisions of the ECHR can exert an effect on the procedure employed for devising precautionary measures for individuals connected to the mafia, only as "intermediate rules" in relation to art. 117 (1) of the Constitution. It is unacceptable though that the Italian judge simply refrains from applying domestic laws that conflict with art. 6 ECHR, as if such provision were EU law, regulating EU matters. A judge should instead raise the question of constitutionality and refer back to the assessment made by the Constitutional Court (as was actually done). In this case, the Constitutional Court held that in the Court of Cassation's judgement, which is limited to questions of legality, the ECHR and ECtHR case-law do not require that the hearing be public, and therefore the current Italian legislation in this issue is not unconstitutional.

A similar argument, regarding the reconstruction of the relationship between domestic law and international and European laws on human rights, is set forth in the Constitutional Court's judgement 236/2011. Judges discussed the legality of the provisions of the law of 5 December 2005, No. 251 that precluded the application of rules regarding the time-barring of offences, more favourable to defendants, in appellate proceedings or before the Court of Cassation (see *2011 Yearbook*, pp. 290-291). The rule requiring retroactive effect of any criminal provision favourable to the defendant is held by recent ECtHR case-law to reflect the principle of non-retroactivity of substantive criminal law (art. 7 ECHR, see in particular, the judgement in *Scoppola v. Italy* (No. 2) of 2009). Art. 7 ECHR, in turn, finds its counterpart in art. 15 (1) of the International Covenant on Civil and Political Rights and is repeated almost *verbatim* in art. 49 CFREU, which likewise reiterates: "If, subsequent to the committing of a criminal offence, the law provides for a lighter penalty, that penalty shall be applicable." The result is a strong drive to see the retroactive application of the law most favourable to defendants, even in domestic law, as an integral part of the principle of legality. International standards in this case even overreach the mandate of art. 25 (2) of the Italian Constitution (which merely forbids retroactive application of punitive rules), and rather restate the general principle set forth in art. 2 (3) of the Italian criminal code. The recent Italian acts shortening the statute of limitations prove in fact to favour the defendant and one can rightfully ask whether they should not be applied to all pending cases, including those that have passed the trial stage. In its judgement, the Constitutional Court, before addressing the merits of the issues, summarises the essential elements of the debate concerning the status of ECHR rules in the Italian legal system and the manner in which they operate as "intermediate rules" with regard to art. 117 (1) of the Constitution. The Court outline the bulk of the arguments discussed in judgement 80/2011. On the merits, in this case too the Constitutional Court upholds an interpretation of Italian legislation at variance with what can be concluded from a perusal of ECtHR case-law. The Constitutional Court notes that, in accordance with recent rulings of the Strasbourg Court, the *lex mitior* (more favourable to the individual) that must entail retroactive effects only is substantive law (the field to which the letter of art. 7 ECHR and of art. 49 CFREU refers). Laws governing criminal procedure do not necessarily apply retroactively, even if they are more favourable to the defendant. When fashioning procedural rules – and consequently also limitation periods – States have wide discretion. Namely, the *favor rei* principle can encounter restrictions in the principles of certainty of judgement, *res judicata*, efficiency of the criminal justice system, and of the protection of the rights and expectations of the persons affected by court decisions (for example, victims of crime). It follows that the provisions of law 251/2005 that place certain limits on the retroactivity of the new statute of limitations do not conflict with art. 7 ECHR and therefore do not breach art. 117 (1) of the Constitution.

The issue was also addressed in order No. 314/2011 of the Constitutional Court, and in judgement No. 46884/2011 of the Court of Cassation. In both cases the courts followed the interpretation set forth by the Constitutional Court in its judgement 236/2011.

The domestic judge cannot waive application of domestic laws conflicting with the ECHR or other international standards other than those of EU law. Furthermore the domestic judge cannot refrain from applying EU secondary law (or request that laws ratifying the EU treaties be ruled unconstitutional) when the latter conflict with other international sources of law. The Council of State (case 4723/2011) stated that, while recognising that the application of EU law by domestic courts encounters the constraints posed by the supreme principles of the Italian Constitution, and that accordingly certain EU secondary law dispositions may be ruled unconstitutional, it should be stressed that a conflict between EU law and other rules of international law (such as those generated by the World Trade Organisation) does not abrogate the European law that the domestic court must apply, nor can it lead to a constitutionality case under domestic law, but will only give rise to the international responsibility/liability of the State and/or of the EU. The same judgement implies that as long as the EU does not accede to the ECHR, direct application of ECHR rules in the guise of EU law is out of the question. Court of Cassation decision 13603/2011 moreover states that it is the court that must decide whether or not to ask the ECJ for a preliminary ruling on the issue of applicability of a domestic law that appears inconsistent with human rights as recognised in the ECHR and the EU law, and that such choice always depends on the impossibility of finding, in a specific case, an interpretation reconciling the national and the EU provisions.

For a decision of a trial court that incorporates the reading endorsed by the Constitutional Court of the relationship between Italian law and international human rights standards, see the order issued by the Court of Tivoli on 1 March 2011.

One might cite in this connection the judgement of the Court of Cassation in a case partially adjudicated by the ECtHR. During the 1996 election campaign, a newspaper had published a politician's statements about another candidate that the latter denounced as defamatory. The criminal case lodged by the offended party had been dismissed, since the Senate had invoked parliamentary immunity (art. 68 of the Constitution), without the judge raising any controversy between branches of the State. The party then filed a civil action and, in parallel, a complaint was filed before the ECtHR that claimed a breach of art. 6 ECHR. On 3 June 2004 the ECtHR issued a judgement (*De Jorio v. Italy*) in which it discerned a disproportionate restriction of the right of access to the courts. The judgement entered in 2002 at the trial of the Italian civil case recognised the immunity granted by the Senate but, on the merits, denied that the statements were defamatory, holding them to be within the bounds of political polemic. An appeal ruling in 2005 fully upheld the trial judgement, expressly denying any relevance to the ECtHR's ruling. The Court of Cassation overturned the Court of Appeal's judgement on the issue of the ECtHR's relevance, stating that "a final ruling by the European Court of Human Rights is immediately enforceable as a domestic judgement." It followed that, even for an Italian court, the immunity granted by art. 68 of the Constitution had no relevance for the judicial determination of the case. Nevertheless, the Court of Cassation held that once defined the case as merely a dispute between two ordinary citizens, it needed not alter its findings: there was no defamation and accordingly it dismissed the claim for damages.

II. Authentic Interpretation Affecting *in pejus* Settled Case-law, and the Principle of Fair Trial

Some cases on which the Constitutional Court or the Court of Cassation ruled, involved the issue of whether certain legislation complied with the principle of fair trial (art. 6 ECHR) and, more generally, with the rule of law. Some legislation, purported as "authentic interpretation" of existing laws, contradicted the case-law that had accumulated over the preceding years and was therefore received as impinging upon the "law in action".

The Constitutional Court (case 1/2011) dealt with the issue of the legality of certain provisions of the 2007 Budget Act (law 296/2006) which contained an authentic interpretation (having retroactive effect) of certain provisions of law 8 August 1995, No. 335 (Reform of the pension system and complementary measures), with the result that an individual entitled to a survivor's pension in the public sector would be paid only 60% of the special supplementary allowance (part of the total pension payment), instead of 100%. On this issue, however, before the legislator intervened, case-law had accumulated that predominantly held that workers who retired on survivors' pensions before the reforms of 1994-1995 were entitled to the entire special supplementary allowance. The Unified Sections of the Court of Cassation upheld this doctrine in a 2002 ruling. The 2006 law therefore harmed survivors' pensioners, with the sole exception of those who had in the meantime obtained a final judgement on the point in their favour. Regarding the constitutionality of the statute of authentic interpretation, the Constitutional Court had itself issued rulings concerning this law in 2008 and 2010. In both cases it held the legislative measure not to be unreasonable. However, the issue of the statute's possible unlawfulness on grounds of breach of art. 6 ECHR as an "intermediate rule" had not yet been broached. The issue under analysis concerned in particular the non-compliance with the "equality of weapons" principle, when a private citizen and the Government stand before the judge, and the latter takes advantage of the new interpretative law. The judgement 1/2011 affirms that the Parliament, in exercising its constitutionally guaranteed duties, may enact laws of authentic interpretation. These differ from laws that innovate and reform previously enacted provisions, in that they are capable of exerting retroactive effects and thus they must apply also in pending law cases. Such retroactive effects need not breach the fair trial principle (art. 6 ECHR), provided that the Parliament is impelled to enact such statutes by "imperative grounds of national interest". The Parliament itself must determine the cogency of the grounds for enacting such statutes on a case-by-case basis. In this particular case, the pension reform of 1995 was intended to harmonise and equalise the various pension regimes (in particular by eliminating certain measures that favoured public employees over those of private companies) and to attain the commitments necessary for the introduction of the single European currency.

The judgement 17076/2011 of the Unified Sections of the Court of Cassation addresses another case elicited by a law of authentic interpretation: that of the l.d. 31 May 2010, No. 78, converted into law, with amendments, with law of 30 July 2010, No. 122 (Urgent measures concerning financial stabilisation and economic competitiveness), amending certain social security provisions contained in the 1997 Budget Act. Art. 1 (208) of that statute provided that people who had more than one job must pay their pension contributions to the pension scheme in charge of their "main line of business". However, it was doubtful whether that rule should also apply to taxpayers who run their own businesses and at the same time hold a temporary job as salaried employees, or instead their registration to the separate pension fund of the National Institute of Social Insurance (INPS) was compulsory. The issue generated extensive litigation and was settled in terms of case-law by a ruling of the Unified Sections of the Court of Cassation of 2010, which adopted the prevalence criterion for this sort of situation. The 2010 statutory exposition, however, reversed this approach, immediately affecting the proceedings still pending between individuals and INPS. The decisions reached in these proceedings were at odds with the "law in action" developed by case-law before the legislator intervened. A new ruling, No. 17076/2011 of the Unified Sections of the Court of Cassation, takes note of the meaning that must henceforth be attributed to the 1996 law, acknowledging the genuinely interpretative nature of the 2010 law, which in effect assigns to the statute one of the possible meanings attributable to it, without altering its scope. As to the possible conflict with art. 6 ECHR, the Court of Cassation merely noted that Parliament enacted the law in question in accordance with art. 70 of the Constitution ("The legislative function is exercised collectively by both Houses"), a rule of constitutional standing whose contents prevail, "in the balancing of values, on those expressed by intermediate parameters [i.e. art. 6 ECHR], which, being contained in ordinary statutes (such as the law ratifying the ECHR [...]), are subordinate within the system of the sources of law."

It seems that the legal arguments summarised above (to which can be added the Constitutional Court's decision 303/2011, which will be discussed in this Part, see Human Rights in Italian Case-law, VI) are not such as to rule out renewed episodes of – at least virtual – conflict with the ECtHR, similar to those that have already broken out regarding this issue in the *Agrati* and *Maggio et al.* cases, which are explained beneath (see in this Part IV, Italy in the Case-law of the European Court of Human Rights, II). In particular, to refer vaguely, providing no details, to the legislative function and to the political and parliamentary discretion in order to justify retroactive interference in events still being considered by the courts might, according to the Strasbourg case-law, constitute restriction of the fair relationship between the judge and the parties. This is especially so as case-law had fostered citizens' expectations in a diametrically opposite direction, and the interference – imposed by means of rules of a merely interpretative nature – favours the State and takes place more than a decade after the statute now being re-interpreted was enacted.

III. Human Dignity, Informed Consent to Health Care Treatment, Medically Assisted Procreation

By judgement 16543/2011 the Court of Cassation ruled on a case involving laparoscopic surgery performed on a woman with reproductive system deficiencies. The laparoscopic surgery then became a laparotomy. The surgeon was later found to have committed no errors. Nonetheless the patient was rendered barren (largely on account of improper post-operative treatment, not amount to any offence however). The point that emerged as crucial in the Court of Cassation's judgement concerns its characterisation of the right to informed consent as a "true and veritable human right", both with respect to the right to individual self-determination and with respect to the right to health (relying on judgement 438/2008 of the Constitutional Court). Indeed, the physician conducted laparotomy on the patient without asking her consent, which had been given merely for the less invasive laparoscopic surgery. Moreover the physician decided to conduct the surgery in order to avoid subjecting the woman to a second anaesthetic. Thus the motive was not the response to a serious threat to the patient's life. In this way the physician violated a right enshrined in the Oviedo Convention (which Italy ratified, as the judge mentioned, by law 28 March 2001, No. 145) and in art. 1 of the Additional Protocol of 1998 to the Convention (on actual ratification by Italy of both instruments, see Part I, International Human Rights Law, III), as well as in art. 3 CFREU. The Court stated, "The duty becomes evident, one that is incumbent on the State and on its institutions, including the judge, to focus on the dimension of the concretely existing human being endowed with inherent dignity. Dignity presides over the fundamental rights, and without dignity those rights might be [...] subjected [to] narrow constraints capable of debasing all their incisiveness. Human dignity constitutes an axiological value that permeates the legal system as a whole and, therefore, *a fortiori*, characterises all ordinary laws."

The Court of Cassation ruled accordingly in judgement 3847/2011, by stating, *inter alia*, that clinics (in this case it was a private one) and attending physicians are bound to inform the citizen of any possible equipment and organisation defect, that, had they been known, might have led the patient to choose a different hospital. The case concerned an indemnity claim for a new-born's severe disability ensuing from the poor monitoring conducted at the private hospital where the birth had occurred.

In 2011 too, the application of law 40/2004 on assisted reproduction saw some interesting developments in the pertinent case-law (see also *2011 Yearbook*, p. 264). In particular, the Court of Naples (judgement of 1 July 2011) held that new-born babies conceived in the United States by means of heterologous fertilisation, a technique that is lawful in the US but forbidden in Italy, should not constitute an obstacle to transcribing the birth certificates of the children in the civil registry of their father's town in Italy. The transcript cannot be deemed subversive of public order in Italy. Indeed, the judge noted, not only is heterologous fertilisation no newcomer to the European legal landscape – of which Italy forms a part – but the prohibition contained in law 40/2004 is not such as to deny the importance (and to justify the negative consequences for the children) of the fundamental principle of procreative responsibility and protection of offspring. Similarly decided, in a case of heterologous fertilisation with a surrogate mother (this time performed in India), the Court of Forlì, in a judgement of 25 October 2011. The judgement, however, orders the attribution of paternity of the twins born in India only to their father (the donor), not to his partner, because she had neither donated the egg nor given birth to the children. The Court of Cassation, for its part, in judgement 46728/2011, ruled that assisted reproduction techniques cannot be used at the request of an inmate who is serving a sentence in accordance with art. 41-*bis* of the Prison Regulations (law 354/1975) unless a disease has been clinically diagnosed (in this case referring to the prisoner's wife). Since that conclusive finding had not been presented, the request was to be dismissed.

The decision of the Court of Varese of 7 December 2011 refers repeatedly to the safeguarding of human dignity on granting the request of an old woman forced to move from her home into a publicly funded health care facility. The court appointed, in addition to her limited guardian ("Amministratore di sostegno"), an extra assistant, who was specifically charged with caring for her pet, a dog, and was instructed to take the dog to see the old lady regularly. The grounds that the court adduces for its decision are firstly respect for the dignity of the elderly and living with disabilities, which demands due consideration for their wishes, and secondly the growing recognition of the importance of pets' contribution to their quality of life, enshrined in particular by the European Convention for the Protection of Pet Animals of 13 November 1987, recently ratified by Italy (law of 4 November 2010, No. 201).

The same Varese judge dismissed (order of 24 October 2011) a motion from the guardian of a person declared incapacitated on account of psychic disability (retarded mental development) to act against her ward who was apparently having frequent sexual intercourse with an acquaintance. The court held that disability does not negate the intimately personal right to sexuality, which cannot be restricted without infringing the freedom and dignity of the individual. Of course situations of abuse, exploitation, commodification and sexual violence would be excluded – none of which was present in this particular case. In conclusion, the guardian was instructed to take the woman to a psychologist and to take whatever measures the psychologist suggested in order to prevent any harm befalling the ward.

Law 164/1982 (Rules on correction of gender assignment) does not address the issue of whether a parent may represent the child to request permission to undergo sex-change surgery and consequently alter the gender datum in the civil registry. The Court of Rome (judgement of 11 March 2011) granted the motion made by the father of a seventeen-year-old who for two years had undergone hormone therapy and had meanwhile permanently assumed a female persona. The request received a positive response. Clinical and scientific expert opinions attested to the surgical treatment as the best way of coping with the malaise produced by gender identity disorder. The parent's request is conceived as a complex act that cannot be accomplished without the minor's consent. The court sees the operation as functional to the assertion of the individual's right to a sexual identity which is, in turn, a specification of the broader right to health, understood as a state of complete physical, mental and social wellbeing.

IV. Asylum, International Protection

In 2011 Italian case-law was divided over the recognition of Greece as a safe State for purposes of regulation 343/2003 EU (Dublin regulation). Indeed a number of TAR judgements quashed orders transferring asylum seekers who were in Italy to Greece, where the Dublin Unit ascertained that they had entered the European area through the Greek border. In support of this decision, ECtHR case-law was cited (in particular *M.S.S. v. Belgium and Greece*, 21 January 2011) as were the statements issued by several Governments, which in recent years have decided to suspend transfers of asylum seekers to Greece invoking the "sovereignty clause" of said regulation: among them are Belgium, the United Kingdom, the Netherlands and Germany. The administrative courts' decisions on this issue were also heavily influenced by the report prepared in 2009 by the Commissioner for Human Rights of the Council of Europe on the condition of refugees and asylum seekers in Greece – CommDH (2009)6 of 4 February 2009. The report found the Greek Government was unable to provide a sufficient level of protection to persons entitled to refugee status or subsidiary protection.

Some of the concurring judgements issued: Lazio TAR, judgements No. 2115/2011, 2116/2011, 2687/2011, 2686/2011, 4173/2011, 4252/2011, 4259/2011, 4260/2011, 4261/2011, 4262/2011, 4264/2011, 4276/2011, 4315/2011, 4319/2011, 4320/2011, 5268/2011, 5278/2011, 5279/2011, 5795/2011, 6517/2011, 6518/2011, 6528/2011, 6531/2011, 6532/2011; Lombardy TAR, judgement 1944/2011.

The Council of State, in its judgement No. 1024/2011, departed from this prevailing view by acknowledging that in Greece a certain change in attitude is discernible, which would persuade one to avoid using the sovereignty clause in a mechanistic way. Accordingly, the high administrative court upheld the decision to transfer an Afghan asylum seeker to Greece. The Lazio TAR for its part banishes all doubts concerning the legality of transferring to Austria under the regulation in question, an Armenian family with three minor children, one of whom had been born only a few months earlier in Italy, since Austria can undoubtedly be considered a "safe Country" (case 7096/2011).

The qualification of the Niger Delta in Nigeria as an area where it is plausible that recipients of humanitarian protection come from was upheld (see Court of Appeals of Rome, judgement 2405/2011). The same is true for the Ivory Coast (see Court of Appeals of Rome, case 963/2011), as well as Bangladesh (see Court of Milan, judgement 9932/2011). On the other hand different considerations are now applicable to Kosovo: an appeal against the denial of recognition of refugee status issued by the competent territorial commission was dismissed by judgement 1096/2011 of the Rome Appeals Court; the Court of Cassation concurs with the view. In its judgement 12614/2011, in particular, this latter remarks that the petitioner, who adduced as grounds for asylum his conversion to Catholicism, lacked credibility, since the territorial commission verified that he knew nothing whatsoever about Jesus.

In the various rulings issued on asylum cases, the Italian courts tend to abide by the narrow interpretation proposed by the Court of Cassation in some recent decisions (for example case 18549/2006). In accordance to this interpretation, since national and EU legislation distinguishes between refugee status on the one hand and international protection on the other, art. 10 (3) of the Constitution – governing the right of asylum – does not provide for any entitlements beyond the mere right to access Italian territory in order to apply for international protection there (see, among others, Court of Milan judgement 2359/2011). However, this by no means entails denial of concrete humanitarian protection to persons seeking asylum. The Court of Cassation (case 3898/2011) found a breach of the law in the decision of the Rome Justice of the Peace denying an appeal lodged by a Liberian citizen against an expulsion order issued by the Prefecture of Rome. The same individual had applied for a residence permit on humanitarian grounds alleging risk of persecution on returning to Liberia, as a result of the constant instability prevailing in that Country. The Court of Cassation, in this context, reminds that art. 19 of lgs.d. 286/1998 states that "in no case can an alien be expelled or subjected to *refoulement* to a Country where the alien may be persecuted on grounds of race, sex, language, nationality, religion, political opinion or personal or social status, or else might run the risk of being sent to another State where the alien is not protected from persecution." This provision entitles the alien with a substantial human right that cannot be disregarded simply by stating that an application for international protection is not expressly listed as a circumstance that precludes expulsion. The deportation order was therefore quashed.

In a case involving a Nigerian asylum seeker threatened in his Country not by Government, but by private individuals from whom however the authorities afforded him no protection, the Court of Cassation recognises in principle the possibility of resorting to protective measures. The Court stresses – consistently with its prior case-law – that the determination of the facts which warrant the granting of international protection cannot be based solely on statements made by the applicant, but rather the territorial commissions and courts of appeal must also play an active role. They therefore have to investigate facts supporting the claim and acquire all documents, including unofficial ones, to reconstruct the actual situation in the Country of origin, since the task at hand is to secure a fundamental right (see case 12939/2011; similarly see also case 12940/2011).

V. Discrimination

A. Gender Discrimination

The Sardinia TAR by judgement 864/2011 invalidated the appointment by the President of the Autonomous Region of Sardinia of 12 councillors to the Regional Government, because the list of appointees did not include any women. The TAR took cognisance of the case in the light of certain articles of the Italian Constitution, namely art. 51 read in conjunction with arts. 2, 3 (on fundamental rights), and 97 (principles on public administration). Such articles are immediately applicable although Sardinia still lacks a regional law implementing the principle of equal opportunity. The judgement also refers to art. 21 and 23 CFREU and art. 117 (7) of the Italian Constitution, which mandates that the principle of equal opportunity be recognised in regional legislation as well. Despite the political nature of appointments to the Regional Government, the court reaffirmed the constraint imposed by the provisions cited on the political discretion of the Regional President. The judge also criticised the obstinacy with which the political body pursued the goal of an all-male cabinet, on the pretext of a Constitutional Court's order in 2009 had pronounced void the Sardinian Autonomy Act of 2008 that forbade either sex from holding more than 60% of the seats in the Regional Cabinet.

The Court of Tivoli dismissed a motion to submit to the Constitutional Court the constitutionality of the current legislation on marital status, which does not allow people to bear their mother's surname next to their father's. The court held that the Constitutional Court had already ruled on the issue, to wit, in judgement 61/2006. In that decision it refused to declare the ban unconstitutional, on the grounds that this would require the Court to modify a number of legal provisions, which would be incompatible with its task of interpreting the laws and not of amending or creating them. At the same time the Constitutional Court denounced the backwardness of Italian law on this issue. The innovations ensuing from the Lisbon Treaty's entry into force are not likely to compel any trial court to refrain from applying domestic laws on grounds of conflict with the ECHR and the CFREU, since the framework of the civil state is not subject to the jurisdiction of EU law (the judgement of the ECJ in C-353/06 is quoted).

At the Court of Varese (judgement of 24 February 2011) proceedings on a tort damages claim related to a prosecution for harassment and threats ended, after summary proceedings, with an acquittal for lack of proof beyond reasonable doubt. The Court discussed violence against women and civil liability. The court noted that, although not sufficient for a conviction, there was sufficient evidence to link the injuries suffered by the plaintiff (a former partner of the attacker) to an act of physical violence, rather than merely a fortuitous accident. Apart from the criminal aspect, physical assault on a woman constitutes in any case a serious breach of human dignity, a constitutionally protected value in any context, including that of family and partner relationships. Use of the civil liability remedy under art. 2043 civil code is necessary to pursue the goal of stamping out violence against women, a priority objective in numerous documents of the EU and the UN. Damage is not only the harm done to the victim's health, but is also the expression of the continuing inequality between women and men. The claim must comprise both damage to health (so-called "biological damage"), and the moral damages connected to the violation of a human right.

The Constitutional Court (case 94/2011) issued judgement on Liguria's regional law of 10 November 2009, No. 52 (Provisions against discrimination related to sexual orientation or gender identity), ruling that the statute does not infringe the rules on the division of powers between the national Government and the Regions. The Prime Minister's Office attacked the regional law maintaining that its norms encroached on the national Government's exclusive jurisdiction in matters concerning civil rights. The Constitutional Court did not hold the statute to be unlawful, neither where it binds the regional executive to ensure that, in matters of regional competence, the services provided by public and private operators be provided without discrimination based on gender, nor where it is committed to legislate in compliance with these principles of non-discrimination. Finally the Court found it constitutionally sound that the impugned regional law assigned to every person of legal age the ability to designate a person (including a possible homosexual partner) who will have access to any health care facilities where the appointer is being cared for to offer any assistance or psychological support he or she may need, and to whom health care staff must furnish all information relating to the patient.

The Court of Ferrara referred to the Constitutional Court the issue of the constitutionality of existing legislation that forbids marriage between individuals of the same sex. On this point, however, order 4/2011 asserts in part the manifest inadmissibility of the application, in part that it is manifestly groundless, as an identical question was decided by judgement 138/2010 (on which see the *2011 Yearbook*, pp. 265-266).

In an action for property and non-property damage to be paid by a person found guilty of manslaughter for causing a traffic accident, the Court of Milan held that, although the relationship is not equivalent to legal marriage as recognised by the State, compensation for moral damage must be paid to the individual who was living with the victim, and was in a steady relationship with him, even if both are of the same sex (case 9965/2011).

B. Racial and Ethnic Discrimination

The Unified Sections of the Court of Cassation Civil Division asserted in judgement 7186/2011, the "absolute" value of the right to freedom from discrimination on racial, ethnic or religious grounds. Art. 44 of lgs.d. 286/1998 (Consolidated immigration act) furnishes a remedy against the violations of this right. The question before the Court of Cassation concerned the issue of whether it is a function incumbent upon the ordinary courts or on the TARs to rule on an allegedly discriminatory conduct on the part of the management of a hospital in Milan. The management had initially announced that only EU citizens could participate in a procedure intended to select staff that would be hired on a permanent basis. The Court of Cassation, without ruling on the merits of the dispute, held that, given the absolute nature of the rights protected and in view of the scope of the cited art. 44, the power to rule on the existence of discriminatory behaviour, order the cessation of this behaviour, remove the effects and possibly order the manager to pay damages, are a matter for the ordinary courts (sitting as a single judge), and not for the administrative ones. This holds even if the conduct in question is attributed to a Government agency, subject in principle to the supervision of the TARs.

Concerning the procedure under art. 44 of lgs.d. 286/1998, the Court of Cassation (order 3670/2011) reiterated that the matter to which it applies is inherently linked to fundamental human rights and therefore the power to adjudicate disputes relating to racial or ethnic discrimination (under cited art. 44 or art. 4 and 4-*bis* of lgs.d. 215/2003 – now art. 28 of lgs.d. 1 September 2011, No. 150) is always vested in the ordinary courts and not the administrative ones, even when the act which constitutes discrimination is a measure of a Government agency. The case concerned the Municipality of Brescia and the Association for Legal Studies on Immigration – ASGI. The latter, after obtaining a court order suppressing the Council's policy of awarding a "baby bonus" only to families where at least one parent was an Italian citizen, had also challenged as equally discriminatory and retaliatory the subsequent Council resolution revoking all baby bonuses.

The Criminal Division of the Court of Cassation (case 563/2011), while applying the aggravating circumstance of the aim of ethnic, racial or religious discrimination and hatred (art. 3 of law 205/1993 – the so-called Mancino act enforcing the International Convention Against

Racial Discrimination), reiterated that for a harsher penalty to be applied, the discriminatory purpose accompanying the criminal conduct may also be "indirect." In this case it was threats made to a person, a non-Jewish scholar of Jewish issues, who was wished treatment similar to that suffered by the Jews under the Nazis. The hateful purpose can be found in likening the victim of this crime to a group against which hatred is expressed on racial, ethnic or religious grounds.

Likewise concerning the same issue, the Court of La Spezia's case 352/2011 dealt with a woman who had insulted her husband calling him names that referred to his national origin and ethnicity. The court found that by doing so the woman had not committed the offence of insulting him with the aggravating factor of ethnic hatred, since by having married him and living with him she had shown the absence of any ethnic prejudice in her behaviour. It may be noted that, apart from the case in point, this idea according to which no racial prejudice can occur within a couple has been criticised by some.

The Council of State issued an important judgement, 6050/2011, which decides on appeals and counter-appeals lodged against a judgement of the TAR of Lazio 6352/2009, which had quashed several presidential orders issued pursuant to the declaration on 21 May 2008, of a state of emergency in the territories of Lazio, Lombardy and Campania in connection with the situation in Roma camps. The Lazio TAR had cancelled the orders, but not the declaration of state of emergency, issued under the law of 24 February 1992, No. 225 (Establishment of the National Civil Protection Service). The judgement on appeal before the Council of State led to recognise the invalidity of that declaration, too. In the opinion of the judges, there were no factual grounds for issuing an emergency decree, namely the actual existence of an emergency and the inability to cope with it by using ordinary means. The terms used in the decree of 21 May 2008 refer to various situations that occurred in the territories of Milan, Rome and Naples that elicited "social alarm" and "risks" to "public order and safety" ensuing from unauthorised Roma settlements. However the decree failed to specify neither the facts that supposedly brought about this extraordinary situation (not even the number of "nomads" on the various territories is stated), nor their causal relation to the problems of coexistence and public order. On the other hand, it does not appear that, by the "emergency situation" to be resolved, what was meant was the exceeding destitution in which the inhabitants of those camps lived. This "humanitarian" issue, addressed in subsequent orders, was nowhere reflected in the decree of 21 May. Nor does the decree mention any attempt made to take ordinary monitoring measures to establish order in the affected areas, which is an additional deficiency of the Government measures. Furthermore the Council of State denies that the decrees can constitute any discriminatory action by the administration against the Roma, since the goals of "ghettoising" and of dealing exclusively with a specific ethnic group were missing. The judges reaffirm the illegality of the orders issued on the basis of the emergency decree by the Commissioners appointed to deal with the emergency in the three Regions in question. They also indicate that the measures taken to regulate life in the new "equipped villages" erected in place of the irregular camps breached the freedom of movement of their inhabitants (art. 16 Const.), for example by providing each resident with an identification badge, restricting access by visitors and requiring signing of a code of conduct, as well as the right to work (art. 4 Const.). The "equipped villages" regulations prescribe that the repeated failure of a resident to accept proposals to get into work designed by Lazio regional offices would result in him or her being asked to leave the village.

C. Discrimination against Persons with Disabilities

The law of 1 March 2006, No. 67, provides that any action constituting direct or indirect discrimination against persons with disabilities may be challenged in court, following the same procedure as that for discriminatory behaviour on racial, ethnic, political or religious grounds under art. 44 of lgs.d. 286/1998. A few months into the 2010-2011 school year, parents at some schools in Milan and an association for the rights of people with disabilities brought a lawsuit against the Ministry of Education and the schools listed because of a drastic reduction in the number of hours of educational support provided to children and young people with disabilities. The Court of Milan (judgement of 4 January 2011) acknowledged, in part relying on the Constitutional Court's judgement 80/2010, that, since the administration had made no mention of any reduction in services provided to the other students at those schools, this measure constituted an indirect form of discrimination against students with disabilities. The court mandated the administration to reinstate the special needs assistant teachers programme to the same strength as during the 2009-2010 school year.

The anti-discrimination procedure was also used, on the initiative of the parents of a girl with disabilities, to obtain from the Court of Rome an order (issued on 24 October 2011) to cease and desist discriminatory treatment against persons with motor disabilities by the city of Rome and by the Rome public transport company (ATAC SpA). They were ordered within 12 months to institute a number of measures to eliminate physical and architectonic barriers that prevent access of persons with disabilities to certain city bus lines and to some stations on the Underground.

In addition to the ruling just mentioned, attained by means of the anti-discrimination procedure, consequences of the Constitutional Court's judgement 80/2010 were also noticeable in the TAR case-law. Some TARs quashed the measures taken by schools to reduce the number of hours of support provided to students with disabilities (see, for example, Lazio TAR judgement 757/2011; Lazio Latina TAR, judgement 417/2011; Campania Salerno TAR, judgements 1407/2011 and 1640/2011; Calabria TAR, case 834/2011). The Sicily TAR (case 2264/2011) ruled against a Municipality that, having failed to approve its 2011 budget, had also failed to appoint the teaching and communication support assistant for a primary school girl, in breach of regional and national disability laws and of the 2006 Convention on the Rights of Persons with Disabilities.

D. Provisions for the Victims of Racial Laws

Administrative courts may hear appeals against the refusal to acknowledge individuals as victims of fascist racial laws under the law of 10 March 1955, No. 96 (measures for the benefit of anti-fascist victims of political persecution or victims of racial persecution and their surviving family members). In its judgement 4580/2011, in particular, the Council of State ruled that an appellant who claimed to have suffered anti-Semitic persecution, was entitled to use as evidence thereof an affidavit dated 2005, stating that in 1943 the appellant was prevented from attending training courses for elementary teachers because of her Jewish background. This document, together with other facts ascertained (her father was Jewish) constitute proof that the appellant qualifies as a beneficiary of this law, even though her name is not registered among those belonging to the Jewish community in Rome: her cancellation from the list was indeed requested by her mother in 1941, presumably to keep her safe from persecution.

Other laws, in addition to that of 1955, provide benefits to former deportees or victims of racial persecution during World War II. In particular, the Lazio TAR (case 5880/2011) clarified that even a person who exhibited a 1944 birth certificate stamped with the words ‘Jewish race’, born just weeks before the liberation of the capital from Nazi occupation (4 June 1944), is entitled to the benefits provided for by the law of 8 July 1971, No. 541. Although he was a new-born at the time the racial laws worked against him, moral damage cannot be denied.

VI. Workers’ Rights

Among the most significant cases tried in 2011 was the one held before the Criminal Court of Turin, for the fire that broke out at the Thyssen Krupp AST plant in Turin on 6 December 2007, causing the death of seven workers. Proceedings at the trial stage (case 31095/2011) ended with the conviction of the chief executive officer (a German citizen) and six other executives of the company for murder with recklessness. This was the first Italian judgement that held that if an employer fails to install the required fire protection systems on company premises and any employee dies as a result thereof, the employer can be considered guilty of murder with recklessness. For this to be determined, the employer must be is aware that the accident is very likely to take place and accepts this outcome in accordance with a conscious decision by means of which he knowingly gave precedence to business and industrial considerations over the lives and safety of workers. Also significant was the fact that the Turin court granted standing to seek damages against the defendant company, not only to the families of deceased workers and to their injured colleagues, but also to various legal persons, including political territorial entities (such as, among others, the Piedmont Region, the Province and the Municipality of Turin, trade unions, "Medicina Democratica" – an NGO –, etc.).

The Constitutional Court's decision 303/2011 likewise concerns the right to work. It discusses the constitutionality of certain provisions of the law of 4 November 2010, No. 183 (Delegation of power to the Government regarding monotonous, hazardous and strenuous work, reorganisation of institutions, holiday leave, acquired rights and permits, the social safety net, employment procurement services, incentives to employment, apprenticeships, female employment, measures against unofficial employment and provisions regarding public employment and labour disputes). Art. 32, paragraphs 5, 6 and 7 of this law provides the standard criteria for calculating the amount due to employees unlawfully hired under temporary contracts which are to be converted into permanent employment contracts. These criteria require compensation to a worker. The compensation is owed regardless of the time worked or the length of litigation, and ranges from a minimum of two and a half times the final monthly salary to a maximum of 12 months'. According to some labour courts and the Court of Cassation itself, these rules conflict with some articles of the Constitution (3, 4, 24, 101, 102 and 111) as well as with art. 117 (1) Const., using as intermediary norm art. 6 ECHR, because the new rule also applies to labour contracts concerning which a litigation is still pending. For these cases, the new legislation requires the court to apply a criterion, which yields to the worker an amount presumably far lower than it would be if applying regular standards (the latter require in principle a compensation including all wages unpaid since the expiry of the fixed-term contract until the worker is actually reintegrated as a permanent employee). The new rules, in addition to degrading the work performed by the employee, by paying it at a flat rate, give no incentive for the employer to settle the litigation, but rather encourage drawing it out. The Constitutional Court did not uphold allegations of unconstitutionality. Firstly the court remarked that the new rules determine with greater precision and reliability the amount of the indemnity payable to a worker illegally hired on a fixed contract, as compared to the existing case-law, which is fairly inconsistent on this point. It also noted that the main instrument of protection introduced by the statute is not so much the flat-rate compensation, as the stabilisation of the employment relationship. Regarding the fact that law 183/2010 interferes with proceedings still under way, in breach of the fair trial principle (art. 6 ECHR – see, in this Part, Human Rights in Italian Case-law, II), the Constitutional Court noted that, unlike other cases involving only public employees, the rule under review affects all employers, public or private. The need to prune many irregular employment situations and to make employment conditions clear-cut is an overriding ground of general interest that warrants, in accordance with ECtHR case-law, the enactment of retroactive rules that sweep away the judicial settlement of pending cases.

In its judgement 13532/2011, the Court of Cassation acquitted a Calabrian employer of charges of virtual enslavement. The employer, the object of precautionary measures for belonging to the mafia, had hired two Romanian immigrants (non-EU citizens at the time of the events) to work as shepherds for a paltry wage (that he eventually failed to pay) and in extremely poor housing conditions. The workers, in effect, were not forced to work, they had regular residence permits and, once they had experienced the intolerable working conditions, were able to leave.

VII. Immigrants' Rights

A. Expulsion of Foreigners and Immigration-related Offences

The ECJ's judgement in *El Dridi* (28 April 2011, C-61/11 – see in this Part, Italy in the Case-law of the Court of Justice of the European Union, I) and the direct applicability of directive 2008/115 of the European Parliament and Council ("Returns directive") had an immediate impact on Italian law. In particular, the courts have begun to deem no longer applicable certain provisions of the Consolidated immigration act (lgs.d. 286/1998) governing the procedures for expulsion and readmission of aliens, that also provided for criminal sanctions for cases of non-compliance. Domestic norms were accordingly replaced with immediately applicable provisions set forth in the EU directive. Thus, the Court of Rome (case 9060/2011), among others, refrained from applying art. 13 and 14 of lgs.d. 286/1998 and likewise disregarded the police orders providing for the removal of a foreigner and barring his re-entry.

The Court of Cassation (case No. 22105 of 28 April 2011) explicitly recognised that Italy's failure to transpose directive 2008/115 by the deadline makes the provisions thereof that are capable of producing immediate effects directly applicable and bars Government authorities from enforcing any domestic law – even that of criminal content – that conflicts with EU law. Among the offences that are thus abrogated are those linked by art. 13 and 14 of lgs.d. 286/1998 to expulsion proceedings. Among the judgements of trial courts that, anticipating the ruling of the Court of Cassation, recognised the abrogating effect on domestic criminal statutes of the not yet transposed EU "Returns directive", and therefore acquitted the defendant, can be mentioned the Court of Turin's judgements No. 1/2011 and 3/2011, and the Court of Palmi's judgement of 17 February 2011.

The Constitutional Court, by order 84/2011, denied as manifestly groundless charges alleging unconstitutionality of art. 10-*bis* of lgs.d. 286/1998, the statute that establishes the criminal offence of illegal entry and stay by immigrants, introduced in Italy's legal system by the so-called 2009 "security package". The penalty provided was a fine of between 5,000 and 10,000 euros, or alternatively expulsion for at least five years. The Court had already upheld the constitutionality of the law in judgement 250/2010 (see *2011 Yearbook*, p. 278). In 2011, the Court also denied as inadmissible other constitutionality issues raised concerning the same article, in some cases in conjunction with art. 16 of lgs.d. 286/1998. See in this respect orders 144/2011, 193/2011 and 306/2011.

The Court of Cassation, by judgement 16453/2011 also declared unenforceable against illegal immigrants the crime of failure to produce personal documents and residence permits, referred to in art. 6 (3) of lgs.d. 286/1998. The offence was instituted by law 94/2009, the so-called "security package", and is punishable by imprisonment for up to one year and a fine of up to 2,000 euros. This offence can in effect only be committed by an individual who actually possesses such documents. A provision that punishes irregular migrants for refusing to display documents that by definition they do not possess is illogical. Irregular immigrants face therefore only the penalties of art. 10-*bis* of aforesaid legislative decree (offence of illegal entry and stay). The Court of Alessandria applied such case-law in its order of 7 April 2011.

It is now well-established in the Italian case-law that when deciding whether or not to renew a residence permit on its expiry, due consideration should be given to the degree of integration that the foreigner has achieved in Italy, especially the establishment of family ties. That is the purport of art. 8 ECHR (see Council of State, judgement of 13 September 2010, No. 6566).

The Court of Cassation (case 8795/2011, see also judgement 19957/2011) states that, despite the wording of art. 4 (3) of lgs.d. 286/1998, a refusal to renew a residence permit for family reasons on grounds of prior convictions for certain offences deemed to constitute impediments to entry in Italy (in this specific case they were drug-trafficking offences) is unlawful, because this ground does not entail *per se* a "real and present threat to public order and safety." Having a criminal record may in fact be offset by the need to keep the family united (protected, among others, by art. 28 of the same lgs.d. 286/1998) and to protect the best interests of under age children (art. 3 Convention on Rights of the Child). The ruling out of all automatic mechanisms stems in particular from EU legislation, namely directive 2003/86/EC.

Similarly, the Criminal Division of the Court of Cassation (case 3607/2011) struck down and referred back for further consideration a judgement whereby the trial court, in addition to convicting a foreigner for criminal conspiracy linked to drug trafficking, had ordered his deportation as a security measure. The convicted person claimed to have a domestic partnership with a woman and minor children of Italian citizenship living in Italy. If this claim were determined to be true, the security measure ordered would be unlawful, because it breaches the alien's right to a personal and family life, protected, among others, by art. 8 ECHR.

Even the administrative expulsion under art. 16 of lgs.d. 286/1998 cannot be ordered against a foreigner married to (although not cohabiting with) an Italian woman by whom he has a daughter. His deportation would constitute, in particular, a breach of art. 9 of the International Convention on the Rights of the Child, since it would deprive the child of one of her parents (see Criminal Division of the Court of Cassation, case 20143/2011).

The Sicily TAR, by a judgement of 24 October 2011, No. 1864, ruled on the case of an alien worker, a legal resident of Italy since 2003, with stable employment and a family in Italy, whose residence permit the Palermo police had refused to renew because of a conviction for selling counterfeit goods, handed down in 2007 but based on events that had occurred before 2002. The TAR struck down the denial on grounds of breach of art. 8 ECHR. The judge described this rule as "directly applicable within our legal system as a consequence of the 'communitarisation' of the ECHR effected by the Amsterdam Treaty [*sic*] (meaning to say "Lisbon Treaty")." The same holds, among others, for judgements No. 418/2011 of the Sicilian TAR and No. 362/2011 of the Campania TAR.

B. The Right to Marriage

The law of 15 July 2009, No. 94 (the so-called 2009 "security package") included an amendment to art. 116 (1) of the civil code under which a foreigner who wishes to marry in Italy must submit a valid residence permit in addition to all other documents required for any couple to marry. According to the Court of Catania, this restriction on the freedom to marry, hampering both aliens and Italians since its intent is to affect the couple as well as the individual, is a breach of arts. 2, 3 and 29 of the Constitution. Moreover it violates art. 16 of the Universal

Declaration of Human Rights, art. 12 ECHR and art. 9 CFREU. The Constitutional Court addressed the issue in judgement 245/2011. The Court noted that Parliament introduced the rule in question for the purpose of combating marriages of convenience arranged to enable the alien spouse to acquire Italian citizenship through marriage. The same goal was also pursued by means of an amendment to the law of 5 February 1992, No. 91 (new rules on citizenship), art. 5 of which allows the alien spouse of an Italian citizen to be naturalised only after two years from their marriage if resident in Italy (tree if resident abroad), and on condition that, at the time citizenship is granted, the spouses have not separated, or dissolved or annulled their marriage, or its civil effects lapsed. In 2002, moreover, the so-called "Bossi-Fini law" provided that residence permits issued to an alien for family reasons shall be withdrawn if it is determined that (s)he married an Italian citizen solely to be able to enter Italy and reside there, or if there was no actual cohabitation after marriage, unless they have children (art. 30 (1-*bis*) lgs.d. 286/1998). Likewise in light of these provisions, the Constitutional Court held depriving irregular residents of the right to marry to be a disproportionate restriction of a fundamental human right that, moreover, will affect not only the foreigner but also the Italian citizen. The amendment to art. 116 (1) of the civil code was accordingly struck down as unconstitutional.

C. The Right to Housing

The TAR of Lombardy (case 3151/2011) recognised as unlawful the refusal by the Municipality of Milan to enter the applicant foreign citizen on the waiting list for the allocation of public housing, on the grounds that the she had spent part of the required term of stable residence in Lombardy (to wit five years) as an irregular resident. In effect the woman, who applied for public housing allocation in 2009, had acquired citizenship of the European Union in 2007, but between approximately 2004 and 2007 had resided and worked illegally in the Region. The Municipality of Milan had relied on this circumstance to deny her registration on the list. On the contrary, the TAR believes that, since the procedure is designed to grant access to a fundamental human right derived from art. 8 ECHR, among other provisions, once the alien has acquired the right (in this case EU citizenship) to reside legally in Italy, the time spent residing and working there in the informal sector should be counted for purposes of the allocation of public housing. The relevant legislation (at the national level, art. 40 of lgs.d. 286/1998 and at the regional level, Lombardy regional law 27/2009), when requiring that the immigrant has fixed abode in and a measure of personal attachment to a given territory, makes no mention of the regular or irregular status of the applicant's presence throughout the period being considered. If this item had been considered, the legislation would have been open to the charge of discrimination based on nationality regarding access to a fundamental right.

D. Social Dangerousness and Rejection of Applications to Extend Residence Permits

The Court of Cassation (case 22983/2011) pronounced itself on the scope of art. 4 (3) of lgs.d. 286/1998 where it provides that the police may deny a foreigner renewal of a residence permit for family reunification when the foreigner poses a real and present threat to State security. The Venice Court of Appeals quashed a similar denial issued by the *Questura* of Belluno (State Police Headquarters) on the grounds that the rule in question refers to a narrow concept of public order and security that does not cover "everyday" police and public safety concerns, but rather concerns at a higher level of Government. In actual fact, analysing the sorts of offences that warrant classifying an alien as dangerous for purposes of admission to or residence in Italy, on the one hand there are references to criminal offences that are characteristic of a "high-level" concept of national security (subversive criminal conspiracy, belonging to armed gangs, devastation, pillage and massacre, civil war...), but on the other hand also to offences related to a breach of the public peace and *ordre public* (enslavement, child prostitution, rape, offences relating to weapons and drugs, murder, armed robbery, extortion, etc.). This interpretation of the notion of State security, more attentive to safety needs of the community, is also more akin, according to the Court of Cassation, to the guarantee that the law must provide for the goods protected by art. 8 ECHR.

The Campania TAR (case 305/2011) acted to apply the provisions of l.d. 78/2009, converted into law 102/2009, on the regularisation of illegal immigrant workers, thus diverging from the prevalent reading (upheld in 2009 by the Council of State). One factor that constitutes an obstacle to the regularisation of an immigrant worker is provided for in the law cited above, to wit a report from the Schengen Information System stating that the alien has committed criminal offences or engaged in other unlawful conduct in other Countries belonging to the Schengen area. Most case-law has construed this requirement as being largely automatic in nature. The Campania TAR on the other hand, proposing a systematic reading of the said domestic provision, holds that only a Schengen alert that, in the judge's opinion, relates to conduct by the alien such that his/her presence may entail an actual threat to public order and safety constitutes an obstacle to regularisation.

E. Fundamental Rights and the Principle of Reciprocity

The Court of Cassation, in its judgement 450/2011, held that, notwithstanding the provisions of art. 16 of the preliminary dispositions to the civil code regarding the status of aliens ("an alien is eligible to enjoy the civil rights granted to citizens on condition of reciprocity and subject to the provisions contained in special laws"), when dealing with fundamental rights derived from art. 2 of the Constitution the reciprocity clause does not apply. The issue the judges faced concerned the possibility to admit the mother of an Albanian national who had been run over and killed in Italy by a vehicle whose driver was unknown, to be compensated by the solidarity fund for the victims of traffic accidents, an Italian fund established by law in 1969 that has no counterpart in Albania, where the hit-and-run victim's mother lived. The Court of Cassation reconstructed in a nutshell, the issue of inviolable rights in the Italian legal system and concluded that, even if an alien's relative is killed, "the compensatory protection (unless derogated by the reciprocity condition), ensuing from the event infringing constitutional values such as the protection of the family and of parental relationship (art. 2, 29 and 30 of the Constitution) that are inviolable human rights, must covers both pecuniary and non-pecuniary damages." On the other hand the reciprocity criterion set forth in art. 16 of the civil code still governs the compensation for property damage (to a vehicle, for example). Accordingly, access to risk protection funds provided for by Italian law may be granted to an alien only if an Italian citizen in the foreigner's Country and in a similar situation can avail him/herself of similar protection.

F. The Social Rights of Immigrants and Regional Policies

Constitutional Court judgement 61/2011 of 25 February 2011 was issued in response to an attack by the Prime Minister's Office to Campania Region law of 8 February 2010, No. 6, (Standards for social, economic and cultural integration of foreigners residing in Campania). The judgement resumes and upholds the approach adopted by the Court in similar cases, namely in judgements 269/2010 and 299/2010. In the instant case the Government found fault with the provisions of the regional law, which appeared to extend social protection measures (access to social services such as reception, public housing, health care and welfare benefits) to aliens residing illegally in Italy, thereby encroaching upon matters of exclusive jurisdiction of national law (art. 117 (2) Const., letters a), b), h) & l). The Constitutional Court dismissed the objection and upheld the lawfulness of regional law. In fact, regional legislation, insofar as it relates to fundamental human rights within the jurisdiction of the regional legislator (welfare, student support schemes, social integration, use of languages, etc.), have no choice but to recognise the rights of illegal aliens. This however does not bestow "even indirectly any lawful status on their presence on the national territory," and consequently in no way impinges on the jurisdiction of the State. Regarding more specific regional legislation concerning setting up reception centres for foreigners who have not found housing independently, even if they are irregular immigrants, the Constitutional Court considers it entirely pertinent to the region's competence in the area of social services (concurring: cases 10/2010 and 269/2010). In other cases concerning allocation of public housing and access to health services, the Court noted that the regional law under scrutiny actually confers no rights on illegal immigrants in addition to the fundamental rights already guaranteed by national law (namely the Consolidated immigration act). Regarding entitlement to social allowances and other welfare benefits of legally resident immigrants, this cannot be limited to holders of a residence permit valid for longer than one year, as the Government would like, because already Constitutional Court judgement 299/2010 had pointed out that such a restriction was unreasonable (on this issue see *2011 Yearbook*, pp. 280-282).

The judgement just cited can be compared to another judgement by the Constitutional Court, namely 8/2011, dismissing in part the objection by the Prime Minister's Office against certain articles of the Emilia-Romagna regional law of 22 December 2009, No. 24. In particular the article of the regional law that recognises the right of all EU citizens to access public and private health services equally and without any discrimination, whether "direct or indirect, on the grounds of race, gender, sexual orientation, language, religion, political opinion, or personal and social status" is not unconstitutional. Nor are the provisions that invoke the principle of non-discrimination, whether direct or indirect, enshrined in EU law. Reference to binding provisions of EU law does not amount to the Region usurping the prerogatives of the State.

In keeping with its judgement 187/2010 (see *2011 Yearbook*, p. 278), the Constitutional Court, by decision 329/2011, ruled that law 388/2000 (2001 Budget Act) is unlawful in so far as it admits payment of children's attendance allowance instituted by law 11 October 1990, No. 289, to minors with disabilities who are not EU citizens only if they hold a residence permit. Indeed, the allowance provided by law, even if contingent on certain income requirements, is not intended to supplement the income of the minor or his family, but to provide for the protection of fundamental rights in the field of health, education and, social and occupational integration, and specifically meets the rights of persons with disabilities under the United Nations Convention of 2006, ratified by Italy by law 18/2009. Accordingly, allowances cannot be granted merely to a narrow category of minors who are long-term residents, since this would constitute discrimination in breach of constitutional provisions and of art. 14 ECHR (an "intermediate rule" to art. 117(1) Const.). The allowance must, on the contrary, be recognised to all alien minors legally residing in Italy.

G. Unaccompanied Foreign Children

Over the years, legislative initiatives and the Constitutional Court have repeatedly modified the legal regime applied to unaccompanied foreign children, a segment of the immigrant population that over the last decade has numbered 5,000 to 10,000 people each year. In particular, the legislation and the relevant case-law have fluctuated for several years regarding the conditions under which a residence permit issued to a minor alien can be "converted" into a different sort of residence permit (for work, study, etc.) when the holder reaches the age of eighteen. This law (art. 32 of lgs.d. 286/1998) was amended in 2002, in 2009, and most recently by law 2 August 2011, No. 129 (conversion into law, with amendments, of l.d. of 23 June 2011, No. 89, on urgent measures to complete the implementation of directive 2004/38/EC on free movement of EU citizens and for the transposition of directive 2008/115/EC on the repatriation of illegal third Country nationals). In particular, the 2009 reform (contained in the "security package", law 94/2009), established the same (restrictive) criteria for converting a residence permit (i.e. at least three years residence in Italy and two years attending social and civil integration programmes) both for unaccompanied minors without any family or social ties in Italy, and for those assigned to a foster family or a reception centre under law 184/1983, or for whom guardians had been appointed in accordance with art. 343 of the civil code. These two categories of children in foster family or structures and under guardianship were previously treated on the same footing as children living in Italy with their legally resident immigrant parents, who upon coming of age, could routinely convert their residence permits obtained in their capacity as members of their respective families into individual residence permits, authorising them to work or follow other pursuits. The provision of art. 32 of lgs.d. 286/1998 as amended by the 2009 "security package" was not considered retroactive by the case-law of the Council of State and the TARs; therefore it did not affect the situation of children taken into care or placed under guardianship in Italy before 8 August 2009 (the date on which that provision took effect). The Constitutional Court (judgement 222/2011) confirms this interpretation and rejects the question of constitutionality posed regarding art. 32 (in the wording that was in force before the amendment of August 2011) and based on the assumption that the new provisions would apply to all foreign minors, even if already taken into foster care or placed under guardianship.

After the 2009 reform, the requirements set forth in law 94/2009 for converting a residence permit given on grounds of minor age into a permit for work or study purpose after the age of 18 (three years' residence and two years' integration programme) also apply to minors in foster care and wards. The Council of State however, in its judgements of 2010 and, in 2011, in judgement 3987/2011, pointed out, as a partial alleviation of the severity of the rule, that the new rules apply only to anyone entering Italy after 8 August 2011, the date of the entry into force of the 2009 security package. Thus, the old regime applied to a Turkish minor who entered Italy on 3 August 2009, at age of 17 and a half. Indeed, "it cannot be demanded that on coming of age the minor has already completed the two-year integration course: rather, it is sufficient to prove that on such date, the plaintiff had been duly admitted to the programme activities and that the programme is running regularly. Likewise, nor is it necessary to prove at least three years residence in Italy, since children under guardianship who entered the Country before the 2009 reform were exempt from this requirement."

Note that in judgement 1784/2011, the Lombardy TAR in Brescia, while adopting the Council of State's argument, nonetheless eventually upheld denial of conversion of a residence permit on the grounds that the appellant entered Italy in June 2009 at the age of 16 years and nine months, but despite having been placed under guardianship in timely fashion, had never undertaken a social and civil integration path. (For other judgements that concur with the Council of State's approach and accordingly deny retroactive application of the 2009 reform, see, among others, Rome, Lazio TAR, judgement 3491/2011; Latina, Lazio TAR, judgement 638/2011; Tuscany TAR, judgement 1344/2011 and Rome, Lazio TAR judgement 2681/2011).

The 2009 legislation was also challenged before the Constitutional Court because its content seemed to conflict with the notion of an unaccompanied foreign minor that can be inferred from EU legislation (in particular directive 2003/9/EC – and consequently to be in breach of art. 117 (1) Const.), as well as with art. 3 and 10 (1) Const. The Court (order 326/2011) is silent on the issue of constitutionality because, after its pronouncement, law 129/2011 was enacted, which reverses the terms of the question, re-establishing a clear distinction between unaccompanied alien minors strictly speaking and those under legal guardianship or in foster care.

Under this new reform, unaccompanied foreign minors who are in foster care or have a guardian and who have received a positive assessment as to their integration by the Committee for Foreign Minors, or else who have been in Italy for at least three years and have participated for at least two years in a social and civic integration project, may obtain a residence permit on attaining majority. The status remains to be clarified of those who, having entered Italy between 8 August 2009 and 6 August 2011, are subject to art. 32 of lgs.d. 286/1998 as amended by the 2009 "security package." The Tuscany TAR (judgement 1469/2011) has strictly applied the rule, by upholding the refusal of conversion of a residence permit of a Kosovar citizen who entered Italy as a minor in early September 2009. The doubts of constitutionality that rely on art. 8 ECHR and on the provisions of the International Convention on the Rights of the Child are dismissed by the court as not being suited to anything more than minimal limitation of the State's exercise of its prerogatives regarding management of migration. Moreover, according to the TAR, several law provisions (including that prohibiting the expulsion of juvenile illegal immigrants) do safeguard the fundamental rights of the child. The same New York Convention, the TAR notes, "does not guarantee [...] the unconditional stay on the territories of the States parties once [children] have reached the age of majority."

The judgement of the TAR of Lazio 7094/2011 addresses an issue relating to unaccompanied minors of Romanian nationality ("neo-EU citizens"). At national level, a special central coordinating agency is charged for their repatriation. The agency had ordered the repatriation to her maternal grandparents of a Romanian girl born in 2008 who had been removed from the parental custody of her mother (a psychic patient) and placed in a reception centre, and who had been decreed adoptable. The appeal brought by the girl's legal guardian complained that the agency's decision had failed to take the minor's best interests into account, since it had ordered her repatriation without any integration plan and without considering the minor's current favourable integration into the community and the prospect of her adoption in Italy. The TAR granted the appeal.

H. Immigrant Children in Need and Temporary Residence Permits for their Parents

Art. 31, para. 3 of the Consolidated immigration act allows the issuance of a temporary residence permit to a foreigner whose presence is deemed essential in order to care for a minor family member in Italy when "serious threats to the minor's mental and physical development" exist. In 2010 the Unified Sections of the Court of Cassation intervened with judgement 21799/2010 to resolve conflicting interpretations of the "serious threats" requirement (see *2011 Yearbook*, p. 285). The criteria established by the Court of Cassation were used by the Brescia Court of Appeals (order of 14 January 2011) to authorise the stay in Italy (for two years), of the Nigerian mother of a child just over one year old. The woman was unable to renew her residence permit after nine years living and working in Italy and married to a fellow Nigerian unqualified to apply for family reunification. Both options alternative to granting permission to stay in Italy provided for by art. 31 of lgs.d. 286/1998, namely either expelling the woman and allowing the child to remain in Italy with its father, or else returning both mother and child to Nigeria, would traumatise to the child, in breach of his "best interests", namely enjoying the presence of both parents.

The judgements of the Court of Cassation (7516/2011 and 7610/2011) assign respectively to the Court of Appeals of Florence and Naples the task of ascertaining whether or not there are criteria that may warrant granting residence permits to parents of foreign children in Italy who have health problems that do not constitute an emergency. The challenged orders of the Courts of Appeals failed to provide analytical grounds based on careful assessments of the cases to justify their denial of the parents' applications. Rather, the decisions were abstractly inspired by a "restrictive" approach. The Juvenile Court of Bari (18 January 2011), on the other hand, chose an interim solution for a family living in a particularly precarious situation, authorising the parent to stay for six months, during which time they should be able to legalise their situation.

I. Aiding and Abetting Illegal Immigration and the Defence of Necessity

A parent who uses a forged personal identity document and circumvents regular family reunification procedures in order to bring his/her diseased minor offspring to Italy to procure medical cures for a disease that cannot be properly treated in their home Country cannot be considered as committing the offence of aiding and abetting illegal immigration (Court of Cassation, Criminal Division, judgement 5061/2011). The mother in question had not in fact assisted a "third party", but her own son; that would constitute a form of "self-aiding and abetting" clearly unrelated to the criminal offence set forth in art. 12 of lgs.d. 286/1998. The Court of Cassation held that quite to the contrary, she had acted properly, considering the situation of necessity (at least presumed) created by the inadequate health facilities available in her homeland and the need for the woman to resume working – her only source of income – in Italy. It should also be noted, the Court added, that the priority in such cases must be assigned to the child's best interests. Accordingly the crime set forth in art. 10-*bis* of lgs.d. 286/1998, of illegal entry or stay in the Italian territory, cannot be configured either.

VII. Criminal Procedure and Enforcement of the Sentence

A. Court Sentencing and the Binding Force of Judgements of the European Court of Human Rights

Judgement 113/2011 of the Constitutional Court may prove to be the final seal on a long case history which has several times seen the Italian

Government called before the monitoring bodies of the CoE (the Commission of Human Rights and then the Committee of Ministers) as a result of failure to adapt domestic legislation to the findings reached by the Strasbourg authorities. When dealing with the *Dorigo* case, the Commission of Human Rights (the organ that complemented the ECtHR prior to the 1998 reform) had found a breach of ECHR rules concerning fair trial. The applicant was convicted in Italy on the basis of statements made during the preliminary investigation in uncontested proceedings and that were never taken up again during subsequent stages of the case. The only way to cure the breach of the ECHR that tainted the judgement, purportedly rendering it unlawful, was a retrial. However, since the judgement had already become final, under Italian law no retrial was possible. Unlike the situation prevailing in many other European legal systems, in fact, in Italy no law provides for retrial of a case in order to enforce a ruling issued by the judicial bodies of the Council of Europe asserting that an ECHR provision was breached in the course of a judicial procedure. The conflict between domestic regulations (in particular art. 630 of the code of criminal procedure concerning review of proceedings) and art. 46 ECHR (an "intermediate rule" with respect to art. 117 (1) Const.), is the subject matter of the judgement in question. Already in 2008 the Constitutional Court was asked to comment on a possible inconsistency in the code of criminal procedure, namely between art. 630 on the one hand, and arts. 3, 10 and 27 Const. on the other. The Court denied any unconstitutionality but advised the legislator to enact a new rule enabling a closed case to be reopened if the ECtHR (or, before 1998, possibly the Council of Europe Commission of Human Rights) found it to be tainted by a breach of the fair trial principle. However this advice never brought fruit. On the other hand, in its judgement 113/2011, using as an intermediary rule art. 46 ECHR, the Constitutional Court actually did assert the unconstitutionality of art. 630 of the code of criminal procedure because it fails to provide, in addition to the conventional retrial remedies, for an *ad hoc* mechanism that enables the reopening of proceedings when this is the only reasonable means of restoring the rights of an individual convicted at a trial that the ECtHR deems unfair on grounds of breach of art. 6 ECHR, or of complying with any guidance from the ECtHR when issuing an interpretative ruling under art. 46 (3) ECHR. The Constitutional Court holds the review proceeding regulated by art. 630 to be the closest, though not identical, to retrial under art. 46 ECHR. This of course does not prevent the Parliament from regulating the matter in a different way.

B. Extradition and the Risk of Ill-treatment

On some occasions the Italian courts have refused extradition or expulsion of alien nationals to Countries when there was a real risk that the person would suffer torture or cruel, inhuman or degrading treatment prohibited by international human rights law (in particular by art. 3 ECHR).

With decision 15578/2011 the Court of Cassation struck down the judgement of the Bologna Court of Appeals granting the extradition of a Belarus citizen sentenced to serve imprisonment with hard labour in her Country. Such a penalty – which is in no way comparable to the community service to which an offender may be sentenced, with his/her consent, under Italian law – constitutes a breach of art. 3 and 4 ECHR, of art. 4 and 5 CFREU and of art. 7 and 8 (3) of the Covenant on Civil and Political Rights. It is also significant that Belarus is the only Country in Europe that is neither a party to the ECHR nor a Member of the Council of Europe. This fact, coupled with the many reports by international intergovernmental and non-governmental organisations denouncing the deficiencies of Belarus' criminal justice and penal systems, should likewise lead to discount the [Belarus] Government's assurances that the woman would not be subject to torture or other inhuman treatment.

Concerning extradition it should be noted that over the last few years, a dispute has been ongoing between Italy and Brazil concerning Italy's request for the extradition of Cesare Battisti, convicted in Italy for extremely serious crimes of a terrorist nature. Battisti escaped from Frosinone prison in 1981 and took refuge in several different Countries including France, where he devoted himself to writing. In 2004 he was arrested and his transfer to Italy was ordered. He managed to escape but he was rearrested in Brazil in 2007. However, the Brazilian authorities (primarily the President of the Republic) denied the extradition request by the Italian Government. In June 2011 the Constitutional Court of Brazil rendered its final judgement upholding the refusal of the extradition request and ordering Battisti's release. The Italian President's spokesman stated that the decisions of the Brazilian political and judicial institutions have "a significance that adversely impact both the duty of compliance with the existing bilateral agreements on extradition between Italy and Brazil and the struggle against terrorism undertaken by Italy in defence of freedom and of democratic institutions, a struggle fully respectful of the rule of law." The Italian Ministry of Foreign Affairs stated that it intends to resort to "every possible further claim before international judicial instances, particularly the International Court of Justice, to pursue the review of a decision that we do not deem consistent with the general principles of law and with the obligations envisaged by international law."

In its judgement 40687/2011 the Court of Cassation quashed the Turin Court of Appeal's judgement that granted the request for extradition of a Moldovan citizen sought for offences of fraud. The Republic of Moldova is a party to the European Convention on Extradition of 1957, and although several judgements of the ECtHR have found deficiencies in its prison system (lack of hygiene, overcrowding, etc.), the Republic of Moldova is not a State in which persons convicted or awaiting trial are systematically subjected to inhuman treatment. Similarly, a Ukrainian citizen's appeal to the Court of Cassation against extradition was rejected: the cases of inhuman treatment that occur in Ukrainian prisons are not the result of any statutory or factual decision by the Ukrainian Government and may be thus appealed in court. Accordingly extradition must be granted (case 26588/2011).

C. The European Arrest Warrant

The Constitutional Court by order 274/2011 ruled on the legality of provisions of the code of criminal procedure governing extradition as well as of law 65/2005, which implements in Italy the European Arrest Warrant directive (Framework decision 2002/584/JHA of the Council). In extradition cases, the aforesaid set of provisions allegedly fails to attribute due importance to the aspect of the extraditable person's stable integration into Italian society if the offence giving rise to the European Arrest Warrant was committed before 7 August 2002. As a matter of fact the 2005 law provides that the new European Arrest Warrant arrangement applies to all requests starting on 1 January 2004. This entails abrogation of previously existing extradition treaties with other European States, but only if such treaties relate to offences committed before the aforesaid date of 2002. Consequently, two persons of the same nationality and charged with or convicted of the same offence may be treated differently (treatment under the European statute is generally more favourable), depending on the date the offence was committed. This approach fails to allow, among other things, for the fact that the time elapsed since the crime was committed is likely to be roughly proportional to the length of the individual's residence in Italy and hence also proportional to his/her degree of integration in Italy. Therefore it disproportionately hits "older" offenders as compared to the "newer" ones. The Constitutional Court however declined to take cognisance of the question, principally on the ground that the claim was formally inadmissible because it asked the Court to issue a ruling amending a law currently in force, a possibility that lay outside the Court's jurisdiction as a court of law.

IX. Children's Rights

In adoption proceedings, the child's right to be heard in court and the stress that should always be placed on his/her best interests are principles that always should guide the judiciary. Among the most significant judgements concerning this issue, one can cite judgement 21651/2011 of the Court of Cassation, which deals with a man's adoption of his wife's daughter born to a previous relationship. The father was unknown. The adoption had been ordered, relying on the minor's consent, which is a necessary prior condition. But it was subsequently revoked by the Court of Appeals at the mother's behest, after the spouses separated. The Court of Cassation, in upholding the outcome of the proceedings, which it held to be consistent with the principle of the minor's best interests, pointed out among others that the "culture of listening to the child," ensuing from the entry into force of both the New York Convention on the Rights of the Child and of the 1996 Strasbourg Convention on the Exercise of the Rights of the Child (as well as art. 24 CFREU) had influenced the adoption reform (law 149/2001), as well as the new rules on shared custody (art. 155-*sexies* of the civil code). Nor does the law state specifically how the minor should be examined in adoption proceedings. The Court may in any case examine a minor directly or indirectly, through an auxiliary expert, who also provides information about the child's capacity for discernment. In the instant case the child, while not participating in the proceedings by means of a special trustee, had been extensively questioned indirectly, and there was no evidence that made the Court of Cassation question the accuracy of the assessments that trial courts had made of the circumstances of the case.

The possibility of, or rather, the need for the minor to take part, possibly represented by a lawyer or a special trustee, applies to all proceedings which concern the minor, even those, like paternity cases, for which the civil code does not mandate the minor's participation. The Constitutional Court, interpreting domestic laws (in particular art. 250 of the civil code) in light of the principles of the Convention on the Rights of the Child and the 1996 Strasbourg Convention, as well as the constitutional provisions on fundamental rights and fair trial, upheld this rule in its judgement 83/2011 and by order 301/2011.

Regarding the duty to interview the child in the course of proceedings enforcing the Hague Convention on the Civil Aspects of International Child Abduction, unless the interview would harm or cause distress to the minor, see the judgements of the Civil Division of the Court of Cassation No. 13241/2011 and No. 17201/2011 (see also *2011 Yearbook*, p. 284).

In a case decided by the Appeals Court of Milan on 26 January 2011, the mother of an 8-year-old boy in the shared custody of his separated parents had decided to give the child a religious instruction. The father had then challenged the mother's initiative before the Court of Varese. The Court of Varese had thereupon refused to order discontinuance of the child's religious education course. The father appealed to the Appeals Court of Milan. The child's attendance at catechism classes conflicted with the parents' shared decision not to christen the child and not to give him any form of religious upbringing. The mother's unilateral decision, subjected only in perfunctory fashion to her former husband's consent, constituted a breach of their commitment to share equally in the child's education. The Court of Appeals recognised that a suitable way to resolve the dispute would have been to hear the child's untrammelled opinion. Nonetheless the court believed that in that specific case interviewing the child was unadvisable because of his age and his aversion to being involved in parental disputes. The judgement concluded by reprimanding the mother and ordering that the minor continue to attend religious instruction, which had already lasted for over a year, and the interruption of which might have had a negative influence on the minor's psycho-social development.

A conflict between child protection and freedom of the press was found in two identical judgements of the Council of State (1276/2011 and 1277/2011) which finally put an end to the dispute between the Communications Regulatory Authority (AGCOM) and RAI Italian Radio and Television Inc., following an appeal by RAI against a fine issued it for broadcasting a report on law enforcement against child pornography, containing extremely explicit images and commentary, on its pre-watershed news programmes on the State broadcaster's "TG1" and "TG3". The Court points out that in the case at bar, the requirement to protect minors, as set forth in art. 31 (2) Const. and in the 1989 Convention on the Rights of the Child and incorporated, together with other domestic provisions, in the service contract between the Ministry of Communications and RAI that was in force at the time the event occurred (27 September 2000), should certainly override the right to information and reporting. The producers of the television programme should have taken all the precautions that the topic required both regarding protection of minors, on account of the delicate phase of psycho-physical and moral development that they are experiencing, and out of respect for the role and sensitivity of parents and of adults in general.

The Council of State (case 7694/2011) likewise denied an appeal by RTI Inc. against a fine imposed by AGCOM for reports shown on the "Italia 1" television network evening news relating to various offences involving children, reported in their news programmes or in trailers advertising them aired in September and November 2004 and on two dates in May 2005, before the watershed and featuring particularly foul language and shocking images.

Court of Cassation judgement No. 3572/2011, regarding the recognition in Italy of an adoption made abroad by a unmarried person, reiterates the doctrine of domestic legislation and case-law, namely by ruling out the legitimising effect of such adoption: an adoption legitimises only if performed by two spouses joined in wedlock – although this does not prevent the legislator from amending this principle in the future by allowing individuals to adopt children with legitimising effects, just as this option is not ruled out, *inter alia*, by the Strasbourg Convention of 1967 on the Adoption of Minors.

X. The Rights of Persons with Disabilities and of Non-autonomous Persons

During 2011, both the TARs (i.e. Lombardy TAR, judgements 362/2011 and 1424/2011; Veneto TAR, judgement 950/2011), and the Council of State (cases 551/2011, 1607/2011 & 5185/ 2011), reaffirmed the principle, disregarded by some regional laws and accordingly unapplied by local authorities, that the financial standing of an individual used to calculate the extent to which such individual shares the cost of certain social and health services (namely integrated social and health treatments whether conducted at home or in residential facilities) provided to severely disabled persons and to non-autonomous persons over the age of 65, is the financial standing of the person assisted, as determined by his/her Equivalent Financial Standing Indicator (ISEE). In no way shall be taken into account the financial capacity (again calculated according to the ISEE) of persons liable under art. 433 of the civil code, for providing support to the non-autonomous or disable persons (namely spouse, children and other descendants, relatives-in-law and siblings). That ruling, which undoubtedly appears to weaken the role of family solidarity in sharing the costs incurred by State agencies to provide assistance to the person requiring it, is justified by the choice made by law (in particular lgs.d. of 31 March 1998, No. 109, as amended by lgs.d. of 3 May 2000, No. 130, a law held to be immediately applicable) to enhance the individual dignity of persons who are not self-sufficient because of old age or disability. If the assets of the assisted individual are insufficient to cover the expense, costs must be borne by the Government agency in charge of providing services, irrespective of the wealth of his or her relatives. Note that the Tuscany TAR, faced with a similar issue, called into question the constitutionality of the regional law on social services, because this statute, unlike others, specifically required that family members of dependent persons taken on by the social services for social and health treatment, pay a share of the costs of care (TAR Tuscany, judgement 1795/2011).

Aforementioned judgement 1607/2011 of the Council of State also stated that in light of a constitutionally oriented reading of the legislation currently in force, local authorities (Municipalities and Provinces) should bear the costs of school transport not only for pupils with disabilities attending compulsory schooling, but also for those attending the upper level of secondary school. Among other courts, the Lombardy TAR applied this standard in its judgement 1044/2011.

According to the Apulia TAR (case 63/2011) it is unlawful to dismiss an application to use the three days per month allowed to assist a severely disabled relative under law 104/1992 on the grounds that the applicant lives far away from the prospective beneficiary of the assistance, which would entail failure to attain the requirement of continuity of the care given. The TAR interprets the requirement of continuity of the care as referring to its systematic character and appropriateness. These criteria are consistent with a substantial geographical distance. The institutions where a caregiver works, especially in case of military or police units, must accept the organisational challenges that recognition of the right to assist generate as the sacrifice necessary in order to protect the right to health of persons with disabilities.

The Court of Cassation (cases 7889/2011 and 17740/2011) reiterates the imperative character to be attributed to the provisions of law 68/1999 (Rules for the employment of the disabled). The duty of placing persons with disabilities to work in various sectors, including teaching in public schools, must always be implemented. The right to work must not be circumvented by administrative regulations.

Judgement 2945/2011 of the Civil Division of the Court of Cassation upholds a judgement of the Lecce Court of Appeals which had pronounced void a contract between an elderly woman and a person who, in exchange for the sale of the bare ownership of a property, had assumed duties of material and moral assistance for the benefit of the counterparty. The ground adduced for nullity was that the likely future condition of the old lady's health was not unpredictable in nature and therefore the transaction was not synallagmatic (the lady actually died about a year later). The grounds that the Court of Cassation adduced for the ruling (which was handed down almost twenty years after the conclusion of the contract it pronounced void) apart from domestic rules of governing legal transactions, and in particular contracts based on unknown factors, include the recognition of the rights of the elderly set forth by art. 25 CFREU (which in turn is based on art. 23 of the European Social Charter and the Community Charter of Fundamental Social Rights of Workers). The CFREU provision, meant to be directly enforceable, makes it mandatory to protect the elderly from the dire consequences for them and their heirs of entering into unfair care contracts.

The Lombardy TAR (judgement 2294/2011) ruled on a case that in some ways is the mirror image of the one just considered. The court ruled on an application lodged by an elderly person who had asked the Municipality of Milan to defray the cost of her admission to a residential facility, on grounds of her poor health and social standing and her poverty. However the request was submitted to the Municipality a few weeks after she had transferred to her grandchildren (who were also disabled) an apartment she owned. The TAR, upholding the reject of her admission application, remarked that the appellant "requested provision of public services in the field of social rights must be considered in close connection to the duty of solidarity under art. 2 of the Constitution. But this is irrelevant in a situation where a party has voluntarily placed herself in a state of objective need which did not previously exist."

XI. Expropriations and the Right to Peaceful Enjoyment of Property

Some months after the Constitutional Court's adoption of judgement 293/2010 (see *2011 Yearbook*, pp. 294-296) which found for the illegitimacy of art. 43 of d.p.r. 327/2001 (Consolidated law on expropriations), regulating the so-called *acquisizione sanante* (acquisition remedying past irregularities) of private property which had been subjected to *de facto* expropriation by a public body, the Government, through l.d. 6 July 2011, No. 98, made into law 111/2011, reintroduced this legal provision, although with some significant changes. Art. 42-*bis* thus inserted into the d.p.r. of 2001 provides that if the public administration has built on private land without regularly expropriating it, and if it is considered necessary for it to be devoted to a public purpose and suitable supporting justification is given, the administration may add the land to its assets, not only through purchase (or by initiating regular expropriation proceedings), but also through the procedure described by the new article, which will have no retroactive effect and must provide for payment of fair indemnity to the private party (accordingly not full compensation) for pecuniary and non-pecuniary damage. Non-pecuniary damage is determined by the law at the flat rate of 10% of the land's market value.

The case-law that developed after the Constitutional Court's decision temporarily voiding expropriations remedying past irregularities, had followed differing interpretations of existing legislation. Some judicial decisions took care to protect the interest of the public administrations, others paid more attention to the interests of the private owner of assets acquired illegally by the administration (see for example judgements 676/2011, 804/2011 and 3298/2011 of the Council of State). Since the law-decree cited, several judgements by TARs and the Council of State have applied the new system (for example: Council of State judgement 5813/2011; Campania TAR, cases 5635/2011 and 5764/2011). The solutions proposed by the Government and those hitherto applied by the courts and the relevant case-law of the ECtHR are rather divergent. The ECtHR protects with greater rigor the individual's right to peaceful enjoyment of property (art. 1 of Protocol I ECHR). The afore-cited judgement of the Constitutional Court had opted not to make any deep analysis of this particular aspect of the measures adopted by the Government (art. 43 of d.p.r. 327/2001), which had been found unconstitutional on grounds of its failure to abide by the instructions set forth by the Parliament (art. 76 Const.). It is possible that further ECtHR rulings may bring up the issue again.

Meanwhile, in its judgement 181/2011, the Constitutional Court amplified on the constitutionally correct criteria for determining the sums that the

State must pay when it expropriates land suitable for building on grounds of public interest. These criteria now require "real compensation" to the private owner (see judgement 348/2007 of the Constitutional Court issued in the light of the protection afforded to property rights in the ECHR), also in the case of farmland. For the latter, the laws currently in effect calculate the indemnity due for expropriated land on the basis of an abstract notion of "average agricultural value". The provisions referring to average agricultural value should be considered unconstitutional and replaced in accordance with a constitutionally-based interpretation of the legislation, to include the value of the crops actually grown on the land, which will be for the court to determine.

Regarding expropriation (and thus regarding the guarantee of the right to peaceful enjoyment of property), judgement 338/2011 of the Constitutional Court also pronounced unconstitutional the mechanism under laws currently in effect that might rule out any compensation to individuals for the expropriation of properties on which no municipal real estate tax has been paid.

XII. The Reasonable Length of Judicial Proceedings, Mediation in Civil Disputes

During 2011, dozens of rulings by the Court of Cassation dealt with claims against Appeals Court rulings enforcing the so-called "Pinto act" (law 89/2001) on the excessive duration of court proceedings. Some parties, in particular, challenged the interpretation of the Italian courts which calculates fair compensation only on that part of the overall duration of the proceedings that exceeds the average duration, and likewise complain that the Italian courts do not systematically allocate an additional sum ("bonus") when the proceedings in question relate to matters of particular impact on the life of the person involved, namely cases involving labour disputes or those related to social security or welfare benefits. In both respects, Italian case-law diverges from the parameters issued by the ECtHR, to the detriment of the citizen. In a number of rulings, the Civil Division of the Court of Cassation has dismissed these claims, arguing that the Italian courts are in compliance with law 89/2001 ("Pinto act"), which without a doubt can be considered as a whole, fully suited to assuring the principle of reasonable duration of proceedings under art. 6 ECHR.

In this regard see, among others, the following judgements of the Civil Division of the Court of Cassation: 731/2011, 5996/2011, 5998/2011, 6139/2011, 6140/2011, 6141/2011, 6142/2011, 6143/2011, 6144/2011, 6145/2011, 6821/2011, 6822/2011, 6823/2011, 6824/2011, 6827/2011, 6846/2011, 6847/2011, 6848/2011, 6958/2011, 6959/2011, 6960/2011, 6961/2011, 6962/2011, 6963/2011, 6964/2011, 6965/2011, 6966/2011, 7095/2011, 7096/2011, 7143/2011, 7290/2011, 7291/2011, 7677/2011, 7678/2011, 7679/2011, 7807/2011, 7809/2011, 7810/2011, 7908/2011,

7909/2011, 7910/2011, 7911/2011, 7917/2011, 7918/2011, 7991/2011, 8118/2011, 8902/2011, 8907/2011, 8908/2011, 8910/2011, 8917/2011, 9012/2011, 9013/2011, 9014/2011, 9022/2011, 9023/2011, 9024/2011, 9814/2011, 9815/2011, 10785/2011, 11112/2011, 11113/2011, 11114/2011, 11115/2011, 11116/2011, 11336/2011, 11337/2011, 12611/2011, 12612/2011, 12613/2011, 12728/2011, 18236/2011, 18277/2011, 18278/2011, 18279/2011, 22337/2011, 30128/2011, 30129/2011, 30130/2011.

Regarding the failure to award a bonus in labour litigation, many of these decisions (the bulk of the actions had been brought by the same law firm) state, among other things, that awarding such bonus is not automatic and that the judge is not required to give specific grounds for not awarding it. In all judgements cited, the Court of Cassation, in accordance with the position adopted by the Constitutional Court, also commands the court to apply domestic law (i.e. the "Pinto act") instead of using quantification parameters for the compensation directly taken from ECtHR case-law as the claimants required, alleging that the ECHR was "communitarised".

On the issue of a statute of limitations restricting the right to bring actions under the "Pinto act" for excessively lengthy proceedings, there is no consensus within the Court of Cassation. Most of the judgements (starting with 27719/2011, also upheld by judgements 478/2011, 725/2011 and 12373/2011) hold that if a claim for fair compensation is brought within the statutory term, it may be based on cases that lasted for a decade or more. Other case-law, by contrast, applies a ten-year statute of limitations to such claims. Accordingly compensation may be paid only for the last ten years during which proceedings took place. Decision 21380/2011 of the Civil Division of the Court of Cassation requested that the Unified Sections clarify the issue.

During the year many TARs, the Lazio TAR and the Council of State handed down numerous judgements demanding that the Government comply promptly with Appeals Court or Court of Cassation rulings that found proceedings unreasonably lengthy and awarded compensation therefore. In this area, the Trentino-Alto Adige TAR upheld in its judgement 181/2011 that, under art. 112 (2), letter c) of the new code of administrative procedure (lgs.d. of 2 July 2010, No. 104), the proper venue is the TAR that affirmed the breach of law. The same Trentino-Alto Adige TAR, in its judgement 305/2011 which deals with the Ministry of Justice's compliance with the order issued by the Court of Appeals of Trent, denounced as unacceptable the fact that after the judge had taken 17 years and six months to rule on a trivial dispute, 18 months after the Court of Appeal's ruling, the Government had not yet paid any compensation to the plaintiff. The TAR therefore decided to forward its decision to the Regional Prosecutor of the Court of Auditors, assuming that the dilatory and negligent conduct of the relevant officials might be associated with accounting misdeeds. It is worthy of note that the Court of Cassation affirmed its own case-law in accordance with which proceedings for breach of the "Pinto act" are distinct from those established to enforce the judgement thereof and accordingly possible excessive length of the latter should be recorded and evaluated separately (see case 2396/2011).

It should be noted that during 2011, and on the basis of certain provisions of the code of administrative procedure (lgs.d. 104/2010, art. 26, as amended by the lgs.d. of 15 November 2011, No. 195), case-law held that the "Pinto act" had been accompanied, in an effort to induce the judiciary to handle cases more swiftly, by the addition of a new rule commanding the party vanquished in any proceedings which were objectively unsustainable, to pay the prevailing party a fair sum set by the court (the courts referred to "damages for lawful judicial conduct") (see, for example, Lazio TAR judgement 8915/2011, that mentions judgement 3083/2011 to the Court of Cassation). An amendment to the provision enacted through lgs.d. 195/2011, however, quantified more precisely the amount owed ("by no less than twice and not more than five times the costs due for submitting the initial complaint"), classifying it as a fine; the Court expressly attributed this penalty to "reckless" behaviour by the party to the case.

Furthermore Court of Cassation judgement 15250/2011 rules that the only persons with standing to bring an action under the "Pinto act" are those who can be fairly deemed victims of the breach of the right to an expeditious trial as set forth in art. 6 ECHR. The Court then asserts that not everyone is harmed by an unreasonably lengthy trial involving other people. The case in point was a claim for reasonable compensation submitted by the manager of a joint-stock company in connection with a dispute to which the company was a party. The complaint was rejected and the Court of Cassation upheld the denial.

Again in connection with the "Pinto act", the Court of Cassation has remarked in several of its rulings (for example case 15251/2011) that, under the interpretation given by the Constitutional Court to the bankruptcy law (Constitutional Court ruling of 7 July 2010, No. 279), a person declared bankrupt is entitled to lodge a claim for fair compensation on grounds of the excessively lengthy proceedings in which he was involved, within the term of six months commencing on the fifteenth day following his receipt of notice reporting the filing of the order closing the bankruptcy, and not on the fifteenth day following the filing of the latter.

Court of Cassation judgement 5759/2011 is noteworthy on account of the particular facts of the case. It ruled on an appeal brought by the Ministry of Economy and Finance against a decision by the Court of Appeals of Catanzaro, which, under the Pinto law, had awarded more than 21,000 euros in compensation to the heirs of a citizen whose trial concerning his claim for a war pension had lasted from 1968 to 2006. The Ministry challenged this ruling because it made no allowance for the fact that the right to fair compensation for excessive length of proceedings is legally based on art. 6 ECHR as construed by the ECtHR and that the latter's jurisdiction to hear actions brought by individuals alleging breaches of this rule by Italy began only on 1 August 1973, namely the date on which Italy consented to proceedings initiated by an individual party's complaint and to the ECtHR's compulsory jurisdiction. Consequently, the Court ruled, 5,000 euros (i.e. 1,000 euros per year for the time span 1968-1973) must be subtracted from the compensation.

In its judgement 5752/2011, the Court of Cassation rules, among other things, that the compensation due on account of excessively lengthy proceedings may include compensation for non-economic loss even when the beneficiary of such indemnity is a legal person. The moral or psychological harm that must be considered is, of course, that endured by the individuals who constitute or run the legal person in question.

Regarding any non-economic loss ensuing from excessively lengthy proceedings, the Court of Cassation specified, upholding its own prior case-law, that, although such loss must be expressly asserted by the party, it may always be granted, unless it appears that the excessive duration of proceedings was intentionally pursued as a conscious procedural gambit by a party to the case (case 4822/2011).

One of the major reforms introduced in 2010 in the field of civil justice was mandatory mediation as an extrajudicial mechanism for settling disputes that might otherwise engage the attention of the courts. The lgs.d. of 4 March, 2010, No. 28 (Implementation art. 60 of the law of 18 June 2009, No. 69 *in re* mediation in civil and commercial disputes) was challenged on grounds of alleged unconstitutionality in the context of certain procedures. The Court of Catanzaro, in particular (in a ruling dated 14 December 2011), dismissed an unconstitutionality motion according to which, in particular, the insertion of a "filter" controlling access to the judicial protection of rights, namely in the form of mandatory settlement negotiations – which are moreover applicable only to certain categories of disputes and not to all – allegedly breaches the CFREU (arts. 47, 51, 52 and 53) as well as art. 6 (2) TEU, and art. 6 ECHR could also be recalled, as "intermediate rule". The Court found the challenge manifestly devoid of grounds, since the ECJ had already acknowledged the lawfulness of compulsory conciliation proceedings, provided they meet certain conditions, which are set forth in lgs.d. 28/2010. Among these conditions are: that the conciliation proposal submitted by the mediator not be binding, that mediators' remuneration be determined by law and not be too onerous, that the time frame within which attempts at mediation are conducted be brief, and that mediation proceedings do not apply to interim injunction. As compulsory mediation is intended to alleviate the courts' workload and abbreviate civil proceedings, it is hailed as a substantial contribution to ensuring the fundamental right of access to the courts.

XIII. Human Rights, the Rule of Law and Mayoral Orders

Judgement 115/2011 of the Constitutional Court ruled on an issue referred to it by the Veneto TAR (in the course of a lawsuit brought by an anti-racist association in the town of Selvazzano Dentro), concerning the constitutionality of a provision of the Consolidated law on local Government (lgs.d. of 18 August 2001, No. 267) included in the 2008 "security package" (lgs.d. 92/2008, converted, with amendments, into law 125/2008). The relevant provision empowered the Mayor, in his or her capacity as a government official, to issue written orders, specifying the grounds therefor, for measures "even extraordinary and urgent, in accordance with the general principles of the legal system in order to prevent and eliminate serious threats to public safety and urban security" (art. 54 (4) of aforementioned lgs.d. 267/2001). The amendment introduced in 2008 consists of adding the word 'even', with the effect that mayors' powers to issue ordinances were extended to encompass matters of regular administration, which, while they must respect the limits of the law, can cover virtually any field, having as a purpose very general goals such as the prevention and elimination of dangers and damage to public safety and urban security. The Court observed that "[i]t is not sufficient that the law devotes the power thus granted to the protection of an asset or a value, but it is essential that its exercise be defined in terms of its content and methods [...]. The mayoral ordinances affected by this ruling, by virtue of their purpose [...], impinge upon the general sphere of individuals' and communities' freedom, by setting behavioural requirements, imposing prohibitions, prescribing obligations to act and to refrain from acting, that, albeit intended to protect important public goods, nonetheless impose to a greater or lesser extent restrictions on the individuals in question". The Italian Constitution, inspired by the fundamental principles of legality and democracy, requires that no obligation of a personal or financial nature may be imposed on any person except by law (art. 23 Const.). The Minister of the Interior's decree of 5 August 2008 provides some guidance as to substance and procedure with respect to the exercise of the mayors' power to issue ordinances, but obviously cannot replace a law. The power to issue ordinances, owing to the manner in which it is regulated by art. 54 of lgs.d. 267/2011, also breaches art. 97 Const., and the very principle of equality of citizens. It is in fact now common to experience situations in which certain rights and freedoms are regulated differently depending on one's location within the Country, and not by virtue of any law (a general, nation-wide and binding law, subject to democratic control and to the judicial scrutiny of the Constitutional Court), but depending on choices made by different local authorities.

XIV. International Crimes and the Immunity of Foreign States from National Jurisdiction

Again in 2011, the Court of Cassation ruled on the issue of immunity of foreign States before the Italian courts in connection to breaches of international law and the law of armed conflict committed during World War II (see *2011 Yearbook*, p. 249). In accordance with the *Ferrini* case (judgement of the Unified Criminal Sections of the Court of Cassation, 5044/2004), Germany must pay compensation to the victims of numerous breaches of peremptory norms of international law committed by the Nazis (including slavery and forced labour, reprisals against civilians contrary to humanitarian law and other crimes against humanity). In the reasoning of the Court, Germany is barred from pleading sovereign immunity to refuse to pay such compensation. During the 1990s some Greek courts ruled thus. The Court of Appeals of Florence in 2006 and 2008 furthermore ordered enforcement of a judgement issued in Greece that could not be carried out in that State for lack of a required governmental approval. The Court of Cassation's ruling 11163/2011 upholds as correct the decision made by the Court of Appeals of Florence to recognise as enforceable in Italy the judgement issued in 1997 by the Greek Court of Livadeia that ordered Germany to pay the Province of Vojotia, as representative of the civilian victims of a Nazi massacre, a sum as compensation, and subjected real estate belonging to Germany but located in Italy to restrictive measures. The Court of Cassation stated that such judgement was not contrary to Italian legal order in which the principle of absolute immunity of foreign States from civil jurisdiction of domestic courts succumbs when the foreign State is responsible for breaches of peremptory norms of international law. The Court of Cassation held that, regardless of the fact that the issue of legality under international law of such interpretation and Italy's ensuing conduct are both subject to the judgement of the International Court of Justice (whose ruling is expected in the course of 2012), the principle of a fair trial entails that the Italian court should not refrain from ruling on the matter pending the decision of the Hague Court. In any case, the effects of the Italian decision are suspended until the judgement of the International Court of Justice is published, and this by virtue of l.d. 63/2010, converted into law on 23 June 2010, No. 98.

Italy in the Case-law of the European Court of Human Rights

A total of 64,500 applications were lodged to the European Court of Human Rights (ECtHR) during 2011. This represents an increase of more than 3,000 cases over the previous year. 1,511 judgements were decided on the merits; 151,600 cases were still pending at 31 December 2011.

The year 2011 saw, for the case of Italy, a further increase in the number of appeals, which rose from 3,852 in 2010 to 4,733 in the year under review. 84 appeals were decided on the merits, gathered into 45 judgements. In 34 cases the Court found a breach of the ECHR, while in three cases it ruled that no infringement had taken place. In the remaining cases the ECtHR had been asked to rule on the determination of fair compensation with respect to prior decisions.

I. Judgements of the Grand Chamber

In 2011 the Grand Chamber delivered two judgements of particular importance for Italy. Both cases were appealed by Italy before the Grand Chamber after the State had been vanquished before a Chamber.

In its judgement in *Lautsi et al. v. Italy* (18 March 2011) the Grand Chamber of the ECtHR, reversing the judgement issued by the Chamber of the II Division of the Court (*Lautsi et al. v. Italy*, 3 November 2009) makes a final determination that no breach of art. 2 Protocol I ECHR (right to education) took place, with fifteen voting in favour and two against. The applicants (the mother of two pupils in compulsory schooling, also on behalf of the minors), complained that by displaying a crucifix in each classroom the State breaches its duty under aforesaid article of Protocol I to the ECHR to "respect the right of parents to ensure such [education and teaching] in conformity with their own religious and philosophical convictions." The "crucifix case" elicited voluble debate both in Italy and elsewhere in Europe. The Chamber's 2009 decision pointed out that the Italian State had breached the Protocol's article because it had failed to abide by the principle of neutrality among different faiths and philosophical convictions, since the regulations (which dated from the time before the Italian Republic existed) required the display of crucifixes in public school classrooms. The Grand Chamber approached the issue by reading Protocol I, art. 2 ECHR in conjunction with art. 9 ECHR. The duty to "respect" parents' right to educate their children in a manner consistent with their beliefs does not mean that parents can ask the State to organise the school system to educate students in accordance with the particular religious or cultural attitudes of parents. Furthermore, in this matter States enjoy a broad margin of discretion, as shown by the fact that, according to the Court, European States follow different policies regarding issues such as the presence or absence of religious symbols in schools. The education provided by the State may propagate certain philosophical or religious values, but it must do so in an objective, critical and pluralistic manner, refraining from indoctrination and proselytism. In this specific case, the Court noted that the crucifix is certainly a religious symbol, but expressive of a broader tradition that does not have a merely denominational character. Furthermore, although visible in the classroom, it remains a "passive" symbol, since it is not connected to any particular educational content in school, and much less does it entail a process of indoctrination. Consequently it is not a *powerful external symbol* like the Islamic veil worn by a teacher in a certain Swiss school, nor does it imply compulsory teaching of the Christian religion. Moreover, according to information provided by the Italian State, in public schools pupils are educated to be tolerant and to interact with various cultures. No discrimination exists concerning the use of non-Christian religious symbols by pupils. Accordingly, the Grand Chamber concluded that the display of crucifixes does not exceed an acceptable exercise of the national Government's margin of discretion. The two dissenting judges stressed the positive duty of States to assume a position of strict neutrality towards religious or philosophical beliefs present in a multicultural society like that of Europe, especially when working in the field of education, and that this neutrality must be reflected not only in the subjects taught but also the environment in which educational activity takes place and the manner in which it is organised.

The other judgement issued by the Grand Chamber was *Giuliani and Gaggio vs. Italy* (24 March 2011), which partially reverses the previous ruling of the Chamber of the IV Division (*Giuliani and Gaggio vs. Italy*, 25 August 2009), thus releasing Italy from any responsibility for a breach of art. 2 ECHR. The most significant items of the operative part of the ruling were approved with 10 votes in favour and 7 judges against. On other issues the judges voted 13 to 4. The case involves, as is well known, the killing of a demonstrator – Carlo Giuliani – by a *carabiniere* during the violence that took place during the G8 summit in Genoa on 20 July 2001. The Genoa events were not limited to Giuliani's death. On the contrary, many other acts of serious violence occurred, which gave rise to several criminal proceedings in Italy. Even though the ECtHR's judgement is limited to a single incident, upon assessing the implementation of the positive and negative obligations under art. 2 ECHR, the sum total of police operations conducted by the national Government in those days was also examined. The Chamber, in its 2009 judgement subsequently appealed by the Italian Government, had determined Italy's responsibility concerning the procedural obligations entailed by art. 2 ECHR, and noted deficiencies in the procedure of establishing the events that led to Giuliani's death. As regards the breach of the substantive aspects of art. 2 ECHR (fair and proportionate use of lethal force by the police officer who fired and by the security apparatus as a whole) the judgement denied any breach of the standards of art. 2 ECHR.

The judgement of the Grand Chamber, more complex than that of 2009, established that Italy had substantially complied with the standards on the legitimate use of force. The Grand Chamber upheld the characterisation (also by the Italian judge) of Giuliani's killing as an act of self-defence. On the other hand, the Grand Chamber modifies the findings on the procedural aspect of the fulfilment of art. 2 ECHR, acknowledging that the Italian authorities had not contravened their duty to investigate the circumstances of the protester's death in an effective, independent and timely manner, in compliance with the victim's family members' right to participate (within legal limits) in the judicial proceedings. The criticisms voiced by the dissenting judges concern both the finding that the use of lethal force by the police officer who shot Giuliani was lawful, and the compliance with art. 2 ECHR of Italian legislation regarding the use of violence to enforce public order, both regarding planning and organisation of the police and riot control operations, and finally the efficiency and completeness of the criminal investigations undertaken. The decision that art. 13 ECHR was not infringed was also criticised (the determination not to open criminal proceedings for Giuliani's death deprived his family of the possibility of becoming a civil plaintiff in the case); on the other hand, the decision was unanimously adopted not to examine the question of the breach of art. 3 ECHR (inhuman treatment) and 6 ECHR (access to the courts). Finally the idea of censuring the Italian Government for lack of cooperation with the ECtHR was dismissed.

II. Interpretative Laws Affecting Ongoing Proceedings

Some ECtHR judgements dealt with issues on a matter of considerable systematic significance and of a certain importance for their practical consequences. Among them is breach of the fair-trial principle and of the rule-of-law principle itself (in particular, the constraints that exercise of the judicial function imposes on the legislative branch) wrought by legislative initiatives presented in guise of "interpretation" that interfere retrospectively with matters that are yet *sub iudice*. On the emergence of a latent conflict on this topic between the ECtHR and Italian case-law, see in this Part, Human Rights in Italian Case-law, II.

In its judgement of 7 July 2011 in *Agrati et al. v. Italy*, the Court joined several appeals (including one signed by more than 121 persons), which concerned the alleged breach by Italy of art. 6 ECHR (fair trial) in connection with the effects of the law of 23 December 2005, No. 266 (the 2006 Budget Act). Art. 1 (218) of the said law provided for a so-called "authentic interpretation" of the provisions of a previous law from 1999, ordering the transfer to State employ of school administrative, technical and auxiliary staff (i.e., the non-teaching school staff) hitherto employed by local authorities. The transfer of personnel provided for by the 1999 law had not in fact settled exhaustively to what extent the seniority that they had earned working for local government would be reflected in their new pay scales at the Ministry of Education. Indeed, after their transfer their wages fell and many of them sought redress in court. The case-law in some cases had favoured awarding the workers supplementary allowances to their new wages. In other cases courts failed to furnish any remedy. The applicants belong to a group of workers who, not having previously obtained a final judgement, were adversely affected by the consequences of the 2006 Budget Act, which required that the provisions enacted in 1999 be interpreted to the detriment of the non-teaching school staff's demands. Since 2006, therefore, particularly on the basis of a number of 2008 Court of Cassation rulings, case-law less favourable to these workers' interests has been upheld. Those workers among them who in the meantime had been paid additional wages by virtue of favourable court rulings, were ordered to refund such sums. The core issue of the complaint before the ECtHR is therefore above all the legality, under the fair trial principle enshrined in art. 6 ECHR, of the legislative measure that, before the pending proceedings on this matter were concluded, imposed on the courts a statute retroactively requiring a particular interpretation of the provision at issue in this case, namely one favouring the (financial) interests of the State. Note that the Constitutional Court had twice ruled on the point in judgements 234/2007 and 311/2009, in both cases affirming the lawfulness of the law of authentic interpretation. The fact that it was enacted on a matter that was actually *sub iudice*, according to the Constitutional Court, also relying on the ECtHR precedents, does not constitute an automatic breach of the fair trial principle, if there are "grounds of overriding public interest" that speak in its favour.

The ECtHR's ruling in *Agrati* nevertheless challenges the very existence of these "grounds of overriding public interest" which alone could justify such restriction on the principles of rule of law and fair trial. Accordingly the ECtHR's ruling in *Agrati* questions the concept that the 2005 act was a purely interpretative law, since its content was far more detailed than that of the 1999 law, and can scarcely be deemed "implicit" in the latter and inferred through interpretation. The "authentic interpretation" statute was furthermore enacted over five years after the law that it purported to clarify and after a majority of judges (including the Court of Cassation) had developed a consistent case-law regarding the issues it dealt with that was diametrically opposed to the "authentic interpretation". In essence, the change wrought by the 2006 Budget Act resembled a retroactive tax amnesty (as the Court of Cassation itself noted in its judgement of 8 August 2011, No. 17076, *see above*). Consequently, the Strasbourg Court ascertained the breach by the State of art. 6 ECHR. The Court also remarks on the breach of art. 1 (1) Protocol I ECHR (right to peaceful enjoyment of property) finding also in this case non-compliance with the international standard. Because in fact the legislative measure enacted by the State had no other purpose than to comply with the 1999 law by reducing the Government's financial outlay on non-teaching school staff once they had been converted into employees of the Ministry of Education, this measure constitutes a disproportionate unfavourable interference with the legitimate expectations on the part of the employees transferred to Government employ to acknowledgement of the seniority that they had earned over the entire length of their employment by local government. The Court, however, refrains from quantifying the amount of fair compensation payable by the Italian Government to the applicants, and instead refers this task to subsequent proceedings, while expressing hopes for a friendly settlement between the applicants and the Government.

On 6 September 2011 the ECJ (Grand Chamber) ruled in case C-108/10 on the controversy that had served as a backdrop to the *Agrati* case (see in this Part, Italy in the Case-law of the Court of Justice of the European Union, III). The ECJ did not see fit to resume discussing the issue of consistency between the 2006 Budget Act and art. 6 ECHR (in conjunction with art. 6 TEU and art. 46, 47 and 52 CFREU), which had been the topic of the ECtHR's judgement.

A similar situation occurs in *Maggio et al. v. Italy* (judgement of 31 May 2011). The dispute concerned the effects of a provision contained in the 2007 Budget Act (law 296/2006) which, while claiming to make an authentic interpretation of a law dating back to 1968 transposing agreements between Italy and Switzerland of previous years, provided that the pension paid by Italian Social Security to Italian citizens who had worked in Switzerland was to be calculated on the basis of contributions actually paid to the Swiss social security fund, multiplied by a coefficient (contribution-based system), and not according to the earning-related schemes. In this way, these workers' pensions were reduced to the same level as the pensions earned by those retiring in the same year who had worked in Italy. In the years prior to 2007, however, the prevailing Italian case-law (also supported by a ruling of the Court of Cassation in 2004) had interpreted the law then in force differently, namely ruling that Italian workers in Switzerland could opt for an Italian pension based on the more generous earning-related system then in force in Italy. The five applicants, former Italian workers in Switzerland, lodged a complaint before the ECtHR to seek the recognition of the harm they had sustained from the 2006 law, which reversed the case-law that had developed over the years on that issue and brought about a reduction of their pensions by 20 to 25%. In previous years they had moved the Italian courts to calculate their Italian pensions (earned in Switzerland) at the more favourable rate to which they felt entitled, but after enactment of the 2006 Act, their motion was denied. In 2008 the Constitutional Court had found the legislative measure exerting retroactive effects to be constitutional, albeit acknowledging that it was not merely interpretative in nature, but rather, innovative. According to the applicants, the rights breached by the Italian State were that to a fair trial (art. 6 ECHR), as the 2006 law had innovated compared to an established case-law, and that to property (art. 1 of Protocol I ECHR), as a legitimate expectation of a larger pension had been frustrated. Art. 14 ECHR was likewise cited, since the new law discriminated unreasonably between retirees whose claims had been granted by a final judgement in their favour before 2006, and those who, after the 2006 law, could no longer rely on such favourable treatment.

The Strasbourg court reiterates that the rule-of-law principle and the notion of a fair trial (art. 6 ECHR) in general rule out any interference by the legislator in the administration of justice designed to influence the outcome of court proceedings still in progress. Grounds of overriding public interest may justify such an intervention, but these cannot consist simply in the need for budgetary savings. As for arguing a need to eliminate the privileges of pensioners who had worked in Switzerland, this was not deemed by the ECtHR sufficient grounds to warrant legislation exerting a retroactive effect. A breach of art. 6 ECHR was accordingly found. Regarding the breach of art. 1 Protocol I ECHR, the Court holds on the contrary that the reduction of the pension, albeit large, is not large enough to constitute an impairment of the right to a pension, also bearing in mind that during their working lives the appellants had actually paid far less in contributions than those paid by workers in Italy. As for art. 14 ECHR, the Court denies the existence of discrimination and acknowledges that in matters such as pensions, assignment to one bracket or another is almost inevitably in some way arbitrary.

III. The Right to Life and Not to Be Subject to Inhuman Treatment

Apart from the Giuliani case, art. 2 ECHR was relevant to one other ECtHR case affecting Italy. This is the judgement in the case *Alikaj v. Italy* handed down on 29 March 2011. The facts underlying the case concern the death of a young Albanian, Julian Alikaj, who was killed by a shot fired by a policeman during the night between 2 and 3 December 1997. The youth, along with three other countrymen, was in a car (later found to have been stolen), driving along the Milan-Bergamo motorway. About midnight a highway police patrol became suspicious of the way the car was being driven and began to pursue it. The Albanians' car stopped and its occupants got out and fled on foot. The police likewise alighted from their vehicle and began pursuing the fugitives without a torch, off the motorway lanes and began shooting. A bullet struck Alikaj in the heart. The first investigations were conducted by police officers belonging to the same detachment as those who had conducted the operation. The prosecutor and the coroner arrived on site some two hours after the events. The proceedings against the policeman who had fired concluded in a first acquittal, because the killing was deemed purely accidental (the policeman's gun allegedly fired accidentally when he stumbled and fell while advancing through the darkness on ground made slippery by rain). Later the case bounced back and forth between jurisdictions between the District criminal Court and the Court of Assizes, and eventually in 2006 the shooter was convicted for manslaughter. The fault consisted in undertaking the pursuit in difficult conditions and in having fired a number of shots in the dark at the fugitives (the witnesses alleged about six shots). The Court deemed the policeman's youth and his standing as a law enforcement officer to be mitigating circumstances and noted that the statute of limitations had expired. The policeman was not subjected to any disciplinary measure of any kind. The Court of Cassation upheld the trial court's findings in 2008. In 2010 the Court of Appeals of Venice, by virtue of the "Pinto law", awarded Julian Alikaj's parents 15,000 euros as compensation for the excessively lengthy proceedings.

The complaint was lodged before the ECtHR in 2008. The Court found that the State had infringed in numerous respects its duty to protect the right to life. Firstly, the use of firearm detonations to stop persons who can by no means be considered particularly dangerous is contrary to the standards on the use of lethal force set forth in art. 2 ECHR. Even more so if the pursuit, gun in hand, took place on slippery ground and in the dark. The ECtHR also noted failure to regulate on the part of the State, since it found no specific regulations regarding the use of firearms by the police in similar circumstances. Accordingly Italy breached art. 2 ECHR in its substantive aspect (positive and negative obligations). From the standpoint of procedure, the ECtHR remarked that staff personnel belonging to the same department as the policeman who had fired conducted the first on-site inspections. The same applies to the subsequent criminal investigation, although the police acted under the prosecutor's instructions. This circumstance is likewise criticised in the judgements of the Italian court. Furthermore the criminal proceedings appear to have concluded more than 11 years after the events, by application of the statute of limitations. The fact that belonging to the police was not considered a factor which could render judgement on the policeman's conduct any harsher, but rather was treated as a mitigating factor, should also be criticised. In conclusion, the Court believes that "far from having acted with rigor, the penal system, judging by its performance in this case, was incapable of exerting any deterrent force likely to prevent effectively other unlawful acts such as those reported in the application." The ECtHR awarded the applicants (the parents and Julian Alikaj's two sisters) a total of 130,000 euros as fair compensation for moral damages. Apart from a refund for the cost of repatriation of the body, no pecuniary damage was found to have been sustained.

Another case in which Italy was found guilty was *Toumi v. Italy* (judgement of 5 April 2011 which is final). The case concerned a breach of art. 3 ECHR (prohibition of torture). The events greatly resemble those in *Trabelsi v. Italy* (see *2011 Yearbook*, p. 306). The complaint was lodged by a Tunisian citizen who had been convicted in Italy for crimes of international terrorism. Released in May 2009, he was at once transferred to the Crotone deportation centre to be sent back to Tunisia. In the meantime Toumi learned that he had also been convicted *in absentia* for fraud by a Tunisian court. The man lodged a complaint before the ECtHR and the Registry of the Court asked the Italian Government, as an interim measure under art. 39 of the ECtHR's Rules, to stay enforcement of the expulsion measure. Toumi also applied for asylum. The application was dismissed and the dismissal challenged before the Court of Cassation; proceedings were still ongoing when judgement was rendered. The ECtHR indicated to the Italian authorities a second interim measure requesting a stay of deportation, in the context of which the 2008 *Saadi v. Italy* case was also mentioned. Tunisia is notorious for torturing and mistreating prisoners and detainees. Despite these requests, the expulsion was carried out on 2 August 2009.

The ECtHR analysed the case in light of its well-established case-law regarding art. 3 ECHR. In particular, the ECtHR dismisses explanations based on assurances given by the Tunisian authorities to the Italian State promising their strict compliance with international human rights standards in its treatment of the person expelled. The futility of such diplomatic assurances can be readily ascertained by reading a recent report by the UN Special Rapporteur on the promotion and protection of human rights and fundamental freedoms while counter-terrorism, Martin Scheinin, which notes the discrepancy between what the law says about the protection of detainees and citizens suspected of terrorist activities and the reality of their actual treatment by the Tunisian police in particular. The ECtHR concludes that any expulsion to Tunisia of a person in Toumi's position exposes the individual to substantial risk of inhuman treatment and torture. (In fact, Toumi complains of having been tortured for three days after his arrival in Tunis. He was later released, but was then charged with committing crimes of terrorism abroad).

In addition to violating art. 3 ECHR, Italy also breached art. 34 ECHR, by failing to abide by the request for stay of deportation. As a result of the State's conduct, the applicant was unable to exercise all his procedural rights in connection with proceedings at the Strasbourg court and, most significantly, the ECtHR's judgement cannot be enforced because the applicant is located in a State that is not a party to the ECHR. The Chamber decided (against the vote of three judges) not to deal with the issue of violation of art. 8 ECHR. Fair compensation was set at 15,000 euros.

Art. 3 ECHR was violated likewise in *Sarigiannis v. Italy*. In this case, the Italian police briefly detained a French family in the customs offices at Rome Fiumicino airport. During their 2-hour detention the travellers sustained slight injuries in a scuffle with the Italian police. The ECtHR established that there was no violation of art. 5 (1) ECHR, since, as the Italian judge who investigated the facts found, the applicants' behaviour had fully justified the police's suspicions and they had been uncooperative. However, with respect to art. 3 ECHR, the fact that, during their brief detention in the customs offices in the company of four police officers, two members of the family sustained head injuries, is inconsistent with police measures intended merely to contain and soothe them. Accordingly the State could not prove that the use of force against the applicants was proportionate and consequently a breach of art. 3 ECHR was founded.

In *Schuchter v. Italy*, case 68476/10, of 1 October 2011, the ECtHR dismissed as manifestly ill-founded the complaint of a German citizen, a resident of Italy of many years' standing, whose extradition had been requested by the United States for complicity in numerous financial crimes. The woman was arrested in 2009; between 2009 and 2010 the Rome Court of Appeals and the Court of Cassation both granted extradition despite her poor state of health, both bodily and mental (depression and anorexia). The Ministry of Justice issued an extradition order, whose enforcement however remained in abeyance on grounds of health. In 2011 the Lazio TAR affirmed that the measure was lawful and enforceable. The appeal lodged before the Council of State (still pending) could not suspend the execution of the extradition order. Mrs Schuchter then resorted to the Strasbourg Court alleging a violation by Italy of arts. 2 and 3 ECHR as well as of art. 6 ECHR. Art. 2 ECHR would be allegedly breached because, on the basis of known facts of record, the American prison system is unable to care adequately for female prisoners in her state of health. Art. 3 ECHR would be allegedly breached because the US sentencing guidelines applicable to the offences with which she is charged might lead to her being given a sentence practically corresponding to life imprisonment without hope of release, which would constitute inhuman treatment. The same applies to certain forms of medical treatment (e.g. forced feeding) that might await her. Furthermore in view of the applicant's health (in a few days' detention in Italy she lost about 6 kg.), incarceration itself would be inhuman treatment. Finally, art. 6 ECHR would be allegedly breached because of the non-public character of the extradition proceedings. The ECtHR deems the appeal to be admissible (since a domestic appeal before the Council of State does not automatically suspend extradition), but manifestly ill-founded. In particular, in accordance with

ECHR case-law, life imprisonment constitutes inhuman treatment only if it is neither *de jure* nor *de facto* irreducible, and this condition is not fulfilled by the American judicial system. Moreover, the American judicial system provides safeguards that satisfy the health standards prescribed by the Convention. Press reports submitted by the applicant do not suffice to prove otherwise. Nothing, moreover, suggests that American physicians are permitted to practice forced feeding except in cases where this is necessary to save the patient's life. As for Italian extradition proceedings closed to the public, ECtHR case-law holds them to be consistent with the right to a fair trial.

IV. Unlawful Detention and Prisoners' Rights

Seferovic v. Italy concerns a case of detention for 43 days in a deportation centre of a Bosnian woman with no identity papers who had lived in a nomad camp near Rome since 1995. Her transfer to the Ponte Galeria centre (Rome) took place on 11 November 2003, less than two months after the woman had given birth to a son who died a few weeks later. During her stay at the deportation centre it emerged that she was actually a legal resident, since in 1999 she had filed a request for asylum which was dismissed but whose dismissal was never reported to her lawyer. She consequently believed in good faith that she was staying legally in the Country pending determination of the sort of protection she was to receive. On 24 December 2003 the Court ordered her release, and only in 2006 would she be granted refugee status. The Court also finds that the woman's transfer to the expulsion centre was illegal because it took place before the expiry of the six-month term after the birth of the child required by art. 19 of lgs.d. 286/1998. The fact that the baby later died did not entail loss of such a guarantee, that is intended for the mother's protection. The ECtHR determined that, apart from the charge brought by the applicant against the Italian police authorities of having lured her under false pretences to their offices, the story is deemed, according to the Strasbourg case-law, to be a case of "clear and serious irregularities" in application of the provision in art. 5 (1) letter f) ECHR, i.e. the rule which allows the arrest or detention of a person to prevent unauthorised entry onto national territory or to carry out an expulsion or extradition procedure. Moreover, the ECtHR noted that the Italian legal system provides no basis to seek a remedy for unjust detention in a case like Seferovic's. The Italian case-law does not indeed consider art. 5 (5) ECHR ("Everyone who has been the victim of arrest or detention in contravention of the provisions of this article shall have an enforceable right to compensation.") to be directly enforceable. Consequently the ECtHR also found a breach of art. 5 (5) ECHR. The ECtHR set fair compensation at 7,500 euros.

In the third *Scoppola v. Italy* case (on which see *2011 Yearbook*, p. 304) the ECtHR ruled, in line with the case-law in *Hirst v. United Kingdom*, that application of Italian criminal law prescribing the loss of political rights as an accessory penalty to sentences of imprisonment exceeding a certain threshold violates the ECHR. In case of a prison sentence of at least five years or life sentence, the accessory penalty is disqualification from public office and perpetual loss of political rights (right to vote and to stand for office); for sentences over three years, disqualification from public office lasts five years (see art. 28 and 29 of the criminal code). The applicant, sentenced to life imprisonment, later reduced to imprisonment for 30 years, complained that the automatic application of such an additional sanction involves a disproportionate restriction of the right protected by art. 3 Protocol I ECHR. The Court's decision reflects the *Hirst* judgement, which was harshly criticised in the United Kingdom. The Italian Government in any case appealed that judgement, and so the Grand Chamber will have to pronounce itself on the issue.

In *Di Cecco v. Italy* (case 28169/06), a prisoner convicted of terrorism, complained that his correspondence had been unlawfully opened and its content read by prison officers, including his application to the Strasbourg Court, in breach of art. 8 ECHR. Indeed the application form and other correspondence with the convicted felon's lawyer regarding his ECtHR case bear the censor's stamp. This occurred in clear violation of the provisions of domestic legislation, namely art. 18-*ter* (2) of law 354/21975 (Prison law), enacted by means of law 95/2004. The ECtHR, in keeping with its established case-law, found that there had been violation of the right to privacy and also noted that the current complaint procedure to the supervising judge for breaches of the confidentiality of letters addressed to the ECtHR is ineffectual, since it can only be enforced *ex post factum*. The Court then denied that certain delays or gaps in the Italian courts' replies to the appellant's complaints were breaches of the right to access a court under art. 6 ECHR.

V. Protection of Rights by the Courts

A. Right of Access to a Court and of Fair Trial

The case *Menarini Diagnostics s.r.l. v. Italy* involves Italy's compliance with the individual's right, enshrined in art. 6 (1) ECHR, to have his case involving a sanction of a certain magnitude, heard by a court capable of fully exercising its jurisdiction. The Antitrust Authority (AGCM) fined the Menarini pharmaceutical company six million euros for anti-competitive practices, for having cooperated with other companies in order to maintain prices levels of certain diagnostic tests for diabetes. The company challenged imposition of the fine before the TAR of Lazio. The latter, on upholding the penalty imposed by the AGCM, noted that on the specific subject of competition its jurisdiction is weakened and limited to a "common sense" review of the decisions made by the competent independent Authority. Menarini Diagnostics srl. contested that decision, noting that the TAR, by conforming slavishly to the decisions of the Authority, had failed in its duty to exercise its judicial function. The Council of State rejected the appeal and so did the Court of Cassation in 2008, on the grounds that the control exercised by the judges on the AGCM's decisions is certainly of jurisdictional nature, even if the court is not entitled to replace the agency in exercising the latter's discretionary powers. The ECtHR states firstly that, in accordance with its own case-law – and therefore, irrespective of its status under domestic law – the sanction imposed by the AGCM can be characterised as penal. Therefore, art. 6 (1) ECHR applies. It is therefore a penalty not imposed by a court. Nonetheless the procedure allows for a court to review the decision imposing the fine. In order for the guarantee of art. 6 ECHR to be fulfilled, that court must have full jurisdiction over the matters alleged. The ECtHR remarks that the administrative judge to whom the Competition Authority's decisions are appealed need not merely verify the legality of the measures adopted, but may also examine whether they are warranted and proportionate, inspect the technical evaluations, and finally enquire into the appropriateness of the penalty imposed. It follows that there was no breach by Italy of art. 6 (1) ECHR. It is worthy of note, as the dissenting ECtHR judge observed, that the recent statute reforming the administrative procedure has enlarged the judge's role in judicial review of penalties imposed by administrative agencies, including independent authorities.

> The ECtHR, in *Capitani and Campanella v. Italy*, reaffirmed its earlier rulings (see, *inter alia*, *Bocellari v. Italy* and *Rizza v. Italy* of 2002) under which proceedings held *in camera* (and not in public) as prescribed for the application of precautionary measures in their various stages, breaches the principle of publicity of the proceedings. Regarding the limited application that the Italian courts give to this ruling of the ECtHR, see in this Part, Human Rights in Italian Case-law, I.

In the judgement *Guadagnino v. Italy and France* the ECtHR ruled on the issue of limits to the State's immunity before the civil courts of a foreign State. The issue is raised by an Italian, a former employee of the French School of Rome, who had resorted to the Italian courts to attack firstly her employer's restructuring of her pay scale, and later the legality of her dismissal on reaching the age limit. In both cases, the Court of Cassation – which took part merely for purposes of preliminary determination of the proper jurisdiction – ruled that jurisdiction belonged to the French courts, not the Italian ones. However when the action was brought before French courts, it was dismissed for lack of jurisdiction. The applicant complained that no judge would try her case because both Italy and France lacked jurisdiction. The ECtHR examined the issue applying its own case-law and some rules of international law it deemed representative of the prevailing doctrine regarding immunity of States (in particular the 2004 Convention on Jurisdictional Immunities of States and Their Property). Applying these principles, the ECtHR concluded that the Italian State had no ground to claim that the French School was immune from its jurisdiction on a labour issue concerning an Italian citizen, since, while implying an interference in the management of a entity that is a segment of a foreign State, the case did not call into question the greater interests of France. In addition to establishing a fair compensation to be borne by Italy, the judgement also states that "when an individual is a victim, as in this case, of proceedings that breach the guarantees of art. 6 ECHR, in principle, a suitable remedy is the holding of a new trial or the reopening of the tainted proceedings, on application by the affected party."

B. Parliamentary Immunity

The case *Onorato v. Italy*, 24 May 2011, relates to another episode of conflict between the ECHR and the effects of applying art. 68 Const., concerning parliamentary immunity (see *2011 Yearbook*, p. 309). The facts concern alleged defamation of the applicant, a judge at the Court of Cassation, by Senator Dell'Utri. The latter, in interviews given to newspapers such as "Il Giornale" and "Il Corriere della Sera", supposedly accused the judge of failing to consider the exculpatory evidence in a trial for tax offences in which Dell'Utri was the defendant. In his statements, the senator rebuked the judge of having "a Communist background." While some proceedings for libel were instituted, the Senate's Parliamentary Immunity Commission stated that the deeds with which Dell'Utri was charged were covered by parliamentary immunity, including statements issued outside Parliament. As a result, the charges were dismissed. A case brought by the Milan judges before the Constitutional Court concerning conflict between branches of State could not be examined on the merits because it was submitted after the deadline had expired. The applicant, justice Onorato, asked the ECtHR to determine whether such an episode constituted a violation committed by Italy of a citizen's right to have his case adjudicated by a court. The ECtHR, having searched its case-law (including the *De Jorio* case: see in this Part, Human Rights in Italian Case-law, I), concluded that, at least regarding the statements that attacked the applicant personally and did not concern the political controversy between Parliament and the Judiciary, the mechanism that had deprived justice Onorato of any opportunity to plead his case before a court was a disproportionate application of the parliamentary immunity principle (in other respects, perfectly legitimate and democratic).

C. Excessive Length of Proceedings

As usual, many ECtHR judgements concerned "Pinto on Pinto" cases, in which namely the applicants asked the European Court to recognise their right to have adjudicated in a timely manner their claims brought before Italian courts to seek compensation for the excessive length of the original proceedings. The leading case in this matter is *Cocchiarella v. Italy*, decided by the Grand Chamber in 2006. In this respect, mentioning also judgements *Salvatore et al.* (18 January 2011), *Capriati* (26 July 2011), *Pascarella et al.* (20 September 2011), *Truocchio* (4 October 2011), *Selvaggio et al.* (18 October 2011), *Giusti* (18 October 2011, in this case the Pinto proceedings held in Italy had concluded with the acknowledgment of excessively lengthy proceedings, but no compensation was awarded. The ECtHR awarded 6,300 euros in non-pecuniary damages). In *Facchiano and Maio* (15 November 2011) the ECtHR awarded compensation to the applicants although they had stated, upon the entry into force of the "Pinto law", that they intended to use this procedure and discontinue the procedure at the Strasbourg Court; eventually however they did not drop the complaint before ECtHR. *Ce. Di. Sa. Fortore s. n. c. Diagnostica medica chirurgica v. Italy* (27 September 2011), despite dealing with excessively lengthy proceedings, is not strictly speaking a "Pinto on Pinto" case.

VI. The Right to Family Life

The judgement in *Sneersone and Kampanella v. Italy* involves a complex case of enforcement of the Convention on the Civil Aspects of International Child Abduction, whose principles are supplemented for EU Member States by regulation 2201/2003 of 27 November 2003. The case was brought before the ECtHR by a Latvian citizen and her son. The latter was born in Italy in 2002 and his father was an Italian citizen. The couple decided to separate and the Juvenile Court of Rome awarded custody to the mother. During the following years, the father became concerned that the mother might take the child with her to Latvia and failed to provide regular financial support to the mother and child, who relied mainly on assistance from the wife's mother, who lived in Riga. In 2006, the mother decided to return to her homeland and took her son with her, in breach of agreements regarding the other parent's visitation rights approved by the Italian court.

There followed a number of procedural incidents culminating, on the one hand, in a judgement of the Juvenile Court of Rome (21 April 2008) that, enforcing the international and European law referred to above, assigned to the father sole custody of his son and ordered the minor's return to Italy (the decision was upheld in 2009 by the Court of Appeals of Rome; no record of any appeal to the Court of Cassation); and secondly, in the opinion issued by the European Commission, in response to a referral by Latvia in the context of proceedings for infringement under art. 259 TFEU (formerly art. 227 of the Treaty on European Union), which notes that Italy, in giving effect to regulation 2201/2003, among other things, failed to give adequate weight to the opinions of the minor's mother, failed to consider the many psychological assessments that advised against removing the child from his mother and neglected to interview the child directly.

The ECtHR examined the issue from the standpoint of a possible breach of art. 8 ECHR, in light of its case-law as expressed in particular in *Neulinger and Shuruk v. Switzerland* (2010 Grand Chamber case). According to the ECtHR the judgements of the Italian courts merely apply the principles established by international standards without however giving due consideration to the child's best interest. In particular, no account is taken of the fact that the return of the child to Italy would lead to his final separation from his mother, who does not have the financial means to make long trips and does not speak a word of Italian, and consequently would be unable to establish herself independently in the Country. The measures ordered by the courts to permit the joint exercise of parenting are clearly insufficient (the mother is allowed to stay with the child for 15 to 30 days in the first year after moving to Italy and thereafter for one month during the summer every two years). In conclusion, the ECtHR condemns Italy for restricting the applicants' right to family life in a manner disproportionate to what is necessary in a democratic society. Regarding procedural aspects of art. 8 ECHR (including failure to hear the child in person), the ECtHR found insufficient evidence to determine a breach.

VII. Property Rights, "Indirect Expropriations", Fair Compensation

In application of settled case-law that finds contrary to art. 1 of Protocol I ECHR the manner in which the Government decide substantially to its own advantage cases of "indirect expropriation" that occurred in past years (see in particular the case *Guiso-Gallisay v. Italy* of 22 December 2009), numerous rulings issued by the ECtHR in 2011 end with a finding that the Italian State violated the right to peaceful enjoyment of property and afford the applicants a just satisfaction. See judgements *Farina, Fiorello, Ventorino, Santinelli et al.* (all of 17 May 2011); *Iandoli, De Stefano et al., Casolaro Camilletti, Rivera and Bonaventura* (all of 14 June), *De Caterina et al.* (18 June); *Maioli, Macri et al.* (12 July); *Paleari* and *Pozzi* (both of 26 July).

Equally large is the number of decisions that, in accordance with earlier rulings that had found Italy in breach of the ECHR, determine the amount of just satisfaction. Worth mentioning are the cases *Giacobbe et al.*, *Genovese et al.*, *Quattrone* (1 February); *Plalam s.p.a.* (8 February – the merits of the case are mentioned in the *2011 Yearbook*, p. 301); *Ucci* (17 February); *G.N. et al.* (15 March – a friendly settlement was reached); *Dedda and Fragassi* (12 April); *Di Marco* (10 April); *Notarnicola* (12 April).

On the issue of property rights (in this case the right to just satisfaction) it is worth recalling the Court's ruling in *Celano et al. v. Italy* (7 June 2011), which declared the case inadmissible because domestic remedies had not been exhausted. The applicants were physicians formerly undergoing specialisation at "La Sapienza" University in Rome. The dispute concerned the failure to adjust the sums paid for scholarships awarded to graduates for a number of years and the non-payment of social security contributions by their employers. The Court emphasises that the issue of whether the domestic law of a State provides or not effective and appropriate remedies to protect rights, should be considered by reference to the situation as it was when the application was lodged with the Court, and not to the situation at any subsequent time. In fact, at the time the applicants lodged the complaint (2007) there had not been a consolidated jurisprudence unfavourable to the applicants' claim, since most proceedings were still pending.

Italy in the Case-law of the Court of Justice of the European Union

This section presents the most significant decisions dealing with human rights issues adopted by the Court of Justice of the European Union (ECJ) in 2011 and concerning Italy. The ECJ, apart from the cases relating to Italy, in 2011 applied the Charter of Fundamental Rights (CFREU) in numerous decisions, thus enriching its case-law on human rights.

Concerning this latter type of decision, and with particular regard to the issue of discrimination, it is worth mentioning: judgement C-236/09 of 1 March 2011, in which the ECJ holds that the differences in insurance premiums and benefits arising from the use of sex as a factor in the calculation constitutes discrimination; judgement C-447/09 of 13 September 2011, in which the Court ruled that terminating airline pilots' employment relationship when they attain 60 years of age constitutes a discrimination on grounds of age; judgement C-147/08 of 10 May 2011, that ruled that the equality principle is breached by any difference, *ceteris paribus*, between the pension arrangements afforded a married couple and those afforded a same-sex civil union. Interesting because of its aspect dealing with protection of privacy is the judgement of 25 October 2011 (joined cases C-509/09 and C-161/10) which rules that in the event of an alleged infringement of personality rights by means of content placed online on an internet website the victim may bring an action for liability, in respect of all the damage caused, before the court of the Member State in which the centre of his interest is based. As to the standing of victims in criminal proceedings, the Court, while restating the importance of the victim's opinion in all proceedings and likewise in determining the form and level of the offender's penalty, in its judgement of 15 September 2011 (joined cases C-483/09 and C-1/10) ruled that EU law does not preclude the imposition of a mandatory injunction to stay away for a minimum period, even when the victim of the crime opposes the application of such a measure.

Other important decisions concern citizenship rights. Among them, judgement C-34/09 of 8 March 2011, ruled that EU citizenship precludes a Member State to refuse a third Country national upon whom his minor children, who are European Union citizens, are dependent, a right of residence in the Member State of residence and nationality of those children, and from refusing to grant a work permit to that third Country national, in so far as such decisions deprive those children of the genuine enjoyment of the substance of the rights attaching to the status of European Union citizen.

In the field of sanctions for terrorism and on the basis of the *Kadi* case, worthy of note is the case of the People's Mojahedin Organisation of Iran (C-27/9 P of 21 December 2011), in which the Court dismissed the appeal lodged by France against a judgement of Court of First Instance of the European Communities that ruled that the People's Mojahedin Organisation of Iran should be struck from the European list of terrorist organisations, on the grounds that the Council had adopted its decision violating the Organisation's rights to defence.

Regarding issues involving bioethics and bio-law, in its judgement C-34/10 of 18 October 2011, the ECJ upheld the exclusion from patentability of processes that use stem cells obtained from a human embryo at the blastocyst stage and entail destruction of the human embryos. In particular, the German Federal Court of Justice, the referring court in the case, when deciding whether a German patent complied with directive 98/44EC, which provides for the exclusion from patentability the use of human embryos for industrial or commercial purposes, asked the Luxembourg Court to elucidate the notion of human embryo. The Court, stressing that it was not called upon to broach questions of a medical or ethical nature, but must restrict itself to a legal interpretation of the relevant provisions of the directive, concluded that: 1) the concept of "human embryo" within the meaning of art. 6(2)(c) of the directive must be understood in a wide sense; 2) the exclusion from patentability of scientific research activities involving the use of human embryos, as only is patentable its use for therapeutic or diagnostic purposes which is applied to the human embryo and is useful to it; 3) an invention requiring the prior destruction of human embryos or their use as base material is excluded from patentability.

Finally, regarding the application of the "Returns directive", a French case very similar to the *El Dridi* case (on which see next section) is the *Achunhbabian* case of 6 December 2011 (C-329/11). In this judgement the Court states that the legislation of a Member States is inconsistent with directive 2008/115 if it represses illegal stays by criminal sanctions, in so far as that legislation permits the imprisonment of a third-Country national who, though staying illegally in the territory of the said Member State and not being willing to leave that territory voluntarily, has not been subject to the coercive measures referred to in art. 8 of the "Returns directive" and has not, in the event of placing in detention with a view to the preparation and implementation of his removal, reached the expiry of the maximum duration of that detention.

I. Application of the "Return Directive"

On 28 April 2011 the ECJ (case C-61/11 PPU) entered its judgement in the case of Hassen El Dridi, which had been referred by the Court of Appeals of Trent on 2 February 2011 in the form of a reference for an urgent preliminary ruling (criminal proceedings against Hassen El Dridi, alias Karim Soufi). The issue of interpretation facing the Italian domestic court concerned whether art. 14, paragraph 5-*ter* of the Consolidated immigration act (lgs.d. 286/1998), enacted as part of the 2009 "security package" (law of 15 July 2009, No. 94), was consistent with EU law. This provision, in force since the summer of 2009, states that a foreign national who remains illegally and without valid grounds on the territory of the State, contrary to the order issued by the *Questore* to leave the territory of the State within five days, shall be liable to a term of imprisonment of one to four years. Such orders are issued whenever an illegal immigrant cannot be held in an Identification and Expulsion Centre or for any reason the expulsion or return by deportation by the law enforcement authorities cannot be carried out. The alien is subjected to summary trial and, if convicted a new expulsion order with deportation by the law enforcement authorities is issued. However, if deportation is still not possible the foreign national is again ordered to leave the territory of the State within five days. If this order too is disregarded, the illegal immigrant may be sentenced to up to five years' imprisonment.

The task facing the judges of the Luxembourg Court was to evaluate the consistency of the Italian legislation on returning illegally staying third-Country nationals with EU law, in particular with directive 2008/115 (the so-called "Returns directive"). The fact that Italy had not yet transposed the directive into domestic law by the end of the period prescribed (25 December 2010) did not prevent the Court from ruling on the substance of the case, since the Court had acknowledged that the directive's provisions exerted a direct vertical effect and, by virtue of being unconditional and sufficiently precise, they may be relied on by individuals before domestic courts even in the absence of transposition. Regarding the merits of the issue referred to it, the Court noted firstly that directive 2008/115 is intended to achieve "the establishment of an effective removal and repatriation policy, based on common standards, for persons to be returned in a humane manner and with full respect for their fundamental rights and dignity" (as stated in the second introductory recital). Among the underlying principles that it introduces are those of giving priority to voluntary departure and resorting to coercive measures as a last resort; of granting illegal aliens an appropriate period for voluntary departure of between seven and thirty days, unless special circumstances exist, such as the risk of absconding or if the person concerned poses a risk to public security or national security. If the obligation to return or the repatriation order have not been complied with, the national Government, in order to perform the expulsion, is authorised to take all necessary measures including, if required, coercive means, provided that they are proportionate and in accordance with fundamental rights. For the purpose of removal, a third-Country national may be kept in detention for a limited period not exceeding 18 months in specialised detention facility or, in any event, in prison accommodation separated from ordinary prisoners. In every case, to avoid breaching the fundamental right to individual freedom, detention should not exceed a reasonable term.

Although the Court then finds that the directive allows the national Government to adopt all coercive measures necessary to carry out the removal of a third-Country national, including criminal sanctions aimed at dissuading those nationals from remaining illegally on those States' territory, it states that such measures cannot jeopardise the attainment of the Union law's objectives'. Since directive 2008/115 is intended to establish an effective policy of removal and repatriation of illegally staying third-Country nationals (voluntarily if possible), Italy is precluded from enacting a legislation which attributes to the immigrant the responsibility for its own authorities' inability to carry out the expulsion by imposing to him/her a sentence of imprisonment, because this rules jeopardise the achievement of the objectives pursued by a directive and, therefore, deprive it of its effectiveness. In the light of the foregoing, art. 14, paragraph 5-*ter* of the Consolidated immigration act, providing for a prison sentence for illegally staying third-Country nationals in the event of refusal to obey an order to leave the territory of the State, should not be applied by national courts as it is contrary to EU law.

In light of the *erga omnes* character of the Court's judgements and the primacy of EU law over domestic law, the legal effects of the *El Dridi* case can be summarised as follows: acquittal of defendants in pending proceedings because the fact did not exist, even if the chief of police's unfulfilled order was prior to the date by which Italy would have had to transpose the directive; application of *favor rei* to the portions of conduct already consummated before that date; case-by-case assessment of judgements that had already become final (see in this Part, Human Rights in Italian Case-law, VII, A).

II. Means of Obtaining Evidence during Criminal Proceedings from Minors who are Victims of Crime

By its ruling of 21 December 2011 (C-507/2010) the Court of Justice of the European Union decided on a reference for a preliminary ruling submitted by the Court of Florence in 2010 (criminal proceedings against a person suspected of having committed acts of a sexual nature on his minor daughter). The questions referred in the context of the preliminary ruling concerned the compatibility of Italian criminal procedural rules applicable to a minor victim with the provisions of Council Framework decision No. 2001/220/JHA on the standing of victims in criminal proceedings.

The Court of Florence, in particular, asked the ECJ to rule on the compliance with EU law of the Italian code of criminal procedure which, on the one hand, under art. 392, paragraph 1-*bis*, 398, paragraph 5-*bis*, and 394, imposes no obligation on the Public Prosecutor to take any action on a request by a victim that use be made of the *incidente probatorio* (a pre-trial taking of evidence) and, on the other hand, does not allow the victim to bring an appeal before a court against a refusal by the Public Prosecutor to comply with that request. The Court of Luxembourg in particular was to determine whether such legislation conflicts with the objectives set out in art. 2, 3 and 8 of Council Framework decision No. 2001/220/JHA, which require that Member States undertake to ensure for all victims treatment affording them "due respect for the dignity of the individual", the opportunity to "to be heard during proceedings and to supply evidence", as well as to ensure a "specific treatment best suited to their circumstances" and, whenever appropriate, protection "from the effects of giving evidence in open court", and that they should enjoy, "by decision taken by the court", the right "to testify in a manner which will enable this objective to be achieved, by any appropriate means compatible with its basic legal principles."

According to the ECJ, even though Member States are required to take specific measures to assist victims who are particularly vulnerable, national authorities have wide discretion in implementing the objectives of the framework decision and that, in the Italian case, the margin of discretion does not appear to have been infringed. Not only is it not conceivable that victims may be entitled to a right to be heard and give evidence under the arrangements of the *incidente probatorio*, but the fact that in the Italian criminal justice system, it is for the Public Prosecutor to decide whether to submit to the competent court the victim's request for use of this form of taking evidence at the pre-trial stage, "can be regarded as part of the logic of a system in which the Public Prosecutor is a judicial body with responsibility for bringing prosecutions".

III. Salary Treatment of Workers in the Event of a Transfer

In its judgement of 6 September 2011, in *Scattolon v. MIUR* (C-108/10), the Court of Justice of the EU considers the reference for a preliminary ruling submitted by the Court of Venice on February 26, 2010. The reference has been made in the context of the proceedings between Ms Scattolon and the Ministry of Education, Universities and Research concerning non-recognition, when Ms Scattolon was transferred to work for that Ministry, of the length of service that she had completed with her original employer working as an ATA (administrative, technical and auxiliary) employee.

The referring court asked the Court of Luxembourg in particular to determine whether the taking over by a public authority of a Member State, of staff employed by another public authority entrusted with the task of supplying schools with auxiliary services, constitutes the "transfer of an undertaking" within the meaning of EU legislation on maintaining the rights of workers. The judges, after answering in the affirmative to this first question, examined the issue of the consistency of the worker's transfer with the contents of the directives. The directive's aim is to avoid workers being placed, solely by reason of a transfer to another employer, in an unfavourable position compared with that which they previously enjoyed. In this case, the fact that, rather than recognising that length of service as such and in its entirety, the Ministry calculated a 'notional' length of service for each transferred worker, was considered as contrary to EU law to the extent that the worker was not assured of preserving rights acquired during previous employment. Having determined this however, the Court stated that it is for the national court to verify whether the applicant in the main proceedings suffered a loss of salary at the time of her transfer, since only a domestic judge is in a position to assess in each case whether such alleged harm actually occurred. The subject matter of this ruling resembles the case referred to the European Court of Human Rights that gave rise to the *Agrati* judgement (applications 43549/08, 6107/09 and 5087/09), issued by the ECtHR only a few months previously. But whereas the Luxembourg Court dealt with the aspect of the case concerning the maintenance of the rights of workers in the event of a transfer of an undertaking, for the ECtHR the main issue was the retrospective application of the law providing for an "authentic interpretation" of the legal provision that disposed the transfer of the worker (see in this Part, II, B).

IV. Liability of Member States for Infringements of European Union Law by One of their Courts Adjudicating at Last Instance

In case C-379/10, decided by judgement on 24 November 2011, the ECJ grants on the merits the European Commission's action brought against Italy, inasmuch as Italian legislation on the reparation of damage caused in the exercise of judicial functions and the civil liability of judges (law of April 13, 1988, No. 117) has failed to fulfil its obligations under the general principal of the liability of Member States for infringements of European Union law by one of their courts adjudicating at last instance.

According to the ECJ, the Italian statute, by excluding all liability of the Italian State for damage caused to individuals through an infringement of EU law on the part of a court adjudicating at last instance when that infringement results from an interpretation of the rules of law or an assessment of the facts and evidence carried out by that court and therefore by limiting that liability to cases of intentional fault or serious misconduct of judges, is inconsistent with EU law.

Such liability, the Court notes, must be met regardless of which Government agency caused the damage, and even if the judiciary was at fault. Specifically, the limitations by the Italian legislature of the State's liability for mistakes in the application of EU law by courts of last instance preclude, according to the judges of Luxembourg, the realisation of an effective judicial protection of the rights the European Union confers on individuals.

Should Italy fail to abide by the ECJ's ruling, the European Commission may again bring the matter before the Court of Justice seeking to have penalty payments.

Index

Table of Cases

Italian case-law

Constitutional Court

Court of Cassation, Civil Division

Court of Cassation, Penal Division

Supreme Administrative Council (Consiglio di Stato)

Regional Administrative Tribunals (TAR)

Ordinary Tribunals

European Court of Human Rights

Court of Justice of the European Union

European Committee on Social Rights

Research and Editorial Committee

Andrea Cofelice, MA in Institutions and Policies of Human Rights and Peace, University of Padua. PhD Candidate in Political Science – Comparative and European Politics, University of Siena.

Paola Degani, Aggregate Professor of Human Rights and Women Condition in the Master's Degree Programme in Institutions and Policies of Human Rights and Peace at the University of Padua. In the same University, she also teaches Public Policies and Human Rights.

Pietro de Perini, MA in Institutions and Policies of Human Rights and Peace, University of Padua. PhD Candidate, Department of International Politics, City University London.

Paolo De Stefani, Aggregate Professor of International Protection of Human Rights in the Master's Degree Programme in Institutions and Policies of Human Rights and Peace at the University of Padua. In the same University he also teaches International Criminal and Humanitarian Law. He is National Director for Italy of the European Master in Human Rights and Democratisation (E.MA).

Marco Mascia, Associate Professor of International Relations and Jean Monnet Chair in Political System of the European Union at the University of Padua. In the same University he is Director of the Interdepartmental Centre on Human Rights and the Rights of Peoples, Chair of the Master's Degree Programme in Institutions and Policies of Human Rights and Peace, Coordinator of the European Centre of Excellence Jean Monnet.

Antonio Papisca, Professor Emeritus of the University of Padua where he teaches International Organisation of Human Rights and Peace in the Master's Degree in Institutions and Policies of Human Rights and Peace and holds the UNESCO Chair "Human Rights, Democracy and Peace". Director of the Review "Pace diritti umani/Peace human rights", published by Marsilio (Venice), he promoted in 1982 the establishment of the Interdepartmental Centre on Human Rights and the Rights of Peoples within the University of Padua. In the period between 1994 and 2002 he has been member of the Italian Inter-Ministerial Committee for Human Rights at the Ministry of Foreign Affairs and of the Italian Human Rights Commission at the Presidency of the Council of Ministers.

Claudia Pividori, MA in Institutions and Policies of Human Rights and Peace, University of Padua. PhD Candidate in International Order and Human Rights, University of Rome – La Sapienza.

Human Rights Studies

Among the broad structural transformation processes at the global level, the international legal recognition of human rights occupies an exceptionally prominent position. The dimensions of this process include standard setting, the functioning of sophisticated machineries for the promotion and protection of human rights, the development of a specific international case-law as well as new priorities of the political agenda.

The human rights paradigm is at the heart of a new set of interrelated principles, which are equally valid at both the domestic and the international levels – such as the rule of law, democratic principles and the responsibility to protect – and of great strategic visions, as human development and human security. New functions, such as human rights monitoring, election observation, fact-finding and inquiry have already been admitted to international practice.

This series intends to foster the publication of volumes that investigate the multiple facets of a strongly evolving reality, and stimulate the production of new and innovative ideas. It offers to highlight how the human rights paradigm is at times used and at times disregarded or exploited in cases and situations that regard among others those belonging to vulnerable groups (immigrants, asylum seekers, persons with disabilities), NGOs and human rights defenders' advocacy, intercultural dialogue, governance of world economy, bio-technologies and peace operations. Those studies which adopt inter- and trans-disciplinary approaches, in accordance with the fundamental principle of interdependence and indivisibility of civil, political, economic, social and cultural rights, will be favored.